HOW TO PLAY AND TEACH BASKETBALL

HOW TO PLAY
AND TEACH

ASSOCIATION PRESS • **NEW YORK**

BASKETBALL

REVISED EDITION

FRANKLIN ALFRED LINDEBURG

WITH A FOREWORD BY

JOHN W. BUNN

How to Play and Teach Basketball

———

Copyright © 1967 by
National Board of Young Men's Christian Associations

———

Association Press, 291 Broadway, New York, N. Y.   10007

Second Printing

Standard Book Number: 8096-1667-X
Library of Congress catalog card number: 67-28541

PRINTED IN THE UNITED STATES OF AMERICA

This book is dedicated to
my wife Cora
and my children
Kathryn Ann, Franklin, Jr., and Cynthia Joan
for their continued interest and
inspirational enthusiasm.

Foreword

HOW TO PLAY AND TEACH BASKETBALL is a book designed as a textbook for the professional preparation of coaches of basketball. It is an excellent reference book for those who are coaching. The thoroughness and simplicity of its coverage make it a valuable handbook for the youngster who is learning to play the game.

The book not only deals with individual techniques and bases of team offense and defense but also traces the development of the game from its beginning and deals with such important items as strategy, conditioning, scouting, selecting the team, and administrative duties of the coach. It presents basketball in its broader aspects rather than limiting discussion to a specific plan or system of play. Particular features of the book are its rich supply of references, excellent summaries, study questions, and projects for additional study. These features enhance its value as a textbook.

The author, Dr. Franklin A. Lindeburg, is well qualified to write a book of this kind. He has had a wide playing and coaching experience in high school, college, and the armed services. He is active as an official and as a leader of officials' organizations. He is presently intercollegiate athletic director at the University of California, Riverside, where he introduced the game and has developed it in a period of eight years to a strong competitive game in that area. His most unique quality is that he is a student of the game and a highly qualified teacher. He writes from this rich background. Of the few books which have been prepared as textbooks, his is most outstanding.

JOHN W. BUNN
Former Coach and Athletic
Director, Springfield College,
Springfield, Massachusetts

Preface

This book is written for basketball players, teachers, and coaches who have expressed a need for a basketball textbook. With this objective in mind, the author has prepared a text, and reference book, which deals with the modern game of basketball.

The material in this book comes from many sources: books and articles; friends; the enemy—my opponents; conferences and clinics; games and players; and, in short, from every contact I have had with the game of basketball.

The author is indebted to numerous individuals and organizations for their assistance in the preparation of this book.

Gratitude and appreciation are given to authors and publishers who have granted permission to quote.

Numerous materials have been generously offered for use. In each case, specific credit is given where this material appears.

I am indebted to Dr. Jack E. Hewitt of the University of California at Riverside, whose enthusiastic assistance aided materially in the preparation of this manuscript.

Greatly appreciated are the time and effort given by players Tim Oleno, Bill Sands, and Dale Decker, who so graciously posed for the pictures.

Credit and gratitude are given to Dwain Lewis, Assistant Basketball Coach, University of California at Riverside, for his aid and technical skill, which were needed in taking the pictures.

The author is deeply grateful for the assistance given by his wife, Mrs. Cora Lindeburg, and by Miss Evelyn Roddy and Mrs. LaClaire Brown, whose assistance in typing, editing, and preparing the manuscript went far beyond the call of duty for ordinary technical assistance.

Also I would like to pay tribute to each player and coach with whom I have been associated, because it is from them that I have developed an appreciation and a philosophy of basketball and of life.

F.A.L.

Contents

TWO
The Coach—A Teacher

THREE

The Coach—An Administrator

FOUR
Individual Defensive Fundamentals

SIX
Individual Offensive Fundamentals

SEVEN
Team Offense

EIGHT

Strategy of the Game

NINE
Scouting and Game Statistics

TEN
Conditioning and Training

List of Illustrations

List of Charts

List of Figures

KEY TO FIGURES

Player with the ball ①●

Pass – – – – – – – →

Path of player ————→

Dribble 〰〰〰〰→

Screen ————————)

Shot ················→

Pivot or turn ↰

Offensive players ① ② ③ ④ ⑤

Defensive players ① ② ③ ④ ⑤

Player in new position ⌊1⌋ ⌊2⌋

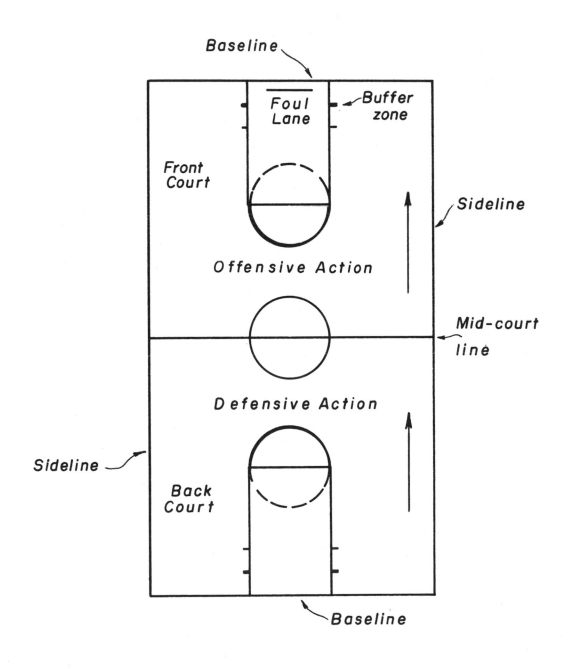

Baseline

Foul Lane

Buffer zone

Front Court

Sideline

Offensive Action

Mid-court line

Defensive Action

Sideline

Back Court

Baseline

CHAPTER 1: Introduction to Basketball

Basketball is a game that is played by thousands and watched by millions of spectators throughout the world. Within the span of a little more than half a century, the sport has become so popular that it is played in over 95 per cent of all the high schools in the United States, and over one hundred million spectators watch their favorite high school teams compete. Almost four hundred junior college teams play for the benefit of some eight million fans, while over eight hundred four-year colleges sponsor teams for more than thirteen million spectators. Uncounted thousands watch or play basketball on service teams, in municipal and recreation leagues, on "Y" teams and in "sand-lot" games. It is played in foreign countries throughout the world, and games played outdoors have drawn an audience of forty thousand people.[1] Basketball is one of the international sports introduced into the Olympic Games in 1936 because of its popularity in countries world-wide.

Backboards are commonplace in parks and lots or on garages, testifying further to the widespread enthusiasm shown for this relatively new sport. In certain parts of the United States, such as Indiana, with its "Hoosier" zeal for basketball, almost an entire town of loyal rooters will follow its team to the state finals, while some towns boast of high school gyms that actually seat more than the total population of the incorporated town itself.[2] This indicates the growth of, and interest in, the game of basketball in the twentieth century in the United States and throughout the world.

► Naismith's Dream

In 1891 the quest for a new game came about, due to a number of circumstances. A need came from the YMCA directors who were aware that their members were losing interest in the body-building type of exercise being conducted in Y gymnastic classes. College students participated in football in the fall and track and baseball in the spring, but had only gymnastics and marching during the winter season when they were confined indoors. Something interesting, exciting, thrilling to play and watch, was needed to fill this void.

Dr. Luther Halsey Gulick, senior secretary of the National YMCA Physical Education Department and head of Physical Education at the International YMCA Training School, now Springfield College, in Massachusetts, recognized this need and proposed it to a seminar class in psychology as a "need for some game that would be interesting, easy to learn, and easy to play in the winter by artificial light."[3] Subse-

quently James Naismith, one of the members of that class and then a young instructor, was assigned an unruly class which obviously no longer cared for gymnastics and marching. In an effort to make the class more appealing, various recreation games such as 3-deep or sailors tag were played; but interest again lagged, and it was necessary to turn to a new game.

Naismith tried football, soccer, and lacrosse in a space of 65 by 45 feet, but each in turn failed because they were all too rough to be played inside within four confining walls. He realized that any attempt to modify an old game would result in failure and that a new principle was the answer.

After much thought, Naismith decided, "All we have to do is to take the factors of our known games and recombine them, and we will have the game we are

[1] Bill Mokray, "Basketball Attendance," *1957 Basketball Yearbook*, (36th ed.; Malden, Mass.: Converse Rubber Co.), p. 22.

[2] Mokray, *loc. cit.*

[3] James A. Naismith, *Basketball—Its Origin and Development* (New York: Association Press, 1941), p. 33.

DR. JAMES NAISMITH, THE INVENTOR OF BASKETBALL (*Courtesy, Naismith Memorial Basketball Hall of Fame, Springfield, Mass.*)

looking for."[4] With this idea in mind Naismith then attacked the problem in an organized fashion. He came to the conclusion that all team games used a ball; therefore, the new game would require some type of ball. "I then considered a large ball that could be easily handled and which almost anyone could catch and throw with very little practice. I decided that the ball should be large and light, one that could be easily handled and yet could not be concealed."[5]

The main point of interest of the various popular games of the day was considered. In football and rugby tackling was necessary, because the player ran with the ball. This pointed out a new principle: the player could not run with the ball, but he could bat or throw it in any direction.

The next item considered was an objective for the players, and this involved some sort of a goal or target. And in Naismith's words: "I thought that if the goal were horizontal instead of vertical, the players would be compelled to throw the ball in an arc; and force, which made for roughness, would be of no value."[6] Naismith desired boxes 18 inches square; but when he was ready to play the first game, only two peach baskets were available. They were nailed one at either end of the gym, high up on the lower rail of the balcony, so that the players could not stop the ball from entering.

Fundamental Principles

Five fundamental principles were developed in the formation of the game:[7]

1. There must be a ball: it should be large, light, and handled with the hands.

THE FIRST BASKETBALL TEAM (*Courtesy, Naismith Memorial Basketball Hall of Fame, Springfield, Mass.*)

[4] Naismith, *loc. cit.*
[5] Naismith, *op. cit.*, p. 40.
[6] *Ibid.*, p. 48.
[7] *Ibid.*, p. 62.

Original Basketball Rules

Basketball Rules, January 15, 1892
by
James Naismith, Originator of the Game

The goals are a couple of baskets or boxes about fifteen inches diameter across the opening, and about fifteen inches deep. These are suspended, one at each end of the grounds, about ten feet from the floor. The object of the game is to put the ball into your opponent's goal. This may be done by throwing the ball from any part of the grounds, with one or both hands, under the following conditions and rules:

The ball to be an ordinary Association football.

1. The ball may be thrown in any direction with one or both hands.

2. The ball may be batted in any direction with one or both hands (never with the fist).

3. A player cannot run with the ball. The player must throw it from the spot on which he catches it, allowance to be made for a man who catches the ball when running at a good speed if he tries to stop.

4. The ball must be held in or between the hands. The arms or body must not be used for holding it.

5. No shouldering, holding, pushing, tripping, or striking in any way the person of an opponent shall be allowed; the first infringement of this rule by any player shall count as a foul, the second shall disqualify to injure the person for the whole of the game, no substitute allowed.

6. A foul is striking at the ball with the fist, violation of Rules 3, 4, and such as described in Rule 5.

7. If either side makes three consecutive fouls, it shall count a goal for the opponents. (Consecutive means without the opponents in the meantime making a foul.)

8. A goal shall be made when the ball is thrown or batted from the grounds into the basket and stays there, providing those defending the goal do not touch or disturb the goal. If the ball rests on the edges and the opponent moves the basket, it shall count as a goal.

9. When the ball goes out of bounds, it shall be thrown into the field of play by the person first touching it. In case of a dispute, the umpire shall call a foul on that side.

10. The umpire shall be judge of the men and shall note the fouls and notify the referee when three consecutive fouls have been made. He shall have power to disqualify men according to Rule 5.

11. The referee shall be judge of the ball and shall decide when the ball is in play, in bounds, and to which side it belongs, and shall keep time. He shall decide when a goal has been made and keep account of the goals, with any other duties that are usually performed by a referee.

12. The time shall be two fifteen-minute halves, with five-minute rest between.

13. The side making the most goals in that time shall be declared the winner. In case of a draw, the game may, by agreement of the captains, be continued until another goal is made.

The number composing a team depends largely on the size of the floor space, but it may range from three on a side to forty. The fewer players down to three, the more scientific it may be made; but the more players, the more fun. The men may be arranged according to the idea of the captain, but it has been found that a GOAL keeper, two GUARDS, three Center MEN, two WINGS, and a HOME man stationed in the above order from the goal is the best.

It shall be the duty of the goal keeper and the two guards to prevent the opponents from scoring. The duty of the wing man and the home man is to put the ball into the opponent's goal, and the center men shall feed the ball forward to the man who has the best opportunity; thus nine men make the best number for a team.

We would advise the director to keep a good firm grasp on the ruling for awhile at first.

2. There shall be no running with the ball.

3. No man on either team shall be restricted from getting the ball at any time that it is in play.

4. Both teams are to occupy the same area.

5. The goal shall be horizontal and elevated.

The first game was played in the winter of 1891 with a soccer ball, nine men on a team, and under a set of thirteen typewritten rules. The players were mature men with beards, mustaches, long pants, and shirts with short sleeves.

Raymond P. Kaighm, member of the class in which Naismith introduced his new game in December, 1891, stated: "None of us who participated in the old Training School gym at Springfield had the remotest idea that in a few short years basketball would sweep around the world, bringing health, fun, and excitement to millions of youth and their elders."[8]

It is interesting to note that a member of the class, Frank Mahon, suggested that the new game be called Naismith ball, which James Naismith immediately rejected. The student then offered the name basket ball, and so the game of basketball was born.

Interest in the Game Spreads

The YMCA, the Army, and Navy were the primary agents in aiding the spread of basketball. The YMCA Training School fostered the growth in two ways. First,

The *Triangle*, the school paper, printed a description of the game and the rules in January, 1892. This paper went to the branches of the YMCA all over the country; and as these branches were looking desperately for some activity that would interest their members, they quickly accepted the game.[9]

Secondly, as the *Triangle* spread the word of the new game via the printed page, the students of the Training School in turn expanded knowledge of the game as they went to the many different parts of the country to continue Y work:

Basketball owes a great deal to the YMCA, because it was first to recognize the necessity for a winter sport, it furnished the facilities and the opportunity to originate the game, and it was a means of spreading the game over the entire world, as its foreign introductions came largely through the branches of the Association in the various countries.[10]

The first college games came quickly after the game originated, and it is reported that Geneva College played the sport in 1892, as did Iowa and Minnesota.[11] The high schools played the game and often defeated the college squads. The Amateur Athletic Union, athletic clubs, colleges, high schools, churches, settlement houses, and industrial institutions supported teams, and basketball became known throughout the United States.

The YMCA and the Army and Navy were largely responsible for making the various countries of the world conscious of this remarkable new physical activity called basketball. It was soon played in foreign countries wherever the Y had a branch. The military soon found the game to their liking and took it with them wherever they traveled throughout the world. World War I found the American soldiers and sailors playing the game in lands they had never heard of before entering the service, and leaving it in these lands as they returned home.

Soon twenty countries had organized basketball to the extent that they were interested in international competition. The bid to play basketball in the 1932 Olympics failed, but a renewed effort accomplished the task, and basketball was played by twenty-one teams in the 1936 Olympics held in Germany. Through the 1964 Olympics, the United States has won every Olympic championship without losing a single game, but the competition is getting keener as players of the various countries increase their knowledge. skill and experience of the game. Following are two newspaper releases which tell of the United States victories in 1960 and 1964.

U. S. WINS BASKETBALL TITLE, 90-63
(Reprinted from the *Los Angeles Times*)
September 11, 1960
by Paul Zimmerman
Sports Editor

ROME, September 10—Led by Ohio State's amazing Jerry Lucas who hit the hoop for 25 points tonight, the United States scored a 90-63 runaway victory over Brazil in the palatial Palazzo Dello Sport here tonight to win the Olympic basketball championship.

The South Americans, vastly outreached but not outsped, trailed 50-20 at the half.

By defeating Italy, 78-70 Russia won second place with Brazil third.

The predominantly Italian crowd of 16,000 who packed the arena booed vociferously when the USSR took the second step on the victory stand after wildly applauding the Americans.

This was because of the rough semi-finale contest when, at one time, the teams almost came to blows.

The final game never was a contest although it appeared that the officials tried to make it so, constantly giving the Brazilians the edge in the calls.

At game's end, Adrian Smith and Walter Bellamy, hoisted on the shoulders of teammates, cut the nets from the baskets and the United States players divided up the cord for souvenirs.

Lucas received staunch assistance in the scoring from Oscar Robertson, who hit the hoop for a dozen points, but in the final analysis it was the Buck-eye star who set the torrid pace and he received a big hand when taken from the game early in the second half, never to return.

Although Walmir Marques was the top scorer for the Brazilians, the big star on the South American team was Sugar Antonio Salvador.

[8] *Basketball Hall of Fame* (booklet).
[9] Naismith, *op. cit.*, p. 111.
[10] *Ibid.*, p. 115.
[11] D. C. Seaton, I. A. Clayton, et. al., *Physical Education Handbook* (2nd ed.; New York: Prentice-Hall, Inc., 1954), p. 52.

The tallest man on the team—6 ft. 6 in.—Salvador was terrific on rebounds. He was about the only man who could wrest the ball away from the U.S.A. giants under the basket.

While coach Pete Newell kept running in fresh players through the contest the Brazilians substituted sparingly and Salvador played the entire contest.

Bellamy was thrown out of the game in its early stages when his elbow accidentally clipped Amaury Pasos on the chin.

U.S.A. (90)	G	F	P	T	BRAZIL (63)	G	F	P	T
West	2	2	3	6	Pasos	6	5	1	17
Dischinger	4	3	2	11	Marques	7	4	1	18
Lane	3	3	2	9	Bispo	1	0	5	2
Lucas	12	1	2	25	Salvador	5	3	3	13
Robertson	4	4	4	12	Slatk'skas	0	0	5	0
Bellamy	0	0	1	0	De Azevedo	1	0	4	2
Bozzer	1	4	4	6	Blas	0	0	3	0
Haldorsen	0	1	1	1	Domingos	3	2	2	8
Imhoff	2	0	2	4	De Souza	0	1	5	1
Kelly	2	0	5	4	Schall	0	0	5	0
Smith	3	5	2	11	Geraldo	1	0	1	2
Arnette	0	1	2	1					

U.S. BASKETBALL TEAM KEEPS PERFECT RECORD
(Reprinted from the *Riverside Press*)
Friday, Oct. 23, 1964

TOKYO (UP)—Rocked back on their heels by the Russians in the first half, Uncle Sam's stunned basketball forces rallied around play-makers Lucious Jackson and Joe Caldwell to keep their all-time Olympic record unblemished last night with a 73-59 gold medal victory over the surprisingly stubborn Soviets.

Players of both teams shook hands all around after the U.S. rolled to its ninth straight victory without a defeat in the round-robin tournament.

But there was little quarter either given or asked during the 40 minutes of play which had an overflow crowd of 5,000 continually at the edge of its seats.

After trailing through much of the first half, the U.S., which has never lost a single game since basketball first was introduced into the Olympic program in 1936, came back for a 39-31 margin at half-time and then played the Soviets off their feet to go ahead by as much as 18 points, 67-49, with less than six minutes remaining.

For the Russians, who suffered their first defeat of the tournament in nine games but wound up with the silver medal for second place, six foot-one Alexander Travin was the standout.

Earlier, Brazil defeated Puerto Rico, 76-60, for third place.

▶ Changes in the Game

Nat Holman, coach of the City College of New York basketball team for over thirty years and student of the game of basketball, has written:

The principles on which basketball was founded are still fundamental today. Agility rather than strength, teamwork in which the player can exercise his individual iniative, speed and movement, passing and accuracy in scoring make the game popular with both players and spectators.[12]

Although the principles under which basketball was originally played are still basic to the game, tremendous changes have occurred that have influenced the play of the individual and the team. Basketball is now played with skill and finesse, teamwork and strategy, making it the fast, thrilling sport it is.

These changes have gradually come about as the result of a number of factors. The players have increased ability and skill. The individual is a better physical specimen. Coaches, as students of the game, stress the strategy of individual and team play. Scientific principles are considered, and better coaching and teaching methods are used by the average coach.

Skill of Players

Naismith, from personal observation, writes, "Greatest changes in basketball have taken place in the skill with which the game is played."[13] Players today are better fundamentalists; they are all-around players, with ability and skill in all phases of the game from passing and dribbling to shooting and rebounding. To use shooting as the most striking illustration, it is obvious that the player of today is far more proficient in scoring than his counterpart of years ago. Below are figures that indicate the increase in shooting percentage among college players during the past decade.

The shooting percentage for Major-College teams has increased each year since 1928 when all teams averaged only 29.3 per cent. During the 1966-67 season, five Major-College teams shot 50.2 per cent or over and twelve College-Division teams performed over the entire season, hitting over one-half of all field goals attempted.[14]

Major-College Division	FGA	FG	Pct.
U.C.L.A.	1082	2081	.520
St. Peter's	773	1498	.516
Bradley	832	1641	.507
Vanderbilt	834	1654	.504
Tulane	843	1679	.502
College-Division			
Alabama State	874	1555	.562
Winston-Salem (N. C.)	1290	2380	.542
Delaware State	683	1321	.517
Southampton (N. Y.)	828	1603	.517
Norfolk State (Va.)	794	1533	.511
Miles (Ala.)	764	1496	.511
Ft. Valley State (Ga.)	936	1833	.511
St. Paul's (Va.)	660	1295	.510
Cheney State (Pa.)	1006	1979	.508
Abilene Christian (Tex.)	586	1156	.507
Arkansas State	739	1473	.502
Jackson State (Miss.)	1109	2220	.500

12 Nat Holman, *Holman on Basketball* (New York: Crown Publishers, Inc., 1942), p. 1.

13 Naismith, *op. cit.*, p. 76.

14 *Official Basketball Statistics* (National Collegiate Athletic Bureau, New York, 1967).

The technique of shooting the basketball through the hoop has gone through a series of revolutions. Two that are recent and clearly illustrate the point are the advent of the one-hand shot as popularized by Hank Luisetti and the great Stanford teams of 1936-38, and the great weapon of today, the jump shot. In the first case, the one-hand shot enabled a team to obtain more shots during a game, it was more accurate, and it was at least as good a shot as any other used at that time.

Since the end of the World War II, the jump shot has proven itself to be basketball's new potent scoring weapon. Players are shooting it from far and near—from the baseline, from the post, on the run, stationary, facing the basket, and as a turn shot. . . . Now the one-hand shot and the jump shot are taken twenty and thirty feet away from the basket, and the players are not just throwing the ball away; they are shooting and getting a good percentage of hits.[15]

There are now many players with the ability to jump and shoot from twenty-one feet away from the basket, which is at the edge of the circle beyond the foul line (the key). This type of shot has changed offenses, and has resulted in defensive changes. We can look forward to increased dexterity in this area as players gain more knowledge and practice the year round.

Players of Today

The players of today are better equipped physically for the game. They are taller and higher jumpers.

The 1966-67 *Scholastic Coach's* annual All-American high school squad of forty players has eighteen young men who are 6 ft. 6 in. or taller. The range in height is from 5 ft. 10 in. to 7 ft. 2 in. with only five players under 6 ft. 0 in.[16]

The 1966-67 United States Basketball Writers Association All-American Team lists players at 7 ft. 1⅜ in., 6 ft. 9 in., 6 ft. 8½ in., 6 ft. 8 in., 6 ft. 4 in., 6 ft. 3 in., 6 ft. 3 in., 6 ft. 1 in. and 6 ft. 0 in.[17]

Loeffler, in his book on basketball, lists the sizes of college players as "little men including those up to 6 feet 2 inches; the medium-sized men, those from 6 feet 3 inches to 6 feet 7 inches; and the big men, those over 6 feet 8 inches."[18]

Small high schools and small colleges are fortunate to have one medium-sized player on their team by the above scale, but frequently teams from small schools appear with several medium-sized players on the front line who play with agility and co-ordination. The tall player with basketball ability is dominating the game and is proving the saying that a good, big man is definitely better than a good, little man.

A coach used to be very happy with one man at 6 feet 6 inches, but today basketball coaches at the college level want two medium-sized players and one large man on the starting five. Of course, the little

man will always have his place in the game, but to be an exceptional player in this category he must excel in scoring or play-making.

Not only are the players taller but they are jumping higher when shooting and rebounding. Today it is not uncommon to observe a high school team warm-up and see two or three boys of only 6 feet or 6 feet 1 inch "stuff" the ball into the basket when shooting lay-ins. Heavy resistance exercise for basketball players is proving to be a factor in increasing jumping ability.[19]

Thus, not only is the player of today tall but he is jumping higher, and the game is now being played a great deal of the time at the level of the basket.

Coaches Are Students of the Game

Coaches are students of the game, and many hours are spent deliberating on different strategies of offensive and defensive play. Teams are scouted and games are filmed, resulting in special defensives and offenses aimed at the opponent's vulnerable spots. Not only will a team press but they might do it man to man or by a zone. Again, the press might be applied full court, three-quarters court, or half court. Not only will teams present their opponents with any one of the above but they can, and often do, use more than one in a single game. Defense, offense, stalls, fast break—all phases of the game are studied and utilized to the best advantage of the individual player's ability and the team's benefit, because the average coach has the opportunity to become thoroughly indoctrinated with all phases of the game. Coaches' clinics, methods courses at the college level, coaches' association meetings, etc. all enable the coach to become a student of the game if he wants to take advantage of the opportunity.

▶ Evolution of the Rules of the Game

It is interesting to note that from an original set of thirteen rules typewritten on one sheet of paper, there has developed a comprehensive group of fifteen rules, with over one hundred sections to those rules, designed to govern the play of basketball.

Major changes have been concerned with various

---

15 F. A. Lindeburg, "The Jump Shot—Basketball's Potent Weapon," *Athletic Journal*, October, 1957, p. 18.

16 *Scholastic Coach*, May, 1967, pp. 44-46.

17 I. R. McVay, "1966-67 All-American Basketball Team," *Look*, March 21, 1967.

18 Ken Loeffler, *Loeffler on Basketball* (New York: Prentice-Hall, Inc., 1955), p. 22.

19 O'Conner and Sills, "Heavy Resistance Exercises for Basketball Players," *Athletic Journal*, June, 1956, p. 7. Murray and Karpovich report similar results in their book *Weight Training in Athletics* and recommend a program for basketball players.

aspects of the game, but the major changes were concerning primarily the number on a team, out-of-bounds play, penalties and scoring, the dribble, the elimination of the center jump, the ten-second rule, and rules to regulate the play of the tall man.

Number on a Team

When the game was first started, it was with the idea that it should accommodate a number of people; it was the practice, especially when the game was used for recreation after class, to divide the class into two groups, regardless of the number and allow them to play.[20]

It was soon realized that the game was more enjoyable and easier to play and understand with fewer on a team; consequently, in 1893 the rules were amended so that five men played on a side in small gymnasiums and nine in larger areas. In 1897 the rule was standardized to the five players on a team which has remained unchanged to the present time.

Out of Bounds

Originally, the game was played so that when a ball went out of bounds, the player first touching it was entitled to toss it back into play without interference. This caused much scrambling for the ball, especially if it went into a special area, like the running track above the basket. This first touching caused roughness and unnecessary confusion; therefore, in 1913 the rule was restated to read that an opponent of the player who caused the ball to go out of bounds should put it into play.

Penalties and Scoring

Penalties and scoring evolved as follows. The first penalty assessed against the violator was a warning and a violation marked against him. The second penalty disqualified him from play until the next basket had been made. He was not entitled to more than two fouls. To help keep the game from being rough; if three fouls were committed by one team without the other having committed a foul, the team that was fouled would receive one point. This was a very serious penalty, as a goal then counted one point.

The next change was in the value of the field goal from one to three points and each foul one point.

The foul shot came into being and the team fouled tried for a basket twenty feet from the goal. If successful, it counted the same as a goal from the field. Any player who committed two personal fouls was disqualified for the remainder of the game.

Subsequent changes moved the foul shot in from twenty to fifteen feet and limited the value to one point. The field goal became standardized at two points. The number of personal fouls for disqualification went from two to five to four to our present five.

The Dribble

The dribble was originally a defensive measure, and the player was allowed to use only one hand. This soon changed so that he could alternate hands.

In 1901 the dribbler was not allowed to shoot for the basket; but in 1908 this was revoked, and again the player who had been or was dribbling was allowed the opportunity to shoot and score.

The Center Jump

Prior to 1936, whenever a basket was scored the official would recover the ball and proceed to the center of the court for a center jump. The game would resume when the official tossed the ball into the air. The team with a tall man could obtain possession of the ball on this center jump, and the tide of the game could rise or fall depending on whether or not the tall man could control the tip consistently. With this in mind, the rule-makers decided upon a revolutionary scheme which was to allow the team scored upon to obtain possession of the ball after it came through the basket. This enabled each team the opportunity to try for a score after the opponent had scored. It also speeded up the game, as many teams would start running as the basket was made by the opponent and would even recover the ball before it hit the ground—the object being to beat the defensive team down the floor and score.

The Ten-Second Rule

In 1901 the players and coaches discovered the advantage of a five-man defense concentrated under the basket. The opponents soon found that this tight defense was hard to penetrate for a score; consequently, if they were ahead they would stall at their end of the floor and not try to increase their score beyond the lead they had. Making baskets became infrequent, scores were low, and spectator interest lagged as some games became farces with one team trying to outmaneuver the other via the strategy of not attempting to score. They would obtain possession of the ball and not advance it near the opponent's defense. Players sat down, autographed programs, read newspapers, and did not play basketball. In an effort to control this type of action, the ten-second rule was instituted into the rules in 1936. It required a team to move the ball into its front court within ten seconds after recovery. The National Basketball Association of professional teams has gone this one further and required a team to make an attempt at the basket within twenty-four seconds after obtaining possession of the ball. This eliminates stalling, and a team several points behind in the last minutes of play has a good opportunity to win. Several college games have been

[20] Naismith, *op. cit.*, p. 72.

played with some modification of the professional twenty-four-second rule, but to date the college and high school rule-makers have not decided to go in that direction.

The Tall Man's Effect on the Rules

The tall man in basketball has been a constant problem, because he is closer to the basket for rebounding and scoring. A tall man could stand just in front of the basket, receive a high pass and turn and toss the ball into the hoop. In an effort to prevent the tall player from "parking" in an area in front of the bas-

ket, a three-second rule was instituted into the books that stated that a player shall not remain for more than three seconds in the six-foot-wide free throw area between the end line and the foul line. This change occurred in 1936. In 1956, another change was made to move the big man further from the basket, as Bill Russell, then at the University of San Francisco and now player-coach of the Boston Celtics, would funnel the long shots of his teammates into the basket. His 6 ft. 10 in. height, long arms and tremendous ability to jump nullified the six-foot lane. In an effort to move this excellent player and other tall men farther out from the basket, the foul lane was widened to twelve feet. The rules committee made another rule change in 1967 and eliminated the dunk or stuff shot after observing a young 7 ft. 1⅜ in. sophomore basketball genius named Lew Alcinder, All-American from UCLA, dunk with ease and dominate the game. The exception to the following rule which allowed dunking was removed so that

a player shall not (a) Touch the ball or basket when the ball is on or within either basket; nor touch the ball when it (b) is touching the cylinder having the ring as its lower base; or (c) is not touching the cylinder but is in

1891
Association
Football

1905
Rawlings
Varsity

1921
Rawlings
Official
Intercollegiate

1926
41 Panel
Ball

1929
Naismith
Model

1939 V. M. S.
Molded
Doug Mills Model

1962
Rawlings
Basketball

THE EVOLUTION OF THE BASKETBALL (*Courtesy, Rawlings Sporting Goods Company*)

downward flight during a try for a field goal while the entire ball is above the basket ring level and before the ball has touched the ring or the try has ended.[21]

► Changes in Equipment and Facilities

One can imagine a basketball game played in 1895 with a soccer ball, a metal hook for the basket ring, the players in various assortment of uniforms, and the floor pine boards or cement. Today the game is played with the same type of equipment, but it has improved with time and with man's ingenious ability to perfect that with which he works.

The Ball

From the original association football (a soccer ball) has come the modern molded type of leather ball. "It shall be of the molded type. If the panels are leather, they shall be cemented to the spherically molded fabric which surrounds an airtight rubber lining."[22] These balls are expertly made with regard to shape, reaction, and durability. Some are treated with formulas to give better finger traction to improve ball control.

From 1891 to 1894 a soccer ball was used; but in 1894 it was decided that a larger ball was preferred.

This ball was the forerunner of the modern type basketball.

Until 1928 the ball had leather laces concealing a rubber stem and the bladder. In that year, the concealed lace appeared with the needle type valve doing away with the necessity of the leather lace. From this great innovation, which improved the trueness of the bounce, there followed about ten years later the molded ball, which increased the perfection to where it is at the present time.

Recently the rubber basketball has been perfected, which has the feel and appearance of pebbled grain leather. Many high school leagues have adopted this as the official ball for the league play. It is quite similar to the leather ball in feel, bounce, and play, and the rules allow it to be used in high school or YMCA play.

The Bankboard (Backboard)

Originally it was not planned that there would be a bankboard, and none was used until it was discovered that spectators behind the rim were attempting

[21] *Official NCAA Basketball Guide*, 1961, p. 29.
[22] *Ibid.*, p. 8.

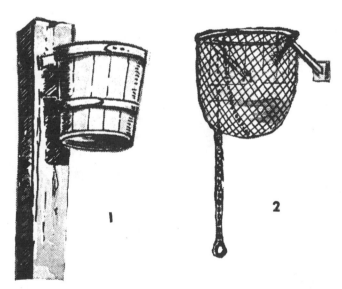

THE EVOLUTION OF THE BANKBOARD (*Reprinted from the 1958 Converse Basketball Yearbook, with permission of the Converse Rubber Company*)

(1) In 1891, Dr. Naismith's original peach basket looked something like this. (2) Later, the goal became a basket without backboard while biased fans deftly directed the ball in or out of the hoop. (3) Then came a bottomless net on a wire backboard and (4) finally, today's glass backboard and familiar shaped net.

First court teams wore standard gym togs, modified football gear, padded baseball pants or indoor .briefs, the latter somewhat like today's uniforms. Knee and elbow pads were common. A soccer ball was first used, then a special ball that had to be hand laced, followed by the laceless ball and finally today's molded basketball.

THE EVOLUTION OF THE BASKETBALL UNIFORM (*Reprinted from the 1958 Converse Basketball Yearbook, with permission of the Converse Rubber Company*)

to deflect the ball away from the basket. A screen wire about 6 by 4 feet was placed behind the basket as a device to keep the spectators away from the ball. Players soon discovered the advantage of banking the ball off the screen, but the sag of the screen made for inaccurate shooting.

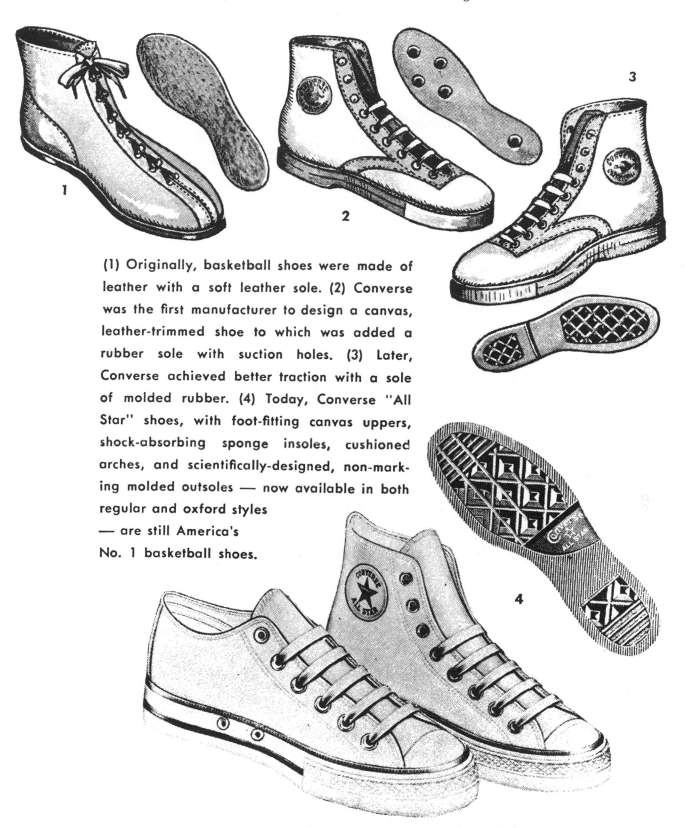

(1) Originally, basketball shoes were made of leather with a soft leather sole. (2) Converse was the first manufacturer to design a canvas, leather-trimmed shoe to which was added a rubber sole with suction holes. (3) Later, Converse achieved better traction with a sole of molded rubber. (4) Today, Converse "All Star" shoes, with foot-fitting canvas uppers, shock-absorbing sponge insoles, cushioned arches, and scientifically-designed, non-marking molded outsoles — now available in both regular and oxford styles — are still America's No. 1 basketball shoes.

THE EVOLUTION OF THE BASKETBALL SHOE (*Reprinted from the 1958 Converse Basket-ball Yearbook, with permission of the Converse Rubber Company*)

In 1906 plate glass was introduced, but in 1916 the glass was done away with and the bankboards were painted white.

Today fan-shaped as well as rectangular bankboards 6 by 4 feet are used. The fan-shaped board came into existence when the floors were extended from 90 by 50 to 94 by 50, so that the baskets and bankboards were each two feet more inside the playing floor. The fan shape eliminated the corners, and players could score easier from the baseline.

Today the transparent rectangular bankboard is used. Either type is all right for other games, but the rules specify that when new equipment is being installed for high school or YMCA games, the fan-shaped bankboard be used.

The Uniform

The modern uniform is far removed from the long-sleeved shirts and long pants of mustached players in the early 1890's. Today the uniform is designed for fast play. It does not bind or restrict the movements of the player and is easily distinguished by its contrasting colors.

Shirts are tailored to fit and are made of fine materials such as nylon, durene, rayon, and cotton or combinations of these materials to provide the best qualities for the heavy use.

Pants are styled to fit the fast-moving player and to stand hard wear. Such fine materials as nylon combat cloth, skinner satin, nylon satin, rayon satin and tackle twill are available.

The modern basketball shoe is usually made of heavy army duck cloth with non-slip molded outsoles. The shoe may be of the high type or the low-cut, ankle-high style. Most manufacturers make shoes with a good last and provide inner lining, some sort of a cushioned inner sole, and arch support.

The Court

Although basketball can be played in any area which is large enough for a backboard and level enough to bounce the ball, the basketball games of today are generally played in well-lighted, well-marked and well-equipped gymnasiums. The optimum sizes range from 84 to 94 feet in length and 50 feet in width. This is quite a contrast from the original games, which were played in small gymnasiums and large rooms, on pine or cement floors, with no out-of-bounds markings and inadequate light. The majority of high school and college gyms now have well-finished maple floors, are adequately marked, are without obstructions, and have ample room surrounding the court for spectators and officials—as exemplified by the beautiful Kansas City Municipal Auditorium, which is the scene of many famous basketball tournaments.

THE GYMNASIUM WHERE BASKETBALL WAS FIRST PLAYED—December, 1891, Springfield, Mass. (*Courtesy, Naismith Memorial Basketball Hall of Fame, Springfield, Mass.*)

Kansas City Municipal Auditorium (Courtesy, Hillyard Chemical Company, St. Joseph, Mo.)

► Summary

Basketball, from its inception in 1891, has developed into a tremendously popular world-wide sport. James Naismith, the inventor, started with five principles and thirteen simple rules; and although the basic fundamental principles are still the same, the game has evolved to where the rules have become more or less standardized, so that the game would be easily recognized as basketball no matter where it is played.

By means of man's inventive genius, facilities and equipment have undergone changes so that today excited, screaming fans can watch two collegiate teams play on a shining maple floor under thousands of candlepower of light. The baskets are on glass backboards, and the floor is clearly marked with proper lines.

This popular game of basketball is America's contribution to the world of sports, and is played by thousands and watched by millions. In its development, and in addition to the evolution of the rules, there have come about systems of offense, styles of defense, strategies of play, and other ramifications of development, such as increased knowledge of the sport by the individual coach, increased skill of the individual player, and improved teaching techniques by the coach. These factors indicate that this relatively young sport has come a long way in a short period of time.

► Study Questions

1. What were the factors in our society during the late 1800's which presented the problem of needing a new game?
2. What conditions have influenced the high scores in basketball games?
3. How has the tall man influenced the evolution of the basketball rules?
4. What caused the rapid spread of basketball throughout the United States?
5. Why did Naismith discard rugby and football in favor of inventing a new game?
6. When was basketball introduced into the Olympic Games?
7. How did the elimination of the center jump after a score influence the scores of basketball games?
8. Why was a bankboard added to the game of basketball?
9. What influenced the change in the out-of-bounds rules?

► Projects for Additional Study

1. Search in back copies of newspapers, magazines, or journals for stories of the original beginnings or reports of basketball games prior to 1900. Contrast with articles of today.
2. Select a particular item of basketball equipment and trace the development of that object from the time it was first introduced to the present time.
3. Contrast the five original fundamental principles of basketball with those of soccer, baseball, or football.
4. Trace in chronological order the evolution of one of the major rules of the game of basketball.
5. Survey a community and determine the extent to which basketball is played and watched during a particular season.
6. Contrast the original thirteen rules with the present fifteen. What major items have been eliminated or added?

► Selected References

Allen, Forrest C. *Better Basketball*. New York: McGraw-Hill Book Co., 1937. Deals with the beginnings of basketball, the development of the game, and Allen's interesting tales as basketball coach at Kansas.

Athletic Journal. Evanston, Ill.: Athletic Journal Publishing Co. Contains many basketball articles which cover all phases of the game.

Holman, Nathan. *Holman in Basketball*. New York: Crown Publishers, Inc., 1950. Is concerned with basketball from "horse and buggy days to the streamlined style." Interesting tales of early basketball days are included.

Mokray, Bill. "Basketball Attendance," *1957 Basketball Yearbook* (36th ed.). Converse Rubber Co., Malden, Mass. Article on basketball attendance which illustrates the tremendous interest in the playing and watching of the game.

Naismith, James A. *Basketball—Its Origin and Development*. New York: Association Press, 1941. Naismith's own account of the birth of basketball and its evolution.

National Collegiate Athletic Association. *Basketball Guide, 1961*. New York: The National Collegiate Athletic Bureau. The official rules book and record book of college basketball.

Newell, Pete, and Benington, John. *Basketball Methods*. New York: The Ronald Press Co., 1962. Contains an excellent, concise statement on the development of the modern game of basketball.

Scholastic Coach. New York: Scholastic Magazines, Inc. Contains many basketball articles which cover all phases of the game.

Terrell, Roy. "The American Game," *Sports Illustrated*, December 9, 1957, p. 26. A popular article which deals with basketball as a collegiate sport.

U. S. Navy. *Basketball*. Annapolis, Md.: United States Naval Institute, 1943. A brief discussion of the beginnings of basketball followed by basketball as offered and played in the service.

CHAPTER 2: The Coach—A Teacher

To coach, one must be a teacher. The coach instructs, and in doing so endeavors to impart knowledge to his students, the players. The good coach will get the most out of his material as the good teacher would obtain the best effort of his students.

A coach must have a philosophy of life geared to sportsmanship and recognition of the fact that one team will win while the other *must* lose. A coach must be concerned with applying the principles of the laws of learning in his teaching, so that his methods have scientific foundations. A coach must be concerned with the psychology of coaching an individual who becomes a member of a team, as in doing so the player must subject his self-interest to the welfare and benefit of the entire team. A coach must be able to select the team and form the best combination into a working, co-operating, co-ordinated unit of five. A coach must select the offense, the defense, and the practice drills. A coach must be concerned with the various teaching devices or aids such as films and recorders. A coach must be interested in and informed about the research and tests used in basketball. A coach must be continuously seeking self-improvement and professional advancement.

► Coaching—A Philosophy of Life

The statement "As he lives so will he coach,"[1] is one which is observed wherever a coach is in action. The distinctive qualities of individuality which make up a person's character do not remain hidden, but are expressed in every act and deed. For this reason, it behooves the coach to develop a philosophy, a way of life, which is concerned with his proper conduct and actions at all times when working with individuals and groups or before large audiences.

Professional Pride

The attitude of the coach toward his professional duties is an integral aspect of coaching, and one which cannot be escaped.

The team. To place a basketball team on the court ready to play a game is not sufficient for the best coach. Professional pride urges him to teach so that the team is a well-coached, well-behaved group of individuals, of which—win or lose—he can be proud.

Victory spirit. To inculcate a team with the "they can't beat us" spirit is a wonderful achievement. Given two teams of equal ability, the team with the victory spirit will win, because they will not admit defeat and will play accordingly. The coach's actions, voice, and enthusiasm will spread to the players; and if it is of the "victory spirit" type, he will have done his job well.

Praise or criticism. A coach's acceptance or rejection of praise or criticism should be done in a professional manner. Remember, the coach is the teacher only; he did not shoot the baskets or play the defense. Credit where credit is due, plus modesty, is always a good course of action.

Rules of the game. The rules of basketball are designed so that both teams play under similar conditions. The coach should know the rules and instruct his players to play strictly according to the rules. There is no place in basketball for illegal tactics or the skirting of the rules, and the coach should never condone such actions.

Discipline. The coach should expect certain conduct and actions from the players, which should be specifically stated and understood by each individual player.

---

[1] Everett S. Dean, *Progressive Basketball* (New York: Prentice-Hall, Inc., 1950), p. 1.

Set down the rules, abide by them, and disciplinary problems should be minor. Although each coach will act toward discipline as his character dictates, the players should know the rules of conduct and should be able to expect a firm, uniform course of action regarding these rules from the coach.

Players' health. The health of any player on the team should be considered above all things. If there is any doubt whether or not a player should participate in a game or in practice, the coach should receive a doctor's recommendation. This protects both the coach and the player and leaves no area for doubt.

Successful leadership. To be able to lead a group of players into a game, through league play or over an entire season, is an inspiration to a coach. But even more thrilling is the knowledge that your leadership has been successful in bringing out the best in the team. Successful leadership should always be strived for and worked toward.

Ideals. Each coach should have a set of ideals toward which he is always striving. High ideals, high standards, can always be aspired for as they offer a goal, an aim in view for the coach and the team. Examples are an undefeated season, the league championship, excellence in defense, precision in offense, high-percentage shooting, or exemplary conduct of the team under trying circumstances.

Service to community. To coach is to be in the public eye; consequently, time must be given to community service. Speechmaking, committee service, and the like are expected, and the coach should serve whenever possible within the limits of his teaching and coaching position.

Parents. The coach should always make it a point to meet parents and talk with them about their boy and his progress in school and on the basketball team. Honest appraisal and sincerity should enable the coach to explain the boy's place on the team.

Faculty. The coach is a member of the faculty and should attend the meetings and take a regular place, assuming his responsibility as a member of the teaching staff. Many matters are brought to the attention of the faculty which concern the students, players, and faculty, and each coach should be prepared to state his case and defend or recommend, whatever the case may be. As a regular member of the faculty, the coach should dress and act the part at all times.

Press. The public's opinion of a coach, a team, or an institution is often obtained through the medium of the newspaper, radio, and television. Representatives of these important media of public information should be treated with respect and given information regarding games, items of public interest, and the like. It is probably a good method of procedure to wait five minutes or so after a game before expressing opinions of the game, the officials, or the opposition. During these few minutes a coach can collect his thoughts and be more certain to have his composure. Simple rules of honesty and frankness will be appreciated by representatives of the press; and their views, which every coach wants to be favorable, will reflect this wholesome attitude. When discussing controversial topics, apply the quotation "Do unto others as you would have them do unto you," and you will have good press relations.

Sportsmanship

The manner in which the coach conducts himself will soon be reflected in the opinions and actions of others. "If athletes and coaches do not conduct themselves in a sportsmanlike manner, athletics are not worthwhile but are a destructive influence and not justifiable."[2] The coach will come into contact and have dealings with many different individuals under both pleasant and trying circumstances, and his conduct and attitude should always reflect a sportsmanlike manner which involves honest rivalry and graceful acceptance of the results.

Players. The actions of the coach are observed, and often copied, by the team members; consequently, it is necessary for the coach to act with a high degree of sportsmanship and regard for all those with whom he comes into contact. In addition to developing a code of good sportsmanship for his own actions, the coach should set up general expected rules of conduct by which the players are expected to abide. Examples are proper acknowledgment of a foul, playing the game according to the rules, polite and respectable actions toward the officials, and graceful acceptance of the results of the game. In the long run, the actions and manners of the players in a game will reflect on the coach; hence, the adoption of a code of good sportsmanship for himself and his team is a necessity.

Opponents. Frequent contact with the players of the opposing team is made before and after the game, in the dressing rooms as well as on the playing court, and as a winning or losing coach. If the coach conducts himself with dignity, is polite, sincere, and friendly, he will have done his job well.

Opposing coach. Minimum essentials regarding the opposing coach would be to act the part of a gracious host or guest. The visiting coach should be greeted and shown his accommodations. After the game the losing coach, no matter how difficult the task may seem, should congratulate the winning coach.

Officials. The officials are a part of the game, functioning to make certain that the game is played according to the rules; when this is realized by the coach, he will temper his judgment of officials with

2 Clair Bee, *The Science of Coaching* (New York: A. S. Barnes & Co., 1942), p. 43.

reason. Before the game the officials should be met and introduced to the opposing coach. Any necessary discussion during the game should be as gentleman to gentleman, even though one or the other might have reason to be angry or perturbed. As a general rule, it is a good idea to refrain from discussing specific play rulings or interpretations until both concerned have had a "cooling off" period. Many times a short wait will make a bitter conversation unnecessary, because with collected thoughts and less emotion the matter will then be regarded as only one incidental part of an entire basketball game and not worthy of debate. Adequate private accommodations should be provided for officials so that they are able to dress, officiate the game, shower, and redress without undue interference by players, coaches, and other team personnel. This in itself will assist relations with officials and help maintain good relations.

Character of the Coach

The way people and players see the coach as an individual is important, and every possible effort should be made to make the picture an acceptable one.

Some coaches are characterized by their actions, dress, or some similar characteristic—such as chewing on a towel; always wearing a particular hat, tie, or suit; making a running talking commentary of the game; baiting officials; or starting feuds with opponents. In some instances, the item which characterizes the coach is harmless; in some cases, it enhances his position; and often it is unprofessional and has no place in basketball.

Good sportsmanship, professional pride, and a professional attitude towards basketball and coaching are positive foundations upon which any coach would be proud to base his character.

► Psychology of Coaching

The coach sets the stage, chooses the cast, and teaches them their lines and actions. How well he does his job is demonstrated in basketball competition. Coaching or teaching is the organizing of learning experiences; and the coach, in his efforts to instruct his players, must be aware of the best teaching methods and use them accordingly. The good coach will get quick, lasting results.

Laws of Learning

Laws of learning are so called because their results are universally obtained and the procedure will, if properly applied by the coach, increase both the scope and depth of the player's learning.

The law of readiness. "Students learn best when they are ready to learn—when they have reached the proper growth level (maturation) and have a keen desire to find out. The learner is ready when he can learn readily with ease, succeeds, and is spurred on by his own ambitious desire to master what he attempts."[3] The player should be given drills, fundamental patterns, etc. with which he can succeed, which are commensurate with his ability level, so that success is obtained. Also, the coach can motivate the learner and instill the ambition to succeed which will assist the learning procedure.

The law of exercise. "We learn from experience. The more frequently we practice, the faster we will learn, but *only* if we practice the right way."[4] Correct demonstrations of the proper way to do a fundamental; individual assistance and corrections, plus a clear explanation of why it is done this way—then practice will impress the correct movement pattern on the learner. Correct action, insight into why an action is performed a certain way, and repeated practice will pay off with rapid learning.

The law of effect. "Trial attempts will produce a positive reaction if the student has had a pleasurable experience that was difficult enough to challenge him and meaningful enough to have been considered important, even to be desired."[5] When satisfaction results, usually from success, that action is strengthened. From this law comes the important fact that the coach should praise and note the success of an action which in turn relates satisfaction to the learner.

Application of the Laws of Learning

A scientific approach to specific teaching situations necessitates applying the laws of learning. The individual and the team will learn through experiences; and when the experiences are presented in a scientific manner, the acquisition of the skill is more liable to come about easily, in such a way that the effect will last.

Illustrations of how the laws of learning can be applied to coaching basketball are offered by Dean.[6]

The Whole and Part Method of Teaching

Let us apply this law of learning to the short shot. It would be well to demonstrate the whole method first, in order to give the players a clear picture of the execution of the shot. The coach or captain and senior players should do the demonstration. The players have seen the whole picture of the execution of the shot and are now ready to learn the shot by steps. The breakdown will start with the take-off, and each succeeding part of the shot will be practiced.

Clear and Simple Presentations of Teachings

A coach should not talk in generalities when explaining fundamentals and plays, but instead should give detailed

---

[3] M. Vannier and H. F. Fait, *Teaching Physical Education* (Philadelphia: W. B. Saunders Co., 1957), p. 39.
[4] Vannier and Fait, *loc. cit.*
[5] Vannier and Fait, *op. cit.*, p. 40.
[6] Dean, *op. cit.*, pp. 45-48.

explanations. However, do not become complex in coaching methods for fear of confusing the players.

Proper Progression in Teaching Fundamentals

It is considered effective coaching to show progression in teaching fundamentals. In teaching the fundamentals of passing, the coach would choose an elementary stationary drill, without opposition, to set up a favorable learning situation. The next step would be an action drill, and the next a drill with opposition. A fourth progressive step would be an actual game condition drill such as two against two, or three against three. The final sequence would be real scrimmage. In this manner, players find it easier to learn the skills of the game.

Proper Progression in Team Organization

Much time should be given to the co-ordination of plays, offenses, and defenses. In assembling an offense, it is considered better teaching to start with one-man, two-man and three-man plays before drilling in the complete offense. The part method is used in teaching the players the offense.

The Use of Competitive Drills

Competitive drills make practice more interesting for the players. It teaches the habit of competition and gives players more opportunity to play under fire. These drills make for quicker development of the player, and make him a more relaxed performer.

Repetition in Coaching

This is an important law of learning. Coaches should repeat explanations, drills, and practices until the lesson is well learned. Do not take too much for granted in coaching. Do not hesitate to repeat.

Stimulating and Interesting Methods of Coaching

The play spirit of the squad must be maintained in order to get the best results. Many coaches forget this important coaching point because of the pressure of a long, hard season. The retention of this spirit, once gotten, is a real test of the ability of any coach.

Some of the ways to interject interest in practice follow: (1) Make practices short and snappy. (2) Have competition in most drills. (3) Make drills game-like. (4) Put fun in some of the drills—see *Fun in Fundamentals,* Chapter 2, p. 66. (5) Permit players to select own defense to be used in some games. (6) Give most-valuable-player awards, highest-free-throw-percentage awards (7) Use seniors as player-coaches early in the season. (8) Take players to see college games and big double-headers. (9) Give a sufficient number of days off from practice to make players want more practice. (10) Have some optional practices.

Analytical and Corrective Methods

One of the hardest jobs for a coach is to realize the individual differences of his players in scrimmage, and how and when to make corrections. Movies provide a good medium for individual and team corrections.

Learn by Doing

This important law of learning is often violated, because some coaches do not have sufficient scrimmage. Since scrimmage is the exact game condition, it should not be neglected, even for fundamentals.

Use of Simplified Fundamental Drills

Fundamental drills should not be involved, but rather of simple construction. In this way, players can apply themselves more to the learning of the fundamental than to the learning of the drill.

Use of Segregated Parts of Team Play for Fundamental Drills

Actual parts of the offense, such as two-man and three-man plays, should be lifted and used as fundamental drills. By following this plan, there is concomitant learning by the players, such as the learning of the play itself, the timing, the fundamentals necessary to execute the play, learning one another's playing habits, condition, and so on.

Developing Receptive Attitude, or a Will to Learn

This is one of the fine arts of coaching and teaching. The attitudes of ambition, desire to learn, will to win, fair play, and unselfishness are all related to the subject. Obstacles in the path of the development of those attitudes are anger, fear, confusion, and an unco-operative spirit.

Acquisition of a Skill

A skill is acquired when an individual learns a co-ordinated series of responses which are performed with proficiency. Basic principles in the acquisition of skill are offered which should serve as guides when teaching the fundamentals of basketball.[7]

1. *Stress the correct performance at the start.*

2. *Concentrate on the actual task to be learned.*

3. *Learn in units, not piecemeal.* The natural rhythm of the entire skill should be learned as a unit.

4. *Space learning trials.* The learning period should be short enough to avoid fatigue, boredom, and interference effects, but long enough to avoid wasting time in getting warmed up to the task.

5. *Overlearn. Do not count on barely learning the task.* A skill performed in public must be overlearned to prevent its being broken up by stage fright or distraction.

6. *Speed or accuracy.* This is resolved in each particular situation. A correct pattern must be practiced from the start; therefore, the particular skill must be analyzed. If performance is the same at high speed as at low, accuracy can be stressed; but if the performance is different at different speeds, accuracy must be sacrificed for speed.

7. *How much guidance?* Guidance is needed at the start to help establish the correct pattern and to avoid errors. After the correct pattern is learned, the learner should get help when it is needed, but self-reliance must be cultivated.

8. *Motivation.* Enthusiasm and real desire to progress are factors which distinguish the mediocre from

---

7 E. G. Boring, H. S. Langfeld, and H. P. Weld, *Foundations of Psychology* (New York: McGraw-Hill Book Co., 1951), p. 161.

the exceptional learner of skills. Knowledge of the results, competition with self and others are useful motivating devices.

Teaching a Motor Skill

There are four principles involved in teaching a motor skill. These are listed below, with the explanation of teaching a jump shot as an example:

Explanation. An explanation of what is to be learned. "The jump shot is being presented to you as one of the most potent scoring methods in basketball. It is easy to accomplish, is hard to block, and is very accurate."

Demonstration. A demonstration of what is to be taught. "Here is how the jump shot is done. Certain points should be stressed: Come to a complete stop before jumping, jump straight up in the air; cradle the ball on the fingers of the left hand, propel the ball with the fingers of your right hand and wrist; concentrate on the target and follow through."

Practice. Organize the group for practice. "Three on a ball, line up here and practice."

Evaluate progress and make corrections. "Note number made, check where misses go, and indicate if not progressing." Coach makes corrections when necessary.

The Importance of Fundamentals and Drills

Fundamentals are the basic skills necessary to play the game of basketball, and drills are the techniques by which the coach teaches the fundamentals. The importance of fundamentals cannot be stressed enough. Shooting, passing, dribbling, rebounding, individual defense, and the like are all necessary to play the game. Each player should be taught the basics of the game in the correct manner, and the players should be expected to learn and play them up to capacity. Some players will excel in one area and some in another, but each player should be expected to play up to a specific capacity in each. *Sound performance of fundamentals is the foundation of a good, sound game.*

Daily performance of the basic fundamentals is necessary to accomplish a high degree of skill. This is done by means of drills. Drills should be selected for specific reasons. Offered are five guides, or rules, which should be used in selecting or planning drills.[8]

1. The drill should be as simple as possible if it is to be used as a drill only.
2. A drill is more useful if it can be adapted to the teaching and practice of a great number of techniques.
3. The drill should, if possible, be made into a game and should be informal at all times.
4. The drill, if possible, should be taken from a part of the offensive-defensive system that is used.
5. As few drills as possible should be used.

The guides or rules for the selection of drills should be used as criteria for choosing drills. As a particular drill is selected, it should be judged against the framework of the above criteria and the drill used or discarded, depending upon whether or not it meets with the desired criteria.

The Player as an Individual

Just because the coach is concerned with a squad of some twelve players, he should not neglect the fact that he is dealing with twelve individuals. The learner is an individual with specific characteristics regarding intelligence, age, height, weight, previous training, well-being, emotional state, physical ability, and the like. No two individuals will be the same, and from year to year the composition of the team and squad will vary. The coach should realize this situation and be conscious of the characteristics of each player in every teaching and coaching situation. The emotional boy should be calmed down, while the lethargic player needs prodding. Some individuals need praise when learning, while others will require what almost amounts to a kick in the pants. Some teams, because of their composition, are naturally aggressive and need little in the way of a pep talk, while others need a spirited speech to be raised up to a high competitive spirit. As soon as the coach realizes the situation, he should act accordingly and get the most out of the individual, the team, and the squad by the proper approach to each.

Game Psychology

Each basketball game is only one in the entire season, but it will be recorded in the win-loss column when the game is over. Consequently—whether the game is a practice or league affair—it is important, and every attempt should be made to obtain the best effort out of the players. In an attempt to do so, the coach should approach each game with an idea in mind, a theme which is used to stress and point up the importance of the game, in an effort to gain a victory. Although each coach will experience different situations, following are suggested items which may be used as themes to develop enthusiasm, spirit, and the desire to win among the players.

Our tough defense will stop their scoring.

Better percentage shooting will give us more points.

This special defense will do the trick.

This play pattern will score for us.

Concentrate on each foul shot. Each one is worth one point.

[8] John W. Bunn, *Basketball Methods* (New York: The Macmillan Co., 1939), p. 73.

We are favored, but don't let that influence you, as we will need to outscore our opponents to win.

The opponents are favored, but a supreme effort can do the job.

The theme should be stressed during practices and by notices and signs posted on the bulletin board and walls of the locker room several days before the game. Soon the players will be imbibed with the idea. Their interest in the point which has been stressed will carry over into the game and, if developed properly, assist in gaining a victory. This theme idea should not be confused with game strategy, which deals with matching players, special defenses, etc., which are dealt with under game strategy.

► Teaching Aids

There are various teaching aids which assist the coach in getting the information across to the players or help the coach accumulate data.

Films

Films can be used as a teaching aid in a variety of ways. Pictures can be taken of scrimmages and games, and the players can then be shown in detail exactly what they are doing. Films of outstanding players, plays, or teams in action can be obtained which are excellent teaching techniques on how it should be done. Movies of opponents can be taken or borrowed which, when viewed by the coach and players, serve as a scouting report on the players and team. The last use to which movies are placed is as a public relations media. They can be shown to outside groups to indicate to them how your team has performed.

Moving pictures of high school games of four eight-minute quarters taken at 24 frames per second require approximately a thousand feet of film. A three-minute overtime consumes an additional hundred-foot reel.

College games with their twenty-minute halves, when taken at 24 frames per second, require from 1250 to 1300 feet for an entire game.

Video-TV

Video-TV is now available and the game, practices or individuals performing specific skills can be filmed on tape and played back immediately or at a later date for review and correction by the coach and players. This excellent teaching device can be used in place of or supplemental to motion picture filming.

Recorders

The coach or an assistant can make a tape recording of practice sessions, games, and scrimmages in which strong and weak points are noted. This information can then be transposed to charts, so that both the coach and players can be appraised of each player's actions.

Skull Meetings or Chalk Talks

Meetings during which specific play situations are outlined or drawn on the board assist in portraying to the players what is to be given on the floor. This is a means of presenting situations, explaining why, and the like, which assists the individual player in better understanding the complexities of basketball.

It is an excellent teaching technique to visualize, by means of a chalk talk, new material which is to be given to the squad. The players, by seeing it on the board, obtain an understanding of the entire situation and each player's part in the scheme of things. This material, which is later presented on the playing court, will be more readily absorbed and accomplished by the team and players.

Basketball Notebook

It is possible to compile pertinent information concerning basketball and important facts which the coach desires to put across to the team into a notebook which can be issued to each player on the team to read and study. An outline of a basketball notebook follows:

1. Introduction
   Pertinent information about importance of reading and studying notebook
2. Schedule
   Season's schedule
3. Practice schedule
   Days and times of practice
4. Training and conditioning
   Training rules and conditioning plans
5. Studying
   Eligibility rules and necessity to develop good study habits
6. Offenses
   Complete outline of offenses with accompanying diagrams
   a. Fast break
   b. Patterns vs. man-to-man defenses
   c. Patterns vs. zone defenses
   d. Combating presses
7. Defenses
   Complete outline of defenses
   a. Man-to-man
   b. Man-to-man sag
   c. Press
   d. Special situations
      (1) guarding man on post
      (2) 1 on 2
      (3) 2 on 3

8. Special play situations
Diagrams and explanations of special plays
   a. free throw—defensive positions
   b. free throw—offensive positions
   c. out-of-bounds plays
   d. jump ball—defensive positions
   e. jump ball—offensive positions
9. Fundamental Skills
Brief description of the fundamental skills and their importance
   a. foul shooting
   b. shooting
   c. dribbling
   d. passing
   e. footwork
   f. rebounding

► Cutting the Squad, Selecting the Team

One of the most difficult and trying tasks confronting the basketball coach is that of having to cut the squad and, in doing so, to eliminate boys who have the desire but not the ability. In addition to cutting the squad, there is the problem of placing the players in the proper positions and then selecting the best five to form the team. In an effort to make the arduous task easier, every attempt should be made to scrutinize the players in as many different areas as is feasible.

Characteristics of a Good Basketball Player

The individual characteristics or qualities which indicate a good basketball player are numerous. Following is a comprehensive list categorized according to physical, mental, social, and emotional ability.

Physical ability. Co-ordination—Speed—Size—Agility—Condition—Ability—Reaction.

Mental ability. Knowledge—Interest in basketball—Willingness to learn and apply self—Mental alertness—Quick thinking—Confidence.

Social ability. Loyalty to coach, squad, and school—Likes to play basketball—Co-operative member of group—Ability to be a leader.

Emotional ability. Judgment—Good disposition—Self-control—Fighting spirit—Will to win.

The qualities of a good basketball player derived from the above list can be presented according to abilities:

Fundamental basketball ability. The ability to shoot, pass, dribble, rebound, and do all the necessary fundamentals which indicate a well-rounded basketball player.

Speed and co-ordination ability. The ability of the player in relation to his speed in running, cutting, and stopping, in addition to quickness in hands and arms.

Playing height ability. The ability of a player to play "tall" regardless of his size. This refers to the height of a basketball player in relation to his jumping ability. The well-co-ordinated 6-foot-2-inch athlete is often more effective and plays taller than the awkward 6-foot-6-inch giant.

Intelligence ability. The ability to be mentally alert, willing to learn, and able to apply self with regard to both basketball and schoolwork.

Social ability. The ability to be a co-operative member of a group and to have loyalty to the coach, squad, and school.

Emotional ability. The ability to have good judgment and self-control, along with a fighting spirit and the will to win.

Determining the Player's Ability

The coach will observe the players in a number of different situations, and he should compile information on each player at every opportunity. Scrimmages, drills, games, tests, and any other situations in which the boy is observed as a basketball player or an individual in society should be used for objective or subjective information.

While a great majority of the characteristics which go into making a good basketball player must be judged subjectively, such as spirit and co-operation, those dealing with physical ability (like speed and shooting ability) can be measured and recorded from performances in drills, scrimmages, and tests.

Individual performance. Some of the items of individual performance which are used as criteria for judging one player's ability against that of another can be recorded as positive criteria. When performing these acts, the player is given credit according to the accomplishment. Chart I indicates a form on which such data can be collected during scrimmages and practice.

The shooting ability of the player is easily ascertained by noting the shooting percentage figured from the shots taken and made. Also important is whether or not the shots taken were good percentage shots or from a poor position on the floor. The shot chart, in Chapter 9, will reveal this information, which is then transferred to Chart I. Foul shooting ability is recorded, and percentages easily indicate those who have the ability.

Obtaining possession of the ball is an important item in a basketball game, and the player who gets the ball one way or another is proving his value to the team. Offensive and defensive rebounding, intercepted passes, recovery of a fumble, or recovery of a jump ball are all items which can be recorded.

Assists in which a player makes a direct pass to another who subsequently scores, the first player being directly responsible for helping produce the score,

BASKETBALL INDIVIDUAL STATISTICS CHART

GAME: _____ DATE: _____

PLAYED AT _____

Name	Field Goals	Foul Shots	Offensive Rebounds	Defensive Rebounds	Lost Possession	Gained Possession	Assists	Tech. Pers. Fouls

CHART I.

indicate the players with an ability to see open players and get the ball to them.

Negative criteria can also be recorded in which the act, because it is to the detriment of the team, is counted against the player.

Among the negative actions are those in which the player is directly responsible for losing possession of the ball by fumbles, bad passes, or violations. Also to be considered are personal and technical fouls which give the opponents free opportunities to score. This information can be recorded on Chart I.

There are many basketball tests which can be used to help a coach in his analysis of the players, to substantiate a selection, to supplement other data, or to be used as a standard in which different abilities of basketball players can be rated. The following tests are compiled and thoroughly explained by Dean:[9]

Practice Free-Throw Graph	Penny-Cup Test
	A Perception Test
Game Free-Throw Graph	Peripheral-Vision Test
	Dr. Carlson's Fatigue Test
The Reaction-Times Test	Jump and Reach Test
	Knowledge Tests

D. E. Chambers[10] offers the following tests for indicating basketball ability.

1. Dribble Test for Ball-Handling. Three chairs, twenty-two feet apart. Ball on the first chair. Pick up ball and dribble with favored hand entirely around each chair and then straight back to start. Total time in seconds.

2. Repeat test number one with unfavored hand.

3. Shooting Skills for Timing, Speed, Accuracy, Reaction, Co-ordination, and Judgment. Chair with ball on it at foul line. Take ball and shoot from under the basket, eight on one side, eight on the other. Total time from start to end of twenty-fourth shot.

4. Testing Rebound Judgment and Speed. Jump to target eighteen inches above reach. Both feet on ground—reach as high as possible. Jump ten times and touch target. Total time in seconds.

5. Passing—Receiving Reaction Test. Position: line nine feet from wall. Pass ball against wall with chest pass fifteen times. Total time in seconds.

After all the data has been gathered, the coach is faced with the problem of rating and ranking the boys in the various positions. Herein lies the art of good coaching: the ability to place the right boy in the correct place so that there is no doubt as to the validity of the decision. What makes this act difficult is that a group of individuals is being judged, and although one boy might be a better performer in the fundamentals of the game, another might be superior in spirit, fight, and determination. The actual playing ability supported by valid data, plus the coach's subjective opinion of the less tangible qualities, should give the coach confidence that the selections are correct and that each boy has been given the proper rating and position on the squad.

Size and Composition

Another factor which is necessary to consider in this area is the over-all size of the team and the composition regarding players in various positions and classes in school.

Some schools will have a turnout which will be so small that no reduction in the numbers of players is necessary, while others will have fifty to a hundred trying out for one team. Certain factors should be considered which, although general, can be used as guides.

1. The number on a team should be such that they receive adequate supervision and instruction by the available coaching staff. When only one coach is available, this number usually varies from ten to fifteen players.

2. The squad should be so composed so that there is an even number of players in the various positions. A balanced squad would carry six forwards, six guards, and three centers—making three distinct teams, or a total of fifteen players.

3. The squad should be so composed that seniors, juniors, and sophomores, and sometimes freshmen, are represented. This ensures returning players on which to build future teams.

4. No senior should be carried on the team unless he is among the first seven or eight players on the team. It is a wise precaution to have junior, sophomore, and freshman reserves who do not play very much basketball, as they can look forward to moving up or to playing during the next season. Seniors who have no obvious future are more liable to be discontented and present a problem to the coach. Eliminate the problem before the situation develops.

Methods of Cutting the Squad

Following are two suggested methods of cutting the squad. Both are recommended, as each cares for the feelings of the player and accomplishes the difficult chore for the coach.

The first method is for the coach to announce during practice that the squad is to be cut. Players whose names appear on the list posted are on the squad. Those whose names do not appear did not make the team at this tryout. Those not making the team are encouraged to practice and participate in as much basketball as possible, preferably on organized teams

9 Dean, op. cit., pp. 71-82.
10 D. E. Chambers, "Testing for Basketball Ability," Scholastic Coach, October, 1952, p. 36.

in a league such as in an intramural league, recreation league, etc. It should be emphasized that every boy is welcome to return for a tryout next season. Any boy should feel free to discuss the case should he have any questions regarding his ability.

The second method involves more effort on the part of the coach, but leaves no doubt in the mind of the boy as to why he was cut. The coach talks to each boy individually and privately and tells him that he had to be cut from the squad; the player is encouraged to try out next season and to develop his ability by practicing and playing basketball.

Selecting Combinations

As early in the season as possible, the starting five should be placed in a unit, so that they can become accustomed to one another and develop into a co-operating, co-ordinated unit. The more they play and practice together, the better they will function as a smooth working five.

Each coach must develop criteria for the various positions in his offense and defense. An illustration is as follows: *Center*—tall, tough rebounder, can shoot with back to basket, and is good in passing off. *Forwards*—mobile and rangy, good shooters, good rebounders, and good passers. *Guards*—fast, good passers, good drivers, and good outside shooters. While some coaches are fortunate in that they have a selection of good players to fit the criteria, others must fit together the five boys with the best ability.

There are two important items that should be considered when selecting the first five. These involve having a team quarterback and having a spirited leader on the floor. Frequently these qualities come in the same outstanding individual, but more often they are found in two separate individuals.

Basketball, with its changing defenses and strategy, is difficult to coach; and each team, to accomplish the purposes as set forth by the coach, must be quarterbacked by one of the players who is alert, a quick thinker, one who has a good knowledge of the offense and defense and of basketball. It is usually one of the guards who is in the position to quarterback the team, to set the offense and attack the opponents. In this case, it is sometimes more profitable to sacrifice ability for a quarterback.

One of the players on the first five should be a spirited leader, one who spurs the team on regardless of whether the team is behind or ahead. Occasionally more than one of these exceptional players occur on a team. When this is the case, the coach is indeed fortunate.

The Captain

There are several methods utilized in selecting or appointing a captain.

The first does it in a democratic manner as the team elects the captain for the entire season. This can be done at the conclusion of one season for the next or at the beginning of the season. This captain for the year is elected by popular acclaim, but it is possible, particularly when the election is held at the end of the season to become effective the next season, that this player might not make the first team. If this happens, the coach would have to appoint a playing captain.

The second procedure is for the coach to appoint a game captain to act as floor leader, usually from among the first five, to act as captain for the game. The coach has the opportunity, when using this method, to pick the inspirational leader, the quarterback, or the deserving player who has been playing good basketball. At the end of the season, under this plan, an honorary team captain is elected for that year.

▶ Research in Basketball

There is a definite need for basic research in basketball, and there are many areas in which the individual coach can experiment and broaden the horizons. The sport of basketball is a relatively new one, and opportunities are available to the coach with an inquisitive nature.

Areas in which research is needed involve changes in the rules, teaching techniques, fundamentals, criteria for player selection, training and conditioning, diet, equipment, systems of offense and defense, and practically any other phase of basketball.

The research committee of the National Association of Basketball Coaches of the United States is continually carrying on research projects in an effort to improve the game. Individual coaches are encouraged to participate.

One does not have to be a statistician to gather and summarize data. If the data collected needs statistical treatment for analysis, there is always someone available in each school system to lend a hand if the coach is not statistically inclined.

Another important item concerning research is that once collected, summarized, and analyzed, it should be disseminated so that everyone in the field can profit. This usually means a presentation at a conference, clinic, or convention, or publication in a magazine or journal.

▶ Professional Advancement

In addition to the basic education in the field of basketball, the coach should strive to keep abreast of the rapid growth of knowledge, techniques, and strategies of the game of basketball and further his knowledge by: attending clinics, coaching schools, and conferences; reading current published material;

being an informed member of the National Association of Basketball Coaches of the United States; and knowing of the place and function of the Naismith Memorial Basketball Hall of Fame.

Clinics, Coaching Schools, and Conferences

There are pre-season, post-season, and summer clinics, coaching schools, and conferences dealing with all phases of basketball. The best teachers and coaches present material which is informative, interesting, and valuable. There are no secrets in basketball; consequently, every effort should be made to discover how successful coaches have achieved success. Methods, teaching techniques, strategy, offenses, defenses, and the like all add to the fund of information of the coach.

Published Material

Reading in the field will keep one abreast of the current trends in basketball. Many books and magazines are available dealing with all aspects of basket-

ball. Each coach should be a subscriber of a national coaching magazine, and new books should be obtained and read as they are published.

National Association of Basketball Coaches in the United States

The Bulletin is the official organ of the National Association of Basketball Coaches. In it appear the proceedings of the Association's annual meeting, plus diversified material concerning all aspects of basketball.

Naismith Memorial Basketball Hall of Fame

It is in the Naismith Memorial Basketball Hall of Fame that all the records of basketball will repose. Supporting and knowing of this important part of basketball is the duty of each and every coach in the country. It is located at Springfield, Massachusetts, and in it are listed the members of the Basketball Hall of Fame, plus the history and records of basketball from its inception in 1891 to the present.

NAISMITH MEMORIAL BASKETBALL HALL OF FAME (*Courtesy, Naismith Memorial Basketball Hall of Fame, Springfield, Mass.*)

► Summary

The profession of coaching basketball is actually one of teaching individuals, forming them into units, and placing the finished product in a competitive game situation. The coach is responsible for every aspect of this teaching situation from the beginning to the end. The coach should have professional pride in his coaching, and his sportsmanship and actions should be above reproach.

Scientific teaching methods and techniques will insure good teaching and quick, lasting results.

Objective as well as subjective judgments are made when selecting the squad, placing the players in the proper positions, and forming the five-man team; sufficient data should be utilized so that there is no doubt that the choices made were valid ones.

Because basketball coaching is competitive and the game of basketball has so many ramifications in its methods, strategies, rules, and playing of the game, each coach of necessity must keep up by reading current material and attending basketball clinics, conferences, etc. Self-encouraged professional advancement is a must.

► Study Questions

1. List the three Laws of Learning and give illustrations of how they are applied to a specific learning situation in basketball.
2. Why are fundamentals important in basketball?
3. The coach should have certain principles of action in regard to sportsmanship. What are they?
4. What four procedures are necessary in the teaching of a skill?
5. Why is it necessary to select the first five early?
6. What specific methods can be used to determine a player's ability?
7. Outline a method you would use when cutting the squad from thirty-three to fifteen players.
8. Why are subjective characteristics of a good basketball player so important in selecting a team?

► Projects for Additional Study

1. Take a specific skill in basketball and explain how the Laws of Learning are applied.
2. List three specific areas where research is needed in basketball.
3. Outline one research topic.
4. Theoretically compose your idea of a perfect basketball team by listing specific characteristics for each position.
5. Interview a basketball coach and ask him his methods of cutting the squad and what determining factors he uses in composing the first five.
6. Search the national coaching magazines for two articles which further the knowledge of basketball. In what respect are they enlightening?
7. Select a basketball motor skill and explain how you plan to teach it to a group of fifteen players so that it meets the criteria for the acquisition of a motor skill.

8. Explain one characteristic of a coach in your area which characterizes him. Is this good, bad, or harmless?

9. What is the basis for your selection of a particular drill to be used in practice?

► Selected References

American Association for Health, Physical Education and Recreation. *Research Methods Applied to—Health, Physical Education and Recreation.* Washington, D. C.: AAHPER, 1949. A comprehensive coverage of the nature and methods of research in physical activities.

Auerback, Arnold. *Basketball for the Player, the Fan and the Coach.* New York: Pocket Books, Inc., 1952. An excellent list of general and specific coaching suggestions.

Bee, Clair. *The Science of Coaching.* New York: A. S. Barnes & Co., 1942. Excellent material on philosophy, teaching principles, and choosing the squad.

Bonder, James B. *How to Be a Successful Coach.* New York: Prentice-Hall, Inc., 1958. Fine material on how to be a successful coach.

Boring, E. G., Langfield, H. S., and Weld, H. P. *Foundations of Psychology.* New York: John Wiley & Sons, Inc., 1948. Good coverage of all aspects of the learning situation.

Brownell, C. L., and Hagman, E. P. *Physical Education—Foundations and Principles.* New York: McGraw-Hill Book Co., 1951. Fine explanation of the nature of the individual.

Bunn, John W. *Basketball Methods.* New York: The Macmillan Co., 1939. Excellent on general coverage of coaching, philosophy, methods, principles, and choosing the team.

Dashiell, J. F. *Fundamentals of General Psychology.* New York: Houghton Mifflin Co., 1937. Complete look at the fundamentals and conditions of learning.

Davis. E., and Lawther, J. D. *Successful Teaching in Physical Education.* New York: Prentice-Hall, Inc., 1948. Approaches to teaching, the nature of the pupil, and how the pupil learns are fully treated.

Dean, Everett S. *Progressive Basketball.* New York: Prentice-Hall, Inc., 1950. Excellent coverage of coaching, basketball philosophy, methods, principles, and choosing the team.

Newell, Pete, and Benington, John. *Basketball Methods.* New York: The Ronald Press Co., 1962. Outstanding presentation of philosophy and coaching theory, coaching methods and techniques, and coaching problems.

Newsom, Heber. *Basketball for the High School Coach and the Physical Education Teacher.* Dubuque, Iowa: William C. Brown Co., 1952. The basketball coach and his problems, philosophy, laws of learning, and teaching methods are offered for the high school coach and teacher.

Ramsay, Jack. *Pressure Basketball.* Englewood Cliffs, N. J.: Prentice-Hall, Inc., 1964. Good comments on the philosophy of coaching and coaching the game.

Vannier, M., and Fait, H. F. *Teaching Physical Education.* Philadelphia: W. P. Saunders Co., 1957. Very fine material on understanding the student, learning, and techniques of successful teaching.

Wooden, John R. *Practical Modern Basketball.* New York: The Ronald Press Co., 1966. Fine coverage of the philosophy of teaching and coaching.

Woodward, R. S. *Experimental Psychology.* New York: Henry Holt & Co., 1938. A comprehensive coverage of practice and skill, learning and reaction time.

CHAPTER 3: The Coach — an Administrator

Although the coach of a basketball team is primarily responsible for placing a team on the floor ready to compete in a basketball game, he naturally assumes other duties allied with coaching, which range from eligibility checks on the athletes to the purchase and maintenance of athletic equipment. These behind-the-scene administrative duties in basketball are assumed by the coach and/or his assistants; when accomplished with efficiency, they ease the coaching task.

▶ Preparing for the Season

There are certain minimum essentials which each coach has to be conscious of and care for in preparing for the basketball season. Among these are the schedules of games, the pre-season practice schedule, the in-season practices, the post-season summary, organization for individual practices, and minimum requirements for playing the first game.

Season's Schedule of Games

The basketball season, with its schedule of games starting in December and ending in February, is split with vacation periods and holidays and runs through parts of two semesters of school. In addition, the entire season is long in that practice starts in mid-October for colleges and approximately the beginning of November for the high schools and does not end until the end of February. Certain factors must be considered when planning the season's schedule of practice and league games.

1. The total number of games allowed, such as twenty for a high school team or twenty-six for a team in the National Collegiate Athletic Association.
2. The total number of league games and their place in the schedule.
3. The number of games to be played each week and the days on which they are customarily played.
4. Arranging for suitable practice games leading up to the league schedule and placing practice games into open dates during league play.
5. The desirability of a trip or two each season.
6. Agreements from year to year with opponents on a home and home basis in which the dates of the games remain at approximately the same place in the calendar.

7. Tournaments: pre-season, holiday, or post-season.
8. Scrimmages with opponents which are or are not counted in the total number of games in the season.
9. Alumni game, if one is held. Pre-season, post-season, or holiday.

It is recommended that when the season's schedule has been completed it be duplicated and sent to the athletic director or basketball coach of each school appearing on the schedule. This procedure will eliminate mistakes and misunderstandings and will provide all people concerned with information regarding the opponents you play and when.

Enclosed with the schedule should appear a general information sheet[1] for the convenience and use of those teams, coaches, and officials visiting your school. On the following page is a suggested schedule form.

Pre-Season Practice Schedule

The pre-season practice schedule runs from the first day of practice to the first basketball game. It is during this period of time that the coach prepares the players for the schedule of games. He teaches fundamentals, conditions the players, and presents the offensive and defensive systems of play; the squad is cut, players are selected for various positions, and the starting five are molded together.

Because there is much to do in a limited time, efficiency in planning practices and deciding what is to be offered is necessary. A skeleton outline of the entire pre-season practice schedule can be laid out with the major items to be presented included. The remainder

---

[1] Shown on page 57. Courtesy of Art Gallon, Basketball Coach, University of California, Santa Barbara.

	Mon.	Tu.	Wed.	Th.	Fri.
Oct. - Nov.	30 Medical Examination	31 Medical Examination	1 Practice Starts	2	3
Nov.	6 Offense vs. Man-to-Man	7	8 Fast Break Pattern	9 Free Throw Offense and Defense	10
Nov.	13 Team Defense	14	15 Offense vs. Presses	16 Jump Ball Offense and Defense	17
Nov.	20 Pressing Defense	21 Out-of-Bounds Play	22 Game Scrimmage	23 Thanksgiving No Practice	24 Practice Saturday Morning
Nov. - Dec.	27	28 Game Scrimmage	29	30 Team Pictures	1 First Game

Fig. 1. Pre-Season Practice Schedule. Week-to-week practice schedule. Important items are listed.

GENERAL INFORMATION SHEET

(Name of School)
_____
(Location)
_____

It is our hope that the following information will be useful to you during your future trip to _____(name of school)_____. We are looking forward to having your team here this season. If we can in any way help make your stay enjoyable, please feel free to contact us.

Schedule. A copy of our schedule is enclosed. If you have not sent your schedule to us, we would appreciate a copy.

Playing facilities. Gymnasium is located _____(on campus)_____. Regulation court, glass backboards, ample clearance on end and side lines. Capacity _____(2000)_____

Time. Preliminary games start at _____(6:00)_____ P.M. and varsity games at _____(8:00)_____ P.M. At least one-half hour will be allotted for warm-up practice on the floor.

Pre-game practice. Arrangements for workouts can be made if requested well in advance.

Colors. _____(Blue and Gold)_____ : _____(White)_____ at Home and _____(Blue)_____ on the road.

Balls. _____(Name of ball)_____ will be used. Upon request, six clean practice balls will be provided for pre-game warm-up.

Complimentary tickets. Visiting team is entitled to thirty. Please contact _____(name and address)_____

Scouting tickets. Contact _____(name and address)_____ .

Players entrance. Players and officials will enter _____(location)_____. A manager will direct you to your dressing facilities.

Dressing facilities. A room with a blackboard is available adjacent to the training quarters. Feel free to use the training quarters or ask for whatever you may need.

Publicity. Contact _____(name and address)_____ for all information regarding our team and school.

Housing. Contact _____(name and address)_____ for assistance with motel or hotel accommodations.

Transportation service. (List location and accessibility of):
Airport:
Train:
Bus:
Main highways to major cities:

Sincerely,

_____
Basketball Coach

of the planning can best be accomplished on a week-to-week basis. Figure 1 shows such a worksheet.

Following are suggestions which can be used as guides in planning the pre-season practice schedule:

Minimum essentials required for the first game are placed in the skeleton outline with what is believed to be sufficient time for learning allotted.

Pre-season practice schedules will vary for a particular coach depending upon the number of returning veterans and the ability of the boys out for the squad; consequently, it will vary from year to year and school to school.

Sufficient scrimmage time should be allotted so that the players learn to react in a game situation.

At the end of each week, an evaluation of the practices should be made and the next week's workouts changed accordingly.

A judicious balance between fundamentals and offensive and defensive maneuvers should be maintained.

In-Season Practice Schedule

The practice schedule during the regular season is influenced by a number of factors, each of which must be considered when planning individual practice sessions. Although there should be a general plan in preparation for each game, the individual day is planned, and what transpires that day will influence the next day's practice. Following are items which should be considered in planning practice sessions during the in-season schedule.

Number of practices before a particular game.

Number and distribution of games during the week.

How well team and individuals played and the results of the last game.

Specific preparation for the next game.

Light practice with plenty of shooting the day before a game.

On day immediately after a game—light practice for those who played and heavy practice for those who did not.

Inclusion of fundamentals as need indicates.

Inclusion of chalk talk as necessary.

A skeleton outline of a weekly practice schedule with games on Tuesday and Friday follows:

Monday
Moderately heavy practice
Chalk talk on previous game
Chalk talk on coming game
Practice:
1. Offensive and defensive fundamentals as previous game and coming game indicate a need
2. Offense team play
3. Defense team play

Tuesday
Game—no practice

Wednesday
Moderately heavy practice—light for those who played most of last game
Chalk talk on previous game
Chalk talk on coming game
1. Offense and defense fundamentals as previous game and coming game indicate a need
2. Offense—team play
3. Defense—team play

Thursday
Light practice
Fundamentals—plenty of shooting
Offensive review
Defensive review

Friday
Game—no practice

Post-Season Schedule

Administrative duties at the completion of the season are anticlimactical; consequently, the following list of items is offered as a check list of what should be done.

1. Summary of the season: season's record; statistics, individual and team.

2. Recommendations for awards.

3. Collection and tabulation of all equipment. Note number, size, and condition of equipment.

4. Cleaning, repair, and storage of all equipment.

5. Recommendation as to what equipment is needed for the coming year with respect to what is on hand and usable.

Methods of Organizing Practices

Individual Practice Schedules
Ideally, each practice session will include the following:

Warm-up. This includes the period of time during which the players are reporting to practice and the drill or drills which are used to stimulate the players physically and mentally for the concentrated practice to follow.

An excellent way to utilize the period before the first drills is for the coach to work individually with those who report early. Many valuable individual defensive and offensive fundamentals can be profitably practiced under the watchful eye of the coach.

Players can be matched together to practice maneuvers they would use in a game, or individually they can be guided and encouraged to work independently to strengthen their weak fundamentals.

Offensive fundamentals. Offensive fundamentals are usually taught in drills, and those utilized should be the ones which are important and need stressing at that particular practice. Foul shooting as well as shooting in general should be practiced each and every day of practice.

Defensive fundamentals. Continued stress and practice on defensive fundamentals will pay off in a team which plays defense with pride and efficiency. Again, those fundamentals practiced are the ones which are important to the particular day in preparation for the next game.

Team defense. This phase of practice is concerned with co-ordinating the team effort in defense. It is during this phase of practice that the team is prepared to meet the offensive attack of the opponents. Stress on strengthening weak individuals or faulty team efforts is given at this time.

Team offense. The co-ordinated effort of the team to advance the ball down the court and to make an attempt at the basket is the team offense. Certain aspects of the team offense are presented each day at practice, with the entire offense being readied for the next game.

Some coaches stress particular phases of offense and practice them daily. Examples would be regular sessions on the fast break or set patterns to be played against man-to-man defenses.

In addition to the material to be covered in each individual practice, other factors should be considered.

Length of Practice Period

It is generally agreed that after an hour and a half of concentrated practice, the amount gained by the players is not worth the practice time. Practice time is thoroughly utilized, entire squad is kept busy, and practice runs smoothly from one phase to another.

Generally speaking, the practice the day before a game is shorter than usual, running from one hour to an hour and fifteen minutes in length.

Distribution of Time

The amount of time allocated to each phase of practice depends upon what the individual team members need practice on and what the coach feels is essential for the team. Here experience and individual preference are important. Following is a typical Wednesday's practice for a Friday night game.

4:15-4:30	Individual work with centers on defense
4:30-4:40	Lay-in drill
4:40-5:00	Offensive fundamentals
	One-on-one shot and follow
	Shooting foul shots
5:00-5:10	Defensive fundamentals
	Guarding the dribbler
5:10-5:35	Team defense
	Two vs. three
	Team defense for next game (five vs. five)
5:35-6:00	Team offense
	Patterns vs. opponents' zone and man-to-man defenses
	Fast break pattern, full court
	Foul shooting

Suggestions for Effective Practices

So that the players learn quickly and effectively and so that basketball practices do not become routine and dull, the following suggestions are offered:

1. Use scientific teaching methods to put the material across to the players.

2. Use competition in practice and drills. This element of competition will bring out the spirit and enthusiasm from the players and make practices more like a natural, competitive game situation.

3. Set up specific game situations, so that the team becomes accustomed to these highly competitive moments in a basketball game. Examples would be: defense behind two points with forty-five seconds to go; offense ahead three points with a minute to go; or offense behind one point with fifteen seconds to go. Each situation presents a different case in strategy and team play, and teaches the proper actions at the proper time.

4. Control scrimmages. Feel free to stop scrimmages, to make corrections and explain why such an action was or was not necessary. A mistake is then corrected before it becomes a habit.

5. Play games. Play games and bring out the enthusiasm and competition resulting from competitive activities. This simulates game conditions and makes practices interesting.

6. End the practice on a high note, so that everyone leaves happy and eager to return for the next day's practice.

Analysis of Practice

At the conclusion of each practice, the outcomes should be analyzed to determine whether what was anticipated resulted. If certain aspects of the game were not learned or practiced adequately, they should be planned into the next day's schedule.

First Day of Practice

The first day of practice is an important one to both the coach and the players. The coach is interested in developing the individuals in the group into a basketball team, and the players are eager to play on the team. This first session should be stimulating and informative.

So that all the players know the philosophy, policies,

and practices of the coach, he should set forth certain principles as guides for action by the individual members of the squad. Although each coach will enforce discipline in his own manner and have different rules and regulations, certain items should be presented to the squad at the first day of practice.

Schedule of games and season's outlook.

Time of practice.

Eligibility rules.

Training rules and conditioning.

Method of team cut.

Trips, players' actions and appearance.

Procedure and treatment of injuries.

New rules.

When the above have been presented to the players, there is no excuse for not following the training rules, for appearing in the incorrect clothing, reporting late for practice, etc.

In becoming a member of a team, each player must subject his self-interest to the welfare of the team. This act requires self-discipline on the part of each player and knowledge of the rules and regulations he must follow in order to be a member of the squad. "To be a good team member, one often must sacrifice his own immediate interest for the welfare of the group. This is definitely a part of the psychological and religious principle that if a man would find himself he must sacrifice for something bigger than himself."[2]

Minimum Requirements for the First Game

Before the first basketball game of the season, each team should be prepared for certain minimum essentials. These essentials comprise what is necessary to meet the opposition in a regulation basketball game.

Should a team be lacking in one of these essentials, it is liable to jeopardize the opportunity to win. A good example of this would be the team which did not know how to combat a press. Another illustration would be the squad which lost the opportunity of gaining possession of the ball on jump balls. In a close game, essentials such as these could be the determining factors.

Offensive Essentials

Fast break from each recovery of the ball: rebound, intercepted pass, out of bounds, free throw, or score by opponents.

Attacking the opponents' set defense whether it be man-to-man, zone, or a combination of the two.

Attacking the opponents' press, which could be man-to-man or zone.

Jump ball positions when your team can control the tip.

Out-of-bounds play, the minimum being to get the ball safely in bounds while the optimum would be a play from the baseline.

Positions on a free throw line when your team is shooting.

A semi-control system of play or a complete stall offense.

Fundamentals necessary to accomplish the above which will include: shooting, rebounding, passing, dribbling, and footwork.

Defensive Essentials

Co-ordinated team defense.

Pressing defense to utilize when behind late in the game.

Positions on the free throw line when on defense.

Positions on a jump ball when the opposition is almost certain to obtain the tip.

Fundamentals necessary to accomplish the above, which include: guarding the man with the ball in various positions on the floor; guarding the man without the ball no matter where he is on the court; defensive stance and footwork.

▶ Preparing for the Game

There are certain details which are necessary to administer in preparing for each specific game. Each is important and should not be forgotten, as each has its place in the playing of the game.

Pre-Game Preparation

It is during this period of time in which the scouting report is utilized in preparing the team offensively, defensively, and mentally for the game. (See Chapter 9, "Scouting and Game Statistics.")

Pre-Game Talk

The pre-game talk sets the stage for the action to follow. Certain essential items should be included.

1. The starting line-up.
2. Offense.
3. Defense.
4. Special defensive assignments.
5. Team captain.

It is recommended that important points which are to be emphasized be placed on a blackboard. This re-emphasis will influence the individual player and team regarding that important point, and then this item is more likely to be remembered and carried out.

[2] C. C. Noble, "The Moral and Spiritual Implications of School Athletics." *J. Ed. Socio.*, XXVIII (February, 1955) pp. 260-62.

Pre-Game Warm-Up

Several methods are utilized in taking the pre-game warm-up and each has its advantages.

First Method

Warm-up with a fundamental drill such as lay-ins.
Shooting drill.
Pre-game talk.
Starting team shoots and each player takes at least five foul shots.

Second Method

Pre-game talk.
Warm-up with lay-in drill.
Shooting drill—shot and follow.
Starting five shoot and take at least five foul shots.

Third Method

Special warm-up drill with passing and cutting. No shooting.
Shooting drill—shot and follow.
Vigorous lay-in warm-up drill.
Starting five shoot and take at least five foul shots.

Regardless of what method is used in the pre-game warm-up, certain items are to be considered which will make the warm-up period run smoothly.

1. Have a set procedure, so that each member of the team knows what he is supposed to do.

2. Have a definite time schedule and stick to it, so that each phase of the period will receive its full time allotment.

3. Players not on the starting team should practice their foul shots when in the shooting drill.

4. When shooting foul shots, players should work in pairs: one shooting while the other rebounds and tosses the ball back to the shooter.

5. When in the shooting drill, those players who do not have a ball should stay away from under the basket. This gives the four, five, or six players with basketballs the opportunity to shoot from their favorite spot, recover the ball, and shoot several more times without running into a congested area under the basket.

Half-Time Procedure

The half-time period always appears to be too short, a period during which time the players receive a much needed rest and, in addition, are informed of certain specific information which will make the second-half play purposeful and profitable.

A set procedure is recommended, so that a maximum effort can be made within a minimum period of time.

The team should quickly go to the dressing room and rest. During this period of time the coach:

Checks the score book for number of fouls on own team and on opponent's and determines leading scorer on each team.

Checks the shot charts to determine area or pattern of opponents' shots and own areas of scores.

Refers to the short form Scouting Report (Fig. 147) which was prepared during the first half and reveals specific items of offensive and defensive information concerning the opponent.

The coach then joins the team in the dressing room and gives them whatever information regarding his own team play and opponents' team play will help the second-half effort.

Tells players of fouls and fouls on opponents.

Informs players of leading scorer on each team.

Indicates opponents' offense and makes necessary defensive adjustments.

Indicates opponents' defense and makes recommendations concerning offensive adjustments.

Informs team of second-half starting line-up.

Half-Time Warm-Up

After the half-time talk, it is a customary procedure for the team to return to the floor and take a period of three to four minutes of shooting practice before resuming the game. Some coaches have the entire squad shoot, while others bench all except the seven or eight who are to play most of the second half. The first method is recommended as long as the starting group receives sufficient practice to make them confident that they are ready to go.

Special practice on foul shooting, shooting from particular areas of the floor, and the like should be done as the need indicates or upon recommendation of the coach because of inaccuracy during the first half.

After the Game

Before the vivid memory of the game is over, certain information should be noted, for the benefit of the players and so that information can be compiled on what that particular coach uses. This is gathered from the short form Scouting Report which was compiled during the game.

Offensive patterns are diagramed. Types of defenses used are noted. Special play situations such as out of bounds, jump ball, and free throws are diagramed. This report can then be used as a rough scouting report for the next year.

Individual comments regarding especially good plays or notes for improving play are compiled for the next chalk talk, so that each member of the team can be informed of his progress and have his mistakes corrected.

► Scouting

"By scouting is meant the observing and analyzing of an opponent's play in relation to the effect that it will have on the play of your team. It involves not only the study of an opponent when that opponent is playing another team but more particularly when your team is playing that opponent."[3] Thus, teams are scouted when they play other opponents in preparation for a specific game, and information on the opponent is compiled every time the team plays.

Scouting reports are obtained by several methods: personal observation, movies, paid scout, observing a team while playing that team, or by word of mouth from another coach or individual who has played or seen the team play.

Some individuals are not able to obtain scouting reports; hence, information compiled each time that opponent is played becomes a valuable source of knowledge on that particular team.

Scouting, scouting forms, and analysis and use of the report are covered in Chapter 9.

► The Basketball Budget

A budget is a detailed statement of expenses and income. When preparing this detailed account of how you desire to spend the money for the basketball team, the policies of the individual institution must be followed. Income is usually the responsibility of a school official other than the coach.

Items of expense are placed in specific categories, and when approved by the governing body (student body, administration, athletic control board, etc.), money can be spent for the items as requested.

Following are items which should be considered when preparing the expense items of a budget.

College Team

Awards. Number and cost.

Cleaning. Game and practice uniforms and other equipment are enumerated, plus the number of times cleaned, cost per cleaning, and number of items to be cleaned.

Entry fees. Fees for tournaments.

Equipment. Number, item of equipment, make or style number, and unit cost.

Film. Number of games to be filmed, cost of film and operator.

Guarantees. Amount of money guaranteed opponents.

Insurance. Number of players to be insured and cost per player.

Lodging. Total number of nights, cost per room, and number in traveling party.

Meals. Total number of meals (breakfast, lunch, dinner), cost per meal, number in traveling party.

Officials. Number of officials per game, number of home games, and cost per official per game.

Repair of equipment. Estimate on repair which would include equipment and uniforms.

Scouting. Method used in scouting and costs.

Transportation for trips. Automobile, buses, train, or airplane. Mileage and cost per mile.

Miscellaneous. Any items not included in the above. Itemize.

Emergency fund. A certain set amount to be spent for items not accounted for in the budget.

High School Team

Following is a typical high school basketball budget.[4] The revenue for basketball comes from two major sources: the Associated Students and the School Board. This budget is made up with a long-range plan for the purchase of uniforms which covers some eight years and a complete turnover of white and green game uniforms for a "B" team, a junior varsity, and the varsity.

Equipment

"B" team white uniforms	Medical supplies
Six basketballs	Practice "T" shirts
Long socks	Knee pads
Scorebooks	Miscellaneous

Officials	*Films*
Tournament Fees	*Scouting*
Cleaning and Repairs	*Transportation*

Junior College Team

Long-range purchase of equipment with colored game uniform, white game uniform, warm-up pants, and warm-up shirts being purchased on consecutive years within budget limitations.[5]

Equipment

Shoe laces	Practice pants
Basketballs	Scrimmage shirts
Wool socks	Warm-up pants
Cotton socks	Shoes
Practice shirt	Supporters

Laundry and Repairs	*Scouting*
Medical and Insurance	*Travel*
Overhead	*Meals*
Ticket takers	*Miscellaneous*
Custodians	*Officials*

[3] John Bunn, *Basketball Methods* (New York: The Macmillan Co., 1939), p. 99.

[4] Courtesy, Orrin Rife, former Basketball Coach, Polytechnic High School, Riverside, California.

[5] Courtesy, John Matulich, former basketball coach, Riverside City College, Riverside, California.

► Equipment

The items of equipment necessary for a basketball team are few and when well cared for last a reasonably long period of time. Usually each team is equipped with one white and one colored uniform plus a warm-up outfit.

Essential Items of Equipment

Basketballs	Shoes
Uniforms	Socks
White jersey and pants	Supporter
Colored jersey and pants	Training supplies
Warm-up jersey	

Additional Items of Equipment

Warm-up "T" type of	Colored socks
jersey	Ankle-length
Knee pads	Knee-length

Selection of Basketball Equipment

It is generally agreed that the purchase of good quality merchandise will pay dividends in good usage and easy maintenance. Following are six general categories that the buyer usually keeps in mind when he selects equipment.[6]

Design and Material

Utility and Cost of Maintenance

Safety Factor and Protection Equipment

Quality and Workmanship

Source of Supply

Price

Each of the above items is important, but to be especially considered are design and material, utility and cost of maintenance, quality and workmanship, and price.

The design and material should be the first concern of the purchaser. The design should fit one of the purposes of the uniform, and that is player and team identification. In accomplishing this purpose, contrasting colors are important, as well as a basic practical design for play ability. The uniforms should be tailored so that they fit well and give freedom of movement.

Many materials are available such as the new synthetics. Chart II offers a comparison of the common materials now in use. Utility and cost of maintenance are considered, and it is at this point that great consideration should be given to the type of material used in the construction of the item.

Equipment should be purchased on the basis of utility and meeting specific game needs, and should be easy and relatively inexpensive to maintain.

Workmanship is to be expected in good quality merchandise. As a result, purchase from reputable firms is the only guarantee of good quality and workmanship.

The price is often the determining factor in the purchase of equipment—although it should be the last thing considered; all items should be weighed before selection is made. Good quality will cost more, but because of low maintenance and durability features, will actually cost less in the long run.

Sizing of Basketball Uniforms

The uniform serves two purposes: comfortably covering the body and easy team and player identification. In no way should the uniform restrict the movements of the player. Charts III, IV, V, and VI indicate proper sizes and quantities to order for the normal high school or college team.

The usual procedure in issuing game uniforms is to properly outfit the first five, then the second five, and so on. This procedure guarantees proper fit for the players who will be doing most of the playing.

Purchase

There are two systems utilized in purchasing basketball uniforms. The first and most common is to purchase a complete set of jerseys and pants and repeat in several years. With a long-range purchase plan in view, it is possible to more or less stabilize the uniform purchases in this manner. An example would be to purchase a complete set of white uniforms the first year, the next year a colored set, and the third year a warm-up uniform. Then repeat. The old uniforms are turned over to the junior varsity or another team for their use.

The second method is to wear the uniforms for two years and then add approximately six replacements each year or every other year. If a good style is adopted, this method is an economical one, as there is never a complete set purchased after the start. Worn uniforms are discarded and new ones with similar numbers replace them.

When purchasing items of equipment in excess of approximately $25.00, it is economical to place the order on bid. Commercial firms are competitive, and from 10 to 40 per cent can be saved with this method of purchase. It is important when placing an order out for bid to give a thorough description of the article, so that what is desired is received, or at least an equivalent item.

Paying reputable firms for purchases within ten days usually results in a 2 per cent saving and is a good business practice. Process receipt of bills and

---

[6] *How to Budget, Select and Order Athletic Equipment.* Athletic Goods Manufacturers Association, Chicago, Ill., 1958, page 17.

FABRIC AND KNIT MATERIALS COMPARISON CHART

FABRICS	General Characteristics	Color Characteristics	Cleaning Qualities	Wear Index	Uses in Uniforms
Nylon Combat Cloth	Specially constructed twill weave of all Nylon. Great strength. Drapes well. Smooth slick surface. Very tightly woven. High sheen.	True athletic colors. Rather translucent in light colors.	A satisfactory fabric to clean. Bleaching may change colors. Repeated cleaning tends to subdue colors.	Abrasion-A Tensile-A	Excellent for football and basketball pants. White basketball pants should be lined.
Nylon Satin	Lighter than Combat Cloth. Great strength. Drapes well. Smooth slick surface. Tightly woven. High sheen.	True athletic colors. Rather translucent in light colors.	A satisfactory fabric to clean. Bleaching may change colors. Repeated cleaning tends to subdue colors.	Abrasion-A Tensile-A	Excellent for football and basketball pants. White basketball pants should be lined. Good for warm-up jackets.
Tackle Twill	Woven of high tenacity rayon yarn. Great strength for an all rayon fabric. Drapes neatly.	Colors excellent. All shades true and good.	An excellent fabric to clean. Excessive brushing will subdue the original sheen.	Abrasion-A Tensile-A	Excellent for basketball pants and basketball warm-up clothing.
Jockey Satin	Rayon faced, cotton reinforced fabric. High lustre. Good strength. Drapes well.	Colors brilliant and true. Most beautiful colors of any athletic fabric.	Excellent care should be taken to retain original high sheen.	Abrasion-C Tensile-B	Excellent for basketball pants.
Cramerton Army Cloth	Finest quality all cotton fabric. Combed mercerized yarns. Excellent wearing qualities. Good strength. Sanforized.	Colors deep and true.	Excellent.	Abrasion-B Tensile-B	Excellent for moderately priced football game and practice pants, and for basketball pants.
Rayon Satin	Rayon reinforced with cotton. Not as high lustre as Jockey Satin. Good strength. Drapes well. High sheen.	Colors bright and true.	Colors fast. Will withstand repeated cleaning satisfactorily.	Abrasion-C Tensile-B	Good for basketball pants and warm-up clothing.
Hi-Glo Acetate Satin	A lustrous acetate, high sheen. Satisfactory strength and draping qualities.	Colors brilliant and true.	Colors commercially fast. Must be cleaned with care.	Abrasion-C Tensile-C	Good for basketball pants and warm-up clothing.
Gabro-Cloth	Medium quality. Sanforized all cotton twill weave.	Colors true.	Washable.	Abrasion-C Tensile-C	Recommended for softball uniforms and boys football pants.

KNIT MATERIALS

	General Characteristics	Color Characteristics	Cleaning Qualities	Wear Index	Uses in Uniforms
All Coylon	An all nylon stretch material. Lightweight. Combines strength of Nylon with stretch of rubber. Excellent fit and elasticity.	Colors bright and true.	Cleans well. High temperatures should be avoided.	Abrasion-A Strength-A	Excellent for football pants and jerseys.
Coylon and Durene	A stretch yarn. Combines strength of Nylon with stretch of rubber. Excellent fit and elasticity. Wears well.	Colors bright and true. Subdued sheen.	Cleans well. High temperatrues should be avoided.	Abrasion-A Strength-A	An excellent material for football jerseys, basketball shirts, and athletic stockings.
Nylon and Durene	A balanced combination of Nylon and Durene. Lightweight, yet has great strength. Excellent elasticity. Good fit.	Colors bright and true.	An excellent fabric to clean.	Abrasion-A Strength-A	Very popular for both football jerseys and basketball shirts.
Durene and Rayon	A medium weight, moderately priced, knit material with satisfactory elasticity. Wears well.	Colors brilliant and true.	An exceptionally fine material to clean.	Abrasion-B Strength-B	Excellent for basketball shirts; very popular for basketball warm-up clothing.
Cotton and Rayon	A well balanced combination of cotton and rayon. Fits well. Good sheen.	Colors in all shades are bright and true.	A good material to clean. Tends to lose sheen after repeated cleaning.	Abrasion-C Strength-C	Popular in football jerseys and basketball shirts.
All Durene	A medium weight knit material. Wears well.	Colors bright and true. Subdued lustre.	A very good fabric to clean.	Abrasion-C Strength-C	Fine for football jerseys. Particularly suited for use in hot weather.
Stretch-Tex	A Rayon covered rubber knit fabric designed for great elasticity. A medium heavy weight knit material with two-way stretch for snug fit.	High lustre colors.	Great care should be taken in cleaning. Do not dry clean any garment containing inserts of this material. Wet clean only and air dry.	Abrasion-B Strength-B	Suited for all-knit football pants, knit inserts, and backs of half and half pants.
Waffle Weave	A Rayon and Durene specially knitted material. Lightweight knitted in three-color patterns.	A very colorful material for basketball uniforms. Colors brilliant and true.	Excellent cleaning qualities. Slight shrinkage should be expected.	Abrasion-C Strength-C	Used for trim on basketball shirts, inserts on basketball pants, and for warm-up shirts and inserts on basketball warm-up clothing.
V-Knit	A specially knitted Durene and Coylon fabric. Lightweight.	Available in solid colors or in two-color combinations in which second color appears as a contrasting color V-design. Colors brilliant and true.	Excellent cleaning qualities. Slight shrinkage should be expected.	Abrasion-C Strength-C	Used for trim on basketball shirts, inserts on basketball pants, and for warm-up shirts and inserts on warm-up clothing.
Ivy Knit	A specially knitted Durene and Coylon fabric. Lightweight.	A very colorful material. Available in seven different three-color combinations.	Excellent cleaning qualities. Slight shrinkage should be expected.	Abrasion-C Strength-C	Used for trim on basketball shirts, inserts on basketball pants, and for warm-up shirts and inserts on warm-up clothing.
Nyl-Knit	A specially knitted Nylon fabric. Extremely lightweight.	Colors bright and true.	Excellent cleaning qualities.	Abrasion-A Strength-A	Used on front of CSL and CSH Half and Half football pants, and in 19S Knit Shells.

NOTES

1. Wear index ratings show comparative qualities based on top material in each category. One fabric is rated against another fabric, and one knit material is rated against another knit material.
2. Abrasion tests conducted on standard Taber Abraser Wear Tester using CS-10 Calibrase Wheels and 500 gram weight.
3. Tensile tests conducted according to ASTM Test Method D39-49.
4. Ball-Burst (strength) test conducted according to ASTM Test Method D231-46.
5. Knit materials listed are knitted in Rawlings own knitting department. Absolute control is maintained over quality of yarns used and quality of dyes. All characteristics and qualities listed are applicable only to Rawlings Knit Materials.

Special Note on Football Practice Pants

Rawlings Football Practice Pants are available in Half and Half Style (Scrimmage Cloth front with Cotton and Nylon or Stretch-Tex back), Army Duck fabric, and Cotton and Nylon Knit. All of these pants are durable and all are washable. They should be washed at least once a week, and dried out completely before being used again.

CHART II. FABRIC AND KNIT MATERIALS COMPARISON CHART

BASKETBALL SHIRTS

Basketball shirts are made to actual size. Size 38 fits a player measuring 38 inches around the chest.

Extra length shirts should be ordered for players who are 6'2" or more in height. One to two inches longer than regular is recommended for players 6'2" to 6'5"; three to four inches longer for players 6'6" to 6'8"; and five to six inches for players 6'9" and taller.

COLLEGE

Shirt Size		34	36	38	40	42
Quantity	12		1	5	5	1
	15		2	5	6	2
	20	1	4	6	7	2

HIGH SCHOOL

Shirt Size		34	36	38	40	42
Quantity	12	2	3	4	3	
	15	2	4	5	3	1
	18	2	5	6	4	1

CHART III. SIZING BASKETBALL SHIRTS (*Courtesy, Rawlings Sporting Goods Company*)

BASKETBALL PANTS

Basketball pants are made to actual size. Size 34 is made for a player with a 34 inch waist. It is recommended that a notation be made on your order in the case of an unusually tall player so that special allowance can be made for his height.

COLLEGE

Pant Size		30	32	34	36	38	40
Quantity	12	1	4	4	2	1	
	15	1	4	5	3	1	1
	20	1	5	7	4	2	1

HIGH SCHOOL

Pant Size		28	30	32	34	36	38
Quantity	12	1	3	5	2	1	
	15	1	3	6	3	1	1
	18	1	4	7	4	1	1

CHART IV. SIZING BASKETBALL PANTS (*Courtesy, Rawlings Sporting Goods Company*)

BASKETBALL SHOES

Basketball shoes come in one width and are ordinarily fitted one-half to one size smaller than dress shoes. They should be fitted so that the foot will not slide in the shoe on sudden stops.

COLLEGE

Shoe Size		8	8½	9	9½	10	10½	11	11½	12	12½
Quantity	12	1	1	2	2	2	1	1	1		
	15	1	1	2	3	3	2	1	1	1	
	20	1	2	2	3	3	3	3	1	1	1

HIGH SCHOOL

Shoe Size		7½	8	8½	9	9½	10	10½	11	11½	12
Quantity	12	1	1	2	2	2	2	1	1		
	15	1	1	2	3	3	2	1	1	1	
	18	1	2	2	3	3	3	1	1	1	1

CHART V. SIZING BASKETBALL SHOES (*Courtesy, Rawlings Sporting Goods Company*)

BASKETBALL WARM-UPS

To insure complete freedom of motion for the player, a fabric warm-up jacket generally should be ordered two sizes larger than actual chest measurement. For a player 6'7" or taller the jacket should be three sizes larger than chest measurement.

Knit warm-up shirts should be ordered one size larger than actual chest measurement and, for a player 6'7" or taller, two sizes larger than chest measurement.

Extra length warm-up jackets should be ordered for unusually tall players.

Fabric warm-up pants come in three lengths—short, medium and long. The short size (28½" inseam) will fit players less than 5'9"; medium (30½" inseam) will fit players 5'9" to 6' tall; long (32½" inseam) is for players more than 6' tall.

FABRIC WARM-UP JACKETS—COLLEGE

Jacket Size		38	40	42	44	46
Quantity	12	2	3	4	2	1
	15	2	4	5	3	1
	20	2	6	7	4	1

FABRIC WARM-UP JACKETS—HIGH SCHOOL

Jacket Size		38	40	42	44	46
Quantity	12	3	4	4	1	
	15	3	5	6	1	
	18	3	6	7	1	1

KNIT WARM-UP SHIRTS—COLLEGE

Shirt Size		38	40	42	44	46
Quantity	12	3	4	3	2	
	15	3	6	3	3	
	20	4	7	5	3	1

KNIT WARM-UP SHIRTS—HIGH SCHOOL

Shirt Size		36	38	40	42	44
Quantity	12	3	5	3	1	
	15	4	6	4	1	
	18	4	6	6	1	1

WARM-UP PANTS—COLLEGE

Pant Size		30	32	34	36	38	40
Quantity	12	1	4	4	2	1	
	15	1	4	5	3	1	1
	20	1	5	7	4	2	1

WARM-UP PANTS—HIGH SCHOOL

Pant Size		28	30	32	34	36	38
Quantity	12	1	3	5	2	1	
	15	1	3	6	3	1	1
	18	1	4	7	4	1	1

CHART VI. SIZING BASKETBALL WARM-UPS (*Courtesy, Rawlings Sporting Goods Company*)

acknowledgment of the receipt of items quickly, so that this savings can be made.

Repair

Constant surveillance so that rips, broken buttons, loose buckles, etc. are discovered before major damage is done is necessary during the regular season.

Periodically during the season, and as soon as the season is over, the uniforms should be cleaned and then inspected thoroughly to discover where repair is necessary.

All repair work should be accomplished before the uniforms are stored.

Storage

Equipment that is properly stored will not deteriorate and will be in as good condition as when put away.

At the end of the season the uniforms are cleaned, repaired, and packed away until the next season. Several methods are utilized when storing athletic equipment, and the objective should be to leave the equipment in such condition that it will be in good shape when unpacked in the fall.

The uniforms should be hung on hangers in the storage room or, as is recommended, packed in boxes and stored.

► Managers

A good manager is a tremendous asset to a coach, because he can assume numerous routine duties and thus relieve the coach of many minor headaches.

It is an excellent idea to develop a managerial system in which, in addition to a senior manager, there are one or two assistant managers who are learning and working toward the senior manager's position. This type of system perpetuates itself, and there is always an experienced manager or two to select from for the senior manager's job.

Duties and Responsibilities

The more competent the manager, the more responsibility he can assume. Smart, experienced managers can do many tasks with the coach occasionally supervising to be certain the tasks are accomplished.

Each coaching situation will present different problems, making for varied duties and responsibilities of a team manager. Following is an outline which indicates what can be worked out as a check sheet for the manager so that his duties and responsibilities are clearly outlined.[7]

During Practice Sessions

1. Issue basketballs as soon as floor is available.
2. Keep spectators off floor during practice.
3. Keep basketballs in bag or rack when not in use.
4. At the end of practice, replace all equipment and turn off the lights.
5. One manager is to be in charge of the towel room until all players are out.
6. Manager be available to time, chart shots, or score scrimmages.

During Home Games

1. Issue game equipment, game suits and warm-ups.
2. Inflate game and practice balls.
3. Have available at bench: first aid kit, scorebook, shot charts, chalk, pencils, extra timers clock, towels, and whatever is used to prevent shoes from slipping.
4. One manager to be in charge of bench: balls, towels, first aid kit, and warm-up uniforms.
5. One manager to be in charge of shot charts, score, or time as is necessary.
6. At completion of game, collect all equipment, check it in, and return to its proper place.

Games Away from Home

1. Check all equipment before leaving: basketballs, uniforms, score book, shot charts, chalk and pencils, training kit.
2. Issue uniforms.
3. One manager is to be responsible for bench.
4. One manager is to be responsible for scoring or charting shots as is necessary.
5. Check all equipment before leaving for home.
6. Upon returning home, replace all equipment in its proper place.

Miscellaneous Duties

1. Periodically clean the basketballs.
2. Be a team statistician.
3. Periodically send uniforms to the cleaners.
4. Assist coach in marking equipment.
5. Thoroughly check all equipment and pack for storage.
6. Keep duplicate shot chart for opponents. Give at half time and at the end of game.

► Trips

The basketball season is one of many trips, and frequently the trips are of the overnight variety. Immediately, the coach is faced with the problem of having to supervise a group of young men over a prolonged period of time. Also to be reckoned with is the type of travel, overnight accommodations, meals, the players' conduct and attire, and handling of equipment.

Type of Travel

Basketball teams commonly travel by bus, automobile, train, and airplane. Travel arrangements are often made by the school administration, but frequently the coach is responsible. Several items of importance should be considered.

The departure should be timed so that the arrival time is sufficiently in advance of the game to allow the players an opportunity to rest and relax before going onto the playing floor.

---

[7] F. A. Lindeburg, "The Basketball Manager," *Athletic Journal*, October, 1954, p. 22.

Trips should be planned so that a minimum of time is lost from classes.

Meals

Meals are arranged in two different and distinct methods. First, the coach sets the menu, and the entire squad eats the same food. Second, each player is allowed to order what he desires within limits of common sense and economy. Generally speaking, the former method is preferred before a game, while the latter arrangement serves well when not preceding a game.

The coach, manager, or assistant usually pays the bill; but occasionally it is necessary, particularly on trips when the team splits up for recreational or educational sub-trips, to give each player a stated amount of money and let him pay for what he orders.

Policies should be set within the athletic department, so that the method of ordering and paying for meals is established.

Chapter 10 presents additional information on this important phase of basketball.

Players' Conduct and Attire

No matter where the players are, they represent the institution for which they play. Consequently, their conduct should be above reproach at all times. Conduct becoming a gentleman is what is desired, and the coach should leave no doubt as to what he expects.

It is becoming more apparent as time passes that coaches are aware of their teams' appearance on trips; as a result, high school, junior college, and college teams are traveling in slacks, coat, shirt, and tie. The feeling is that if a player looks like a gentleman, he is more likely to act like one. This should be expected, and there is no reason why a team cannot make as good an appearance off the basketball court as on it.

▶ Medical Examination

The player's welfare should be placed above any other consideration in basketball.

Before any player is allowed to report to practice, he should receive a thorough physical examination by a medical doctor. This should include checking the heart and blood pressure, and the general physical condition of the player. This would include hernia, deformities, and a recheck of previous injuries.

Should a player be injured, he should be placed under the care of a doctor and not returned to practice until released by the doctor.

Proper check by a doctor of the player's physical condition and a check any time there is a doubt about the player's ability to play will free the coach from decisions not in his realm of responsibilities. Also, it is better to have a player out for a game being treated than to use him for that important game and then lose him for the remainder of the season.

▶ Eligibility

Robert Gordon Sproul, President Emeritus of the University of California has stated, "We would rather have students playing at being athletes than have athletes playing at being students."

This statement is one which clearly illustrates the case of an education first and extracurricular activities second. Basketball players are in school for an education, and nothing should jeopardize this opportunity. Studying and playing basketball are compatible, and each player should be made to realize the importance and place of each.

Eligibility Standards

Methods of checking eligibility and standards of eligibility vary from a liberal one, in which anyone in school is eligible, to a strict standard, in which the student has to be passing in all subjects to be eligible. Following are typical eligibility standards and systems of checking:

High School

To be eligible to play basketball, the player must have passed four subjects the previous semester and be passing four in the current semester. A weekly check is made during the season, and players not passing in sufficient subjects are ineligible and not allowed to play until they are passing in four subjects.

Junior College

To be eligible, the student must have passed ten units of academic work plus physical education in the previous semester and be passing in ten units plus physical education in the current semester. Weekly checks are made, with eligibility being declared every two weeks. The weekly check is, in effect, a warning to give the boy another week to bring up his grades.

College

To be eligible, a student must have passed in ten units of academic work the previous semester and be enrolled in at least twelve units the current semester. No mid-semester check is made, although deficiency notices serve as a warning.

The above illustrates what is being done. No matter what the standards, the coach should periodically remind the players of their educational opportunities and necessity of maintaining their grades at a high level to be able to go into the vocation of their choice. Eligibility will then be a matter of course.

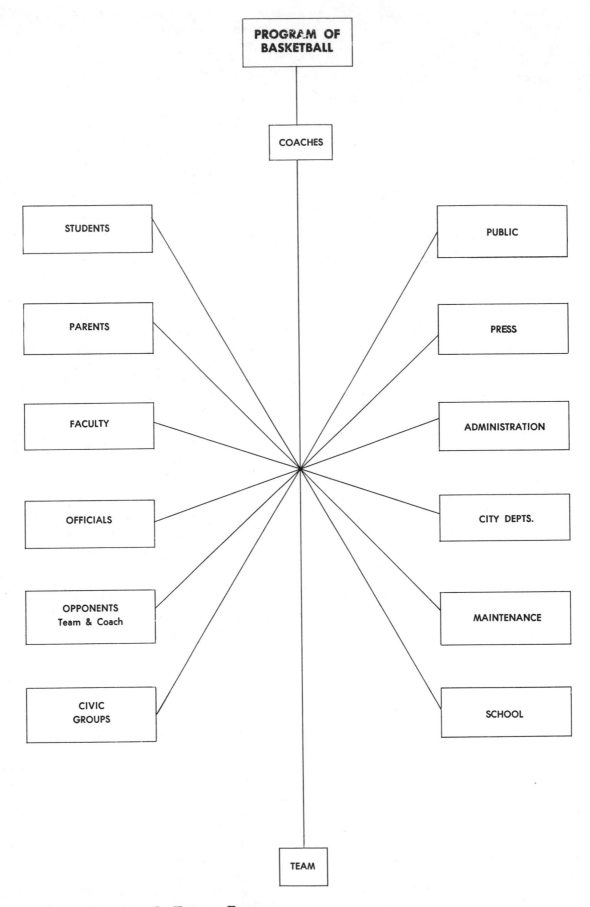

CHART VII. PUBLIC RELATIONS—IT TOUCHES EVERYONE

► Public Relations and Publicity

Public relations extends into more areas and to more people than one realizes. Chart VII portrays the far-reaching effects and the various people who are influenced by the actions of the coach and the team. These actions do not merely stem from games, but result from every contact any individual has with each and every aspect of the entire basketball program, whether it be during a game, while traveling, or during practice sessions.

Each coach has the obligation to maintain good public relations for his team and school, and to provide information for publicity to the newspapers, radio, and television as the case may be.

Pre-season information in the form of a brochure to newspapers, radio, and television stations will give these media of publicity necessary information to be able to report on the teams accurately.

The following informative material is usually found in a comprehensive brochure.

1. Team roster with name, number, position, height, weight, age, class, major, and high school or junior college attended.
2. Schedule of games.
3. General information about school, including enrollment, conference, and administration.
4. Coaches.
5. Previous season's results.
6. Season's outlook.
7. Player sketches with pictures.
8. Individual and team records.
9. Previous record of opponents' scores of games played with this year's team.
10. Freshman roster.
11. Freshman schedule.

Colleges frequently send out comprehensive brochures, but when these are not available at the high school level, information should be submitted with respect to team roster, schedule, information on the coaches, and previous season's results. These should be considered the minimum information.

Some newspapers are able to send reporters to cover games, while others depend upon the individual school reporting the event and notifying the paper of the results before the publication deadline. This is usually accomplished by telephone, with the newspaper personnel writing the story.

Pre-game releases can be written and submitted to newspapers in the form of news releases. Chart VIII indicates a typical release which is sent to newspapers, opponents, and radio stations for their use.

Important information can be transmitted by telephone to the newspaper, with the sports reporter writing the story.

Chart IX indicates what is necessary when compiling information for the release of a story for a game. This form can be utilized by the coach in giving material to school newspapers and the public newspapers, radio, and television stations for their use in disseminating the information as they see fit.

Whether written by a news service or a student or phoned in by the coach, this submitting of news is a valuable and important aspect of publicity and public relations.

Faculty

As a member of the school's faculty, each coach should endeavor to be a dependable member of school staff.

Attendance at faculty meetings, attire in proper dress, and assuming normal obligations as a member of the faculty are the normal courses of action. No individual should place himself above the group; each should do his share as one of the faculty.

Co-operation with the faculty on discipline, eligibility, and other related school matters will make the academic members of the faculty more co-operative and sympathetic to the varied problems of the coach.

Speeches

The successful coach will be deluged with requests to give talks or speeches to service clubs, award banquets, and numerous other groups.

This important public relations phase of the job should be realized, as well as the tremendous values which can result from contacts with members of the community.

Of course, one can accept only those which do not conflict with regular duties; but when there is no conflict, every attempt should be made to accept the invitation.

Most invitations will come with a suggested topic. When the coach is left with the choice, he should consider the group, as well as the appropriateness of the material, in choosing his subject.

It goes without saying that what is important is how the speaker is accepted. This reflects not only on the coach but on the team and the institution which they represent.

Remember that what is said is as important as how it is said. A well-prepared, well-presented, timely talk will be very effective, and always valuable from the public relations standpoint.

University of Redlands

NEWS BUREAU
PYRAMID 3-2121

By Bill Bruns

SUBJECT __Basketball__

DATE FOR RELEASE __Immediate__

PICTURE __No__

Its third straight SCIAC championship already sewed up, the University of Redlands will concentrate on making Occidental its 29th straight league victim Saturday night in the UR gym. Tip-off will be at 8:15.

Though two league games remain, Redlands cinched the SCIAC title Tuesday night by knocking off second place Pomona, 59-49. Pomona, Oxy, and Whittier now share second place with 4-3 records while the Bulldogs stand unscathed at 8-0.

Redlands' long winning streak will be sorely tested by Oxy. The Tigers, who fell to Redlands in the first round 72-64, are fresh from a 71-58 upset of Whittier last week.

Oxy is led by 6-11 Doug Willsie, the league's second highest scorer and top rebounder. Guard Larry Edwards, fifth in the league in scoring, gives the Tigers good outside shooting.

Classy Jack Schroeder continues to pace Redlands in brilliant fashion. The 6-7 center leads the Bulldogs in scoring with an 18.3 average and in rebounding with 10.3 per game.

Schroeder is at his best in key games, and Saturday's will be one. In the first round he held Willsie to a scant 10 points while scoring 29 himself.

Sparking Redlands from his guard spot will be shifty Gary Smith, the league's most accurate all-around shooter. Smith is having quite a sophomore year, sporting a 14.1 average.

Rugged Jim Clark and George Newmyer, both 6-4, will be at the forwards for Redlands while Dave Miller will be at the other guard.

CHART VIII. A NEWS RELEASE (*Courtesy, University of Redlands, California*)

Sports Information Bulletin

1. Sport_____ Coach_____

2. Game Date_____ Time_____

3. Place_____ Opponent_____

4. Squad
   (If traveling)_____
   Starters (*)
   _____
   _____
   _____
   _____
   _____
   _____
   _____

5. Results of last game played.

   A. Opponent_____

   B. Score_____

   C. Place_____

   D. Outstanding performers_____

6. Results of previous game with this same opponent.

   A. Score_____

   B. Place_____

   C. Remarks_____

7. Current Win-Loss Record _____ _____ _____

8. Statistics, if necessary

   _____ _____

   _____ _____

9. Coach's view of coming game_____
   _____
   _____

CHART IX. SPORTS INFORMATION BULLETIN

► Summary

The basketball coach has many administrative duties in relation to coaching the team. These include preparing for the season, preparing for the game, scouting, budgeting, public relations and publicity, managers and their duties and responsibilities, medical examinations for the players, eligibility, trips, and the purchase, repair, and storage of equipment.

Efficiency in these administrative tasks will ease the coach's burden, as will the delegation of certain responsibilities to managers and assistants.

Especially important is the planning for the season, so that the minimum essentials are learned by the team for the first game. Careful planning of the pre-season practice schedule and the individual day's practice will help accomplish this.

► Study Questions

1. What important factors should be considered during the half time of a basketball game?
2. List the minimum essentials necessary for a team to effectively play the first game.
3. What do you consider when making out a day's practice schedule after a Tuesday game?
4. Certain phases of basketball should be included in each practice session. What are they?
5. Explain how it is possible to play a team and scout them at the same time. Of what use is the material obtained? When is it used?
6. What would be included in the pre-game information that is given to the team?
7. Write a theoretical pre-game basketball release.
8. List during-practice duties of a basketball manager. How do these assist you as coach?

► Projects for Additional Study

1. Make up a theoretical basketball schedule of twenty games with twelve league games. Indicate actual days and dates and note home and away games.
2. Visit a basketball coach and examine an actual basketball budget. Is there continuity from year to year? What limiting factors are there?
3. Lay out a pre-season's practice schedule and include the minimum essentials a team would need to play its first game.
4. List three specific situations you would use in practice to make that practice an effective one.
5. Prepare a talk to the players regarding rules and regulations to be followed by the players as members of a team.
6. Lay out a long-range plan of purchasing uniforms for a varsity and a junior varsity team.
7. Plan a record system for the accounting of basketball equipment. Indicate how it would help in the efficient, economical purchase of new equipment.

► Selected
References

Athletic Journal. Athletic Journal Publishing Co., Evanston, Ill. Publication which includes many fine articles on all phases of coaching.

Bee, Clair. *The Science of Coaching.* New York: A. S. Barnes & Co., 1942. Includes comments on the various phases of practices, coaching methods, and detailed practice schedules.

Bonder, Jim. *How to be a Successful Coach.* New York: Prentice-Hall, Inc., 1960. Thorough treatment regarding handling players and public relations.

Bunn, John W. *Basketball Methods.* New York: The Macmillan Co., 1939. Has samples of practices and comprehensive program of practices.

Dean, Everett S. *Progressive Basketball.* New York: Prentice-Hall Inc., 1950. Covers thoroughly the basketball season, aspects of daily practices, and practice sessions.

How to Budget, Select and Order Athletic Equipment. Athletic Goods Manufacturers Association, Chicago, Ill., 1958, p. 17.

McCreary, Jay. *Winning High School Basketball.* New York: Prentice-Hall, Inc., 1956. Good material regarding the high school coach and public relations, the pre-season program, equipment, the season's schedule, and practice sessions.

McGuire, Frank. *Scholastic Coach,* October, 1956, p. 13. Excellent material on preparing for the game.

Newsom, Heber. *Basketball for the High School Coach and the Physical Education Teacher.* Dubuque, Iowa: Wm. C. Brown Co., 1952. Fine selections on daily practices.

Rawlings. *How to Fit Athletic Equipment.* Rawlings Sporting Goods Co., St. Louis, Mo. Good material on sizes and numbers for high school and college.

————. *The Care and Cleaning of Athletic Equipment.* Rawlings Sporting Goods. Co., St. Louis, Mo. Specific information concerning the cleaning of athletic equipment.

———— *Roundout.* Rawlings Sporting Goods Co., St. Louis, Mo. Publication which deals with all aspects regarding athletic equipment.

Scholastic Coach. Scholastic Magazines, Inc., New York 36, N. Y. Publication which includes many fine articles on all phases of coaching.

U. S. Navy. *Basketball.* Annapolis, Md.: United States Naval Institute, 1943. Offers lesson plans that can be used when teaching large numbers.

Wooden, John R. *Practical Modern Basketball.* New York: The Ronald Press Co., 1966. Excellent material on all aspects of administering a basketball team.

CHAPTER 4: Individual Defensive Fundamentals

Individual defense is the effort of a member of the defensive team to stop the individual offensive man from obtaining the ball, to stop the offensive men's attack, and to obtain possession of the ball. The individual defensive situation of one man guarding another always arises regardless of the team defense employed. When properly learned and co-ordinated with the other members of the team, this important aspect of defense forms an impregnable barrier which the offensive attack will find difficult to penetrate.

Individual defensive fundamentals are basic to playing team defense; and when coupled with a determined, aggressive spirit, this combination is hard to beat.

► Philosophy

Individual defense is important. It is half of basketball—the team is either on offense or defense. Although individual defense is relatively easy to learn, the average player, and sometimes the coach, does not appreciate its importance. It is one thing to practice shooting and be able to note immediate success and improvement; but on the other hand, one seldom counts the number of good defensive maneuvers a player makes in the course of a game.

The individual skills which are necessary to play good defense are not difficult. They are relatively simple and easy to learn; but each player must be convinced of their importance, so that he will practice diligently with a purpose in mind.

The fact that defense is important and that it is relatively easy to learn points up the issue to the individual coach. Individual defense is important! Individual defense is easy to learn! Individual defense can be rewarding! When these intangible aspects are made known to the players and stressed by the coach, individual defensive fundamentals will be recognized as a very important part of basketball.

The team with strong individual defensive players will consistently play good defense. This stress on defense will enable a good team to excel, an average team to do well, and a squad poor in ability to make a good showing.

Coaches teaching and using zone offenses must be conscious of the fact that good individual defensive fundamentals are essential to zone defenses. Although some individual techniques are different, if a player is well grounded in the basic individual defensive fundamentals, he will easily adapt to any variation of man-to-man or zone defense.

The author is a firm believer that the basis of any defense is individual defensive fundamentals. These should be taught first, so that the player has a good foundation for playing any defense.

► Individual Requisites

Seldom does one player possess all the requisites which go into making a good defensive player; when this does occur, the player will be of exceptional ability. It is possible to improve some of these individual requisites, but usually the individual is blessed with them or he does not possess them at all.

Speed

Speed can be separated into speed afoot and quickness of hands and arms, of which both play an important part in defense.

The player who has speed afoot has the advantage of being able to move quickly from one position on the floor to another and, in many cases, can use speed to make up for other deficiences and even to cover up mistakes.

Speed of hand and arm movement enables a player to harass an opponent, block shots, and deflect passes. This attribute is a valuable one and is not necessarily paired with speed afoot.

Size

Size is a very important factor in individual defense. Given two players of equal ability, the coach will always select the taller of the two.

Size can be gauged in two ways: standing height and reach, and what can be called playing size. Often the tall player with the long reach is not co-ordinated well enough to "play tall." It is the combination of being tall and being able to play tall that makes the difference. Many 6-foot-3-inch basketball players, because of exceptional jumping ability and an accurate sense of timing, are able to rebound with the 6 foot 6, 6 foot 7, or taller players. Playing tall is more important than mere size.

Alertness

The ability to be ready, wide awake, and prepared for action is *alertness*. A player with this ability will not be caught by a surprise action and will always be ready for the unexpected. Alertness will pay off in the intercepted passes and recoveries, and in general good individual defenses.

Spirit

Enthusiastic loyalty to be the best and to do the best typifies a competitive spirit. A player with this inner fire to get the ball, to beat the opponent, to win the game, etc. sometimes overcomes other weak requisites of individual defense. It is this type of individual who will dog an opponent and, although the other player may be superior in size, speed, or ability, never admit defeat and always strive for victory.

Vision

"He plays as if he has eyes in the back of his head," expresses the important aspect of vision. Some individuals have a wide range of sight—so-called peripheral vision—while others see as if wearing blinders. The ability to see a wide portion of the floor will enable the defensive player to avoid screens, observe other players, watch the movement of the ball, and in general see more of what is going on on the basketball floor.

Judgment

The mental process of judging whether or not to do an act involves making instantaneous decisions regarding many variables. For instance, the speed of a passed ball and whether the defensive player can get to the ball before the ball reaches the offensive player, are judgments which must be made instantly or not at all. This ability to make accurate decisions, to be able to rate an opponent, to use good judgment, can enable a player to be very tough on defense.

Adaptability

The ability to adjust or adapt to a new or changing situation indicates adaptability. Many situations occur in basketball in which the individual player is required to adjust his mode of action to combat the opponent or to change a plan of action. Examples would be adopting the proper defensive position against a left-handed opponent, guarding a player who only drives left, or adjusting one's position on the floor against a faster opponent. These adjustments are often easily made by some players, while others find such changes difficult—hence, the importance of being able to adapt easily to the situation at hand. After having guarded an opponent for five minutes a defensive player should be able to answer these basic questions concerning his opponent's basketball ability:

1. What is his favorite type of shot?
2. Is he right- or left-handed?
3. Can he drive either to the right or to the left?
4. Does he drive toward the baseline or toward the middle of the court?
5. Is he a good offensive rebounder?
6. Is he a good defensive rebounder?
7. What are his favorite fakes?

When the above questions concerning the opponent can be answered, the guard should be able to counter them. For instance, if he is right-handed and uses only that hand, the guard can keep his left hand (the one opposite the defensive player's right when facing him) up so that he will find it difficult to shoot. If he drives only to the right, then the guard can play to his left and easily stop the drive. When his favorite shot is known, then it is up to the guard to keep him from getting into position to shoot it. To sum it up, the more that is known about the opponent, the more positive actions the guard can take against him.

Co-ordination

The ability to co-ordinate all parts of the body enables the individual to be an efficiently functioning organism. The well-co-ordinated basketball player will have a harmonious adjustment of his muscles for efficient action. This type of individual will make difficult actions look easy; he will, with his well-co-ordinated muscles, expend a minimum amount of energy to get the job done.

Co-ordination can be improved with exercises and drills. The tall, awkward boy often needs special work with the jump rope, dancing, or special exercises specifically designed for the individual to develop co-ordination. (See Chapter 10.)

▶ Individual Techniques

Position on the Floor

With the exception of guarding a man in the pivot position and special defenses, *the general rule to follow regarding the position of the defensive man in*

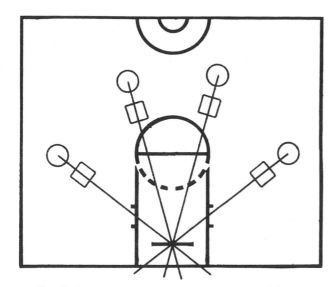

FIG. 2. DEFENSIVE POSITIONS. Men stationed between their men and the basket.

relation to the offensive player is to play between that man and the basket. A line drawn through the center line of the offensive player and the basket would run through the forward foot and forward hand and arm and down the midline of the body of the defensive man. Figure 2 depicts several positions on the floor with the defensive man in the proper position. In each case, the forward foot is the one nearest the sideline. This position makes it difficult for the defensive man to go to the inside and forces his movement to the sideline. If the objective is to force the play to the center of the court, the inside foot should be placed forward.

How close the defensive man plays to his opponent, whether or not the opponent has the ball, depends upon his speed afoot, his opponent's speed, the distance from the basket, distance from the ball, and the type of defense—tight, regular, or sag.

A player who is faster than his opponent can play closer, as his speed will enable him to stay up with his opponent.

If the offensive player does not have the ball, the type of defense usually dictates the distance to be played. A regular man-to-man would necessarily require playing close to the offensive man when he is close to the basket or close to the ball; otherwise, a normal distance of five to six feet is assumed. When a tight defense is being played, the guard is required to stay close to the man, to play close. Regardless of the position of the ball and where the offensive player stations himself, the guard still plays tight.

Another general rule when guarding the man with the ball is the further away from the basket he plays, the greater the distance the guard can move away from him in the direction of the basket. Of course, when the offensive man is within shooting distance, the defensive stance should be taken at touch distance.

Stance

The basic stance in basketball is similar to that of a boxer, with one foot in advance of the other, the toe of the back foot almost opposite the heel of the front foot. The feet should be comfortably spread, no wider than the shoulders apart. The trunk should be erect and the head up with the weight evenly distributed on both feet, so that the player can move quickly in any direction with little shifting of weight. The illustration portrays this defensive position.

When guarding a man with the ball, the defensive man must be prepared to meet a shot, a pass, and possibly a cut or a dribble. As a result, the guard should be ready to close to block or hinder a shot; drop back to guard the dribbler; and, anticipating a pass, move hands in a manner to block or deflect one and then drop back to pick up a cutter. This calls for good balance, good judgment, and a mastery of individual defensive techniques.

The guard should not lunge forward to guard or jump to block a shot. Both of these moves are fatal, as a good offensive man will take advantage of this mistake.

Position and Movement of Hands and Arms

The same hand and arm should be forward as the front foot. This hand is held high to block or hinder a

BASIC DEFENSE STANCE

high pass or a shot. The back hand and arm are held waist high to prevent a dribble in that direction or to block a low pass. The hands should not be held stationary, but should move to hinder and distract the opponent.

Eyes

The defensive player should be continually moving his head to and fro so that he can observe action to his left, his right, and as much as possible to the rear. Proper use of the eyes will enable the defensive player to avoid screens, keep the ball under observation, see his opponent, and know the relative position of his teammates to avoid collisions. Good peripheral vision is an asset; but a player without it, by being alert, observant, and smart, can accomplish the same end.

Voice

The voice serves three distinct purposes in defensive basketball. The first is to "talk it up" to spur your team on. The voice in this case encourages a teammate or the team by calls of "Now we have them," "Keep up the good work," or "Let's score again." On the other hand, when the voice is directed against the opponent, it is for the purpose of discouragement or harassment. Such exclamations for this purpose would be: "Don't shoot," "You can't do it," "I have you—You won't score." The third and very important use of the voice is to *inform* or *warn* players on the team of situations of which they are not conscious. Examples would be a screen, an unguarded player under the basket, and the position of a loose ball. Assisting one another in this manner is another example of smart individual play leading to good teamwork.

The importance of the use of the voice cannot be emphasized too much. In the first instance, it reflects the spirit and attitude of the team, and in the third it indicates intelligent teamwork.

The coach, by pointing out examples of the proper use of the voice or talking to help a player on the team, should strive to inculcate this attribute of individual defense into every player on the squad. A squad that talks will be one in which the five players on the floor are communicating for the good of the team and at the same time presenting a psychological barrier of chatter as a wall in front of the opponents.

Footwork

Footwork is an important aspect of defense because it enables a defensive player to quickly maintain or regain a favorable position on the floor with respect to the opponents.

Short, quick steps should be taken, so that there is never a long period of time in which the weight is on one foot.

A defensive player should never cross his legs. When he does, he places himself in a vulnerable position, so that a smart opponent can take advantage of this entangling stance and cut back to go free. The legs must be uncrossed before the guard can change direction to try to catch his opponent.

When the opponent is moving cross court, a boxer's glide should be used with the first step being taken with the foot on that side. Figure 3 shows the foot movement when guarding a player who is moving cross court from the defensive player's left to right. The first step is with the right foot, then the left, and repeat with short fast shuffling steps. Of course, the reverse is true if the opponent goes in the opposite direction. This maneuver will offer a good balance and afford sufficient speed to keep up with the opponent. Because the guard is in a balance position and is taking short fast steps, he can quickly stop or change direction as necessary.

A different maneuver is necessary when the offensive player cuts or dribbles for the basket to the right of the defensive player. Assuming the right foot is the

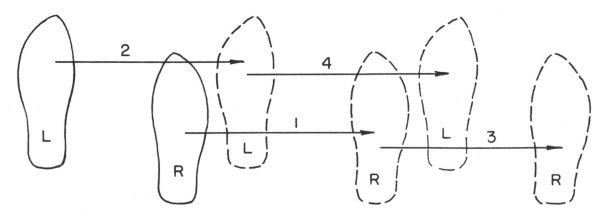

FIG. 3. FOOTWORK: MOVING TO THE RIGHT. When guarding an offensive player who moves across the court, the defensive man first moves his right foot, then his left, right, and left.

front foot, the defensive player pivots on the balls of his feet, pushes off the left foot, and steps with the right foot back and to the right. This maneuver will regain or help maintain position on the opponent and enable the defensive man to assume the boxer's glide. Figure 4 shows this footwork.

It is necessary to change the footwork when the opponent drives or cuts to the defensive man's left when the left foot is forward. Pivot and step with the left foot to the left and back. Follow with the right foot in a boxer's glide. Left, right, left, right. Figure 5 depicts how this should be accomplished.

The boxer's glide is used as long as the defensive player is able to maintain his relative position on the floor, but when this position is lost, the defensive man has no alternative but to run as fast as possible to catch up.

Other important items of defensive footwork use the stop, start, and change of direction.

The *stop* is executed by landing on the balls of the feet with the knees bent and the hips low. The hands and arms are used for balance or harassment of an opponent. A player running at full speed can execute such a stop, but usually fails to do so because he fails to drop his hips low and maintain a low center of gravity.

The *start* may be executed in any direction around the compass, but regardless of the direction of movement, two important movements are necessary. The first is for the player to push off the foot farthest away from the direction he desires to go. The second item involves short choppy steps with the feet pointed in the desired direction. The hands and arms can be used to drive the body around in a pivot as the player starts his initial action.

The *change of direction* involves nothing more than a lowering of the shoulder in the direction the player wants to change to, a press of the planted outside foot, and a drive of the arms to pivot the body in the new direction.

▶ Defensive Techniques

The individual defensive man will come up against some common defensive situations. Proper techniques designed to combat the individual offensive thrusts are basic to individual defense. These involve guarding the man without the ball, guarding the man with the ball, guarding the dribbler, guarding the cutter, guarding the pivot man, guarding two offensive men, and rebounding.

Guarding the Man without the Ball

The position taken while guarding the man without the ball will depend a great deal upon the team defense, but nonetheless there are certain basic principles which can be followed that fit into team play.

1. Stay between the man you are guarding and the basket.

GUARDING THE MAN WITHOUT THE BALL—INSIDE FOOT AND HAND FORWARD

2. The further the man you are guarding is away from the ball, the further you can play away from him toward the basket.

3. The defensive man should play in such a position that he can see both the ball and the man he is

GUARDING THE MAN WITHOUT THE BALL—OUTSIDE FOOT AND HAND FORWARD

guarding. A good rule to follow in this regard is to point one hand at the defensive man and one at the ball. This position will allow a full view of the assigned defensive man, the ball, and the majority of the players on the court.

Two positions are recognized when guarding a man without the ball. In the first, the inside foot is placed forward and the inside hand is held out to block a pass. This position enables the defensive player to observe the offensive player and still keep the movement of the ball in view.

The second stance which is recommended involves placing the outside foot forward, which faces the defensive man toward the ball. The player in this stance plays forward of the line between his man and the basket.

Guarding the Man with the Ball

An offensive player with the ball can do three things: shoot, dribble, or pass. The defensive man has to be prepared to meet any of these eventualities.

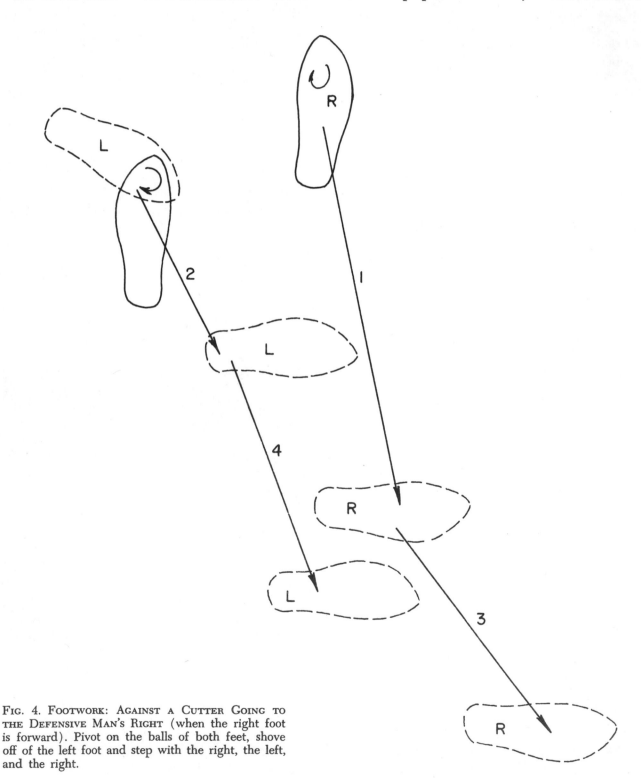

FIG. 4. FOOTWORK: AGAINST A CUTTER GOING TO THE DEFENSIVE MAN'S RIGHT (when the right foot is forward). Pivot on the balls of both feet, shove off of the left foot and step with the right, the left, and the right.

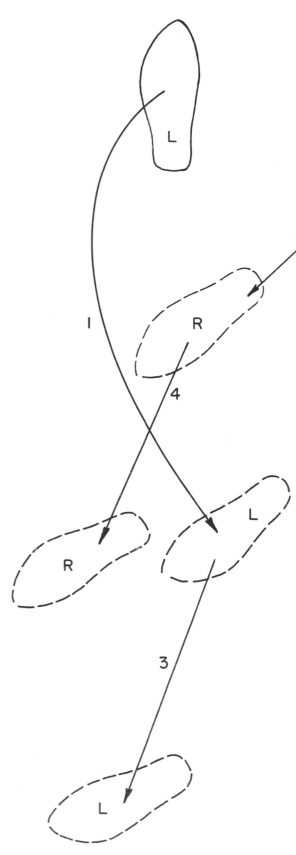

FIG. 5. FOOTWORK: AGAINST A CUTTER GOING TO THE DEFENSIVE MAN'S LEFT (when the left foot is forward). Push off of the left foot, pivot on the right, step with the left and follow with the right, left, and right.

The position a defensive man takes on his opponent will depend upon scouting reports of that player's abilities, the defensive player's estimation of the offensive opponent as an offensive threat, the defensive man's speed compared to the opponent's, and the position on the floor.

Scouting reports will indicate the offensive man's strong features: good jump shooter, shoots well at the head of the key, is the offensive play-maker, drives only to his right, etc. A good defensive man will adapt to these situations and play accordingly.

In this same regard, the defensive man, after playing against an opponent for several minutes, can determine that player's move and adjust accordingly.

If the defensive man is faster than his opponent, he can guard closer and force action in this manner. Speed will enable the defensive man to easily keep a good defensive position in spite of fakes or sudden moves.

A player who is a good shot should be guarded closely. Body position and body balance are important here, because when the defensive man closes in on a good shooter, he becomes vulnerable to a dribble or a pass and cut.

If the man with the ball has stopped his dribble and is close to the basket, the defensive man should move in tighter and play an aggressive defense. On the other hand, when the offensive man is beyond normal shooting distance, the defensive man can drop off and attempt to intercept a pass.

If the opponent shoots, the defensive man should be prepared to screen him out from the basket and prevent losing the rebound; should the opponent dribble, then he is guarded as explained below. When the opponent passes, the guard should immediately retreat a step preparatory to picking up the offensive player should he cut.

Guarding the Dribbler

The main objective when guarding the dribbler is to force him in a predetermined direction and in doing so cause him to stop because he runs up against a sideline, baseline, or teammate.

As soon as the opponent starts his dribble, the defensive player should drop back several quick steps, drop the hand on the side the dribble is going and harass the dribbler with short upward stabbing actions of the hand. The defensive player should force the dribbler in one direction and keep him on that course by staying a half a step ahead. To do this, the defensive player should have the midline of his body at least opposite the front foot of the dribbler.

The defensive player should be conscious of screens and when near one can feel them out by feeling behind with his hands to feel contact. A quick glance or a warning cry from a teammate should alert the guard to a screen.

When the dribbler stops within shooting distance, the defensive man should close on him, because now he can only shoot or pass.

Team defenses usually specify whether the play is to be forced into the center of the court or toward the sideline. Drills should be used that will practice what is to be accomplished in a game.

Guarding the Cutter

Guarding the cutter presents a situation similar to that of guarding a dribbler; but instead of harassing the ball, the guard keeps the hand which is on the ball side up to prevent or deflect a pass.

One successful technique against a cutter is for the guard to move legally into the path the cutter desires to take and, in doing so, force the offensive man to vary his path and disrupt the timing of the cut. This movement is accomplished by the guard moving quickly back toward the basket as the first action, then a slide into the path of the cutter—to be a legal movement, the guard must establish a legal position in front of the cutter before the cutter arrives at the cut-off spot. It is not necessary to establish a firm position on the court, but the guard might continue to slide to force the cutter around as one would force the dribbler to the sideline.

When playing against a player who is consistently cutting, the guard should play a little further from him than normal. This advantage of a foot or two will give the guard an opportunity to cut off the cutter, or at least maintain a good position on him throughout the cut.

Should the guard fall behind the cutter, he should run to maintain a favorable position and keep the forward hand up to prevent a pass to the cutter.

Guarding the Pivot Man

Each player on the squad should know the principles and methods involved in guarding a player who moves into or stations himself in the vicinity of the free throw lane. Offenses are now so designed that any player can "flash" into the pivot; as a result, every man should be prepared to guard a man in this area.

In general, there are three positions a defensive player can assume when guarding the man in the pivot position, each depending upon the area in which the offensive man plays and the ability and speed of the two players.

Figure 6 indicates the three general areas. The first is close under the basket and extends out to the dotted line of the foul circle, approximately nine feet from the basket. The second area is that between the dotted line of the foul circle and the foul line, from nine to fifteen feet away from the basket. The third area is that beyond the foul circle.

When guarding a player in Area A, the defensive player should stand between the offensive player and the ball. This position is contrary to the general rule of standing between the offensive man and the basket,

GUARDING A MAN IN THE PIVOT POSITION

but when an offensive player is this close to the basket, every attempt should be made to prevent this pivot player from obtaining a pass. One hand is held high, and the difficult task of keeping both the ball and pivot man in view at once is maintained.

The defensive player stands alongside a player in Area B and blocks every attempt to get a pass in. The illustration shows this position, in which the defensive man stations himself on the side the ball is located and holds the front hand up palm out, faces the offensive player, and holds the back hand behind the pivot man as if to throw an arm around him. The front hand bats down the ball as it is passed in. Should a pass get in to this man, the defensive player should immediately reposition himself three feet or so to the rear of the pivot man and between that man and the basket. If an attempt to shoot is made, the defensive man closes in and tries to block the shot, but if other offensive men cut by or the pivot man begins to maneuver, the best position is an arm's length back. A close position is a vulnerable one, in which the offensive man is at an advantage. He knows where the defensive man is and can often fake and make use of maneuvers to get close to the basket and shoot.

Every attempt should be made to prevent a pass to a man in the pivot position, particularly when he is a high scorer or the team uses a pivot type of offense.

Two-on-One

The situation in which two offensive men approach the basket and there is a lone defender should result in a score, but when the defensive player maneuvers properly, he can often force a mistake, delay the opponents until help arrives, or force a long shot.

The opponent with the ball should be stopped at the top edge of the foul circle. To do this the defensive player moves out and bluffs as if he is going to guard this player. As soon as the dribbler places both hands on the ball, the defensive man retreats back

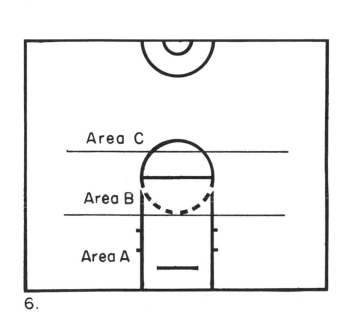

6.

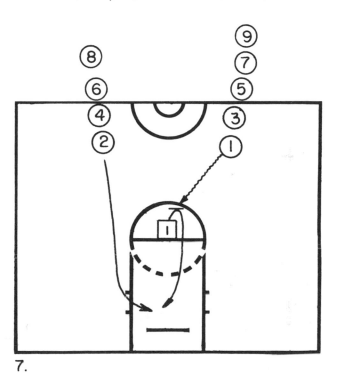

7.

Fig. 6. AREAS OF THE COURT—USED WHEN GUARDING A MAN IN THE PIVOT POSITION. *Area A.* play between man and ball. *Area B.* play alongside pivot man. *Area C.* play behind pivot man.

Fig. 7. TWO-ON-ONE DEFENSIVE DRILL. [1] endeavors to stop the dribbler at the edge of the key and then retreats to prevent a pass in under the basket to ②. This will either force a long shot or stop the attack.

A maneuver in which each defensive man should be proficient is that of shifting from one side of the pivot man to the other when the ball crosses to the other side of the court. The boxer shuffle is used, and when moving from the left to the right side, the right foot moves first, then left, then right, until a favorable position with the front hand held high is reached on the side of the court on which the ball is located.

When the defensive man is in Area C, the best position is between that man and the basket in a regular defense stance.

and in the direction of the remaining offensive player. The player with the ball has two alternatives to choose from within several seconds. His first choice is a pass to the player close to the basket for a good close shot, but good work on the part of the lone defender will cut this off. The second alternative is a shot from beyond the foul line.

The secret of the defensive man's maneuver is to force the dribbler to stop and to retreat rapidly. This is accomplished by moving forward, and as the bluff is made to take the dribble, the weight should be

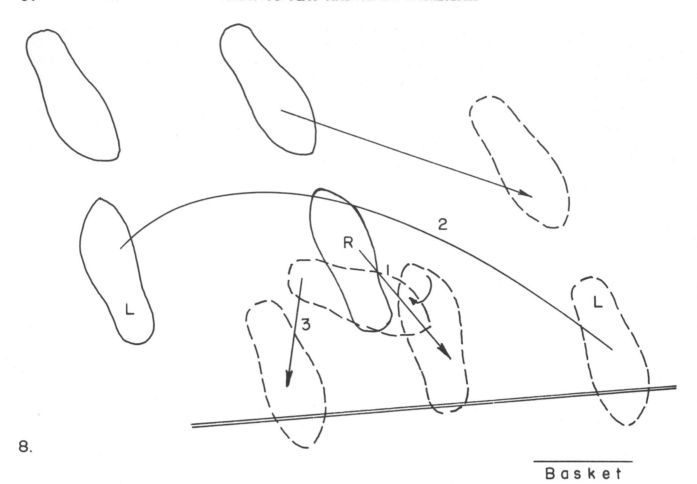

8.

Basket

FIG. 8. FOOTWORK: SCREEN OUT AN OPPONENT WHEN REBOUNDING. As soon as the defensive player discovers which way the offensive man, number ①, decides to go, he steps back with the right foot, pivots, and maintains a position between that defensive man and the basket. Short, fast steps will help maintain this favorable position.

shifted back and the front foot planted and pushed off of at the same instant. This will enable the guard to move in reverse rapidly. As he moves backward, one hand should be waved high to give a barrier to a pass.

An excellent drill to practice this important defensive maneuver is to place a man on defense against two opponents and require him to stay in this position until he has gained possession of the ball five times. Figure 7 indicates the setup for this drill. To make the drill even more interesting, any offensive player who makes a bad pass or misses a shot is immediately placed on defense, and his five counts begin.

Rebounding

Rebounding is one of the important defensive skills, as this manner of obtaining possession of the ball limits the opponents to only one shot at the basket.

Rebounding requires position and proper rebounding techniques. A smaller player with good rebounding ability will often obtain possession of the ball against larger opponents.

The first phase of rebounding consists of gaining

BLOCKING OUT TO REBOUND

position on the offensive player by the defensive player placing himself between the basket and the offensive man. This position is maintained by the guard by moving into the path desired by that offensive player. Figure 8 indicates the proper footwork necessary. Whether the man guarded or one of his teammates shoots, the guard should counter the offensive man's move to the basket. As the defensive man faces his opponent with his back to the basket, he should concentrate on this man's actions. If the offensive man tries to go around the block, the guard should, with short gliding steps, slide across the floor and maintain the position between the basket and the offensive player.

The proper position when blocking out is for the defensive man to spread his feet, allow his butt to protrude, spread elbows wide and hold his hands at shoulder height. This spread position allows for a solid foundation and good movement, and presents a wide obstacle for the offensive man to move out of position or endeavor to go around.

As soon as the guard has attained his advantageous blocking out position, he should quickly locate the ball and move toward where he can rebound it. This period of time between when the guard observes a shot and when he blocks out his opponent and locates the ball should be practiced so that it takes a minimum of time and allows the guard to observe more of the ball in flight.

Actual rebounding is done by jumping up, and if possible slightly forward; head is held up, butt is shoved out in back, legs are spread wide, and the hands are forced vigorously upward to grasp the ball at the top of the guard's jump. As soon as the ball is contacted, it should be moved approximately six inches in any direction to tear it free should an opponent also get his hands on the ball (see illustration). Tall players may hold the ball high overhead, while others should bring it down to chest height and prepare to clear out a pass.

Some players have the faculty to rebound and clear out a pass before touching the ground. This saves precious seconds and often starts a successful fast break.

REBOUNDING THE BALL

Recovery of a Free Ball

There are many times during the course of a game when the basketball is loose: *it is free and belongs to the player or team that gets it.* Of course, the more times one team gets possession of the ball and prevents the opposition from controlling it, the more opportunities that team will have to score.

The most frequent free balls come from fumbles and bad passes. Tough defense and alert "hawking" will cause fumbles by the opponents. Fast, darting, hand action plus good body position will help cause a dribbler to fumble, the passer to toss a bad pass, or a fumble by a player receiving the ball.

A free ball on the floor will end up in a jump ball unless the proper technique is utilized in going after it. The first effort should be to get a position on your opponent so that you can obtain an unobstructed chance at the ball. Secondly, the guard should quickly advance to the ball with low center of gravity and a good solid balanced position. The ball should be scooped up with both hands as if in a rebound and brought into a protected position chest high.

When there is no opportunity to obtain clean possession of the ball, the player must use his judgment as to whether or not a dive for the ball will gain possession, or at least a held ball. This dive for the ball should not be over an opponent, which would draw a foul, but a clean attempt to obtain a free ball.

The least a player should expect from a free ball is a held ball. But with hustle and aggressive action, possession is often obtained.

To practice this technique, the coach can roll or bounce the ball in front of a line of players. The first player properly gains possession of the ball, takes it to the fundamental offensive position and then clears out a pass back to the coach. When the proper technique is attained, the coach can have two lines, the first in each attempting to obtain the free ball. Fouls should be called and clean play stressed.

Intercepting passes is an excellent technique to disrupt the offensive and present an excellent opportunity to score. Pass interception is no haphazard or accidental occurence; it should be studied and planned. The player planning the interception should ask himself: "Does he telegraph the pass? Does he toss soft, slow passes? Does he always pass in the same manner?" Knowing the answers to these questions, plus fast action, will pay dividends. The move to intercept is made just as the ball leaves the passer's hands. The move is anticipated, and should the interception fail, rapid recovery is necessary. The anticipating of fumbles and bad passes and the recovery of the ball will afford the team many more scoring opportunities during the game and will tend to lower the morale of the opponents.

Violations by the Opponents

Probably the easiest way to obtain the ball in basketball is to have the ball awarded to your team out of bounds because the opponents violated a rule of play. Violations can come about because of a mistake, and often a member of your team can cause the opponent to make such a mistake by aggressive play. Common violations are walking, palming the ball, broken dribble, hitting a tip or jump ball illegally and throwing the ball out of bounds.

Harass the opponents into making violations by the use of the voice, by fast hand motions and by determined defensive actions.

ABC's of Individual Defensive Skills

1. The individual should force the opponent to take bad shots.

2. Force dribbler to the outline line.

3. Try to make the dribbler stop.

4. Be prepared for a change of pace or direction.

5. Talk it up.

6. Force an opponent to do the thing the opponent does not want to do.

7. Play the opponent tough and try to force him into mistakes if an opponent is a slow or weak ballhandler.

8. Close in on the dribbler if he has stopped.

9. Force man with the ball to make hurried passes.

10. Take short sliding steps and don't cross the feet.

11. Don't lunge, jump, or dive. Maintain balance.

12. Get in position; never let a man get between you and the basket (except when guarding the center).

13. Know where the ball is at all times.

14. Know your opponent.

15. Be alert—be ready for anything.

16. Hurry back to defense.

17. Be aggressive.

18. When hurrying to cover a man, keep the weight evenly distributed and the trunk erect, so that you can quickly reverse direction.

19. Anticipate a free ball, and get it.

► Summary

Individual defense is relatively easy to learn when given proper emphasis, and the coach as well as the players are convinced of its importance.

Although no one player has all these attributes, an ideal defensive player would be fast on his feet, have quick hands, be tall, be alert, have determined spirit, practice good judgment, be adaptable and be well co-ordinated.

Individual techniques and special guarding situations should be learned and practiced diligently, as these individual defensive fundamentals are the backbone of the team's defense.

► Study
Questions

1. Why is individual defense important?

2. Discuss speed in relation to individual defense.

3. What is the first movement by the guard when a defensive man without the ball cuts for the basket?

4. Explain how you would guard a pivot man who stations himself at the corner of the foul lane and foul line on the same side of the court as the player with the ball.

5. How does guarding the pivot man disobey the axiom of staying between the man and the basket?

6. Where should the weight of the body be located when in the basic stance?

7. When one defensive man is on two offensive men, what is the important maneuver to make after bluffing the man with the ball to a stop? How is it accomplished?

► Projects for
Additional
Study

1. Search the literature and discover two articles dealing specifically with individual defense. What importance do the authors give to defense?

2. Diagram two drills which would aid in the teaching of guarding a man with the ball who can dribble, pass, or shoot.

3. List the individual requisites for individual defense in order of importance and give reasons why you listed the first one first and the last one last.

4. Observe a day's basketball practice and determine to what extent defense is emphasized. Were there any individual defensive drills?

5. Compile a booklet of individual defensive drills: one drill for each situation.

6. Observe a basketball game and, while doing so, pay particular attention to defensive rebounding by the man guarding the offensive player in the pivot position. Is he blocking his man out, what is his technique, and do you have any constructive criticism?

► Selected
References

Auerbach, Arnold. *Basketball for the Player, the Fan and the Coach.* New York: Pocket Books, Inc., 1952. Good hints for the defensive man regarding individual technique.

Bee, Clair. *Drills and Fundamentals.* New York: A. S. Barnes & Co., 1942. Contains excellent basic information on defensive fundamentals and defensive drills.

Bunn, John W. *Basketball Methods.* New York: The Macmillan Co., 1939. Good material on basic methods of individual guarding.

_____. *Basketball Techniques and Team Play.* Englewood Cliffs, N. J.: Prentice-Hall, Inc., 1964. Clear explanation of individual defensive skills.

Dean, Everett S. *Progressive Basketball.* New York: Prentice-Hall, Inc., 1950. Contains 45 individual defensive hints.

Gullion, Blair. *100 Drills for Teaching Basketball Fundamentals.* St. Louis, Missouri: Blair Gullion, 1933.

_____. *Techniques and Tactics of Basketball Defense.* St. Louis, Mo.: Bardgett Printing & Publishing Co., 1951. Very comprehensive coverage of all phases of individual defense. Basic philosophy and ideas are excellent.

Jucker, Ed. *Cincinnati Power Basketball.* Englewood Cliffs, N. J.: Prentice-Hall, Inc., 1962. Good comments on individual pressure defense.

Loeffler, Ken. *Ken Loeffler on Basketball.* New York: Prentice-Hall, Inc., 1955. A successful coach's ideas on individual defensive skills.

McCracken, Branch. *Indiana Basketball*. New York: Prentice-Hall, Inc., 1955. Excellent material in outline form on defensive fundamentals.

McGuire, Frank. *Defensive Basketball*. New York: Prentice-Hall, Inc., 1958. Excellent on philosophy and individual man-to-man defense.

Newell, Pete, and Benington, John. *Basketball Methods*. New York: The Ronald Press Co., 1962. Thorough treatment of individual defense.

Newsom, Heber. *Basketball for the High School Coach and the Physical Education Teacher*. Dubuque, Iowa: Wm. C. Brown Co., 1952. Offers basic information on individual defense.

Pinholster, Garland F. *Encyclopedia of Basketball Drills*. New York: Prentice-Hall, Inc., 1958. Excellent group of drills for all types of individual defensive skills.

————. *Coach's Guide to Modern Basketball Defense*. New York: Prentice-Hall, Inc., 1961. Deals with the importance of defense and the fundamentals necessary for modern defense.

Ramsay, Jack. *Pressure Basketball*. Englewood Cliffs, N. J.: Prentice-Hall, Inc., 1964. Pertinent tips on individual defense.

Rupp, Adolph. *Rupp's Championship Basketball*. New York: Prentice-Hall, Inc., 1948. Deals with individual defense in a concise, thorough fashion.

U. S. Navy. *Basketball*. Annapolis, Md.: United States Naval Institute, 1943. Good coverage of guarding in specific situations.

Wooden, John R. *Practical Modern Basketball*. New York: The Ronald Press Co., 1966. Individual defense the Wooden way, comprehensive and thorough.

CHAPTER 5: Team Defense

Team defense is the co-ordinated effort of five members of the defensive team to play against their five opponents in an organized method to prevent the opponents from scoring and to obtain possession of the ball. In doing so, team defense is concerned with actions resulting from the offensive team's co-ordinated fast break, organized offense, and stall, and with situations of defending the jump ball, out-of-bounds plays, and free throws. Each of these six situations presents different actions by the offense and requires counter-reactions by members of the defense. To be effective, team defense should be a co-ordinated effort in which each player knows how to react in relation to his teammates. Predetermined actions are practiced in which each player has specific duties, so that in carrying out his assignment, the guard knows how his teammates will move and act. In doing so, all five defensive players can feel confident that their maneuver is at least as effective as that of the offense, and probably more so.

► Basic Principles

Mental Approach to Defense

When determined players are schooled properly in team defense, the opponent will always have a hard time scoring. This is the important principle of team defense. The players must know the part they are to play and, in addition, they must play with the idea in mind that what they are doing will be successful.

There is a common saying, "A good defense is the best offense." This statement has a lot of truth in it. The team that is tough on defense will be a difficult opponent, but there must be an even division between offense and defense for a team to be well balanced. The chapter on defense is presented before the one on offense because the author believes that more importance should be given to this aspect of the game —practice, knowledge, and skill in team defensive fundamentals.

It takes co-operative effort to play on defense, as the five players must act as a unit. To do this, a thorough knowledge of the defense is necessary. Each player must be able to execute the required fundamentals; each teammate must talk it up to help and inspire his teammates; and there has to be a team spirit, or *esprit de corps*. This spirit is developed when each player has confidence in the team's defense and

its capability of doing well against superior opponents. When the entire team has that feeling, *it cannot be beat*.

The team with the proper mental approach to defense will play it with a determined, aggressive spirit. That team will practice defense diligently, and good team defense will result.

Evaluation of Ball Possession

It is obvious that if one team gains possession of the ball more times than its opponent, there will be more opportunities to score by that team; hence, the importance of obtaining the ball and not allowing the offense a good opportunity to score.

Frank McGuire, University of North Carolina, has presented an excellent discussion of possession evaluation.[1]

Possession Evaluation is based upon an average number of points for each possession during a game of both our opponents and ourselves. In a *perfect* game we would average two points for each possession and limit our opponents to zero points for each of their possessions. Obviously, this ideal situation never occurs, but the closer we can approach it, the better. Therefore, we judge our offensive strength in any given game by how closely we approach 2.00 per each possession; how well we played defense is determined by the average number of points

---

[1] Frank McGuire, *Defensive Basketball* (New York: Prentice-Hall, Inc., 1959), p. 11.

per each possession by our opponents. What is a possession?

In defining possession, the first assumption is that a team must have uninterrupted control of the ball. The possession is terminated at the point where this control is lost. For example, when a team shoots, that particular possession is terminated. Thereafter either team has a reasonable chance to get the rebound. If the shooting team regains control via an offensive rebound, it is another possession. The situation of a jump ball is practically identical. The team which had possession and was tied up loses that possession and the team which controls the tip begins a new possession.

We have found that the easiest method to arrive at the total number of possessions both teams have during a game is to count lost possessions. General game statistics reveal the number of times a team shoots and the number of times a team is fouled; therefore, to find the total number of possessions we add to these figures a tabulation of errors which result in loss of the ball. Such errors include bad passes, fumbles, violations, jump ball "tie-ups," and offensive fouls. An offensive foul is not a loss of ball if the goal is awarded to the offender. It actually becomes a defensive foul, since the team which drew the offensive foul would get the ball anyway if the shot was made. The sum of the field goal attempts, times fouled, and the errors will equal the number of each team's possessions. By dividing a team's point total by the team's total possessions, we can determine the average number of points for each possession.

To summarize, possession evaluation is the average number of points scored for each possession during a game calculated for both the opponent and our team. The offensive strength is based on how close to a perfect score of 2.00 per possession our team scores, and defensive strength by how low the opponent's score is kept toward zero.

Possession is control of the ball, and possession evaluation is calculated by counting the number of lost possessions by both teams during the course of the game. These are summarized as follows:

Number of times a team shoots.

Number of times a team is fouled.

Number of errors which result in a loss of the ball. This includes bad passes, fumbles, violations, tie-ups which result in jump balls, and offensive fouls.

The formula for calculating possession evaluation is to total the lost possessions and divide that number into the team's total points.

This excellent method of calculating the average points per possession is indicated in the following theoretical games. North High School lost to South High School 43 to 64.

North High School

61 shots for 36 points from 18 field goals
11 times fouled for 7 points
14 times loss of possession from errors
Total of 86 losses of possession for 43 points

$$\frac{43 \text{ points}}{86 \text{ possessions}} = .50 \text{ points per possession}$$

$$\frac{14 \text{ errors}}{86 \text{ possessions}} = 16.3\% \text{ loss of possession without obtaining a shot at the basket}$$

South High School

72 shots for 52 points from 26 field goals
15 times fouled for 12 points
8 times loss of possession from errors
Total of 95 losses of possession for 64 points

$$\frac{64 \text{ points}}{95 \text{ possessions}} = .67 \text{ points per possession}$$

$$\frac{8 \text{ errors}}{95 \text{ possessions}} = 8.4\% \text{ loss of possession without a shot}$$

It is apparent from the above calculations that South High School was superior in nearly all fields of play. South High School shot field goals at a 36.1 percentage against their opponent's 29.5 per cent. South High was superior in shooting foul shots with an 80 per cent to the opponent's 63.6 per cent. North High had only 61 field goal attempts, while South High had 72. North High fouled and allowed South High 15 foul shots to their 11 shots. South High made fewer errors, in committing only 8 to the opponent's 14, or a total percentage of errors per possession at only 8.4 per cent to North High's 16.3 per cent.

Certain logical conclusions can be gathered from the above facts, and a close scrutiny of individual statistics which contribute to the team totals will indicate to the coach the part each player plays in the total picture. Shooting a high percentage of field goals is important, and if a low percentage is achieved, that team had better obtain many more attempts than the opponents to make up for the poor marksmanship.

Foul shooting is important and often is the deciding factor in close games. Of extreme importance is accurate shooting when there is a one-and-one situation. A team which makes frequent costly mistakes which result in a loss of the ball is forfeiting a chance to score. In the above illustration, North High School errored 14 times, or 16.3 per cent of the times they had possession. A good question to ask would be, is one player contributing to more errors than he should?

Often, when examining statistics such as the above, the coach can assess the strength of his team offensively and defensively compared with that of the opponent. This could result in a change of strategy when teams meet again. Few possessions and many errors could be the result of the opponent's strong defensive rebounding, and a fast break might have contributed to the mistakes. This reflection might result in a change of strategy to a slow, deliberate, set style of play.

Implications of Fouling

A free throw is worth one point against a field goal's two points, but the player shooting a foul shot will shoot at a greater percentage. In fact, a great many players are shooting foul shots at a rate higher than 75 per cent. This means that if a player gets fouled four times during a game, he will then score three points. In this case, three points per four possessions is a .75-point average per possession. This is a higher percentage than a team would make during a regular game possession. A one-and-one foul situation is even more drastic. It enables a team to make two points per possession, which is equal to a field goal score-wise.

Clean basketball plus good judgment in relation to when to foul and when not to foul are important aspects of defense. Situations can be practiced (explained in Chapter Nine, which deals in team strategy) which stimulate game conditions that prepare the player to react correctly to a variety of situations.

Change from Offense to Defense

One basic fundamental essential for good defense is the ability to go quickly from offense to defense. This infrequently practiced defensive technique is an important one, because a step or two in defense can often save a basket or prevent a fast break. Each player should know his place in the scheme of the offense, so that as soon as the opponents obtain possession of the ball—or better still, if the loss of the ball can be anticipated—the offensive player becomes a defensive player.

Each play pattern or scoring play will have a movement toward the basket, and when a shot is taken, certain players will be responsible for being on the offensive board, ready for a long rebound, balancing to go on defense or ready to cut off the outlet pass. Each coach will have definite ideas on these assignments. What is important is that each player follows his assignment and then, anticipating the loss of the ball, immediately goes on defense.

The immediate reaction to defense and rapid movement into the back court becomes automatic and when accompanied by hustle will save what would otherwise be easy baskets by a fast-breaking team.

A simple practice drill is to place a team on the floor in an offensive maneuver with no opposition. The team goes through the maneuver, a shot is taken, and instantly each of the five players reacts by moving into his assigned position. This will insure proper balance and reaction to going to defense. The second team and then the third go through this practice.

The second drill is to place a team on defense with

instructions to fast break at every opportunity. The offensive team goes through a play pattern, balances and, when the ball is lost, goes on defense. Three teams can practice this drill, with one on defense and two alternating on offense practicing going on defense.

Matching Players

One of the distinct advantages of a man-to-man defense is that the coach can match his defensive players against the opponents. The tall man plays the tall center, the best defensive man is assigned the high scoring opponent, speed is pitted against speed, etc. More information on this will be offered in Chapter Eight.

Building the Team Defense

Building the team defense or defenses consists of developing the players' individual defensive skills in the one-on-one situation in all areas of the court. To this is added the two-on-two defensive maneuvers, then three-on-three, four-on-four, and finally five-on-five.

Drills should be employed to teach the directional aspect of the defense, so that the players are capable of forcing the play in a particular direction.

The break from offense to defense is added so that the team can readily change from a position in which they were in possession of the ball and attempting to score to a reverse situation, in which the tables are turned and a co-ordinated effort is necessary.

Defensive situations should be practiced first as a "dummy" or semi-passive effort and learned before a full effort is allowed. Every possible defensive situation likely to be encountered should be practiced. This includes: defensing the jump ball, out-of-bounds play, foul shot, set offense, fast break, and stall.

Several methods are recommended for teaching defense: Team No. 1 stays on defense for ten consecutive offensive tries at the basket. Teams No. 2 and No. 3 alternate in bringing the ball down the court on offense and attempting to score. Teams No. 2 and No. 3 take their turns at defense.

Play one- or two-minute games with the defense one, two, or three points behind, with the score tied, etc. These situations give the players what amount to valuable game situation experiences. Use the clock and scoreboard to make the short games realistic.

Place the No. 1 team on defense and allow teams No. 2 and No. 3 to alternate offensive attacks. Team No. 1 is required to stay on defense until it has obtained possession of the ball ten times. Teams No. 2 and No. 3 then take their turns at defense.

Organize situations in which the out-of-bounds play, the jump ball, and the foul shot are defensed.

Every attempt to get the ball on these situations should be stressed.

Have team No. 3 attempt the scouted opponents' offensive plays first in slow motion against a semi-passive defense, then with both teams going full speed. Team No. 2 would alternate with team No. 1.

Criteria for Selecting the Team Defenses

The basic objective of the team defense is to prevent the opposition from scoring and to obtain possession of the ball. Team defense is the manner in which this is accomplished, and in planning a team defense it is imperative that the team be prepared to meet all possible situations: fast break, jump ball, out-of-bounds, foul shot, and the set play whether it be a regular attack or a stall.

"Various factors influence the coach in the choice of defensive tactics and in the development of *his* defensive plan. Some of these factors are:[2]

1. The training and experience of the coach both as a player and as a coach.

2. The quantity and quality of the material available.

3. The floor conditions usually encountered in games away from home.

4. The type of floor available for home games and practice.

5. The general styles of offensive play which will be encountered on the schedule both at home and away.

6. The ability (in general) of opposing teams to fathom the various types of defenses which the team has utilized in the past.

7. The number or types of defenses which the intelligence of the players will permit."

In addition to the factors explained above, certain fundamental criteria should be adhered to regarding all team defenses. These simple basic principles should serve as guides for selecting the various defenses.

1. *The criterion of co-ordination.* The team playing defense is a co-ordinated unit of five players. Each player knows the actions of his teammates, and there is a thorough understanding by regulars and substitutes of the defense and its variations, if any.

2. *The criterion of simplicity.* The defense must be such that it is easy to comprehend and relatively simple to play. The higher the caliber of the talent and the intelligence of the players, the more complex the defense can be, but simple actions are still basic to good defense.

3. *The criterion of fundamentals.* The fundamentals and actions taught in drills are the same as are used in the defenses.

4. *The criterion of balance.* The defense should have balance so that the offense is contained and so

that the defense is positioned and ready to go on offense when the ball is recovered.

5. *The criterion of flexibility.* The defense is flexible in that variations are possible, so that various matching of defensive vs. offensive players is possible according to ability, speed, and size.

6. *The criterion of timing.* The defense needs to be so synchronized that it operates as a unit whether the players sag, switch, play strict man-to-man, or zone. Each player co-ordinates his movements, being conscious of the actions of his teammates, so that each movement is in rhythm and time.

7. *The criterion of mobility.* The team defense should be so mobile that it quickly makes the transition from offense to defense, players switch men with ease, and individual players have speed in their defensive actions.

8. *The criterion of surprise.* The defense should be so constituted that occasionally it presents a perplexing problem to the offense. It is not what is expected, and its actions have a tendency to upset individual players or the entire offense.

9. *The criterion of confidence.* The team has confidence that its particular defense is the best one for the players' abilities and the one which will prevent the opponents from scoring.

Types of Defenses

Generally speaking, team defenses can be classified as man-to-man, zone, combinations of man-to-man and zone, and pressing defenses. Each classification has its own particular types, such as the 2-1-2 type of zone defense; and in addition, each has distinct strengths and weaknesses. Some defenses are played better by certain types of personnel, while others might surprise or confuse the opponent. Regardless of the classification and type of team defense played, what is important is that it be basically a sound defense and that the players are well schooled in carrying it out to the best of their abilities.

► Man-to-Man Team Defenses

Principle of Man-to-Man Defenses

The principle upon which man-to-man defense is played is that each player is responsible for a particular opponent. Man-to-man defense in this classification refers to the position taken by the players in their own backcourt. Theoretically, if each guard could do a thorough job, the opposition would not score. Because of present-day offenses such as figure-eight con-

---

[2] Blair Gullion, *Techniques and Tactics of Basketball Defense* (St. Louis, Mo.: Bardgett Printing & Publishing Co., 1951), p. 198.

tinuities, which produce moving screens and set screen offenses, the guard has a difficult time staying with his opponent. As a result, variations in man-to-man defenses have resulted which lead to switching, sagging, and other tactical maneuvers designed to combat the effort to separate the guard from the assigned offensive man. This type of defense can be varied from regular, tight, to loose, and the players may exchange men by switching or play strictly man-to-man.

Types of Man-to-Man Defenses

Straight man-to-man. In this straight man-to-man defense, the guard is entirely responsible for his man. There is no changing of opponents except to pick up a free man, which can be done *only in an emergency.*

This man-to-man defense can be played in a variety of ways—tight, regular, or sag. The tight, regular, or sag terms refer to the distance the defensive man plays from his opponent.

Tight man-to-man defense is one in which each defensive man assumes a close guarding stance and endeavors to guard his man so closely that an exchange of passes is very difficult. The purpose is to hinder the play of the opponents and to force them into committing mistakes. Players who are rushed frequently become flustered and forget to play their regular game. This type of defense is used late in the game when behind or as a regular defense when a team is faster than its opponents.

Regular man-to-man defense consists of each guard stationing himself at a normal guarding distance of five to six feet from his opponent. Of course, as the offensive man approaches the basket or has the ball and is within shooting distance, this normal distance closes to a tight position. This defense is played during the normal course of a game.

Sagging or floating man-to-man defense approaches a zone in that the distance played from an opponent increases as the offensive man is farther away from the basket and/or the ball. Figure 9 points out this situation where 4 is ten feet or more away from his opponent toward the basket. 4 is guarding a man who is away from both the basket and the ball. The main objective of this defense is to collapse the guards in toward the basket in order to cut off passes and, more important, to bring rebound strength close to the basket. The sagging man-to-man defense is used against a team that has taller opponents that cut up the middle or that has weak set shooters.

Switching man-to-man defense. The switching type of man-to-man defense can vary from one in which the defensive players exchange opponents (switch) every time the opponents cross to one in which they switch only when a guard has lost his man and a switch becomes necessary.

The switching of men when the opponents are playing near the mid-court area is frequently utilized. This particular man-to-man defense is often used against teams that use a weave or set screen attack.

A switching man-to-man defense can be played with the players guarding their opponents in a regular, tight, or sagging manner depending upon the strategy of the particular game, the time left in the game, and the score.

Maneuvers

General maneuvers are possible or necessary in man-to-man defenses. These include directional defense and methods of evading the screen.

Directional Defense

Directional defense refers to the team effort and individual defensive players' attempts to direct the offensive team in a predetermined direction. This is accomplished by playing a tight defense on one side of the court and loose defense on the other side. When confronting a dribbler, the defensive man assumes a strong position on one side to force the dribbler to the other. The offense will naturally play to the side to which it is easy to pass or move via a dribble by following the line of least resistance, and will thus go in the direction desired by the defense.

Directional defense can be utilized in three general ways: force all play to the sidelines; force all play to the middle of the court, or force all play to either the right or the left.

Play is forced to the sideline with the idea in mind that the player is moving the ball away from the basket and out of good scoring territory. In addition, the sideline assists as a defensive aid, as the man with the ball cannot cross it. A caution is necessary in this regard with reference to guarding the baseline: Although play is forced to the sideline, a drive along the baseline should be prevented, as it is difficult for teammates to assist in the defense of such an offensive maneuver.

When the play is forced to the middle of the court, it is based upon the theory that the man with the ball will always run up against other defensive men and the drive to the sideline or baseline is prevented. An objection to this directional maneuver is that players prefer to shoot, particularly jump shot artists, from the middle areas of the floor in the vicinity of the foul line.

Play can be directed to either the right or the left of the court, and the primary purpose of this move is to direct the play to the strong defensive side and away from a high scorer.

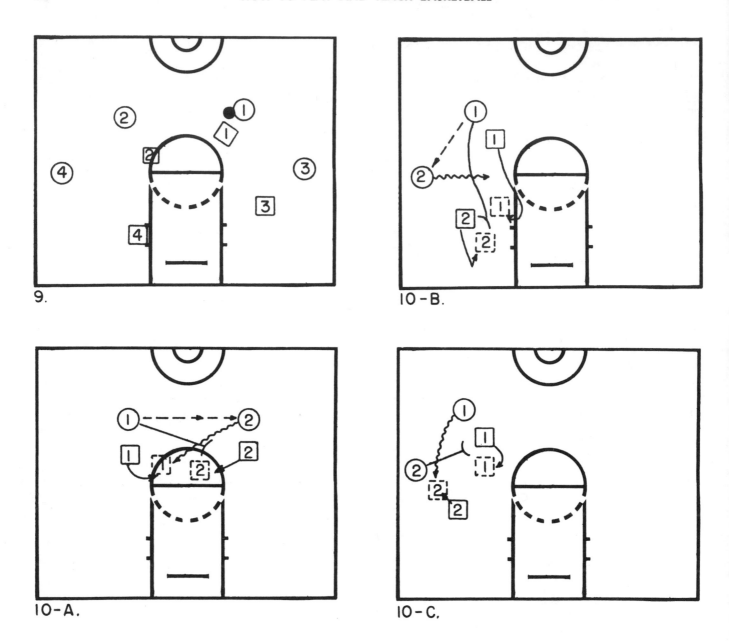

FIG. 9. SAGGING MAN-TO-MAN DEFENSE. With the ball in possession of player ①, ④ sags off toward the basket as far as possible. ② and ③ sag off a step or two.

FIG. 10. MANEUVERS TO COMBAT A SCREEN BY SWITCHING. (A) *Guard-to-guard screen switch.* ① passes to ② and screens. ①, seeing the screen develop, calls "switch." ② immediately drops back a step and assumes a good defensive position on ①. Meanwhile ① closes on ② so that ② cannot shoot or go free. (B) *Guard-to-forward screen switch.* ① passes to ② and screens. ①, seeing the screen being set, calls "switch." ② immediately drops back a step and guards ①. ① assumes a defensive position on ②. (C) *Forward-to-guard screen switch.* ② screens for ①, who has the ball. ②, seeing the screen develop, calls the switch, at which time ① drops back to pick up ② while ② guards ①. (D) *Center-to-forward screen switch.* ⑤ screens for ④. ⑤ calls the switch and picks up ④. ④ drops back and guards ⑤. (E) *Guard-to-forward outside screen switch.* ① passes to ② and cuts to the outside. ②, observing this action, calls "switch" and picks up ①. ① quickly guards ②. (F) *Guard-to-guard screen quick switch.* This switch is similar to that in 10-A except that a switch is called in anticipation of the two offensive men crossing or screening, and the two defensive men pick up their opponents as fast as possible. ① passes to ② and screens. ①, anticipating this action, quick-switches by quickly moving into the path of ② and endeavors to "dig the ball out of the ground" as he meets the dribbler. This quick-switch action is a surprise and can often stymie the screen attempt.

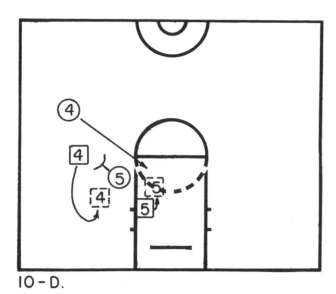

10 - D.

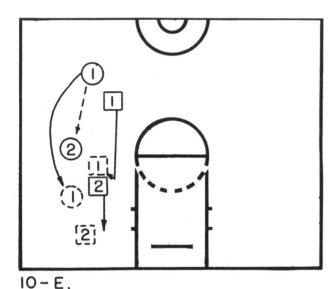

10 - E.

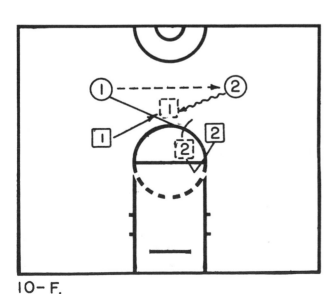

10- F.

Defensing the Screen

The screen is a formidable offensive maneuver, and defensive players should understand the principle of the screen as well as how to combat it. There are two maneuvers used to combat the screen. The first involves switching men on all screens, while the second concerns itself with the maneuvers utilized in evading the screen and staying in a regular man-to-man defensive situation.

Figure 10 (A to F) indicates the various types of screens and the methods of switching men as a means of neutralizing this offensive maneuver.

When playing a man-to-man defense in which there is to be no switching of men, the defensive man can go over the top, fight through, or go behind the screen.

The guard going *over the top* of a screen presents the tightest defensive situation possible, as the defensive man does not allow an opponent or any of his own men to go between the guard and the defensive man with the ball. Figure 11-A indicates how the guard stays with his man by going *over* the top of the screen. This maneuver is recommended for use against teams which shoot after going behind the screen. It should be noted that should the man for whom the screen is applied change his position after setting the screen, any resulting contact would be his responsibility.

Fighting through the screen is the next tightest defensive maneuver, but presents opportunities for a shot over the screen. Figure 11-B indicates this maneuver in which the defensive man goes by the screen and does not allow any other player to get between him and the ball. This method of evading the screen is frequently used against set screens and figure-eight continuities.

Going behind a screen presents the weakest defensive method of evading a screen, as it takes the defensive man a definite period of time to resume his defensive position—during which time the man with the ball has freedom of action. Frequently, this is the only course of action for a defensive man who is suddenly confronted by a screen and his teammate, both of whom are in his desired path to the man with the ball. Figure 11-C presents the method of *going behind* the screen. This maneuver is used only as an emergency measure or in the defense's front court where the offensive man is not in a position to get off a good shot.

ABC's of Man-to-Man Defense

The defensive man should:

1. Know where the ball is as well as where the opponent is located.

2. Be prepared to help a teammate who is in trouble.

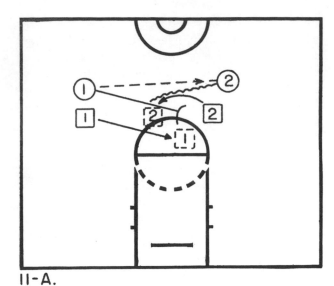

II-A.

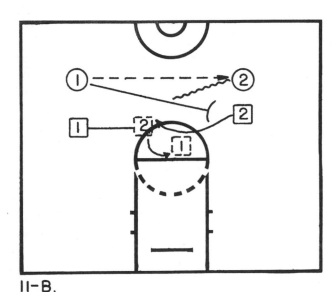

II-B.

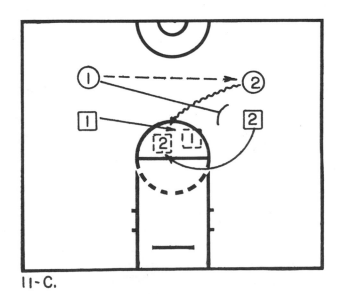

II-C.

3. Sag when guarding a man who is playing across the court from the ball.

4. Talk it up! Encourage as well as warn teammates.

5. Pick up a man. If a man is free and close to the basket area, guard him.

6. Point to the man he is guarding to let the other players know his defensive assignment.

7. Always be alert, even if the ball is across the court from the man he is guarding.

8. Double-team with a teammate on an opponent who gets into the corner of the court.

9. Screen out the man he is guarding every time there is a shot taken.

10. Sag off the man he is guarding to help the man who is guarding that tall center.

Strengths of Man-to-Man Defenses

1. Each player is responsible for a particular opponent.

2. It is possible to match opponents with ability, speed, or size.

3. Each individual player has the responsibility to stop his opponent.

4. It is effective when used late in the game and when behind in the score.

5. It is effective against a team that stalls.

6. It is easily changed over to a pressing defense.

7. It is easy to double up on one opponent.

Weaknesses of Man-to-Man Defenses

1. Men are not usually in a good position to fast break.

FIG. 11. METHODS USED IN DEFENDING A SCREEN AND MAINTAINING THE SAME MAN-TO-MAN GUARDING ASSIGNMENTS. (A) *Over the top*. The guard going over the top of a screen presents the tightest defensive situation possible, as this defensive man does not allow an opponent or any of his own men to come between himself and the man with the ball. As soon as ① sets the screen on ②, ② moves forward and assumes a very tight defensive position on ②, and when ② dribbles ② goes between the set screen and ②. As ② closes on ②, he should be prepared for a dribble in either direction. (B) *Fighting through*. Fighting through the screen is the next tightest defensive maneuver. When ② dribbles around the screen, ② fights between the screen and his own man, player ①. ① has an important role to play, as it is his responsibility to drop back and allow ② a clear path to the man with the ball. (C) *Going behind*. This is the weakest defensive method of evading a screen, as going behind takes the defensive man around the screen and around his own man. ②, as soon as he discovers that a screen is set, drops back and goes around both ① and ① and picks up ② as soon as possible.

2. More fouls may be committed, as there is usually more contact.

3. More energy is used up by following an opponent wherever he goes.

4. There is often a mismatch of ability, size, and speed when men have to switch opponents.

5. Screens are effective.

6. Good footwork and basic individual skills are required of each member of the team.

Basic Man-to-Man Team Defense

Following is an example of a basic man-to-man team defense.

General Objectives

1. Play the opponent strong toward the side of the court to force him to the sideline.

2. Once a man has dribbled, close in on him to stop a shot or a pass. Do not foul.

3. When a pass is made by your opponent, retreat back toward the basket and in the direction of the pass.

4. Teammates will assist and support each other. Support by a quick shift *into* the path of the man who is free or who cuts.

5. Sag off your opponent when he is one, two, or three passes away from the ball. Play as far away from your man as you can toward the basket still being able to cover him closely when he receives a pass.

6. When guarding a man in the pivot position, do not allow him to receive a pass. If he does receive the ball, quickly position yourself between him and the basket and move off several feet.

7. Play your position with reference to the area of the court your opponent is playing. For example:

Area 1 (Fig. 12)

a. Play the man with the ball tight.
b. Make each pass or shot by the opponents difficult.
c. Force everything to the sideline.
d. Go over the top on all screens.
e. Stop a shot even though it leaves your man free.
f. Do not allow your opponent to receive a pass.

Area 2 (Fig. 12)

a. Play man with the ball fairly tight.
b. Slide through on all screens.
c. Encourage opponent to hurry shot.
d. Force opponent to hurry shot.
e. Guard closely only when opponents need two points with seconds to go in the game.

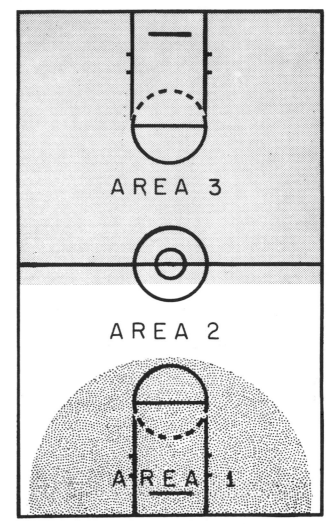

FIG. 12. AREAS OF THE COURT—USED WHEN IN A BASIC MAN-TO-MAN DEFENSE.

Area 3 (Fig 12)

a. Encourage opponents to play with the ball in this area.
b. Drop off and pick up as they enter Area 2.
c. Guard closely only when opponents need two points with seconds to go in the game.
d. Go through or behind on all screens.

Tight Man-to-Man Team Defense

Following is an example of a tight man-to-man defense.

General Objectives

1. This is a special half-court defense.

2. Get the ball. You do not want the opponents to receive a pass, let alone a shot.

3. Pick up opponents as they cross the center line.

4. Play man tight, aggressive, and tough.

5. Force everything to the sidelines.

6. Quick switch on all screens and crosses.

7. Double-team whenever opponent is in corner or near sideline.

8. Force bad passes that can be intercepted.

9. When moving with opponent toward the ball, play high with hand up.

10. This becomes a full-court press when you are behind. Play man high in front court in this case.

11. Take chances. You want the ball. You want to hurry and fluster your opponents.

Type of Personnel

Man-to-man defense requires mobile, fast front men. These ball hawks are usually small of stature, but any size player can play the position provided he is agile and fast.

The man guarding the opponents' pivot man is usually the tallest man on the team and the best rebounder. Frequently, this man is not the agile type, but is a good rebounder. A defensive position close to the basket is the best spot for such a man.

Compared with the center, the side back men are the next best rebounders and are good defensive men. These men should be mobile and fairly agile.

Coaches in school situations where the material is sparse are forced to play the best five players regardless of size and speed and mobility; consequently, the ideal of two fast guards playing in front, backed up by a rough, tall center who is flanked by rangy, fast forwards is only a dream. The coach must fit the boys to the positions according to the best combination.

► Zone Defenses

Principle of Zone Defenses

The principle upon which zone defense is played is that each player plays the ball and, in doing so, is responsible for an area of the court in which he moves in relation to the movement of the ball.

A team playing a zone defense will quickly change from offense to defense, run to their end of the court, and position themselves according to the type of defense to be played.

Zone defenses are named by men stationed in the front, second, and third (if any) line of defense. A 2-1-2 zone defense, for instance, would have: two men, the fast chasers, stationed out in front in the general vicinity of the far edge of the foul circle; one man positioned near the foul line; and two men, the rebounders, standing near the basket on the foul lane lines. Thus, a 2-1-2 zone defense.

Common zone defenses include: 2-1-2, 3-2, 2-3, 1-3-1, 1-2-2, and 2-2-1. Each has its particular alignment on the floor and each, because of the positioning of the men in certain spots on the floor, requires particular types of individuals to play the various positions. Fast, short men are assigned the front or chaser positions, and strong rebounders the back areas.

Players in a zone defense are instructed to closely cover a man with the ball who is in their area. Certain freedom not allowed in man-to-man defenses is encouraged. A man can play high; he can jump to block a shot or a pass because he knows that other players are stationed behind or alongside who can cover the ball or man with the ball should the defensive player be faked out of position.

Once a knowledge of the passing lanes for a particular zone defense is attained, defensive players can shift and move to cut off passes directed into the zone area. This stifles the offensive attempt to penetrate the zone, and the only avenue of attack left to the offense is to pass around the zone and risk long shots over the defense.

Because the defensive players play high and hold their hands and arms up, the zone defense presents a barrier to passing into the zone. This barrier is mental as well as physical; often the offense will not try to penetrate, because it *appears* to be strong and impenetrable. Ideally, when this defensive act is accomplished, the zone defense has fulfilled its mission. Now the concentration of five men near the basket can summon their rebound strength on the one hand and release the other men on the other to start a fast break. One of the distinct advantages of playing a zone defense is that all five men are positioned so that certain ones can be released while others rebound. Always being in the same relative area of the floor helps, as players then know the rebounding responsibility and positions, the clear out passes are made to areas where men are stationed, and other players are released to go down the court in a pattern. Each player is in his defensive position, which remains fairly constant regardless of where the ball goes.

Each particular zone defense has its weak or vulnerable areas. Figure 13 (A to F) indicates these areas as shaded positions of the court.

There are two primary ways or variations of the two in which a team can play a zone defense.

The first is one in which the defense is alerted to offense so that the chasers or front men in the zone are released for a fast break immediately when a shot is taken. This break from defense to offense is predicated on the facts that the back men will gain possession of the ball and clear it to the fast breaking outside men and that because of the fast breaking attack the offense will keep men back to stop the break. *This is a zone defense with an offensive emphasis.* This type of zone defense is played by teams having strong defensive rebounders or against a team that is weak on the offensive board.

On the other hand, the second method stresses *defense until possession of the ball is attained.* In this

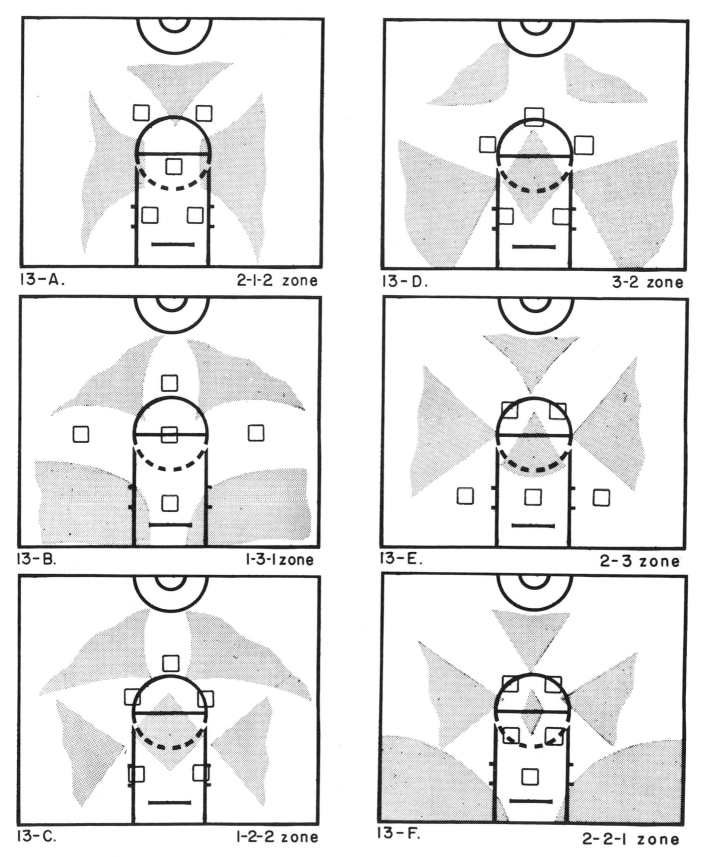

13-A.   2-1-2 zone

13-D.   3-2 zone

13-B.   1-3-1 zone

13-E.   2-3 zone

13-C.   1-2-2 zone

13-F.   2-2-1 zone

Fig. 13. Vulnerable and Weak Areas of Various Zone Defenses as indicated by shaded areas.

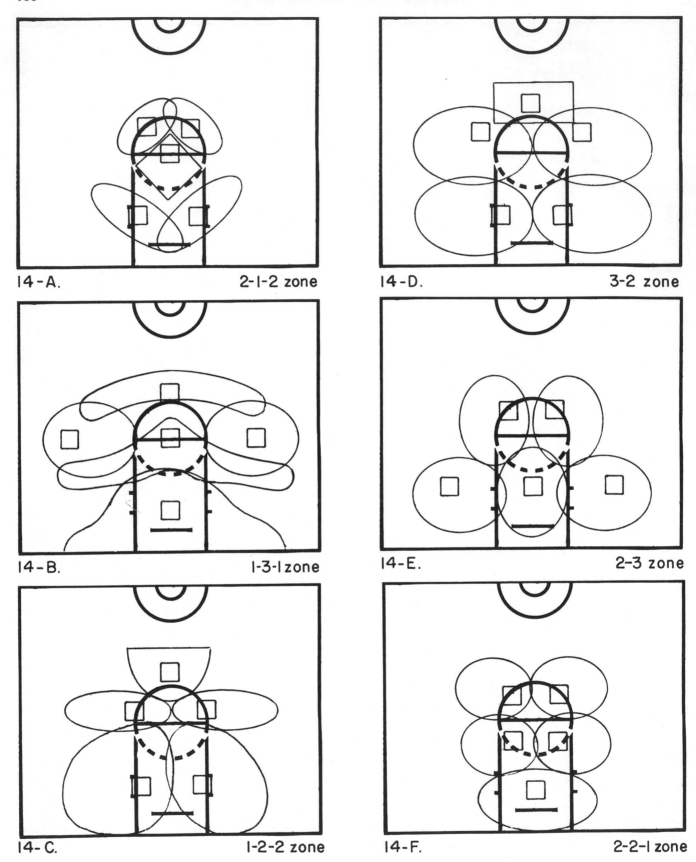

14-A.   2-1-2 zone

14-B.   1-3-1 zone

14-C.   1-2-2 zone

14-D.   3-2 zone

14-E.   2-3 zone

14-F.   2-2-1 zone

FIG. 14. THE SIX COMMON ZONE DEFENSES AND PARTICULAR AREAS OF RESPONSIBILITY FOR EACH MAN.

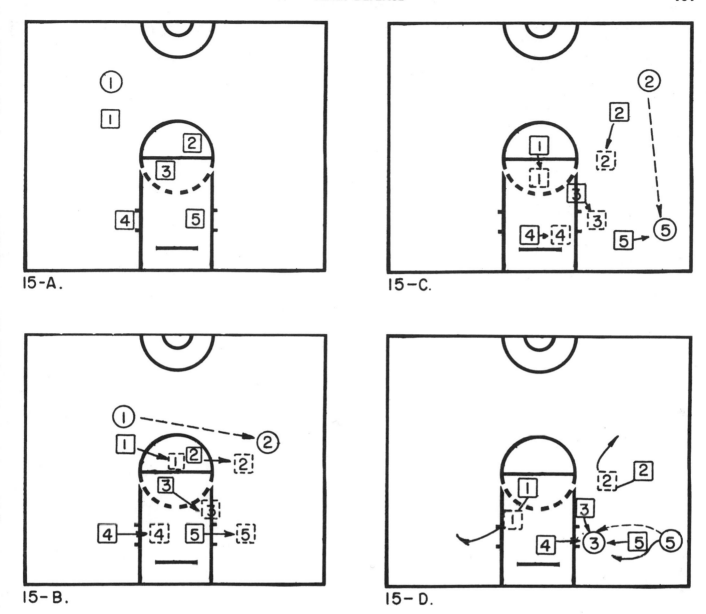

15-A.

15-C.

15-B.

15-D.

FIG. 15. THE 2-1-2 ZONE DEFENSE. Player movement is indicated as the ball is passed from ① to ② to ⑤ and to ③.

zone the defense rings the basket whenever a shot is taken. When, and only when, the ball is recovered do men clear out for a fast break. This type of zone is frequently played against an offensive team that is strong on the offensive boards or by a defensive team that is not particularly strong on its defensive boards and needs all five men in position to recover the rebound.

Types of Zone Defenses

Common types of zone defenses include the 2-1-2, the 3-2, the 2-3, the 1-2-2, the 2-2-1, and the 1-3-1. Figure 14 (A to F) indicates the general areas of responsibilities for the individual player in each of these six types of zone defense.

The 2-1-2 Zone Defense

This defense uses two chasers out in front, one man to guard the middle, and two men back. Figure 15 (A to D) indicates the player movement in relation to the movement of the ball, and shows the original setup when the ball is held at the top of the key, then the shifting of positions when the ball is passed from ① to ②. The new defensive alignment indicated by ⌐⌐ presents a 2-1-2 defense between the ball and the basket. The ball is passed to a man in the corner. Again 2-1-2 defense is formed between the ball and the basket. When the ball is passed into the center of the zone, as is shown in 15-D, the

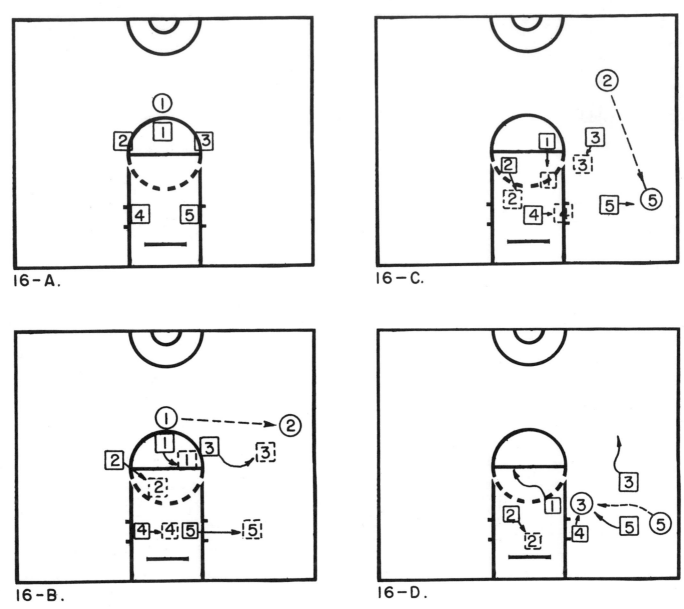

FIG. 16. THE 3-2 ZONE DEFENSE. Player movement is shown as the ball is passed from ① to ② and to ⑤ to ③.

zone collapses around it, brings rebound strength close to the board, and prepares to release the front men to a fast break.

Ideal personnel for this type of zone would include fast men in the front positions. The back defensive positions would be manned by good, tall rebounders. They should be mobile, as they have considerable ground to cover laterally. The center spot would be filled by a mobile center who is a good rebounder.

The center can play the middle position in two ways. He can play the middle strictly as a zone defense and shift according to the movement of the ball. Or he can play his zone, but guard the opposing center man-to-man when he is in this area.

This defense is strong down the middle of the court, and the middle man helps cut down the effectiveness of an opposing center who plays in this area.

The 3-2 Zone Defense

In an effort to present a 3-2 front to the ball, the players in this type of zone shift according to Figure 16 (A to D). Figure 16-D shows how the zone collapses when the ball is passed into its midst.

Ideal personnel would include three fast, mobile front men backed up by two excellent, tall rebounders Because the two back men have considerable area to cover laterally, they should be very mobile.

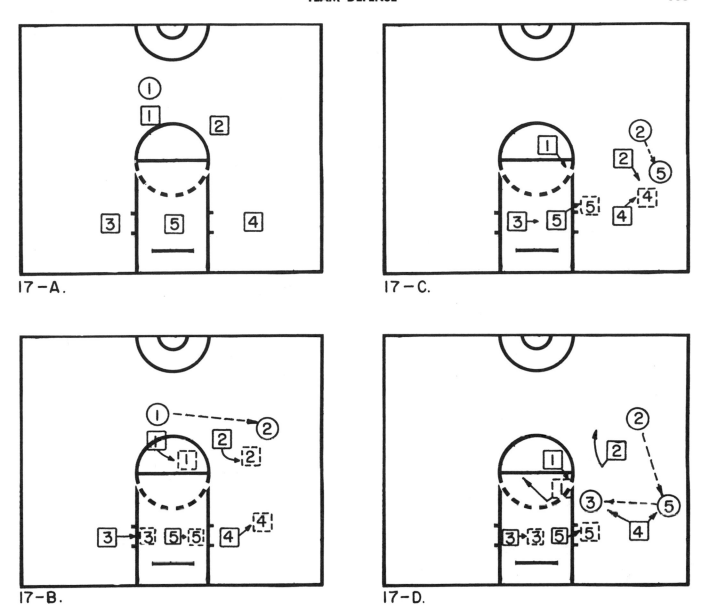

FIG. 17. THE 2-3 ZONE DEFENSE. Player movement is shown as the ball is passed from ① to ② and to ⑤ to ③.

The 2-3 Zone Defense

The 2-3 zone defense places two men as chasers out in front and stations three men along the back line of defense. It should be noted that the two front men have a lot of territory to cover; hence the importance of the two fast men in these positions. Again, Figure 17 (A, B, and C) shows the player movement, while Figure 17-D shows the position when the ball gets into the center of the zone.

The three back men share rebounding responsibilities with the best rebounder in the center at the ⑤ position. The foul line area is especially vulnerable and is one of the weak spots in the defense. It is strong along the back line in defensive rebounding and prevents close shots.

The 1-2-2 Zone Defense

This zone resembles the 3-2 type of zone defense except that it presents a defense more in depth between the ball and the basket. The middle man in the 3-2 defensive front line moves out in front; the other two play closer together to form the 1-2-2 zone defense. Figure 18 (A to D) shows the relative positions of the defensive players in relation to the ball and the movements necessary to get to those spots.

The front man ① in the defense should be fast and mobile. Frequently, this man is the best ball handler and because of this is given the responsibility of leading the fast break. The second two men should be fairly fast. The rear two defensive men ④ and ⑤ of necessity must be mobile, tall, good rebounders.

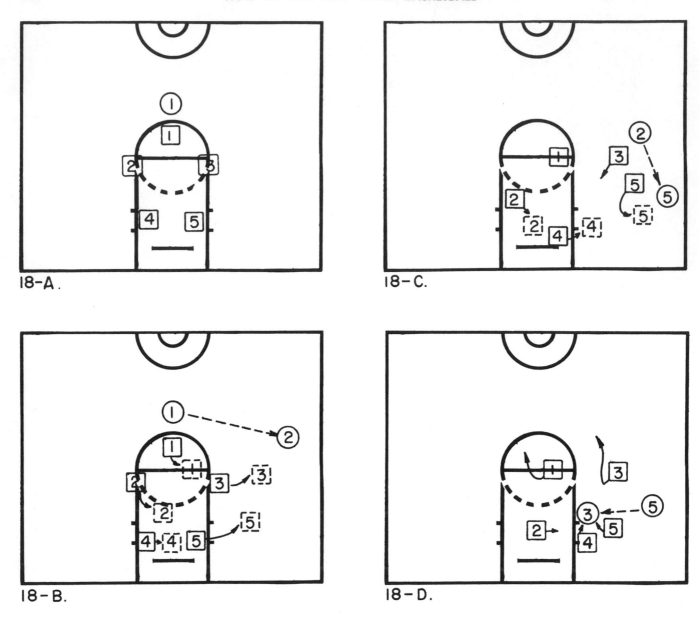

FIG. 18. THE 1-2-2 ZONE DEFENSE. Player movement is shown as the ball is passed from ① to ② to ⑤ and to ③.

The 1-2-2 zone defense is strong down the middle of the court and is effective because of its defense in depth.

The 2-2-1 Zone Defense

This zone defense is a variation of the 2-3 zone in which the back middle man is an especially tall or awkward rebounder and it is necessary to keep him close to the basket. So that the foul line area is covered, the two back men move forward and together. Figure 19 (A, B, and C) indicates the movement of the players as they maintain a 2-2-1 front between the ball and the basket. ⑤ stays in the immediate area of the basket regardless of the movement of the ball. Figure 19-D shows how ① and ② collapse on the ball

as it goes into the middle of the zone or prepare to break, depending upon the situation.

The 2-2-1 zone defense is very strong against short shots and is a good one for a team with a tall, awkward rebounder.

The 1-3-1 Zone Defense

This defense's main objective is always to have a line of three men between the ball and the basket. One man is the chaser and in front, three men are the second line, and one is the rebounder. Number ① of necessity must be a fast, aggressive player who is in excellent condition, because it is his main job to "dog" the ball in the mid-court area. This player will force the offense into mistakes, force high lob passes, or

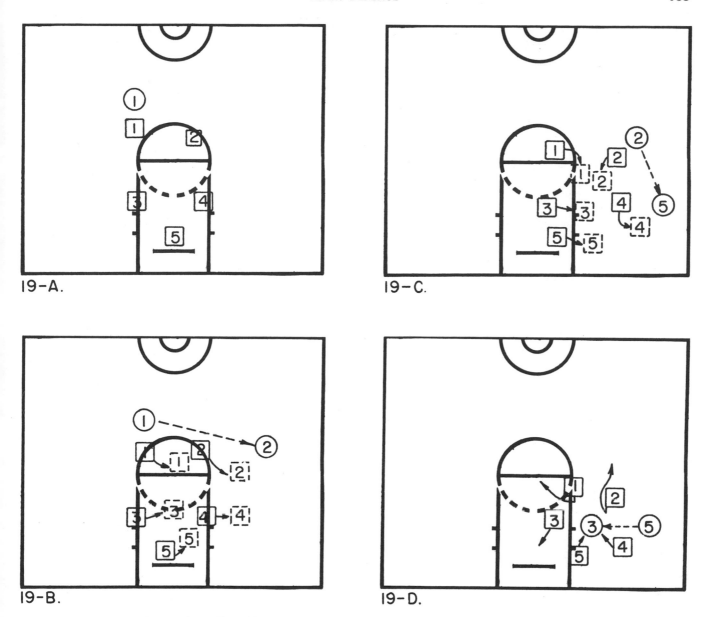

19-A.

19-C.

19-B.

19-D.

FIG. 19. THE 2-2-1 ZONE DEFENSE. Zone movements are portrayed as the ball is passed from ① to ② to ⑤ to ③.

confuse the opposing guards and so hinder their play by aggressively attacking the man with the ball. Figure 20 (A to D) portrays the player movement as the ball is passed from ① to ② and from ② to ③. The area covered by each individual defensive player is quite extensive, making this zone one of the most difficult to teach. Player ① should be fast. ② and ③ should be relatively fast and fair rebounders. ④ is the second best rebounder, while ⑤ is the best. If ⑤ is not particularly fast, he can be placed in the ④ spot and the more mobile ④ placed to play across the back line under the basket.

This particular type of zone defense is very effective in moving into a fast break. ① can go any time a

shot is taken, and ② and ③ are almost always positioned in or near areas where outlet passes are easy to receive. Players ④ and ⑤ assume most of the rebounding burden, which further frees ② and ③.

The 1-3-1 zone defense is particularly strong in the vicinity of the foul line, and in defensive rebounding.

Maneuvers

It is possible, in addition to playing a regular zone defense, to add certain maneuvers which make the zone defense more effective. These include the directional principle, cutting off of the passing lanes, the rebound triangle, the quick release from defense to the fast break, and individual play.

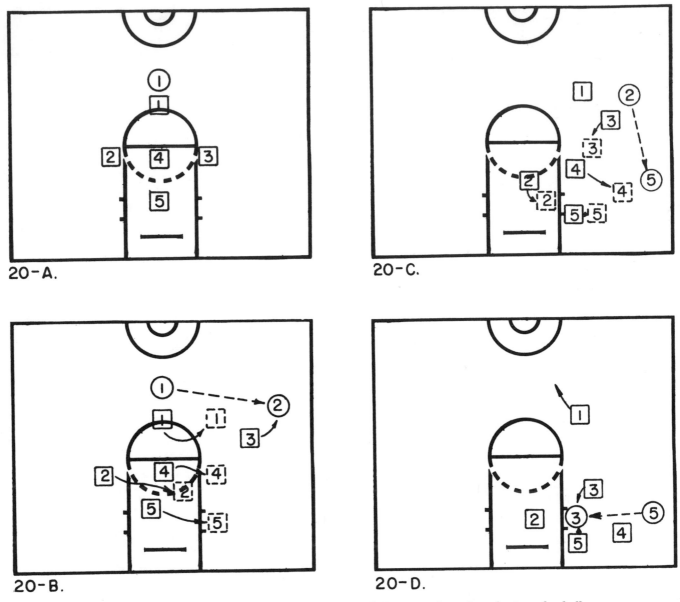

FIG. 20. THE 1-3-1 ZONE DEFENSE. The zone shifts are indicated each time the ball is passed.

Directional Principle

The use of the directional principle incorporated into the zone defense is similar to its use in the man-to-man defense. The ball is directed or guided to a certain side of the court by encouraging passes because of loose guarding on one side of the court and preventing passes by tight defense on the other. This guides or directs the ball in the desired direction. The main purpose behind this directional type of zone defense is to work the ball to a side of the court opposite which a high scorer is stationed. Also, the ball can be directed to the side where strong defensive men are playing. Both conditions favor the defense and make the zone more effective.

Cut Off Passing Lanes

Another advantageous maneuver is for the players in the zone to anticipate where passes into the zone will be directed and so move and play as to cut off or prevent the pass. This maneuver requires each defensive player to know where the offensive players are stationed or anticipate their move to another position. Thus the defensive players play the ball in true zone fashion, but in addition, shift within their area of responsibility with reference to the position of the offensive players. Figure 21 indicates this movement. All players in this defense must be conscious of the normal passing lanes into the zone and must communicate with one another, so that the location of the

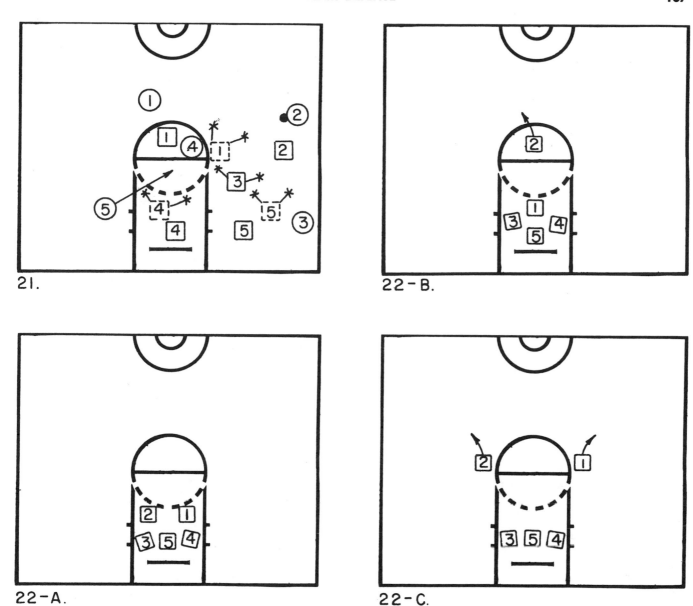

FIG. 21. CUTTING OFF THE PASSING LANES IN A ZONE DEFENSE. Solid figures indicate a normal 2-1-2 zone defense when ② has possession of the ball. Dotted ⌐¬ figures show where these men shift to prevent the ball's being worked inside the zone. These shifts are made in relation to where the offensive men are stationed, to where they might cut, and to where the ball is normally passed into a 2-1-2 zone defense.

FIG. 22. THE REBOUNDING TRIANGLE WITH VARIOUS MEN ASSIGNED TO THE BOARD. (A) Five men on the defensive board. Three close and two for long rebounds. (B) Three and a half men on the defensive board. Three rebounding close in, one for long rebounds, and one ready for a fast break. (C) Three men rebounding.

five offensive players is known by each of the defensive men.

Defensive Triangle

So that the basket is thoroughly covered for rebounding, a defensive triangle is a necessity. The defensive players form the barrier around the basket so that no offensive player can get under. Long rebounds are covered by the other defensive men. Each player in the zone, regardless of the type, has to know his

rebound responsibilities and act each time a shot is taken. It is possible to place five men on the defensive board—three in close and two covering a semi-long rebound. Figure 22-A indicates this position. The usual rebounding plan is to have three men in the triangle, one poised for a long rebound, and one ready to go on a fast break. This situation is usually called three and a half men on the board. The half is the long rebounder. Minimum essentials would place two strong men on the board. Each would be responsible for a side and the front of the basket. Next is the normal three-man triangle pictured in Figure 22-C. Strong defensive screening is necessary so that the defensive triangle, regardless of the number in its make-up, cannot be broken. Each zone defense within the movements of its players should have rules designating those who rebound and where they rebound. Practice on this phase of defense is time well spent. The idea to put forth to the players is *one shot, and one shot only, shall be taken and it shall be from outside the zone.*

The release of specific players to a fast break will depend upon player personnel and the type of zone played. Certain players break to clear-out areas while others are free to "take off" down the court. This should not be a helter-skelter arrangement, but one that has been practiced and is in reality a pattern. More on this subject will appear under "Fast Break."

The ABC's of Zone Defense

The defensive man should:

1. Watch the ball and shift quickly to the assigned position as the ball is passed from man to man.
2. Keep his arms up.
3. Be alert to intercept passes.
4. Move in toward the basket when the ball is passed behind.
5. When the opponents shoot, be prepared either to form a defensive triangle or to receive a quick pass to start a fast break.
6. Talk it up; warn teammates when there is a man in their area.
7. Two-time a man who has the ball between his defensive position and a teammate's area.
8. Close in upon a man who tries to dribble through your zone.
9. Force the opponents to take long shots.
10. Be a little reckless in trying to intercept passes or block shots because the man in the area behind will support you.
11. Be prepared to block any shot taken from his area.
12. Remember that this is not an easy, relaxed defense. Each player must be ready to shift, shift, and shift again each time the ball moves.

Strengths of Zone Defenses

1. Effective against poor long shooters.
2. Effective against poor ball handlers.
3. Effective against the dribbler.
4. Effective against teams that play a set offense.
5. Effective against teams that screen and cut.
6. Players are always in strong rebound positions.
7. Easy to teach, as each player is concerned with the ball and with the guarding of a small portion of the court.

8. Effective for blocking shots, because the outside men know the back men can cover for them if an opponent or the ball gets inside the zone.
9. Effective for intercepting passes.
10. Strong against short shots.
11. Effective when there is a lack of reserve team strength, as it is not a tiring defense.
12. Fewer fouls are called, because there is not as much personal contact as in man-to-man defense.
13. Effective for slow, tall players.
14. Effective on narrow or short courts.
15. Men are in excellent positions to fast break.
16. Good defense when star player is in danger of fouling out.

Weaknesses of Zone Defenses

1. Weak against good ball handlers.
2. Weak against good set shooters.
3. Weak when men do not shift as a team.
4. A large court has a tendency to spread the defense.
5. Weak against the fast break.
6. Not a good defense when behind in score late in the game.
7. Overloading on one or two men puts a great responsibility on those players, and when others come to their assistance, the zone breaks down.
8. If the zone spreads or overshifts, it becomes open for good close shots.
9. Weak when an opponent gets "hot."
10. Weak in covering certain areas of the floor depending upon the type of zone.
11. Cannot pressure the offense.
12. If one player fails to shift, an area is left open.
13. No one player is definitely responsible; therefore, many unnecessary chances are taken.

Basic Team Zone Defense

Following is an example of a basic zone defense. The main objective of this zone defense is to prevent the offense from obtaining a close shot at the basket. It also affords the defensive men the opportunity to screen out the offensive players and to obtain rebounds against tall opponents. In addition, the chasers are in excellent position to start the fast break. Zone defense is work, because each player must move every time the ball moves; consequently, it is effective only when played with aggression and determination.

The zone to be played is a 2-1-2. Rules are as follows:

1. The middle man and the two rebounders will rebound all shots.
2. The chasers will stop the offensive players one step from the edge of the foul circle.
3. The chasers will release for a fast break on each shot.

4. The front men can play high and take chances, as there is always a defensive player behind to give support.

5. Remember the passing lanes into and through this zone and shift to cut them off or to intercept the pass.

6. All five players are cautioned not to spread out. This is a compact 2-1-2 zone defense.

7. The play can, if desired, be directed to the right or left side of the court. This is important should it be decided to take the play opposite a high-scoring forward.

8. When on offense and possession of the ball is lost, a rapid change-over to defense must be made and each player must immediately run to his defensive position.

► Combination Defenses

It is possible to play a defense in which there is a combination of men playing man-to-man and zone defenses. Examples are: the box and one; the diamond and one; front line man-to-man, back line zone; and front line zone, back line man-to-man.

These are special defenses and are employed when there are special circumstances; for instance, in an effort to stop an opponent's high-scoring player or to utilize the special attributes of a player on the defensive team.

The Box and One

This defense is composed of four players playing a 2-2 (box) zone while the remaining player guards the opponent's high scorer man-to-man or is allowed to play free lance as a roamer. The man-to-man defensive player should have special defensive abilities which would enable him to closely guard an outstanding scorer, to intercept passes, and harass the opponents. The advantage of this defense is that the high scorer is guarded man-to-man by a special defensive man, and when he is in the zone of one of the other defensive players, he is guarded by two men. This is a very effective defense, designed to stop a team with a player who takes many shots and scores a majority of his team's points. The front men of the 2-2 zone should be fast, while the two rear rebounders have the entire responsibility of defensive rebounding. Figure 23 indicates the positions taken when the ball is in possession of ②.

The Diamond and One

The diamond and one is a variation of the box in one in which the diamond is a 1-2-1 zone defense and the one is a man-to-man defense applied to the opponent's high scorer or is again allowed to play as a roamer.

Whether to use a box and one or a diamond and one would depend upon the skills of the defensive team. The front man in the 1-2-1 would be the fast chaser. The two men would be mobile players with good rebounding ability. The last line should be manned by an excellent rebounder. Again, the one is a good man-to-man defensive player.

Figure 24 portrays this defense and illustrates the player movement in relation to the ball. The players in the zone shift in relation to the position of the ball, while ① guards ① man-to-man. The players in the zone should double-team ① at every opportunity.

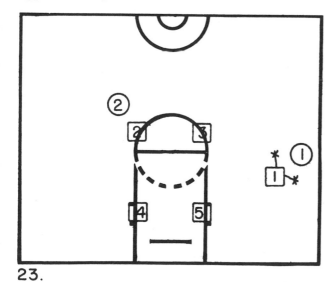

23.

FIG. 23. THE BOX-AND-ONE COMBINATION ZONE AND MAN-TO-MAN DEFENSE. ① plays the opponent's high-scoring player, number ①, man-to-man while the remaining players play a 2-2 or box zone defense.

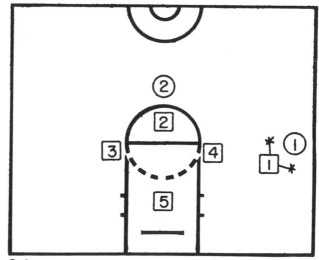

24.

FIG. 24. THE DIAMOND AND ONE COMBINATION ZONE AND MAN-TO-MAN DEFENSE. Defensive man, ①, plays a man-to-man defense on ①, while the other players play a 1-2-1 or diamond zone defense.

Front Line Man-to-Man, Back Line Zone Combination Defense

This special defense can be varied from two to three men in the front line and conversely three to two in the rear line. A combination of two extremely fast, small men with three tall, awkward rebounders would best combine into a two man-to-man–three zone. The man-to-man situation in the front line continues, and when more than three men cut through, one of the chasers follows.

Should the combination be three man-to-man–two zone, one of the three chasers would have to follow a cutter going through. The two rebounders maintain a relatively close position to the basket for rebounding purposes.

Front Line Zone, Back Line Man-to-Man Combination Defense

Again, the combination can vary from two to three men in the front line, depending upon player abilities and the play of the opponents. The front line forms a zone in which their switching leads one to have the impression that it is a switching man-to-man defense. The chasers are in excellent positions to go into a fast break. The front men have quite a range of movement.

Strengths of Combination Defenses

1. The defense can be directed at a particular high-scoring offensive player.

2. Because the combination defense is a special and unusual one, it will often confuse the opposition.

3. The defense can successfully utilize the talents of the defensive team.

4. Both the assets of the man-to-man and zone defenses are realized.

5. It is easy to double-team an opponent.

6. Effective against the dribbler.

7. Effective against the poor long shooters.

8. Often one man can harass the man in the offense, and he still has an organized defense behind him.

Weaknesses of Combination Defenses

1. Weak against good ball handlers.

2. Weak against good set shooters.

3. Weak in covering certain areas of the floor, depending upon the type of defense played.

4. Weak against the fast break.

5. Special abilities are necessary in some positions because of the nature of the defense. Players with these abilities are often not available.

6. When the defense is directed at a particular high-scoring player, other offensive players might get "hot."

7. Special preparation and time are required to develop a special defense.

▶ Pressing Defenses

Principle of Pressing Defenses

A pressing defense is one in which the defensive team guards the opponents in the opponents' back court very tightly and continues to guard them as they try to advance the ball into their front court. The continued *"pressure"* of a tight defense plus the fact that the ball must be brought into the front court within ten seconds frequently upsets the plans of the offensive team. The pressure of a tight defense continually forces the opponents to a course of unaccustomed action and causes them to become confused, play faster than they are able, and make mistakes which enable the defense to score easy baskets. Because of these results, pressing defenses have been developed which are of the man-to-man or zone types of defense.

A pressing defense would be the ideal defense to use the entire game if the personnel were available. It takes players who are aggressive, fast, agile, and in top physical condition, who have a good sense of timing, and who have the ability to handle the ball going at top speed. As the majority of teams do not have the men to fit these qualifications, this type of defense is then used only when behind and it is late in the game. This late-game press presents opportunities for the defense to get the ball and score and also prevents the opponents from easily going into a control type of offense or a stall. The press is also effective against a slow or an inexperienced team.

Presses can be played in two general ways. In the first, the defense is aggressive and makes every effort possible to obtain possession of the ball. This is called the *absolute press.* In the second, the press is more of a bother or a semi-harassing type in which the offense is bothered and is encouraged to play faster but not in a tight, aggressive manner. This is a *harassing press.*

The absolute press would be necessary when behind in the score, late in the game, and could also be played the entire game. The harassing press could not be used late in the game when behind. The players would have to go to an absolute press.

Man-to-Man Press

The man-to-man type of press is started in one of two different ways. In the first, each man can quickly guard the man nearest him as his particular opponent. The second method makes it necessary for the guard to locate the one man for whom he is responsible and

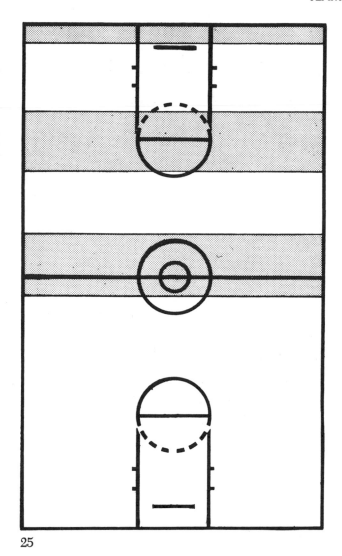

Full Court

3/4 Court

2/3 Court

FIG. 25. PICK-UP POINTS AND FLOOR COVERAGE FOR THE VARIOUS PRESSING DEFENSES. Pick-up points are shown for the full-court, ¾, ⅔, and ½-court presses.

1/2 Court

25

1. Force ball to inside.
2. Play low on a man who has a dribble.
3. Play high on a man who does not have a dribble.
4. Center guards opposing center.
5. Switch on all crosses.
6. Play high on man in front court.
7. Drop back into a man-to-man defense when the press is beaten.

Of course, the above could be changed to no switching or force everything to outside, etc., depending upon the personnel and the desires of the coach.

The man-to-man press can be applied at any position on the floor. A full-court press is one in which the defense guards the offensive men all over the court. Figure 25 indicates the normal pick-up locations for the various presses. The three-quarter- or two-thirds-court press is applied at the offensive team's back court foul line area. The half-court press is put on the opponents one or two steps over the center line. The theory behind this half-court press is threefold. First, there is only a half of the court to guard. Second, the press will quicken the tempo of the opposition. Third, as there are only ten seconds to get the ball across the center line, the defense will make mistakes in their effort to hurry.

A good strategy is to apply a press after a score; otherwise, everyone runs back on defense and the basic back court defense is utilized. This is particularly effective when learning the press, as each player has several seconds in which to find and guard his man while the opponents are putting the ball in play.

Maneuvers

Several maneuvers make the press more effective. The directional principle is one of the most important. The play must be forced either to the outside or the inside. Players guarding men in the offensive team's

to guard that man as soon as possible. The defense plays an aggressive style of play designed to fluster and disturb the opponents.

In this man-to-man press, the players can switch men whenever opponents cross or they can play strictly man-to-man. If a guard loses his man, he should immediately run toward his own foul circle to try to regain a defensive position on his man or pick up another man who might be free. Defensive men double-team offensive players whenever possible to steal the ball, gain a jump ball, or force a pass that can be intercepted.

When building this type of defense, attention is given to one man guarding one offensive man the length of the floor. The defensive man endeavors to force the man with the ball into one desired direction. Two offensive players are then placed against two defensive men with the entire length of the floor to go for a score. Three vs. three, four vs. four, then five are placed against five.

Definite rules are necessary when playing a pressing man-to-man defense. Following are examples:

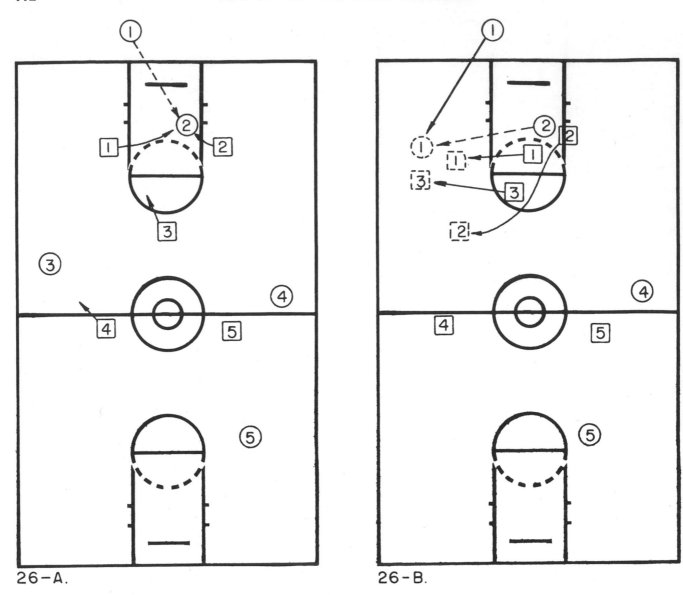

26-A.　　　　　26-B.

FIG. 26. THE 2-1-2 ZONE PRESS. Movements of the players are shown as the ball is passed up the court. In 26-A, ⬜1 and ⬜2 double-team ②) as soon as he gets the ball. ⬜3 moves up and to his left in anticipation of a pass to ③. ② passes back to ① in 26-B, and ⬜1 and ⬜3 double-team ① while ⬜2 falls back in the middle spot. The ball is passed back to ② in 26-C, and ⬜1 and ⬜2 double-team while ⬜3 shifts back to the middle spot. 26-D portrays the situation of ② attempting a long pass to ⑤. ⬜5, anticipating such a play, tries for an interception. ⬜1, ⬜2, and ⬜3 move back and forth and up and back. Should the ball get behind ⬜1, ⬜2, or ⬜3, they run back behind ⬜4 and ⬜5, who would take their place as the front line men.

back court should play alongside or between the ball and the man they are guarding—the object being to force high passes which can be intercepted and to prevent passes if possible. The defense should be instructed either to switch men or to play strictly man-to-man. A quick switch is often successful when timed properly, because it often disrupts the play of the opponent and frequently leads to ball possession by the defense. Defensive players have to be conscious of whether or not the man with the ball has a dribble left. When he can still dribble, he should be played low with upward stabbing motions with the hands.

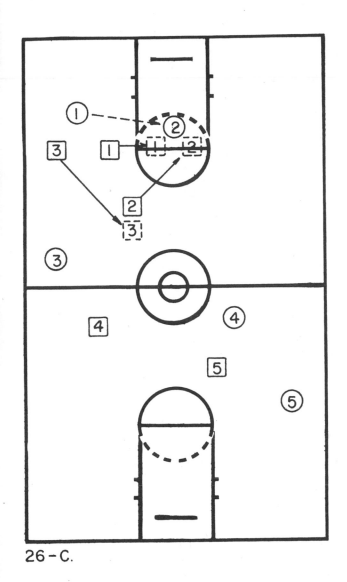

26-C.

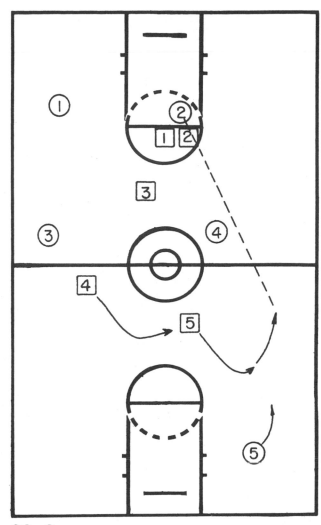

26-D.

As soon as the offensive man has lost his dribble, he should be played high. Hands are waved high to force a lob pass which can be intercepted.

Zone Presses

A zone press is based upon the zone principle of each man playing the ball while guarding specific areas of the floor. As soon as the opponents gain possession of the ball, each man on the defensive team quickly goes to his assigned position on the floor. These positions, which also name the particular type of zone defense, are the 2-1-2 or 2-2-1.

The 2-1-2 Zone Press

In the 2-1-2 pressing zone the two front chasers endeavor to force the man with the ball into a double-team situation or to drive him in a desired direction.

The middle man picks up an open man in his area or the man with the ball should he break through. The two back men intercept passes or take the front man's place should the ball get through. Figure 26 (A to D) shows the player movement as the ball progresses up the court. Every attempt is made to present a 2-1-2 barrier between the ball and the basket at all times.

The 2-2-1 Zone Press

This press is presented as a full-court zone press to be used the entire game. ① and ② team up, and ③ and ④ team up, while ⑤ is the safety man. Every effort is made to double-team, tie up the opponent, cause the offense to speed up and make mistakes. Figure 27 (A to D) shows the player movement in relation to where the ball is located.

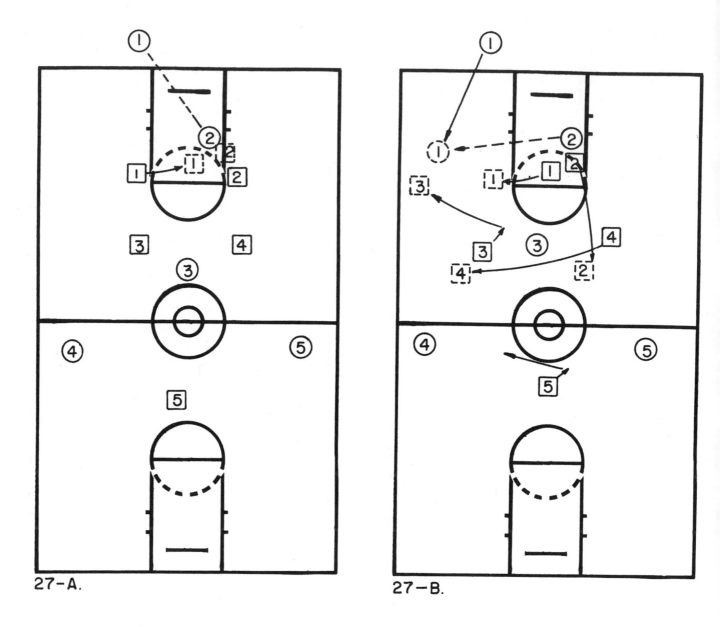

FIG. 27. THE 2-2-1 ZONE PRESS. Diagrams show how the players shift in relation to the movement of the ball. □1 and □2 double-team ②2 as soon as he gets the ball. □3 and □4 shift into the second line of defense. This action is shown in 27-A. In 27-B, □3 and □1 pick up ①1, while □2 and □4 move back to the secondary defensive position. The ball is passed behind the first line of defense to ③3 in 27-C, at which time □2 and □4 double-team him and □1 and □3 move back to become the second line of defense. 27-D portrays the situation of a long pass from ③3 to ⑤5. ⑤5 anticipating such a move tries to intercept, and □2, □3, and □4 hurry back to reform their defense or go on offense if ⑤5 gets the ball.

General rules are as follows:

1. □1 is left forward.
2. □2 is center.
3. □3 and □4 are guards.
4. □5 is right forward.
5. Allow the ball to be tossed into the court.

6. Force everything to the middle of the court.
7. □1 and □2 double-team man with the ball.
8. □3 and □4 take over if ball passes □1 and □2.
9. □1 and □2 replace □3 and □4 when ball goes behind □1 and □2.
10. Press constantly and aggressively; do not foul.

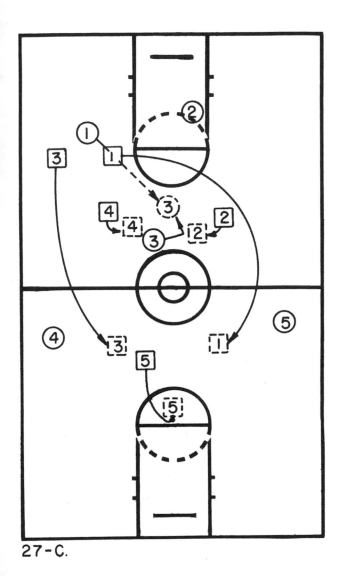

27-C.

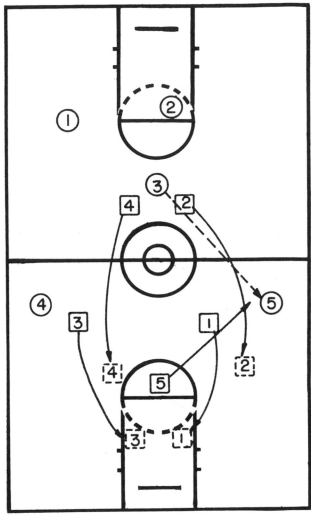

27-D.

11. Anticipate a pass to an open man. Play between open man and the ball. Invite a pass, then intercept it.

12. Defense compresses into a 2-1-2 zone defense at our end of the floor. Go into a man-to-man defense at the first pass.

The 2-3 Half-Court Zone Press

This press is applied two steps across the center line of the court. The defense described is a 2-3 half-court zone press and is shown in Figure 28 (A to D).

Rules for the 2-3 half-court press are as follows:

1. Force ball to center of court.
2. Double-team at every opportunity.
3. Intercept passes.
4. [1] and [2] stop ball two steps across the center line. Double-team man with the ball.
5. [3], [4], and [5] play their areas with reference to

offensive men playing in those areas.

6. Drop back into a 2-3 zone when the offense has successfully moved the ball into their front court.

Learning the Zone Press

The zone press should be first pictured on a blackboard, so that each player obtains a mental picture of what is desired. Basic moves and situations are shown, so that the general idea is put across. Then the same situations are set up on the floor with the players moving in slow motion to each position. When each player has in mind the rules and the movements, then full-court scrimmage is possible. A zone press should be practiced a few minutes each day in order to have the players stay mentally and physically in shape for the rigors of playing it in a complete game.

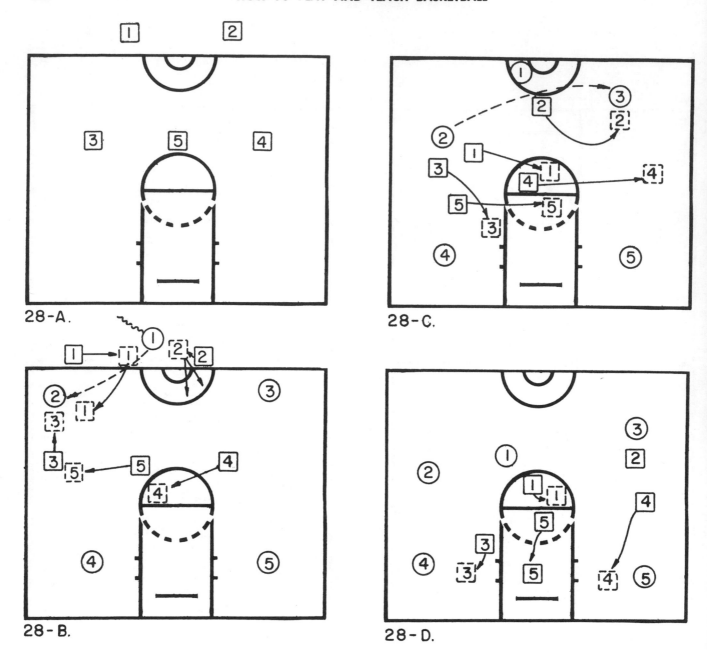

FIG. 28. THE 2-3 HALF-COURT ZONE PRESS. (A) The defensive organization as the opposition moves the ball up to the middle of the court. (B) 1 and 2 double-team 1, who has the ball. Player movement is shown as 1 passes to 2. 4 and 5 shift over to their left as 1 and 3 attack 2. 2 drops back and positions himself in relation to where the offensive players are. (C) The movement as the ball is thrown cross court to 3. The defense again quickly shifts to a 2-3 zone, with 2 guarding 3. (D) The 2-3 pressing zone defense drops back into a regular 2-3 zone, because the offense has been able to bring the ball into their front court and beat the press.

The ABC's of Pressing Defenses

The defensive man should:

1. Take chances and get the ball.

2. Be aggressive.

3. Hurry the opponents into making mistakes.

4. Play low on a man who can still dribble.

5. Play high on a man who cannot dribble.

6. Play high on a man in the opponents' back court.

7. Not be disturbed should the opponents score an easy basket.

8. Be alert to intercept passes.

9. Every man must be in top shape. Do not loaf.

10. Talk it up. Help teammates.

11. Know which direction you are forcing the ball, then direct it there.

12. Know whether you are going to switch or play strictly man-to-man. Then do it that way every time.

13. Know that this defense will get the ball many times; therefore, do not throw it away, but play offense in an organized manner.

14. Be poised; no matter what the circumstances, play as you are coached.

The Strengths of Pressing Defenses

1. Excellent as a basic team defense if personnel is available.

2. Effective late in game when behind in the score.

3. Effective against slow teams.

4. Players can be matched according to speed and ability.

5. Effective against teams not in top condition.

6. Enables the pressing team to score easy baskets when passes are intercepted.

7. Helps team spirit.

8. Effective against a team manned by weak guards.

9. Forces the opponents to make mistakes such as bad passes or fumbles which would not ordinarily occur.

10. Often the offense will panic and several quick baskets will result.

11. Speeds up tempo of own defense and attacks.

The Weaknesses of Pressing Defenses

1. Requires speed and aggressiveness.

2. More than five players are necessary.

3. Team must be in top physical condition.

4. Can cause excess fouling because of the aggressive, fast type of play.

5. A good dribbler can often beat the press.

6. Defense might panic if the opponents score several quick baskets.

7. Requires good team spirit, hard work, and cooperation among the players.

8. Defense takes chances and, in doing so, will leave men and areas of the court open.

9. The leading players are liable to foul out of the game.

► Special Situations

Special situations exist when the entire team or one or two players must act together in a predetermined course of action, such as during foul shooting, the fast break, out-of-bounds plays, jump balls, three on two, defensing the big man, and the like. These situations occur very quickly, and unless each player knows what he is to do as well as what his teammates are to do, the offense will have a tremendous advantage.

Defense the Big Man

Two major ideas prevail regarding the defensing of a big high-scoring center, and they are usually based upon the philosophy of the coach and his personnel. The first idea is that the big man will score his thirty points or so a game regardless of the defense; consequently, play him normally, but do not allow any of the other offensive men to score. The second idea is a direct opposite of the first. The big man usually scores thirty points or so, but we will stop him by special maneuvers even though our defense is weakened against the remaining members of the opposition. Under the first idea, the regular defense is utilized, with the person assigned to guard the big man endeavoring to stop passes into that high scorer and, on shots, attempting to screen out the big man to cut down his offensive rebounds.

Specific information on guarding the pivot man appears in Chapter 4, and this procedure holds even for the very big man. Several strategies can be utilized which will cut down the effectiveness of the big man.

First, prevent the big man from receiving a pass. This responsibility rests jointly with the player guarding the big man and the player guarding the man with the ball. Every attempt is made to direct the pass in other directions or to block the pass into this man.

Second, the pivot man should be forced into areas of the court where, if he receives the ball, he will be at a disadvantage. The man guarding the pivot man has this responsibility. He should force the big man to go where the big man does not want to go.

Third, the team defense can assist should the ball get in to the pivot man. The weak-side forward can sag off his man and attack or guard the pivot man from the rear. The man guarding the center can play high with confidence, knowing that the back door offensive maneuver for the pivot man is guarded. Sagging front men can often bother the pivot man, particularly when he plays at the top of the foul line. Zone defenses which position a man in the area of the foul line are relatively strong in this regard. The 1-3-1, 2-1-2 and the 2-3 are examples of such defenses. Combination defenses lend themselves to such a special assignment. The box and one or diamond and one are excellent. The one man plays the pivot player man-to-man, while the other players play a box zone or a diamond zone defense. Whenever the big man is in the center of a combination defense such as this, he is guarded specifically man-to-man by one guard and is, in addition, surrounded by the remaining defensive players. Any one of those men playing zone defense can collapse on the center and bother him or help him in the defense against him.

Personnel will in many cases determine the type of defense to use against the big man, but regardless of the type, the entire team must be well organized and prepared to defend against the big man.

Defense the Fast Break

Stopping the fast break is a very important part of the defensive team effort. As the fast break can produce many easy baskets, it can be very demoralizing for the opponents; therefore, every effort possible should be made to stop it.

There are three phases in defensing the fast break. The first phase involves an offensive effort to maneuver the men who start the fast break from their normal positions and to rebound strongly when a shot is taken. It is possible to maneuver strong defensive rebounders away from the basket or take the opponents' fast break lead men in under the basket or to the corners of the court. A zone defense, of course, defeats this maneuver as the zone men will not follow the individual offensive men. A strong rebound effort on the offensive board will discourage the defense from releasing their chasers on each shot. Three and a half or four men on the board will often accomplish this purpose regardless of the type of defense.

The second phase is concerned with stopping the first pass at its inception or at its termination point. The outlet pass can often be stopped by aggressive defensive play by the man nearest the rebounder. If the pass cannot be stopped or blocked, the next best thing would be to delay its start. Each team generally has one or two areas to which men go to receive an outlet pass. This outlet area can be covered by a guard, or men to whom outlet passes are normally thrown can be closely guarded, so that the first pass is not successfully cleared. When the first pass is stopped or delayed, the remaining team members have time to go to their assigned areas to stop the outlet pass or to hustle back on defense.

The third phase involves the change from offense to defense. This is coupled with phase one and two, as some players might be involved in those maneuvers. As soon as a man, whether he is assigned to the offensive boards or not, discovers that the ball has gone over to the opponents, he should react immediately. He first thinks of tying up the rebounder or of covering an outlet area, and if these are not his assignments or not possible, he should run to his foul line to establish a line of defense. A team effort in each phase of stopping the fast break will limit the opponents' easy scores, and they will find it difficult to obtain the advantage of an easy basket or of outnumbering the defense 2 to 1, 3 to 2 or 4 to 3.

Defense the Out-of-Bounds Play

As the opponents do not have to wait for an official to touch a ball out of bounds when it is in their back court, they can grab the ball and *go* for an easy two points. When this situation occurs, the defense should react quickly and revert to defense by quickly running back to their back court and forming a defense.

When the opponents take the ball out of bounds in their front court, they have five seconds to toss it to a player inside the playing area. With this in mind, it pays to try to bother the player taking the ball out of bounds by shouting at him and waving hands in his face to obstruct his vision and to block his pass. Because of set screen plays, some coaches advocate using a zone defense when a team takes the ball out of bounds under its own basket. This helps counteract screen plays. The players in a man-to-man defense must be conscious of screens and fast cuts and react quickly to stop a scoring play.

Defense the Free Throw

The defensive team is now assigned the two inside positions when the opponents are awarded a free throw. This advantageous position is often lost because of poor defense on the part of these men. Figure 29 indicates the feet position and the steps these two defensive men should take to effectively screen out their opponents. The man on the right side steps into the lane with his left foot, while the man on the left side steps with his right foot. This places these two men in a controlling position on short rebounds.

The second position which must be defended is that of a long rebound or a tap back to the foul shooter. Figure 29 also indicates this situation and the movement by ③ to cover the foul shooter and the long rebound in the lane.

These stepping maneuvers can be effectively practiced when the team is practicing foul shooting. It will relieve the monotony and instill the correct step and position in each player.

Defense the Stall

No coach or team likes to go into the closing minutes of a basketball game behind in the score, as the team ahead has the tremendous advantage of being able to play control ball or to go into a complete stall.

The first attempt to combat this situation is a full-court press. Every attempt is made to hurry the opponents, to force mistakes, and to obtain possession of the ball. Once the opponents have worked the ball into their front court, an aggressive, determined man-to-man defense is the best solution to a very bad situation. Every attempt should be made to double-team

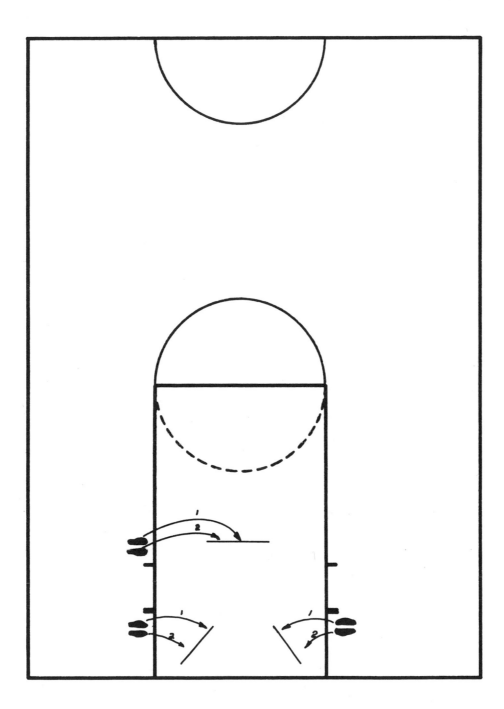

FIG. 29. DEFENSING THE FOUL SHOT. The proper steps are indicated which are necessary for good defensive rebounding positions.

the opponents should two offensive men cross or come close together. Every attempt to intercept or bat down passes should be made. The defense should go all out to get the ball. Once possession is obtained, a good attempt to score should be made. Often a hard-earned possession is tossed away by a poor percentage shot.

This situation can be practiced by holding one- or two-minute games with one team ahead by one or two points. This realistic situation will point out to the players the necessity of breaking the stall.

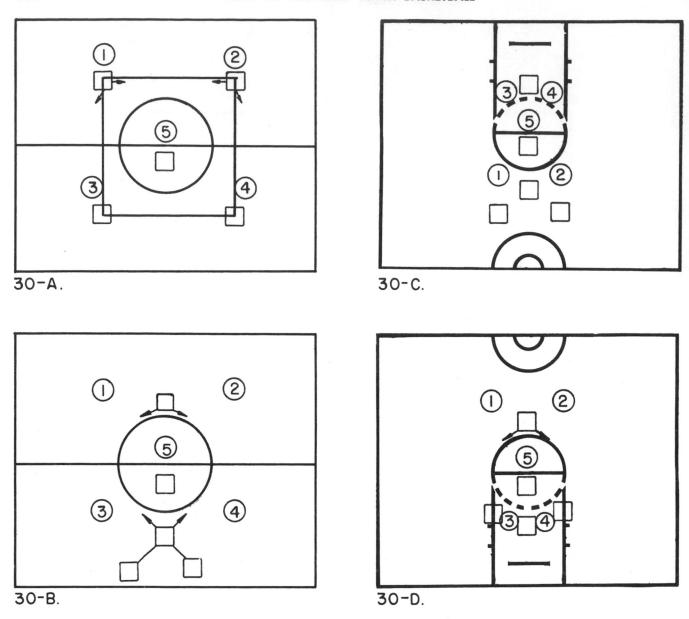

30-A.

30-B.

30-C.

30-D.

FIG. 30. DEFENSING THE JUMP BALL AT THE CENTER CIRCLE, OFFENSIVE FOUL LINE, AND DEFENSIVE FOUL CIRCLE. (A) The box position. (B) The strong Y formation, which places three men between the ball and the basket. (C) Jump Ball positions at the offensive foul line. (D) Defensive line-up at the back court foul line.

Defense the Jump Ball

This aspect of basketball is important and should be emphasized, so that your team will obtain more than its share of jump balls. Three situations exist which of necessity must be planned. These are a jump ball at the center of the court, a jump ball at the back court (defensive) foul line, and a jump ball at the team's front court foul line. It is of special concern when a tall man who will probably get the tip is to jump against your team. These defensive situations are a concern of the team defense. The defense should line up properly in a "prearranged" manner and, although they are on the defensive because the opponent will get the jump, should play to end up in possession of the ball or at least prevent a quick, easy basket by the opponents.

Numerous positions are possible when defending against a tall man who is certain to get the tip. The proper placement, player movement, and aggressive attempts to get the batted ball can often result in possession.

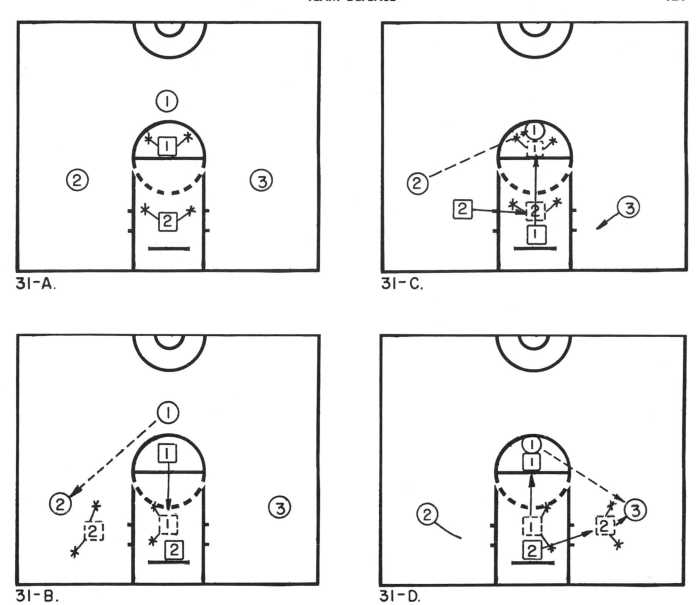

FIG. 31. TWO-MAN ZONE DEFENSE AGAINST THREE OPPONENTS. ①̲ and ②̲ position themselves in a tandem formation, with ①̲ at the top of the foul line and ②̲ a step in front of the basket. ①̲'s movement is back toward the basket and forward to the foul line, while ②̲ moves from side to side. The first three diagrams show this teamwork. ① passes to ②. Immediately ②̲ moves sideways to cover ② while ①̲ faces to the side the ball was passed and quickly moves to the position ②̲ formerly was in. ①̲ keeps his arms up to prevent a pass from ② to ③. When ② passes back to ①, ①̲ and ②̲ quickly shift back to their original positions. (D) The movement of the ball from ① to ③. ②̲ moves sideways to take ③, and ①̲ slides back to an under the basket position.

Figure 30-A indicates a box formation at the center circle, with the defensive men stationed between their men and the basket. A very strong defensive line-up is shown in Figure 30-B. In this position, the men at the edge of the circle can break to either side in an attempt to get the ball, and the two back men can prevent a fast break attempt.

When there is a defensive jump ball at the offensive basket, a fast break can be prevented and an effort made to get the ball by a formation as is portrayed in Figure 30-C.

Figure 30-D shows the defensive line-up at the back court foul line. The opponent is not allowed to have a man near the basket who has an open side. The ball in this case will have to be batted to the side, and the front man might guess correctly and obtain possession.

Two Defensive Men on Three Offensive Men

A fast break will often produce a situation in which three offensive men are placed against only two defensive men. The defensive men must fight these three men off until help arrives or at least force a long low percentage shot. Under no circumstances should a lay-in shot be allowed. Co-ordinated effort by the two defensive men will often stop or stall such an attack by the use of a two-man zone defense. A team using this three-on-two pattern must score within one or two passes, because defensive help is certain to arrive by that time; consequently, the two defensive men should talk it up, shift properly, and hustle to force passes and to prevent a good shot. Figure 31 (A to D) illustrates this type of zone defense.

Team Rebounding

Each defense, regardless of the type, should have specific responsibilities regarding rebounding. The ideal situation is to have a defensive triangle concentrated at the basket every time the opponents shoot. This will assist in obtaining possession of the ball and will prevent second shots by the offense.

Team personnel and the ability of the opponents will determine who rebounds where. When necessary, all five men might be required to cover the board. The usual case though is to have three men in the triangle and one long rebounder, with the remaining player preparing to fast break.

Defensive rebounding can be practiced to good advantage by assigning one team to offense and one to defense. The offense works a play and takes a shot. The defense moves to the assigned positions, rebounds, and makes the first pass out for a fast break. This drill will easily indicate whether or not each player is doing his assigned job.

► Summary

Team defense is the co-ordinated effort of each member of the team to prevent the offense from scoring and to obtain possession of the ball. For convenience, defenses have been classified as man-to-man, zone, combination of man-to-man and zone, and pressing defenses. In addition to basic team defenses, special situations frequently arise which require the immediate co-ordination of several or all the members of the team. These include defensing: the big man, the fast break, the out-of-bounds play, the free throw, the stall, the jump ball, the three-on-two, and organized team rebounding.

The team that is consistently strong on defense, that realizes the importance of obtaining the ball from the opposition, and that plays with spirit, aggressiveness, and determination will always be a difficult team to defeat.

► Study Questions

1. What is the principle of man-to-man defense: zone defense?
2. How has the screen as an offensive maneuver affected team defenses?
3. What defense would you recommend when your team is behind five points with two minutes to go?
4. Describe the ideal personnel for a 1-3-1 zone defense, a 3-2 zone defense.
5. What abilities in team personnel are necessary for a man-to-man press the entire game?
6. What is the directional principle in defense?
7. Diagram a free throw lane and indicate the defensive positions and the footwork necessary to attain those positions.
8. Describe the method used to stop the fast break.
9. What minimum defenses are necessary for a team which would carry them through the season and enable that team to meet any offensive threat?

10. List, describe, and give examples of five of the criteria for team defense.

11. Define team defense.

12. When two men are defensing three opponents, what are their basic moves?

▶ Projects for Additional Study

1. Contrast the strengths of man-to-man defenses with those of zone defenses. Which defense is basic to playing basketball?

2. Observe a basketball game or scrimmage and determine the defenses used by the two teams. Were the defenses for each team the same or did they vary during the game?

3. What is the main advantage of a half-court zone press over a full-court press? The main disadvantage?

4. Outline the rules for a basic man-to-man full-court press team defense that would be used the entire game.

5. Describe two methods of defensing a big, high-scoring center.

6. Diagram a guard to guard screen and indicate the several methods that are utilized to defense it.

7. Diagram a guard to forward screen and indicate the several methods that are utilized to defense it.

8. Search the literature and report on a specific zone defense and a specific man-to-man defense.

9. What is the basic defense used at your school? Does it vary from year to year?

10. How would you as the coach of a high school team practice defensing the stall? Would substitutions be necessary if you had two slow boys playing when the opponents went into the stall?

11. Describe a theoretical situation in which you would use the directional principle of defense.

12. Review the literature and report on two articles which are based on the philosophy of team defense.

▶ Selected References

Athletic Journal. Athletic Journal Publishing Co., Evanston, Ill. Contains many specific articles dealing with all types of team defenses, philosophy, and principles.

Auerbach, Arnold. *Basketball for the Player, the Fan and the Coach.* New York: Pocket Books, Inc., 1952. Good material on hints and specific instructions for man-to-man defensive team play.

Basketball Coach's Digest. Converse Rubber Co. Yearly journal which contains many specific articles dealing with all types of team defenses, philosophy, and principles.

Bee, Clair, *Man-to-Man Defense and Attack.* New York: A. S. Barnes & Co., 1942. Comprehensive coverage of man-to-man defense.

————. *Zone Defense and Attack.* New York: A. S. Barnes & Co., 1942. Comprehensive coverage of zone defenses.

Bunn, John W. *Basketball Methods.* New York: The Macmillan Co., 1939. Excellent material on defensive philosophy, principles, and specific team defense.

————. *Basketball Techniques and Team Play.* Englewood Cliffs, N. J.: Prentice-Hall, Inc., 1964. Outstanding coverage of a variety of team defenses.

Dean, Everett S. *Progressive Basketball.* New York: Prentice-Hall, Inc., 1950. Thorough discussion of fundamentals of defensive play plus specific team defenses.

Gardner, Jack. *Championship Basketball* with Jack Gardner. New York: Prentice-Hall, Inc., 1961. Complete details as to the Utah system of defenses as coached by Jack Gardner.

Gullion, Blair. *Techniques and Tactics of Basketball Defense*. St. Louis, Mo.: Bardgett Printing & Publishing Co., 1951. Entire book deals with defense. Very detailed and comprehensive coverage.

Hobson, Howard A. *Basketball Illustrated*. New York: A. S. Barnes & Co., 1948. Well-illustrated and easy-to-read section on team defense.

Jucker, Ed. *Cincinnati Power Basketball*. Englewood Cliffs, N. J.: Prentice-Hall, Inc., 1962. Brief, concise material on team defense.

Loeffler, Ken. *Ken Loeffler on Basketball*. New York: Prentice-Hall, Inc., 1955. Loeffler's specific ideas on team defense.

McCracken, Branch. *Indiana Basketball*. New York: Prentice-Hall, Inc., 1955. Fine explanations of Indiana man-to-man defense, switching man-to-man, and zone defenses.

McCreary, Jay. *Winning High School Basketball*. New York: Prentice-Hall, Inc., 1956. High school coach's point of view regarding defense. Good on specific defenses.

McGuire, Frank. *Defensive Basketball*. New York: Prentice-Hall, Inc., 1959. Thorough coverage of developing team defense. Entire book deals with defense.

McLane, Hardin. *Championship Basketball by 12 Great Coaches*. Englewood Cliffs, N.J.: Prentice-Hall, Inc., 1965. Coach Eddie Hickey on team defense. Coach Ray Mears on Tennessee's zone and combination defense. Coach Ben Carnevale on pressing defenses. Coach John R. Wooden on stopping the fast break.

Newell, Pete, and Benington, John. *Basketball Methods*. New York: The Ronald Press Co., 1962. Fine explanations of various man-to-man and zone defenses with the philosophy, theory, and application of pressing defenses.

Newsom, Heber. *Basketball for the High School Coach and the Physical Education Teacher*. Dubuque, Iowa: Wm. C. Brown Co., 1952. Good material on various team defenses.

Pinholster, Garland F. *Coach's Guide to Modern Basketball Defense*. New York: Prentice-Hall, Inc., 1961. Excellent presentation of various team defenses.

Ramsay, Jack. *Pressure Basketball*. Englewood Cliffs, N. J.: Prentice-Hall, Inc., 1964. Excellent discussion of man-to-man defense, the zone press, and standard zone defenses.

Rupp, Adolph F. *Rupp's Championship Basketball*. New York: Prentice-Hall, Inc., 1948. Fine material on man-to-man and zone defense, defensing the fast break, and other defensive situations.

Scholastic Coach. Scholastic Magazines, Inc., New York, N.Y. 10036. Contains many specific articles dealing with all types of team defenses, philosophy, and principles.

U. S. Navy. *Basketball*. Annapolis, Md.: United States Naval Institute, 1943. Thorough coverage on man-to-man, zone, and combination defenses.

Ward, Charles R. *Basketball's Match-up Defense*. Englewood Cliffs, N. J.: Prentice-Hall, Inc., 1964. Entire book deals with one specific general all-purpose defense, the match-up.

Wooden, John R. *Practical Modern Basketball*. New York: The Ronald Press Co., 1966. John Wooden's zone and man presses, his man defense plus explanations of other defenses.

CHAPTER 6: Individual Offensive Fundamentals

Offensive fundamentals embrace the skills necessary to advance the ball into opponents' territory and score. Of the many offensive fundamentals, shooting is the most important. Although shooting is the most important, the remaining offensive fundamentals are not to be minimized. A noted basketball coach has written, "Championship teams have been and will always be teams that have mastered the fundamentals of basketball and enjoy the game."[1]

Each fundamental has its place in the offensive scheme of play, and the well-rounded basketball player is the one who is schooled in each and not just a master of one. In this regard, practice does not always make perfect, but diligent practice on the proper methods will produce good results.

Upon the shoulders of the coach rests the burden of teaching offensive fundamentals and of recognizing the need for practice in the proper area. When the team is weak on passing, for instance, that fundamental should be stressed so that the weak link in the chain of fundamentals becomes strengthened.

▶ Shooting

Shooting is undoubtedly the most important fundamental in the game of basketball. In order to win a game, a team must outscore its opposition, and this is done by being more accurate than the opponent. The rule book states: "The purpose of each team is to throw the ball into its own basket and to prevent the other team from scoring." All other fundamentals, however successfully they are carried out, are for the purpose of obtaining the desired objective of scoring.

The player who is to be a valuable member of a team must be able to score, and this means PRACTICE. This skill should be practiced the year round by the player who wants to become a good shot. Actually, this is one fundamental that most individuals like to practice, and seldom does encouragement seem to be needed. A few minutes of practice two or three times a week the year round will aid in developing the ability to shoot, or once it is developed, this practice will keep the player in tune. Daily practice is necessary, of course, during the basketball season.

Shooting ability depends upon *proper technique, co-ordination, concentration, confidence,* and *relaxation.* Some basketball players are naturally good shots and use a smooth, natural, well-co-ordinated motion. They are able to shoot in almost any manner or form and make a great number of their shots. Players of this type usually have what is expressed as a "soft touch." It is a soft shot that lands lightly and, if it does not go right into the basket, bounces softly on the rim and has a good opportunity of going in. These "soft touch" type of shooters naturally adhere to the above five aspects of shooting ability. On the other hand, the great majority of players are required to learn the important skills involved in shooting, and through practice they develop a "soft touch" style of shooting.

Proper Technique

Each basketball shot contains certain basic principles which, plus the proper technique of that particular shot, result in good shooting ability. Even though many good shooters have unorthodox techniques, these basic principles appear in each type of shot.

---

[1] Blair Gullion, *100 Drills for Teaching Basketball Fundamentals* (St. Louis, Mo.: Blair Gullion, 1933), p. 7.

Target

Whether the target be the front of the rim, back of the rim, or the backboard, the player concentrates on that spot before, during, and after the shot.

Smooth, Rhythmic Action

The act of shooting involves a body movement that is smooth and rhythmic. Jerky, hesitant, uneven body actions will not result in accurate shooting.

Soft Touch

The ball is shot so that it lands—if it misses the center of the basket hole—lightly, and in bouncing softly it has a good opportunity of dropping through the loop. This "soft touch" is accomplished by shooting with a smooth, rhythmic action followed by a natural follow-through which produces a slight backspin to the ball. The backspin plus the forward momentum of the ball counteract each other and cause the ball to remain in or around the basket area as it bounces on the rim.

Follow-Through

This act is a natural continuation of the shot while the eyes are still concentrating on the target. A natural follow-through will guarantee that the ball will go on the course where the original action started. Snapping the wrist down and allowing the ball to leave the fingers while the elbow is bent change the arch, the distance of the shot, the spin on the ball, all of which contribute to poor shooting.

Finger Tip Control

The ball is controlled on the finger tips and not in the palms of the hands. The fingers, through their sensitive nerves, enable the player to control the ball as desired and "feel" the control.

Flight of the Ball

Logical reasoning would enable one to realize that a medium arch produces the greatest percentage of shots. The high-arched shot, when it strikes the rim, will rebound long and not be a "soft touch" shot. On the other hand, a low arch shot must be in just the right place or it will strike the front or back rim and rebound out.

An exception to the medium arch would be to shoot a high-arched shot over a defender. This would be accomplished when the shot has a good percentage chance of scoring.

Natural English

Shots directed at the basket or the backboard should have natural English on them. This result of a good follow-through produces a slight backspin which keeps the ball on flight and reacts consistently the same each time the shot is taken.

An exception to this rule would be special shots where the backboard is used. In this instance it is necessary to place English or spin on the ball to get it onto the board and into the hoop. Shots taken from under the basket and out to the sides often are successful because of special English applied to the ball on special design by the shooter.

Use of Basket or Backboard

It is a general practice for players to shoot directly for the basket when taking shots over eight or ten feet from the basket. Shots from the side along the baseline are executed exactly like one taken from the edge of the foul circle. Short shots are normally taken by bouncing the ball high on the backboard and allowing it to drop into the basket. These include the lay-in, short pivot, and hook shots.

There is an increasing use of the backboard on short jump shots which are taken from in front and to the side of the basket. This is recommended, as the defensive player usually expects the shot to go directly for the basket, and instead it is shot to the side and high on the board.

Co-ordination

Co-ordination is the foundation upon which a good shooter builds the proper muscular actions. A well-co-ordinated individual will, through a kinesthetic sense, "feel" the action; and when successful he repeats the act with the same muscular action. This "getting into the groove" enables the shooter to learn the actions necessary for a successful shot and maintain the form.

Proper technique and repeated practice will enable the not-so-well-co-ordinated player to become proficient in the act of shooting. Practice, practice, and more practice is necessary, but the rewards are great, as making baskets is important.

One important aspect of co-ordination is the judgment of distance. This hand-eye co-ordination comes with split-second timing and, because the basket is only eighteen inches in diameter, does not allow much margin for error. The eye judges the distance from the eye to the target. The co-ordination of the body then follows the directions transmitted to the brain from the eye into force, which is accomplished primarily through the fingers, wrist, and elbow. Regardless of the distance of the shot, the elbow should be straight on the follow-through, as the wrist continues the natural action of the shot.

Concentration

The instant the player realizes he is going to shoot, he should concentrate on the target, think of nothing else, and never take his eyes from that spot until well after the shot is released. In fact, he should concentrate so hard that his eyes open larger. This act of concentration removes all external stimuli, and nothing will be obvious to the shooter except the shot until the act is complete.

Confidence

To have confidence in shooting is important. The player who expects to make the shot will shoot confidently, and in doing so, he will be more likely to follow the proper technique and make a successful

are necessary for an all-around basketball player: the lay-in shot, jump shot, two-hand set shot, one-hand set shot, pivot shot, hook shot, the tip-in shot, and the foul shot.

The Lay-In Shot

The lay-in shot (also known as lay-up, hole, or cripple) is the short one-handed shot that is taken from in front of or to the side of the basket.

It is used by the player who drives, passes, and cuts for a return pass or, in general, by any player who has the opportunity to shoot while moving close to and toward the basket.

THE LAY-IN SHOT

shot. To gain confidence, a player should experience success under game conditions. This calls for shooting in competition and while being harassed by an opponent.

Relaxation

Relaxation is another factor necessary to good shooting. Lack of tenseness in the muscles, which is relaxation, allows the player to naturally accomplish the act of shooting, since that player previously practiced and was successful. Relaxation comes with experience and confidence. Again, the player must experience shooting in game or similar conditions, so that relaxing on a shot is second nature.

Types of Shots

There are variations in the styles of shooting a particular shot just as there are tall, short, and medium size players, but it should be remembered that the objective is to make the shot. Players should develop a style that is natural and easy for them and that conforms to the generally accepted good practices of shooting. Although there are numerous types of shots used in basketball today, the following basic types

The illustration indicates the correct technique for the lay-in shot. The shooter jumps off the left foot and carries the ball up high with both hands, the right hand being on the back of the ball with the fingers well spread. The ball is cushioned on the five fingers and does not rest on the palm or heel of the hand. The shooter springs off the ball of the left foot and drives the right knee high into the air. The body is extended, reaching as high as possible, with the eyes fixed on a spot about eighteen inches above the basket where the shooter will "lay" the ball. When the peak of the jump is reached, the left hand is taken off of the front of the ball, and the ball is placed softly onto the target with the right hand, the ball being under finger-tip control. The follow-through is as high as possible, with the eyes fixed on the target until it passes from view. The shooter lands on both feet and quickly returns to the court.

The spring for the *high jump* comes from the left leg when shooting right-handed, and vice versa. The ball of the left foot should hit the floor hard; added momentum is obtained by driving the right knee hard and high into the air.

The ball leaves the right hand with little or no spin and hits the board as lightly as a feather, or so softly that if it were an egg it would not break. This means that when traveling at top speed, the shooter must pause at the top of his jump and concentrate on holding the ball back so that a soft touch will occur.

The ball should be protected from the opponent by the body and by being carried high and strongly held in both hands.

It is recommended that all lay-in shots be taken by banking the ball off the backboard. If the shooter is coming in directly from in front of the basket, he should take a step to the side, then in toward the basket again, and shoot the ball off the board into the basket. An obvious exception to this would be a player who "dunks" the ball directly into the basket.

Players should learn to shoot naturally with the left hand as well as with the right hand. The shot should be taken with the hand opposite the defensive man; in this way, the player protects the ball with his body.

There are many variations of the lay-in shot: under-hand, when the player goes beyond the basket, or when the shooter shoots with the palm of the hand toward his face. Variations of a particular technique are recommended *only* when the accepted method has been mastered.

Jump Shot

This revolutionary shot may be taken from any position on the court but with best results from within twenty feet. It may be tried from a stationary position or on the run and facing or with the back to the basket.

The ball is held as if the shooter were going to take a lay-up shot with the right hand. The ball is carried high overhead, with the shooting hand on the back of the ball and the fingers well spread. As the ball is moved into shooting position, the shooter should jump

THE JUMP SHOT

straight into the air and concentrate on the target or point of aim. The left hand holds the ball, and at the peak of the jump the right hand and wrist propel the ball toward the basket. The follow-through is with the right hand and arm as the shooter propels the ball off the left hand. After the jump, the shooter should be ready to go back into action immediately. The ball is shot with the elbows as straight as possible, as this will get the ball higher into the air and make it more difficult for the opponent to block. Also, the higher the jump the more difficult for the opponent to block and the more effective the shot will be.

when the shooter is in a stationary position on the floor.

The ball is held in front of the chest as in the fundamental position (see illustration). The feet should be close together and in line or one foot slightly in front of the other. The fingers are spread, and the thumbs point toward one another at the back of the ball, with the elbows in close to the body. The eyes are set on the target, and the ball is released with a wrist-and-finger snap. The fingers should give a slight backspin to the ball. The follow-through is with both hands and arms toward the target. To get

When moving into the shot from a dribble, the shooter *stops completely* and jumps straight into the air. If this is done correctly, the shooter will land exactly where he took off.

If the shooter wants to execute the jump shot starting with his back to the basket, he should turn his body and face to the basket as he jumps; otherwise, the shot is made in the same manner as when facing the basket.

If the shooter is closely guarded and wants to get off a jump shot, he should fake and shoot or drive quickly, stop, and shoot. This will always leave the defensive man guessing and always a half-step or a step behind.

Two-Hand Set Shot

The two-hand set shot, or chest shot, is one of the basic shots in the game of basketball. It is an excellent way to shoot when from twenty to twenty-five feet from the basket. It is a set shot, which is a shot taken

THE TWO-HAND SET SHOT

added distance, the shooter can add the spring of his legs and ankles to the shot.

One-Hand Set Shot

This shot is often substituted for the two-hand set shot and is used close to the basket or from twenty to twenty-five feet away.

The ball is carried from the fundamental position to a position in front of the shooter's face, with the

is pushed toward the basket. The right foot should be slightly in front of the left foot (for right-handed shooters), with the knees flexed and the eyes on the target. The ball is sent on its way by straightening the right elbow and following through with a smooth flip of the wrist. The ball should roll off the top of the fingers, and to do this, the shooter should force his right thumb forward, being certain that the back of the hand is toward the face. To get greater distance,

THE ONE-HAND
SET SHOT

the knees may be straightened from their flexed position, giving added momentum to the shot.

The Pivot Shot

The pivot shot is taken when the player finds himself within fifteen feet of the basket (foul line distance) and his back is to the basket. It is a common shot for those playing center, but it is also a valuable type of shot for any boy playing basketball.

The shooter stands with his back to the basket about six to ten feet away from it, the ball at the fundamental position with the feet well spread and in line. To shoot with the right hand, the shooter pushes off with the right foot, pivots on the left, jumps into the air, and lands with the feet in line and both toes facing the basket. The weight should be forward and the shooter should be ready to go into action immediately. The shot is made exactly as the one-handed set shot except for the body action.

As soon as the shooter knows he wants to shoot, he should fake one way with the ball, head, or head and shoulders and then go the other way for the shot. Locate the target; pivot, place the right hand behind the ball, and hold it there with the left hand. As the shooter faces the basket, he should carry the ball past his right ear and shoot as he would a one-hand set shot. Let the ball go and follow through with the right hand and arm straight toward the basket.

The Hook Shot

The hook shot is a difficult one to master, but is very effective for a player who moves into the pivot position with his back to the basket. It is effective because it is very hard to defend against. It is usually

shooting hand behind the ball, as illustrated. The fingers of the shooting hand should be well spread, pointing up, and the back of the hand should be toward the face. The left hand holds the ball in place on the right hand and is removed just before the ball

THE PIVOT SHOT

taken within fifteen feet of the basket and it is a short, accurate shot.

The hook shot is executed by the shooter starting with his back to the basket (see illustration). To shoot with the right hand, the shooter carries the ball in both hands, pushes off the right foot and pivots on the left. The left hand is taken off the ball and the elbow is carried high in a bent position as the body pivots around to face the basket. With his right elbow straight, the shooter propels the ball with the right hand and wrist in an arc over the top of the head. The body pivots around as the arm follows through, so that the shooter lands on both feet facing the basket ready to rebound, if necessary.

The Tip-In

The tip-in shot is used when a player has the opportunity to tip an offensive rebound up into the air again and into the basket. This is a difficult shot, but an important one, particularly for the tall boy.

The offensive player faces the basket with his feet well spread, knees bent, hands at chest height, and elbows bent and sticking out to the sides (see illustration). From this position, the shooter times his jump so that he is able to tip the ball with the fingers of his right hand at the top of the jump. A slight snap of the wrist will propel the ball back into the air again. It is suggested that the tip be directed to a spot on the backboard similar to where the shooter would lay the ball on a lay-up shot. Follow through with the fingers, wrist, and arm and land ready to jump and tip again.

Players can get the needed finger tip control for the

tip-in shot by simply playing volleyball and by tipping the ball up against the backboard time and time again.

Other Types of Shots

There are other types of shots such as the two-hand overhead and the underhand pivot, but the learning

THE HOOK SHOT

The Foul Shot

This important shot in basketball enables the offensive player to shoot a free throw at the basket unhindered in any way by the opponents. In addition, he has ten seconds of time in which to rest, relax, and prepare himself for the shot and to shoot the ball. With these factors in the shooter's favor, he should make a high percentage of his shots. There are three factors to consider regarding the free throw: the style of shooting, the shot itself, and practicing for the shot. The illustration indicates one method of shooting the foul shot.

Style of Shooting

Successful foul shooters use a variety of styles, with Bill Sharman, formerly of the Boston Celtics, one of the greatest with his one-hand push shot. Rick Barry, San Francisco Warriors, one of the few who shoot underhand, makes approximately 80 per cent. The jump shop style is used to very good advantage by Hal Greer of the Philadelphia 76ers. Most coaches believe that it is a good idea to use the set shot one uses from the floor for the foul shot; in doing so, the player will not have to develop and practice an additional style or type of shot. In addition, coaches are of the opinion that as long as a player hits a good percentage of his foul shots, it is not a good idea to ask him to change his style. On the other hand, when a young boy has the opportunity to start the correct way, it is best that he use the set shot he uses from the floor. The main items to consider are that the shot be a natural one for the shooter, be easy to shoot, and be a shot producing results.

of these should wait until the offensive player is a skilled performer in the more basic ways of scoring two points.

Preparing for the Shot

Many players miss foul shots because they do not have a set routine which will give them a few seconds relaxation and an opportunity to concentrate on a method that is identical for every shot. The use of the five steps listed below will help the shooter to become more or less mechanical, so that he will be able to make a maximum number of shots. The shooter should:

gets only one or at the most two attempts at one time in a game, and it is not natural to stay in the one spot and shoot a great number of shots.

6. Just before practice is over each day, shoot until he makes three in a row. When he can make three in a row in three or four tries, then go to four. After that go on to five and up, until finally he will be able to make ten in a row. When he reaches this stage of development, he will be a good foul shooter.

1. When the referee hands him the ball, PLACE HIS TOE OR TOES JUST BEHIND THE FOUL LINE so that he will not step on or over it and nullify the point scored.

2. BOUNCE THE BALL THREE TIMES to relax his fingers, wrists, and arms.

3. LOOK AT THE TARGET (rim of the basket) for which he aims when he shoots. From now on, the shooter never takes his eyes off the spot until the ball is well on its way.

4. While concentrating on the target, TAKE A BIG BREATH and let it out slowly.

5. SHOOT THE BALL into the basket.

Practicing the Shot

The following are MUSTS in perfecting the proper technique for the foul shot. The shooter should:

1. Practice the foul shot as if he were shooting it in a game.

2. Concentrate on each shot as if the score were tied and his making the shot would enable his team to win the game.

3. Shoot the shot with the same style every time and use the five steps outlined above.

4. Practice when fresh as well as when he is tired. This simulates the game situation of shooting when breathing hard and physically tired after running up and down the floor.

5. Step back from the foul line after each shot. He

THE TIP-IN SHOT

There is no excuse for a poor foul shooter. The player should use the style that is natural for him, follow a set procedure every time he takes a foul shot, and practice until he becomes mechanical and has confidence in his ability to make a high percentage of those he shoots, whether in practice or in a game.

Methods of Improving Foul Shooting

Foul shooting can be improved by practicing under situations which simulate game conditions. This important offensive fundamental should be practiced several times a day during team practice. One of the best times to practice is after a strenuous practice drill, when the players are out of breath and tired. All available baskets should be utilized. Players should be required to move to another basket after several minutes of practice. Also, it is a good idea to leave the ball at the basket; thus players will use a different ball at a different basket. Players not shooting should take their places in the lane and practice footwork, screening, or tipping, depending upon their position in the lane. Following are suggested methods of practicing foul shooting.

The shooter shoots, and if he misses, all players at that basket move one position clockwise. If the shooter makes the shot, he is given an additional attempt, after which all players rotate. A maximum of two shots is allowed each player each time it is his turn to shoot. This type of practice requires concentration on the part of each shooter, as he finds the number of shots he is getting limited. The number of shots allowed without a miss can be increased to three, four, or five, depending upon local conditions.

During the practice, each player shoots twenty or twenty-five shots, and a percentage record is maintained.

Another method is to require each player to make three in a row (or four or ten) before going home. Of course, a time limit is often necessary. It is a good incentive idea to start at three and increase the number each day or week, depending upon the team's ability. In this method, the player rotates every time he misses, and another takes his place at the foul line.

Free throw twenty-one[2] is another method of practicing free throwing in a game situation. Six players comprise a game in which each team has men numbered one through three. Player No. 1 of one team

[2] Stan Watts, *Developing an Offensive Attack in Basketball* (New York: Prentice-Hall, Inc., 1959), p. 135.

starts the game by shooting free throws until he misses or makes three consecutive shots. At this time, a game of three against three goes on until a basket is made. The team not making the field goal sends its next man in line to the foul line; he shoots until he misses or makes three consecutive shots. When a foul is made, a jump ball occurs, or an out-of-bounds situation exists, the next man in line shoots foul shots. A field goal counts two points and a foul shot one. The team making twenty-one points is declared the winner.

Freeze-out free throw practice[3] is another method of practicing free throws under the competitive pressures of a game. The group practicing at one basket follow one another in line. If the first makes a shot, the second must do likewise or be frozen out and disqualified. If the first man misses, the next in line is not disqualified should he miss. The last player remaining is the winner.

An excellent free throw drill is *Distraction*. Each player takes his turn at the free throw line and shoots two shots. While he is shooting, the remaining players try to distract him by waving their arms and talking to him. Each player stays in his position on the lane. The shooter must concentrate or the players will distract him.

The ABC's of Shooting

The player should:

1. *Know when and how to shoot.* It is vitally important for the shooter to know when the opportunity presents a good shot or when it is wiser to pass to a teammate who is in a better position to score. The basketball player should learn all the basic types of shots and develop those best suited to him; he should understand the place for the individual type of shot and practice it under those conditions.

2. *Be relaxed.* Shoot as many times as possible under all conditions, so that it will become a natural act during a game. Relaxation is nothing more than a natural action of the body in which there is no tenseness or rigidity.

3. *Have confidence.* Develop a mental attitude that he is capable of making any shot he attempts. When practicing, the shooter should start in close and move out as he begins to make a good percentage of shots. This will help to develop a confidence in the ability to hit. If the shooter is consistently missing a certain shot, he should move in close and, as he begins to succeed, move out again.

4. *Be ambidextrous.* The shooter should practice shooting with the hand he doesn't normally use, and soon it will be a natural motion for him. When, in practice or in a game, there is a position for a left-handed shot, shoot with the left hand and vice versa. For some individuals this will take a longer time, but if players begin young they will have no trouble and will soon use either hand advantageously.

5. *Concentrate on the target.* It is recommended that when the shooter takes a close shot, he aim at the backboard as a target. When taking a medium or a long shot, he should aim at the rim. The object is to have the ball slide just over the edge of the rim nearest from where he shoots. This spot on the rim is the target. If the ball lands on the rim at this point of aim, the forward momentum will carry the ball into the basket or against the backboard, and there is still a good chance that the ball will go in. As soon as the player is ready to shoot, the eyes should concentrate on the target. Concentrate so hard that the eyes open wider than normal. The shooter should continue to concentrate on this spot until the ball has left his finger tips and is well on its way. This last point is very important, because if the eyes are moved from the target before the ball is released, there is a possibility that the lifting of the head to follow the ball will change the arc of the shot and cause a miss.

Two Regulation Basketballs Fitting into a Regulation Rim

The basket is wider and larger than most people believe. It is eighteen inches in its inside diameter, and two regulation basketballs will fit through this large opening at the same time (see illustration). Knowing this is a larger opening than most players

---

3 *Ibid.*, p. 136.

realize should give each the assurance that there is a pretty big hole into which he will toss the ball.

6. *Have body balance and learn the fundamental position*. Even though each type of shot has its particular body position, each shooter should be in balance, with the ball in two hands and the body in the fundamental position, and only then go into the shot. There are a few exceptions to this, but it remains a basic principle of basketball.

7. *Know the arc of the shot*. The shooter should use a medium arc on all his shots, in order to develop a soft touch and have the ball land softly on the rim or against the backboard. Experimentation and practice are needed to find this arc, but the discovery will result in more shots going in, and those that miss will rebound softly.

8. *Follow through*. Follow through on each shot taken and recover immediately to rebound or to go on defense.

9. *Control the spin of the ball*. Spin the ball as little as possible and use English only when necessary. Snapping the fingers down after a shot will produce excess spin, but a flowing, soft wrist motion will produce a shot with the ball having only a slight reverse spin. This is the ideal result and should be obtained on each shot except the lay-in shot.

10. *Practice*. Practice under conditions that are as close to those in game play as possible. Have a teammate assume a defensive position and wave his hand in the face of the shooter while shooting. Use drills which bring in competition, and play as much basketball as you can. Shooting drills follow which will give an assortment of games for this purpose.

11. *Use speed in getting the ball away*. The best shooter in the world will never make a point in a game if he takes a long time to get the ball away. When the shooter has mastered the various basic shots, he should practice getting the ball away in a hurry. Do not throw the ball away, but shoot it quickly, keeping the ball and the body under control at all times.

12. *Judge distance*. The distance the ball is shot is a matter of eye-muscle co-ordination. Concentrate on the target and straighten your elbow in the follow-through, and you will soon find yourself gauging the distance with surprising accuracy.

13. *Gauge direction*. The direction of the shot is a matter of releasing the ball in a straight line through the body to the basket. If either hand releases too much energy, it will pull the shot off line. If, on a one-hand shot, the shooter consistently hits to one side, he should check to determine whether the ball is rolling off the tip of the fingers and having a slight reverse spin. If not, the technique is incorrect.

Common Mistakes in Shooting

1. Failure to concentrate on the target.

2. Giving excess spin or English on the ball.

3. Not being in good body balance.

4. Hurrying the shot.

5. Not using the proper shot at the correct time.

6. Not faking before shooting, especially when closely guarded.

7. Allowing the elbow to swing away from the body.

8. Not following through so that the elbow stops straight and the wrist flips down.

9. Shooting the ball in too low or too high an arc.

10. Not following the shot or recovering immediately to go on defense.

11. Allowing the ball to rest in the palm of the hand when shooting.

Shooting Drills

Following are a list of shooting drills. Some drills can be used for the practice of different types of shots, while others are specific in their use. The coach should constantly scrutinize the players to see that they are performing the proper techniques. In addition to shooting, other fundamentals such as passing, dribbling, and rebounding are utilized. Every opportunity should be made to have the players execute all fundamentals correctly, regardless of the drill.

Dribble in for a lay-in shot. ① dribbles in and takes a lay-in shot. ② follows and rebounds. One and two play catch as they go to the end of the line. As soon as ① and ② are clear of the basket, ③ and ④ continue the drill with another ball. The angle at which the shooter approaches the basket should be varied from along the baseline to straight down the floor, and also on the left side. To speed up this drill, a line can be stationed on the other side of the court and the two lines alternate taking turns (Fig. 32).

Pass, two steps, and a lay-in shot. Player eight is in possession of the ball and player one breaks for the basket. Eight passes to one, who in turn takes a lay-in shot. Nine rebounds, passes to two, and the drill continues. One goes to the rebound line, while eight goes to the shooting line. The angle at which the shot is taken should vary. Figure 33 shows this drill.

Shooting a lay-in shot with the defensive man harassing the shooter. ① starts the drill with a dribble for the basket. ☐ guards the dribbler in a passive manner, but can shout, stamp feet, or do anything else to hinder the shooter. ☐ rebounds the ball and passes to two, and both ① and ☐ change lines. Players are cautioned against aggressive body contact on the part of the defensive player (Fig. 34).

Lay-in shot from a figure-eight continuity. Two passes to one and cuts in front of one as one dribbles diagonally across the floor. Three moves down the floor to receive a pass from one. One goes in front of

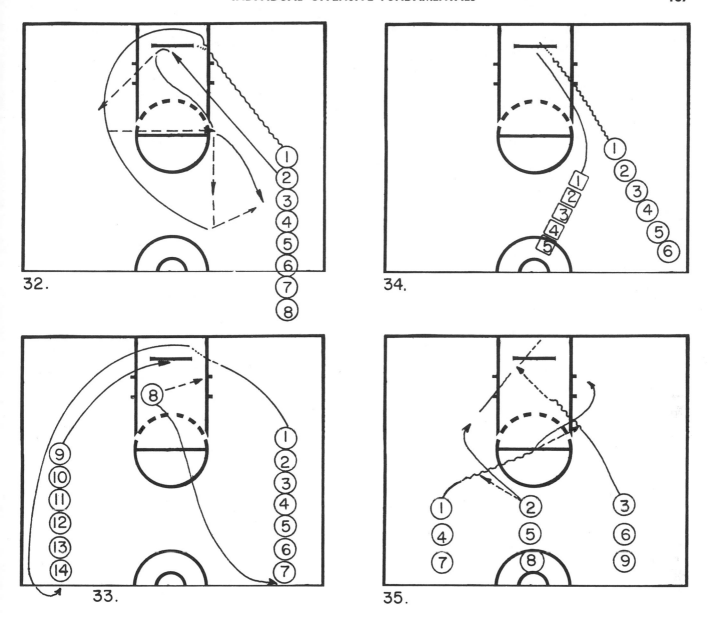

FIG. 32. SHOOTING DRILL: DRIBBLE IN FOR A LAY-IN SHOT. Players in line are paired up. ① dribbles in for a shot while ② follows and rebounds. ① and ② play catch on the way back to the end of line. ③ and ④ follow with a second ball.

FIG. 33. SHOOTING DRILL: PASS, TWO STEPS, AND A LAY-IN SHOT. ⑧ passes to ①, who drives for a lay-in shot. ⑧ goes to end of shooting line, ① to end of rebound line, while ⑨ rebounds and passes to ② as the drill continues.

FIG. 34. SHOOTING DRILL: A LAY-IN SHOT WITH A DEFENSIVE MAN HARASSING THE SHOOTER. ☐1 on defense stands alongside ① and hands ① the ball. ① drives for the basket, with ☐1 trying to distract or hinder the shooter. After the shot, ☐1 rebounds and the players change lines. Players are to be cautioned to avoid unnecessary body contact.

FIG. 35. SHOOTING DRILL: LAY-IN SHOT FROM A FIGURE-EIGHT CONTINUITY. ② passes to ① and cuts between ① and the basket. ① dribbles diagonally across the court and passes to ③, who has cut toward the basket. ① cuts between ③ and the basket. ③ dribbles or passes directly to ② for a lay-in shot. Timing and proper positions are important. Players move a line to the right. The right line moves to the left line.

three and circles to the basket to rebound. Three dribbles diagonally across the floor and passes to two, cutting in for a shot. One and three rebound. Players rotate from line one to two to three to one (Fig. 35).

Jump shot practice with a partner. The shooter starts at position one and shoots until he makes the shot. The partner rebounds and returns the ball. As soon as a shot is made, the shooter moves a step around the arc until he has made a jump shot at each position. The shooter now moves to the second arc and continues on to the third arc. The two partners change positions and resume the drill. Several groups of two can practice at one basket, and if there is an odd number of players, one man can rebound for two shooters. This drill is shown in Figure 36.

Jump shot, dribbler guarded. ① dribbles toward the basket with a man guarding. ① stops sharply, and shoots a jump shot or fakes and shoots. Both players fight for the rebound, pass it to the start of the shooting line and change lines. Players are cautioned to avoid unnecessary body contact. The shooter is urged to stop, go straight up in the air, and recover immediately to rebound (Fig. 37).

Jump shot from behind a screen. ⑥ starts by passing to ① and screening. ① moves behind the screen and takes a jump shot; both ① and ⑥ rebound. The ball is passed to ⑦, who continues the drill, while ⑥ and ① change lines. Figure 38 shows this drill.

Jump shot guarded. ⑥, the defensive man passes the ball to ①, who goes on offense. ⑥ closes on defense, and ① shoots a jump shot. ① rebounds offensively and ⑥ defensively. ① goes to end of line, and ⑥ stays on defense until he obtains the ball five times. See Figure 39 for a diagram of this drill.

Basketball golf. Any type of shot can be taken in this drill. Each player starts at position one and counts the total number of shots required to go the nine holes. As soon as the player shoots, he rebounds and shoots until the ball goes in, and he has then completed that hole. He then moves to the next, etc. Lowest number of shots wins. Figure 40 describes this drill.

Pivot or hook shot. The players line up under the basket with ① in possession of the ball. ① dribbles out six to ten feet from the basket, stops, and executes the shot. He rebounds and gives the ball to the second man in the line. The distance taken and the angle should be varied. When the players are proficient, the second man in line can become a defensive man. The shooter now must fake right and shoot left or vice versa. Both rebound as if in a game. This is shown in Figure 41.

Pivot and hook shot, spot shooting. Mark positions on the floor as they appear in Figure 42. The shooter practices from these positions. A defensive man can be added to make the practice realistic.

Tip-in drill. Players ①, ②, ③, ④, and ⑤ are stationed at the basket as indicated in Figure 43. One of the players tosses the ball up against the backboard, and each player attempts to tip it back in when it comes down on his side. Whenever it goes in the basket, it is tossed up again. After five tips everyone moves one man in a clockwise direction, and the drill continues.

Games Used to Stimulate Good Shooting

Games used to practice shooting simulate game conditions in which the shooter is in a competitive situation, players are shouting and calling, and the shooter is urged to make or miss that particular shot. These games have been found to be excellent techniques to use when practicing shooting.

Game of 21

Players are divided into teams of four or five on a side and lined up an equal distance from the basket. The first player in line shoots from that spot, rebounds the ball, and shoots a follow-in. He then passes to the next player in line, who repeats. Two points are scored for the long shot, one for a lay-in, and three for a clean tip-in. The first team accumulating twenty-one points is declared the winner.

Game of 11

Players are divided into teams of four or five on a team and are lined up an equal distance from the foul circle. The first player in each line dribbles into the foul circle and shoots a jump shot. He rebounds the ball and passes it back to the next player in line, who in turn dribbles into the foul line and shoots a jump shot. Each shot made is scored as one point. The first team scoring eleven points is declared the winner. A variation of this game is to allow a player, after he has rebounded his own shot, to go to the foul line and wave his hands and talk to members of other teams to distract and harass them. He is not allowed to go over the foul line though.

Elimination Shooting

This game eliminates those who fail to keep up with the others. From a designated spot on the floor, each player is allowed a long shot and two follow-in shots to make one. The second time around, each player is allowed one long shot and a follow-in to make one shot. The last round, those not scoring on the first long shot are eliminated. If all miss, another round is taken until one or more score. The last remaining player is declared the winner.

► Ball Handling

The fundamentals of ball handling include the skills of holding the ball in the fundamental position and

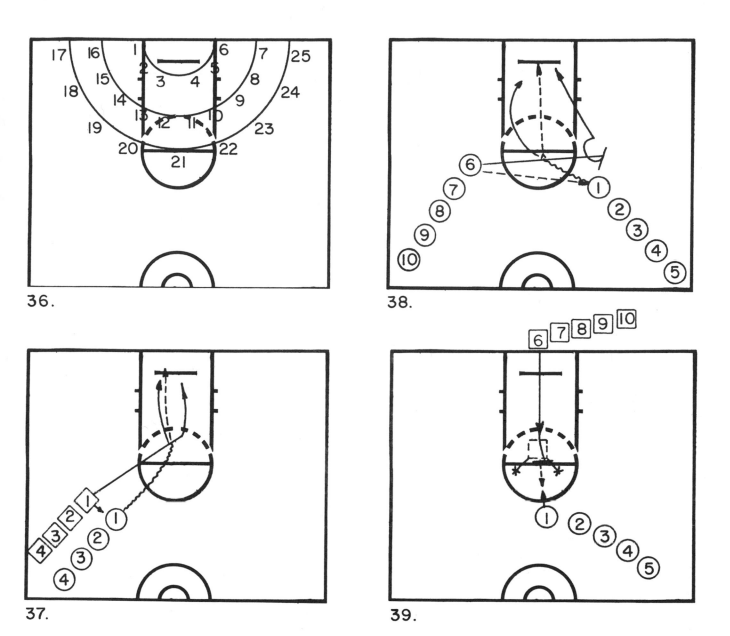

36.

37.

38.

39.

FIG. 36. SHOOTING DRILL: JUMP SHOT PRACTICE WITH A PARTNER. Two players team up with one ball. One shoots while the other rebounds. The first shooter starts about six feet from the basket and shoots until he makes it. He then moves in an arc around the basket. Each player shoots at three distances: six feet, ten feet, and fifteen feet.

FIG. 37. SHOOTING DRILL: JUMP SHOT, DRIBBLER GUARDED. The player on defense hands the ball to ①. ① dribbles toward the basket, and 1 guards him. ① stops, shoots or stops, fakes and shoots a jump shot. Both men rebound, and if ① gets the ball he attempts to shoot again. Players change lines when 1 gets the ball or a basket is made by ①.

FIG. 38. SHOOTING DRILL: JUMP SHOT FROM BEHIND A SCREEN. ⑥ passes to ① and sets an imaginary screen. ① dribbles behind the screen and takes a jump shot. ⑥ rolls off the screen, and both ⑥ and ① rebound. Players change lines and the drill continues.

FIG. 39. SHOOTING DRILL: JUMP SHOT GUARDED. 6 passes to ① and assumes a defensive position. ① fakes and shoots, fakes, fakes and shoots, or shoots, depending upon the actions of the defensive man. Both players rebound aggressively and then change lines.

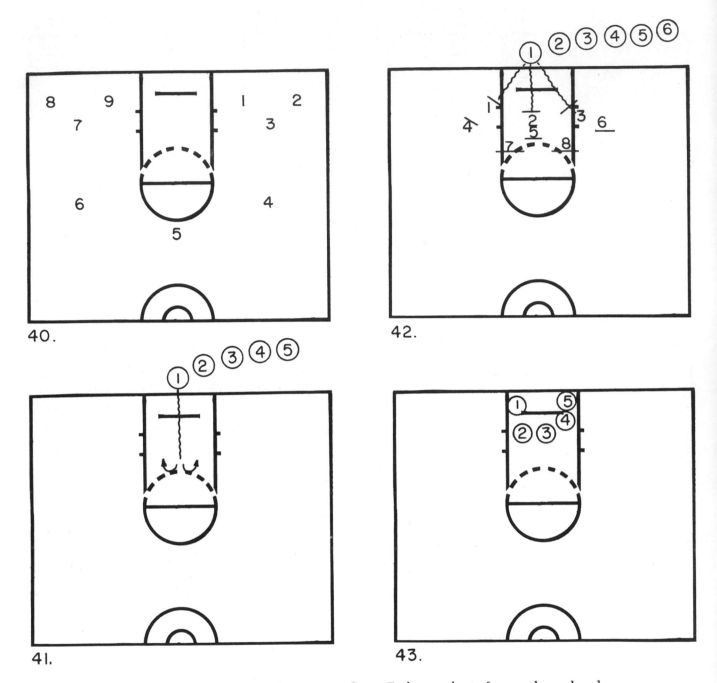

FIG. 40. SHOOTING DRILL: BASKETBALL GOLF. Each man shoots from each numbered spot on the floor. After the first shot, the player rebounds and shoots a follow-in shot. Total number of shots to play nine holes is the player's score. Lowest score wins.

FIG. 41. SHOOTING DRILL: PIVOT OR HOOK SHOT. ① dribbles out in front of the basket and stops. He fakes left and shoots right or vice versa. After the shot, he rebounds, gives the ball to the next one in line, and goes to the end of the line. After the players become proficient, the second man in line can be designated as a defensive man, and he endeavors to block the shot or rebound the ball.

FIG. 42. SHOOTING DRILL: PIVOT OR HOOK SHOT, SPOT SHOOTING. Players dribble to each spot in turn as they are numbered, stop, and take a shot. Each rebounds his own shot.

FIG. 43. SHOOTING DRILL: TIP-IN SHOT. Five players line up around the basket. One of the group tosses the ball up, and each tries to tip the ball back up and in. After five tries, the line moves one man clockwise and the drill resumes.

THE CHEST PASS

THE FUNDAMENTAL POSITION

catching and passing the ball. It goes without saying that an individual who cannot properly handle the ball will never be a good basketball player. Good ball handling enables one player to pass the ball to another so that the team can advance the ball and score.

The Fundamental Position

Whenever a player is in possession of the ball, he must hold it in such a position that the ball is protected from the opponent and at the same time in the proper position ready to pass, dribble, or shoot, whichever is most advantageous at the moment.

This position is one in which the offensive man spreads his feet comfortably, holds the ball opposite his chest, and protects it by bending and slightly spreading his elbows. From this position, the player can pass, dribble, or shoot. Common mistakes in holding the ball are: carrying it too low, which requires the player to raise it to shoot or pass; or carrying the ball too high, which prevents the player from going quickly into a dribble.

Catching the Ball

Catching a pass is a relatively simple skill, but many players disregard some basic principles, thus often making the passer look bad in performance.

The player catching the ball should remember that the ball is a moving object coming with a certain amount of force and spin. With this in mind, he should keep his eyes fixed on the ball until it is firmly grasped

THE BOUNCE PASS

in the hands. The player should relax and catch the ball on the finger tips with the heels of the hands, wrists, and arms, taking the shock of the ball by giving with the force of the impact.

ABC's of Catching the Ball

The player should:

1. Watch the ball until it is firmly in the hands.
2. Catch the ball on the finger tips.
3. Hold the ball between the fingers and thumbs.
4. Catch a low pass with the fingers pointing down and the palms out, catch a high pass with the fingers pointing up and the palms out.
5. Give slightly with the hands, wrists, and arms to ease the shock of the pass.
6. Always move toward the pass except when running or breaking away from the passes toward the basket, as in a fast break.
7. Be prepared to protect the ball with the elbows and body as soon as it is in the player's possession.

Common Mistakes

1. Taking eyes off ball.
2. Catching ball in palms of hands.
3. Not moving toward ball when it is necessary.
4. Starting to pass or shoot before obtaining possession of the ball.

Drills

The drills used in learning the technique of passing the ball are the ones used for those who have difficulty in catching the ball. A simple procedure to be used when working with an individual who is experiencing difficulty in catching the ball is for the coach to stand next to, and observe the actions of, the individual while he and another player play catch.

Passing

Next to shooting, passing is rated as one of the most important fundamentals. To shoot the ball, a player has to obtain the ball, and this is usually done by one

or more passes. A good passer is a valuable asset to any team, because he is able to get the ball by way of a pass to one of his teammates who is in a position to score. One of the statistics maintained in basketball is the *assist*, which gives credit to the player who passes to a teammate who in turn scores. In many cases, the coach values the player who has assists as much as he does the high scorer.

Although there are many different types of passes used in basketball, there are those which are orthodox and basic to playing the game of basketball. These include the chest pass, the two-handed bounce pass, the baseball pass, the overhead pass, and the hand-off pass.

Chest Pass

The chest pass is the most common pass used in basketball. It is used to get the ball to a teammate who is within twenty feet with no opponent in the path of the ball. The chest pass is a good, accurate, swift method of passing the ball.

The pass is executed with the ball held, as in the fundamental position, at the player's chest. The ball is held in both hands with the fingers well spread and the thumbs pointing toward one another on the back of the ball. The elbows are bent and held at the sides. The ball is propelled with a finger, wrist, and arm snap. The follow-through position is with the elbows straight, the palms pointing out, and the fingers pointing toward the target.

Two-Handed Bounce Pass

This type of pass is used to get the ball to a teammate when there is an opponent in the way. The ball is bounced near the feet and under the outstretched arms of the opponent so that he cannot block or intercept the ball.

The pass is identical to the chest pass except that the ball is aimed at a spot on the floor near the defensive player's feet so that it will not be blocked, but will bounce up to the teammate.

When a player is releasing the ball, the pass will come off the floor faster when overspin is created by snapping and rolling the thumbs over the top of the ball as it is released.

THE BASEBALL PASS

This type of pass is the slowest in basketball; consequently, it should be used only when it is certain of success.

In the execution of the bounce pass, it is an excellent technique to fake a shot or a chest pass and then use the bounce pass. This faking action will cause the defensive player to raise up, thereby making this pass easier to get through.

Baseball Pass

The baseball pass is used to throw the ball long distances, as a clear-out pass to start a fast break, or as a pass down the sideline. It should not be used when a defensive player is close, as he will be able to block it, because this type of pass takes a considerable time for the ball to be drawn back behind the head before it is thrown. The ball is thrown as a baseball is thrown (see illustration). The ball is carried behind the ear and head with both hands. With the fingers well spread behind the ball, the throwing hand then tosses the ball from near the ear and follows through so that the ball rolls off the top of the fingers. The ball will curve if thrown side-arm with the ball rolling off the thumb and forefinger. This should be prevented, as it causes an inaccurate pass.

Overhead Pass

The overhead pass is an excellent one to use when passing to a man in the center position. It is also a fine pass for a tall man to use as the opponents find it very difficult to defend against.

The ball is held high overhead with both hands (see illustration). The elbows should be fairly straight and the fingers well spread with the thumbs on the

THE OVERHEAD PASS

back of the ball pointing toward one another. The ball is propelled forward by the hands and wrists in a snapping motion. The fingers follow through as the hands bend at the wrists and point directly toward the target. If added momentum and distance are desired, step forward a half step with one foot.

Hand-off Pass

This pass, or hand-off, is used to give the ball to another player who is cutting closely by, usually at the post or center position.

The ball is held in both hands, protecting it from the opponent with both the body and elbows. The hands should be at the sides of the ball, and the ball is passed by squeezing the spread fingers together just hard enough to force the ball to float up into the air about six inches. This action takes the passer's hands away from the ball and allows the cutter to take the ball without any hindrance. The ball should be given to your teammate while he is still in front because if it is carried to the passer's side, it will be snatched or deflected by the defense. Do not attempt to fake until after the cutter has the ball, because the fake might work and fool your teammate as well as your opponent.

Other Passes

Other passes used in basketball are the hook pass, underhand pass (one and two hands), behind-the-back, roll, and over-the-shoulder toss. These are for the advanced player, but it should be recognized that even some of the greatest players prefer the simple, orthodox passes.

To throw long distances the passer steps with the left foot and throws with the right hand. Following through after the step will enable the passer to toss the ball fifty to sixty feet.

ABC's of Passing

The passer should:

1. Learn the proper passing techniques.
2. Know the correct pass to fit the situation.
3. Adjust the type and speed of pass to the situation.
4. Locate the receiver and then pass accurately.

Passing Drills

Pass the ball to a target on a wall. Ball will bounce back. Good for all types of passes.

Two players play catch, first standing still, then moving. Good for all types of passes.

Star passing drill (Fig. 44). The five players, points on a star, pass the ball to one another and make every attempt to keep the ball from the player in the center.

5. Take pride in his passes; not be fancy, be clever.
6. Pass quickly and accurately with a minimum of motions, so passes will not be telegraphed.
7. Aim the pass at the receiver's chest or chin.
8. Fake and pass; fake one way and pass another.
9. Be ambidextrous.
10. Have control of the ball before passing, but learn to catch and pass in one motion.
11. In the back court, always move toward a pass.
12. Use split vision and not look directly at the receiver, but be certain that he is observed from out of the corner of the passer's eye.
13. Realize that the bounce pass is a slow pass and use it only when absolutely necessary.
14. Lead a player who is moving so that he can catch the ball at chest height and in stride.
15. Be very cautious on throwing cross-court passes and *never* pass the ball under the opponent's basket.
16. Get close to the defensive player, as it is then easier to pass by him.
17. Pass to the receiver on the side away from the defensive man.

Common Mistakes

These are some of the common mistakes which result in bad passes and fumbles.

1. Throwing the ball too hard.
2. Inaccurate pass.
3. Misjudged speed.
4. Poor footwork.
5. Not relaxed.
6. Player tired.
7. Player rattled, confused.
8. Tossing the ball in too high an arc.
9. Using the incorrect pass.
10. Not having control of the ball before passing.

THE HAND-OFF PASS

The man with the ball cannot pass to a man on either side. Fast passing and good faking make this a good drill. Good for all types of passes.

Figure 45 indicates a drill which is used primarily to develop the chest pass and the bounce pass. ① passes to ⑥, who has moved forward to meet the ball. ① goes to his right and to the end of the line. ② moves to meet the ball, and ⑥ passes it, moving to his right to the end of that line.

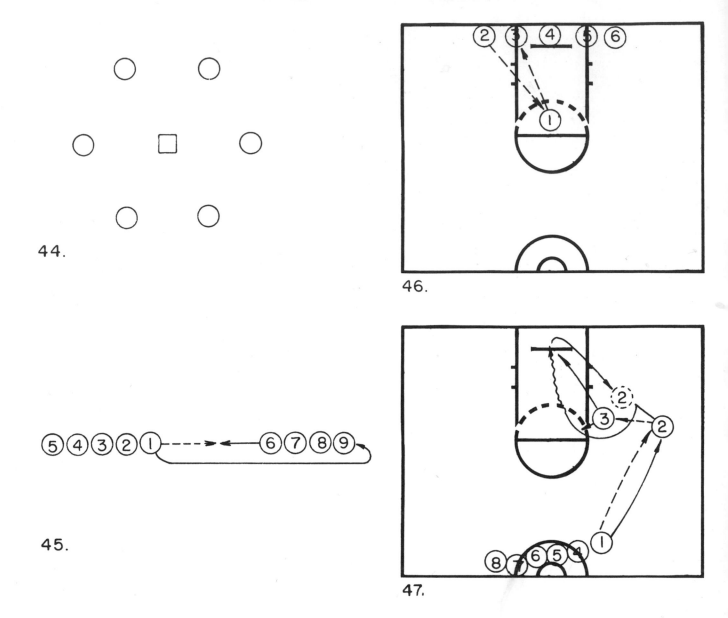

FIG. 44. PASSING DRILL: STAR DRILL. The objective of this drill is to prevent the man in the center from touching the ball. Players use any type of pass, quickly return the pass, and fake and pass. No player can pass the ball to a man on either side. If the man in the middle touches or catches the ball, he takes the place of the player who was responsible.

FIG. 45. PASSING DRILL: BOUNCE PASS. ① bounce-passes to ⑥, who moves to meet the ball. Each player moves to meet the ball, bounce-passes it to the man coming toward him, and goes to the *right* side of the other line and to the end of that line.

FIG. 46. PASSING DRILL: TWO-BALL DRILL. ① stands facing ②, ③, ④, ⑤, and ⑥. ① and ② have basketballs. ① passes to ③, while ② passes to ①. Each player attempts to match the speed and rhythm of the man in front. ① endeavors to pass to each player in turn, but not to a man who has a ball. Each player is given two misses, and then another man goes out in front.

FIG. 47. COMBINATION PASSING DRILL. ① throws a baseball pass to ② and takes ②'s place. ② tosses an overhead pass to ③ and cuts by to receive a hand-off for a drive and a lay-in. ② replaces ③, while ③ goes to the end of the line after he has rebounded and cleared out the ball. This drill can be set up to work from both sides of the court, and one side goes after the other has cleared out of the way.

Two-ball drill (Fig. 46). This drill is an excellent one for practicing the chest pass and developing peripheral vision. ① and ② pass the ball at the same speed. The single man in front, ① in this case, catches and passes one ball, receives the second ball and passes it to another player. Each player should keep the balls moving at the same speed and cadence that the man in front uses with his passes. ① never passes to a man who has a ball, and he endeavors to work up and down the line passing to each man in turn. Two mistakes and ② goes out in front, and ① takes his place next to ⑥.

Combination passing drill (Fig. 47). This drill combines the baseball, the overhead, and the hand-off pass. ① throws a baseball pass to ② and moves to that position. ② tosses the ball to ③ with the overhead pass. ② cuts by ③, and ③ uses a hand-off pass to give him the ball. ② shoots. ③ rebounds, clears a baseball pass to the next man in line, ④, and goes to the end of the line. ② comes back on the court and breaks to the pivot position to receive a pass the second time the drill operates. To speed up this drill, it can be run at the same basket with two groups going at the same time.

► Dribbling

Dribbling is a very important part of basketball when used at the proper time and in the correct manner. The dribble is used to: drive close to the basket for a lay-in shot; to advance the ball; to get the ball out of a congested area; to clear the ball from the defensive goal; to spread the defense; to obtain proper timing of a play; and as **an offensive threat.**

When the dribble is used as an offensive threat, the dribbler can use fakes, changes of direction, and also a change of pace. It is usually at this point that the dribble is abused, because the dribbler becomes too much of a team all by himself. If the opportunity arises to fake and use a dribble drive for the basket, no coach would complain. However, some players do so at every opportunity, regardless of the chances for success, and so destroy team play. The important thing for the offensive man to remember is that dribbling is a very important fundamental to learn, but that it should be used for the good of the team.

In general, there are two ways to dribble: the high and fast method, and the low and dodging technique. In addition, there are special ways in which the player can use these, such as the cross-over dribble, the change of direction, and change of pace.

THE LOW DRIBBLE

High and Fast Dribble

The high and fast dribble is used when the dribbler wants to go somewhere in a hurry and there is no opponent in the way to block or to interfere with the ball. When this type of dribble is used, the body should have a slight crouch, the head should be up, and the ball should be bounced about hip height. The hand should be slightly cupped, the fingers well spread, and only the finger tips should contact the ball. The finger tips should use a controlling touch or push rather than a hit or a bat. The finger tips contact the ball, while the forearm and wrist assist the fingers in adding momentum to the ball. The opposite arm should be carried fairly high for balance and protection.

The dribbler should bounce the ball as far away from the front of his body as possible without over-

extending the reach of the dribbling arm. This will prevent kicking the ball with the knee or toe.

The dribbler should be able to dribble at almost full speed and still control the ball. He should not try to maneuver any faster than he can progress and still have complete control of body and the ball. The dribbler should also be able to see and pass to any of his teammates should one be in the open and in a better position to score or set up a play.

The Low Dribble

The low dribble is used when there are opponents in the area and the dribbler does not want them to be able to touch the ball. An individual would rarely dribble under these circumstances and even then he should be fairly certain of success or it should not be done.

The technique of the low and dodging dribble is identical with the higher dribble except that the body is in a low crouch and the ball is bounced very low to the floor. The ball should be maneuvered fairly close to the body and the free arm and the body help to protect the ball.

Dribbling Maneuvers

The three basic moves that are used to make the dribble an effective weapon in basketball are: the change of pace, the change of direction, and the crossover dribble.

The Change of Pace

This is a method of "faking out" the opponent. The ball is dribbled at a steady rate, and then suddenly the dribbler puts on a burst of speed to carry him away from the man on defense. This trick is usually used when trying to get away from the defense, when advancing the ball, and when driving in for a lay-up shot. It is very effective and many times will allow the dribbler to "cut in" toward the basket when he is head and shoulders ahead of his opponent. This half-step should enable the dribbler to "Go for 2" or advance the ball to where he wants to go.

The Change of Direction

While dribbling, this will enable the dribbler to protect the ball, clear the ball from a congested area, evade an opponent, and be an offensive threat. A slight change of direction with the ball is relatively

THE CROSS-OVER DRIBBLE

easy, but to change direction sharply is another matter. The dribbler turns the palm of his hand in the direction in which he plans to go and contacts the ball on the top and back with a definite controlling movement of the finger tips. He must be certain that he does not illegally "palm" the ball—which is allowing the ball to come to rest in the hand. If the offensive man is planning to turn to the left while dribbling with the right hand, he should plant his right foot, drop the left shoulder, and drive in that direction. This is a very effective maneuver, which will allow the

dribbler to go in any direction as fast as he can cut and change body direction.

The Cross-Over Dribble

This allows the dribbler to change direction sharply when a defensive man is trying to force him to a sideline. It takes good timing, and he must be able to control the ball as well as his body.

The illustration clearly points out this maneuver, as the dribbler dribbles to the right with the right hand while the opponent is ahead and in good defensive

48.

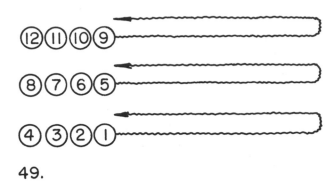

49.

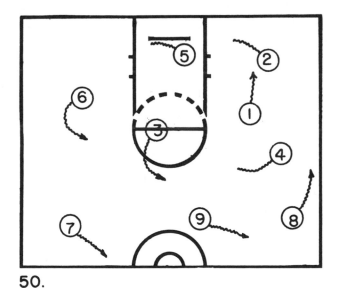

50.

position to force the drive to continue along to the right.

To initiate the cross-over dribble, the man with the ball should not wait until the ball has come to his regular dribbling height, but should control it with the right hand to the left shortly after it comes off the floor. The ball should be aimed at a position on the floor just back of your opponent's rear foot. The left hand now picks up the dribble as the ball comes off the floor and controls the ball so that it is now dribbled off the left side. As the dribbler crosses over the dribble, he changes direction sharply with his body actions as he would normally change direction and protect the ball with his body (ball is now on left side). As the opponent sees this movement develop he will counter to stop it, but controlling the ball in a low dribble and quickly protecting it on the left side will help the dribbler escape the guard.

ABC's of Dribbling

The player should:

1. Dribble only when it will help his team and when he has a good reason to go somewhere on the court with that method.

2. Never dribble when there is a man ahead and open.

3. Keep his head up and look for men to whom he can pass.

4. Learn to start and stop quickly when dribbling.

5. Go only as fast as he can maintain full control of the ball.

6. Practice so that he can dribble with either hand.

7. Practice so that he can dribble to the right or the left.

8. Always dribble with the hand away from the defensive man.

9. Govern the height of the bounce of the dribble by the nearness of the defensive man: the closer they are, the lower the ball, and vice versa.

Common Mistakes

1. Bouncing the ball once every time a player gets the ball. Dribble only when there is somewhere to go.

Fig. 48. Dribbling Drill: Eyes Closed. The first man in each line dribbles toward the opposite line with his eyes closed. When ① dribbles toward ②, ② calls out and guides ① in with his voice. When ② says "Stop," ① stops, passes to ②, and the drill continues.

Fig. 49. Dribbling Drill: Relay Race. Four players compose a team. The first man dribbles with his right hand the length of the floor and returns dribbling with his left. The ball must be handed to the next man in line. First team to finish is the winner.

Fig. 50. Dribbling Drill: Game of Tag. A regular game of tag is played in one half of the court. Each player has a ball, which he must dribble at all times. One player is designated as "it" and remains "it" until he touches another player, who is then "it."

Also, once the dribbler has bounced the ball and caught it, he cannot dribble again.

2. Concentrating on the dribble and not having a clear vision of the floor. Keep head up and eyes open for passing opportunities.

3. Dribbling too fast to adequately control the ball.

4. "Palming" the ball. Control it with a firm press toward the floor with the finger tips.

5. Dribbling with the hand on the inside near the defensive player. The opponent will soon catch on and make the dribble ineffective. Use the hand opposite the defensive player.

Dribbling Drills

Dribble with eyes closed (Fig. 48). ① closes his eyes and starts to dribble across the floor toward the first man in the opposite line, ②. ② keeps up a running chatter of "here, here" or "go left" or "go right." The dribbler tunes in on the voice and dribbles toward it. When ② calls "stop," ① passes him the ball and goes to the end of the line.

Dribbling relay race (Fig. 49). The squad is divided into teams of from four to five on a team. The first man on each team dribbles the length of the floor with his right hand and comes back dribbling with his left. Each player takes his turn, and the first team finished is the winner.

Dribble tag (Fig. 50). Ten or twelve players are each given a basketball. One half of a basketball court is the field of play. One player is designated "It," and the object is for the "It" player to catch another and tag him while still dribbling the ball.

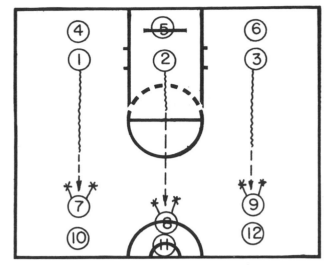

51.

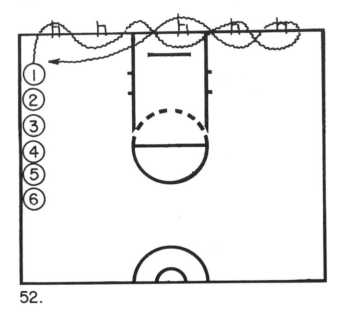

52.

FIG. 51. DRIBBLING DRILL: HEADS UP—WATCH FOR THE SIGNAL. This drill is to teach the dribbler to dribble with his head up so that he can observe men in the clear. The first man in each line dribbles toward the opposite line. The dribbler watches the first man in that line and, when that man thrusts his hands forward, passes him the ball using the same motion as the signal to pass.

FIG. 52. DRIBBLING DRILL: OBSTACLE DRILL. In this drill, the dribbler dribbles around obstacles and back to the starting line. The dribbler should stay low when between obstacles and always dribble with the outside hand. Players, who have to remain with their feet stationary, can be substituted for obstacles. These players hook at the ball with their hands, but cannot move their feet.

FIG. 53. DRIBBLING DRILL: STAY IN CIRCLE. This dribbling drill is a keep-away game. The dribbler and one opponent are placed in a circle. Neither can step on or over the line of the circle. The defensive player endeavors to steal the ball or stop the dribbler from dribbling.

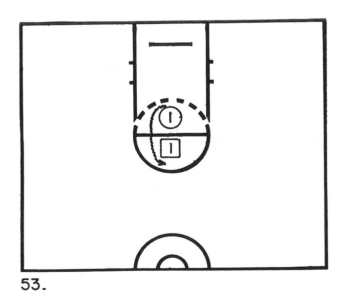

53.

Dribble signal drill. The squad is divided into groups, as in Figure 51. The first in each line dribbles toward the man at the front of the line opposite him. The dribbler watches this man, and when he reaches out with his hands as if to receive a pass, the dribbler passes the ball to him. This drill teaches the dribbler to look and be alert for open men.

Obstacle Dribble. ① starts the drill, as in Figure 52, by dribbling in and out around the obstacles. The dribbler uses the hand away from the man and is constantly changing from one hand to the other. As he passes between players, he should take a low dribble. The men who are obstacles hold their hands out and try for the ball, but they are not allowed to move their feet. Once ① goes around the circle, then the next man goes.

Circle Dribble. This drill, Figure 53, pits one dribbler against a defensive man in a twelve-foot circle at the foul line or at the center of the court. The object is for the dribbler to stay in the circle and protect the ball with his body. The defensive man is also required to stay in the circle.

► Footwork

Speed is very helpful in basketball, but it is not sufficient that a basketball player be just a fast runner. He must know how to start and stop, change direction, change pace, use a rocker step, and pivot and turn. When a player is grounded in these fundamentals, he will be able to free himself for a pass, get open for a good shot, set screens, cut for the basket, and guard his man effectively. These important fundamentals will assist a player who is not particularly fast afoot and will greatly aid the speedster. When playing basketball, a player should move only as fast as he can and still keep the body under control. This is called *maneuverability speed* and is closely allied to footwork. The players should learn the footwork fundamentals thoroughly and speed up their actions as they become sure of themselves. These fundamentals are used when an offensive player has the ball, when one of his teammates has it, and also when it is in the possession of the opponents.

Starts

Starts are practiced from a stationary position or from a slow trot. A player has to get going in a hurry, and the use of the proper technique will help.

The player leans in the direction in which he intends to go, digs his feet into the floor as if he were running in sand, and takes short, choppy steps, lengthening the stride as he moves faster. The arms are used in a pumping motion for balance and to help accelerate to top speed as soon as possible.

Stops

In addition to being able to start, the player should be able to stop quickly without taking unnecessary steps. The most difficult way to stop is the jump stop, or stopping with both feet hitting the floor at the same time. The player hits with both feet simultaneously and well spread. The big secret of this stop is to drop the hips low, as if trying to sit in an imaginary chair, and lean back. The weight should be on the balls of the feet and the heels. The hands and arms are used for balance or for controlling the ball if it is in player possession.

The stride stop is similar to the jump stop except that the feet hit the floor in a one-two count, one in front of the other or alongside.

An excellent way to practice these two methods of stopping is to run up to a chair and stop without touching the chair. The player can increase his speed until he can stop with a stride or jump stop and not shuffle his feet. He can also practice this fundamental in the same manner while dribbling. Coming to a quick stop, controlling the ball, and continuing to dribble at the same time is quite a feat and an excellent maneuver to be able to accomplish.

Change of Direction

The change of direction will allow an offensive man to get free for a pass, to guard an offensive man closely, and to get free for a good shot. Consequently, the basketball player will use this maneuver when on offense and on defense.

When running and wanting to cut to the left, the player plants the right foot firmly on the floor, drops his left shoulder, faces to the left, and steps in that direction with the left foot. The hands and arms are used for balance. Change of direction can be done by crossing one leg over the other and cutting on the inside foot, but the first method is recommended for sharp cuts and for better body position and balance.

It is possible to practice the cut or change of direction when running and dribbling. It has been found that an individual will be a more elusive offensive player and a better defensive player when he can cut sharply and retain his balance. Also, the offensive player will be harder to guard when he zigzags than when he runs in an arc or circles. The defensive player will cut across the arc of the circle and easily catch up. This phase of footwork can be practiced by running down the court and cutting to the left two steps, to the right one step, to the left three steps, etc., so that players can become accustomed to quick zigzag cuts which will successfully help them out-fox their opponents.

The change of direction is frequently used when going to receive a pass. The technique is to start in one direction with one or two steps toward the basket,

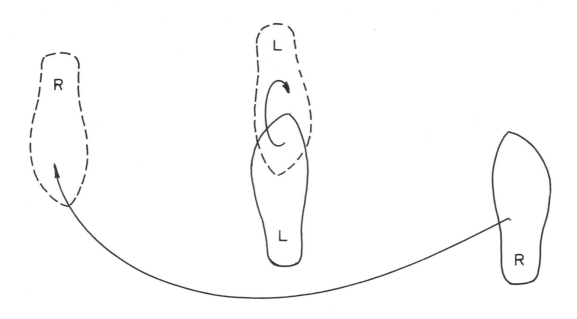

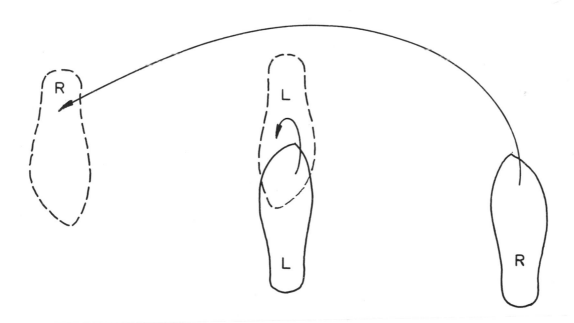

Fig. 54. Footwork: Pivot to the Right. To execute a pivot to the right, the player pivots on the ball of the left foot, pushes off of the right foot to the rear and makes progress to the rear.

Fig. 55. Footwork: Turn to the Left. To execute a turn to the left, the player turns on the ball of the left foot, pushes off of the right foot forward, and makes progress forward.

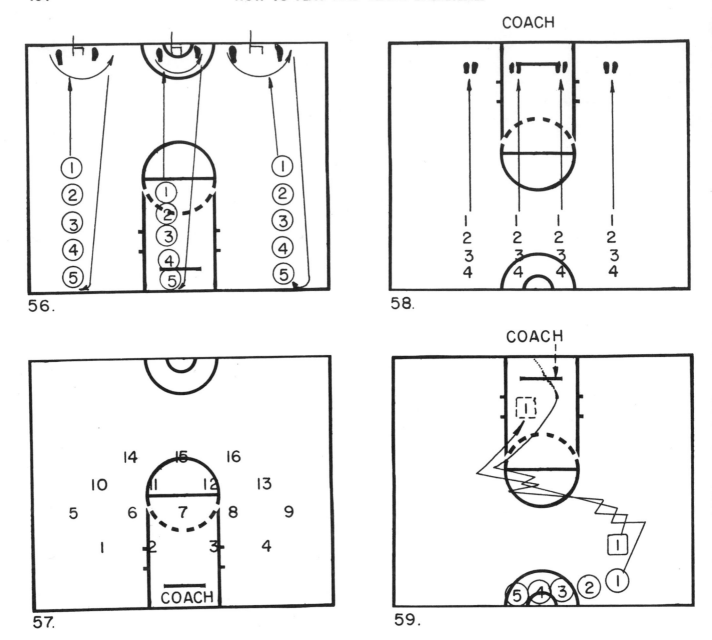

FIG. 56. FOOTWORK DRILL: STOP AND PIVOT. The first man in each line runs to the chair, comes to a jump stop, pivots, and runs back. A combination drill can be developed which includes a dribble to the chair, a stop, a pivot, and a hook pass back to the next man in line.

FIG. 57. FOOTWORK DRILL: MASS PRACTICE. The coach stands in front of the group, and the entire group moves upon the coach's command. It is very obvious when one player goes through the wrong motion.

FIG. 58. FOOTWORK DRILL: STOP AND PIVOT OR TURN. The first man in each line moves to a designated spot on the floor and comes to a jump stop. The coach calls out the type of move, which the players then execute, afterwards returning to the rear of their respective line.

FIG. 59. FOOTWORK DRILL: CHANGE OF DIRECTION. ☐1 defenses ①, who endeavors to get free for a pass and a lay-in shot by making several changes of direction. When ① breaks free, the coach passes him the ball for a shot.

for instance, and then change direction back toward the man with the ball. This cut will force the defensive man to stay between the offensive man and the basket, so that the offensive player will then be clear for a pass when he goes toward the man with the ball. Centers and forwards often use this maneuver to get free for a pass.

Pivots and Turns

Pivots and turns are basic to the footwork of the player and should become habitual, so that their execution becomes automatic. A pivot is accomplished by swinging one foot backward and rotating the body on the ball of the other foot. The body moves backward in a pivot which is sometimes called a reverse pivot. On the other hand, a turn is made by swinging one leg across in front of the other in a forward direction as the player rotates on the ball of the opposite foot. This turn is also called a front pivot. A pivot or a turn can be done as a small arc (45-degree) or in a complete circle, returning to the original starting position.

The pivot is used when a dribbler comes to a stop or is stationary facing a defensive player and wants to protect the ball with his body. It is also used to: change direction when dribbling; screen and roll off; and break away from the basket, pivot, and return to the basket.

A right pivot is executed by keeping the ball of the left foot on the floor, dropping the right shoulder and right hip, and pushing off backward with the right foot and swinging the right elbow vigorously to the rear, as shown in Figure 54. This maneuver should be done in a crouched position and, if the player is in possession of the ball, it should be protected with body and elbows.

The left turn is done from a crouched position with the ball of the left foot remaining on the floor. Drop the left shoulder, push off with the right foot, swing the right leg forward, and thrust the right arm around vigorously (Fig. 55). The turn is commonly used when an offensive player is facing an opponent who is not close to him and he wants to turn forward and have his back to the opponent.

The pivot and turn are practiced to the right and to the left. Each player should be able to do at least a 180-degree maneuver, so that he ends up facing the opposite direction from which he started. The foot remains in contact with the floor at all times. A player can, if he likes, spin like a top on the ball of his foot as long as he keeps that floor contact.

Footwork Drills

Figure 56 indicates a good drill to teach the stop and the pivot. Player ① dribbles to the line, stops, pivots in the required direction, and passes the ball to the next man in line. The first man goes to the end

of the line, while the second man continues the drill. The type of pass can be varied from the chest to the baseball to the hook.

Mass footwork is practiced in Figure 57. The coach stands in front of the group and calls out the maneuver. Players then execute it while the coach watches and makes corrections.

Stop and turn or pivot drill is illustrated in Figure 58. The player runs to the line and executes a stride stop. Then he either pivots or turns as required and returns to the end of the line.

Change of direction drill. The coach stations himself under the basket. Player ① tries to free himself by a change of direction or change of pace to get free for a pass and a shot. Zigzag, cuts, slow-fast actions will free the cutter (Fig. 59).

► Fakes and Feints

A fake or a feint is an action of a player designed to make an opponent believe that something is going to happen, after which something else does. It misleads the opponent and draws him off balance.

Fakes are used by a player both when he has or does not have the ball in his possession. The object is to make the opponent think some action is to occur by the use of the eyes, head, body, legs, arms, hands, or the ball. The actor is performing to fool his opponent. The player uses finesse so that any action he chooses for this purpose will look like a natural basketball act to his opponent.

Play Without the Ball

Fakes and feints without the ball include cutting, stopping, and going free via the back door. When a player does not have the ball, he should be conscious of the necessity of faking so that he can get open to receive a pass or keep a defensive man busy and out of the play. It is more difficult for a player to fake when he does not have the ball; consequently, this type of maneuver should be emphasized.

Cutting and change of direction assist an offensive man in getting free for a pass, but when accompanied by a head-and-shoulder fake, this maneuver becomes more effective. A good maneuver to get free for a pass is for the offensive player to cut a step or two toward the basket and, when the defensive man starts back toward the basket, move toward the man with the ball to receive a pass. Sometimes a head-and-shoulder fake toward the basket is sufficient. The defensive man is kept guessing and is forced to react every time the offensive player moves.

Getting free from a guard by going behind him toward the basket is also called going to the basket by way of the back door. When a defensive man is guarding closely, the offensive man moves toward the ball

THE ROCKER STEP

as if to receive a pass. The defensive man follows closely, and when he is between the ball and the offensive man, the offensive man pivots and cuts for the basket. This maneuver will, if successful once, keep a guard in a more honest position from that time on.

Play with Ball

There are numerous fakes and feints that a player can use when in possession of the ball: fake a pass and dribble; fake a shot and dribble; use a rocker step to drive; pass, fake a cut in one direction and go in another; fake a shot up and go under for a lay-in. There are numerous combinations, with the give and go, the rocker step and the up and under the more frequently used.

The give and go is nothing more than a pass to a teammate and a cut free toward scoring territory. The go is where the fake is important, because it is at this instant that the offensive man can cut free. The head-and-shoulder or one-step fake in one direction is frequently all that is necessary to break free.

The rocker step is one of the most useful maneuvers

when an offensive man is in a one-on-one situation in which he has the ball and is being guarded by an opponent; there is a good chance for a drive to the basket, or to drive and then take a jump shot. This play is a clever offensive maneuver that is actually a back and forth pivot in which the man with the ball tries to get the guard off balance and then drive by him. The illustration shows how the offensive player rocks back and forth by using, in this case, the right foot as the pivot foot. As he rocks the left foot to the rear, he prepares for and fakes a shot. The guard will have to advance to stop the shot as he lifts his left foot, steps close to the guard with his left foot (going by him, not around), dribbles the ball off his right hip, and drives straight for the basket. Should the guard recover quickly and regain a favorable defensive position, the man with the ball can stop quickly and get off a jump shot. If the defensive man is clever and maintains a good position from the start, it is possible to rock several times and perhaps rock back and then take a long shot. This defensive player will be more honest the next time he is in this position, so the drive should be effective when he tries to close quickly to block the shot.

A player should be able to rock with either foot and be able to drive to the right or left, regardless of which foot he is rocking on. There are two important items to remember: dribble the first dribble off the hip so that the body is between the opponent and the ball; and try to go as close to the guard as possible so that the driver goes by, and not around, him.

An excellent maneuver for a player with the ball close to the basket is the up and under. The offensive man fakes a shot, and when the defensive player comes up high to block the shot, the man with the ball goes under and by the guard for a close shot at the basket. Here the important item is the fake of the shot to get the defensive man up high, so that he is faked out by the under maneuver.

ABC's of Faking

The player should:

1. Be an actor and so make the fakes look like natural basketball actions.
2. Use a variety of fakes.
3. Use split-second timing in his fakes.
4. React quickly before the opponent recovers.
5. Use fakes that work on a particular opponent.
6. Learn to fake both when he has the ball and when he does not have the ball.

▶ Obtaining Possession of the Ball

A team can score a field goal only when it has possession of the ball. Consequently, every effort should be made to get the ball from the opponents. Ways to

PREVENTING A HELD BALL

obtain possession of the ball are: by means of a jump ball; by preventing a held ball; by rebounding, offensively and defensively; by getting a free ball or a loose ball or by interception of a pass; by stealing the ball from an opponent; or by violations by the opposition which result in obtaining the ball out of bounds. *The ball belongs to the player or team that gets it,* and every effort should be made to increase players' consciousness of the opportunities and to teach the techniques necessary to carry out the act.

Jump Balls

Each period in the game begins with a center jump; in addition, there are numerous jump balls during the course of any basketball game resulting from held balls.

Individual defensive fundamentals are concerned with the jumper endeavoring to get the tip and the non-jumper obtaining the ball after it has been tipped.

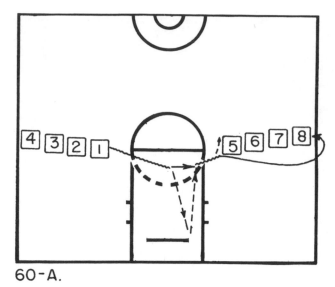

60-A.

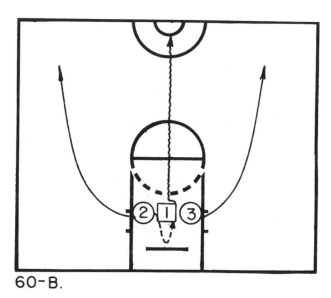

60-B.

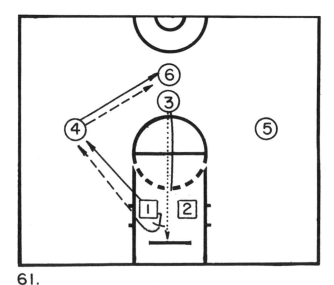

61.

Team efforts are explained in Chapter 7, which deals with team offense and the co-ordinated efforts of the team to obtain possession of the ball on all jump balls.

The jumper should never give up in an attempt to get the tip during jump ball, even if the opponent is taller. The jump should be timed so that the ball is tipped with the finger tips at the maximum height of the jump. The tip should be controlled by the finger tips and guided to a prearranged spot or to the side of one of the teammates on the side away from the defensive man.

Non-jumpers should anticipate the direction of the tip by a teammate or an opponent. The offensive man should screen out the opponent by stepping in front of the opposition and jump to obtain possession of the ball at the top of the leap.

Preventing a Held Ball

When two opponents both have two hands on the ball, the one using the proper technique should obtain the ball and prevent a tie-up. A tried and true technique is to give a quick, steady pull and at the same time turn one hand on top of the ball. Using the arms and back the player uses a sudden jerk to tear the ball free. The entire action should be done immediately upon getting two hands on the ball when the opponent grasps the ball. Immediate action is necessary to prevent a held ball. As soon as possession is definite, the player with the ball should protect the ball with his elbows and body and quickly dribble clear, pass, or shoot. The illustration indicates the position of the hands and body as the ball is jerked free.

FIG. 60. REBOUND DRILL. (A) *Rebound for form.* 1 dribbles into the foul line area and tosses the ball up against the backboard. He rebounds the ball in good form and either passes it to 5 or dribbles and then passes to 5. 5 continues the drill, while 1 goes to the end of the line. (B) *Tear-away drill.* 1 tosses the ball onto the backboard and rebounds it. As 1 comes down, 2 and 3 squeeze him and try to tear the ball out of his hands. 1 pivots between 2 and 3, and when he breaks free 2 and 3 join 1 in a full-court fast break drill. 1, 2, and 3 remain at the far end of the court until the other players have run the drill. Players must be cautioned to try to steal the ball and squeeze the rebounder without causing injury or unnecessary body contact.

FIG. 61. REBOUND DRILL: SIX-MAN DRILL. 3 shoots and rebounds offensively and endeavors to tie up 1 and 2, who rebound defensively. Should 3 gain possession of the ball, he shoots again, but if 1 or 2 gets the ball, they clear it to 5 or 4, whoever is on their side. The ball is then relayed to 6, and the drill continues. 3 takes the place of the player 4 who received clear-out pass. 4 takes the place of 6. Defensive men stay for five tries and are then replaced.

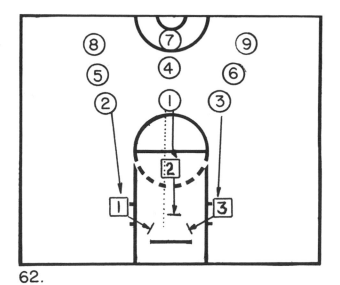

62.

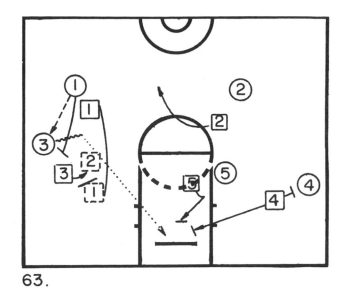

63.

Fig. 62. Rebound Drill: Three vs. Three. This drill presents excellent practice in screening out and rebounding. ①, ②, and ③ rebound defensively after screening out their opponents. ①, ②, or ③ shoots, and all three rebound offensively. If the players on offense get the ball, they try to score and play three-on-three until the defense gets the ball or a basket is made. The defensive men stay on defense until they have gotten the ball five times.

Fig. 63. Rebound Drill: Game Conditions, Five vs. Five. The offensive players run a play and take a shot. The defense screens out and rebounds according to the team defense and team rebounding rules. The defense stays for ten tries at the basket. If a fast break is used, the rebound should be cleared and at least the first pass of the fast break made.

Rebounding

Coaches agree that in general the team which controls the backboard is the one that is going to win the game. With this knowledge in mind, a team should be well grounded in proper defensive and offensive rebounding techniques.

Offensive and defensive rebounding are similar until the player gets his hands on the ball. In the first case, the objective is to get the ball to try to score, but the latter case involves getting the ball so that the opponents will not have a second opportunity to shoot and score.

Offensive rebounding concerns: getting the proper position on the opponent; jumping for the ball; and either tipping the ball back up or obtaining complete control, then taking another shot or passing to a teammate for a shot on an offensive play.

Obtaining the proper position on an opponent requires that as soon as the offensive player or a teammate shoots, every effort be made to obtain a position between the defensive man and the basket. This is the favorable inside position and is obtained by fast, aggressive body and foot movements. The offensive player should make every effort to obtain a position from four to six feet from the basket and hold that position. As soon as the inside position is obtained,

the offensive player should spread out to protect his position, keep the opponent away from the basket, and prepare to jump for the ball. The blocking out position is one in which the player takes a fairly wide stance, spreads the elbows out, and holds his hands in front of his chest with the palms out and the fingers pointing up. The legs can be spread on the jump or straightened, but the hands should be thrust up vigorously. These movements will keep the opponents at a distance and will give the offensive rebounder a good chance to get the ball. The wide stance should form a good foundation, so that the defensive player will be unable to force the offensive rebounder under the basket or from his desirable inside position.

Rebounding takes timing, co-ordination, and the ability to jump. Jumping ability can be improved with specific drills and practice (see Chapter 10). The jump should be timed so that the rebounder obtains possession of the ball at the top of his jump. Co-ordination is necessary, so that the player can obtain the favorable position and be able to position himself correctly and make a good effort to get the ball.

If the offensive player cannot get complete possession of the ball, he should try to tip the ball back into the basket. This shot is described in this chapter. On the other hand, if the offensive man can get possession of the ball, he will then have a good opportunity to immediately jump back up and, by using force and aggressiveness, carry the ball up high with both hands and shoot. If there is no opportunity to tip or shoot, the rebounder should clear the ball to a teammate. He can, in turn, shoot or start another play.

Organized team play of necessity has rebound rules which specify which players will rebound and which will balance to go on defense. This constitutes a co-ordinated team effort and is further explained in Chapter 7.

ABC's of Rebounding

The offensive player should:

1. Screen out the opponent, then rebound. Be aggressive and do not give up.
2. When tall, keep the ball high.
3. Protect the ball with his elbows and body.
4. Clear out the ball quickly by a pass or a dribble.
5. If he is unable to control an offensive rebound, tip the ball back and in.
6. Practice jumping and timing his jump so that he obtains the ball at the top of his jump.
7. Know his place to rebound in the team offensive and defensive rebound plans and patterns.

Rebounding Drills

This very important fundamental cannot be minimized. Players of short stature often out-position and out-rebound players much taller. These techniques can be taught with good practice drills.

Rebound for form. This drill (Fig. 60-A) is excellent to teach and practice rebounding for form.

Tear-away rebound drill. Often players get their hands on the ball, but have it taken away by those with stronger hands. This drill teaches the player to hold onto the ball and clear it. Figure 60-B portrays the drill.

Six-man rebound drill. One offensive man rebounds offensively against two defensive men. Figure 61 indicates this drill, which simulates game conditions.

Three vs. three rebound drill. This drill presents excellent practice in screening out and rebounding. Figure 62 indicates the formation.

Five on five rebound drill. Figure 63 shows this drill. The offensive players run a play and take a shot. The defense screens out and rebounds according to the team defense and team rebounding rules. The defense stays for ten tries at the basket. If a fast break is used, the rebound should be cleared and at least the first pass of the fast break made.

► Summary

Among the individual offensive fundamentals are those which are necessary to advance the ball and to score. Each fundamental has its place in the offensive scheme of play, and the individual basketball player should be well versed in each. Individual offensive fundamentals include: shooting, ball handling, dribbling, footwork, fakes and feints, obtaining possession of the ball, and rebounding.

It is up to the individual coach to determine the need for practice on individual offensive fundamentals, to design the drill used, and to thoroughly indoctrinate the players in its use.

Shooting is the most important fundamental, because a team composed of players who cannot shoot is going to have a difficult time outscoring the opponents.

Although each player should be well grounded in all the fundamentals necessary to play the game, there is never enough time to practice each sufficiently so that all the players become skilled. Judicious planning on the part of the coach is necessary, so that what is needed is practiced.

► Study Questions

1. List those items necessary for a player to have good shooting ability.
2. Explain "finger tip control." Why is it important?
3. When would you advise a player to use English on the ball?
4. Describe the three drills you would use to practice the lay-in shot, the jump shot, and the pivot shot.
5. What are the distinct advantages of the jump shot?

6. List the five steps used as the procedure in shooting the foul shot.

7. What advantages are there in holding the ball in the fundamental position?

8. List several common mistakes made in passing the ball.

9. What disadvantages are there in the promiscuous use of the dribble?

10. Define maneuverability speed.

► Projects for Additional Study

1. Observe a basketball game and record the number and type of shots taken during the game. Total, summarize, and analyze with respect to player and team offense.

2. Diagram five combination drills used to practice passing, shooting, and rebounding.

3. What games can be used when practicing shooting? What are the advantages of games over regular drills?

4. Search the literature for pictures which portray maneuvers that can be executed by an individual player with the ball.

5. Plan a bulletin board display which will emphasize the importance of individual offensive fundamentals.

6. Interview several basketball players and determine their reaction as to how they rebound offensively in regard to the positions they play.

7. As the coach of a high school basketball team, outline the basic individual offensive fundamentals necessary to play a game.

8. Describe thoroughly the technique of shooting a jump shot. What are the most common variations among individual basketball players?

► Selected References

Auerbach, Arnold. *Basketball for the Player, the Fan, and the Coach.* New York: Pocket Books, Inc., 1952. Excellent section on offensive fundamentals.

Bee, Clair. *Drills and Fundamentals.* New York: A. S. Barnes & Co., 1942. Concise coverage of offensive fundamentals with well-chosen drills.

Bunn, John W. *Basketball Methods.* New York: The Macmillan Co., 1939. Outstanding material on individual offensive techniques.

_____. *Basketball Techniques and Team Play.* Englewood Cliffs, N. J.: Prentice-Hall, Inc., 1964. Basic coverage of individual fundamentals.

Dean, Everett S. *Progressive Basketball.* New York: Prentice-Hall, Inc., 1950. Very concise coverage of offensive basketball fundamentals.

Gullion, Blair. *100 Drills for Teaching Basketball Fundamentals.* St. Louis, Mo.: Blair Gullion, 1933. Excellent source of material from which to select offensive drills.

Hobson, Howard, *Basketball Illustrated.* New York: A. S. Barnes & Co., 1948. Well-illustrated and easy-to-read section on individual offensive fundamentals.

Lindeburg, Franklin. "Animated Shooting Drills," *Scholastic Coach,* December, 1953. Shooting drills designed to spruce up the practice.

Loeffler, Ken. *Ken Loeffler on Basketball.* New York: Prentice-Hall, Inc., 1955. Excellent coverage of individual offensive skills.

McCracken, Branch. *Indiana Basketball.* New York: Prentice-Hall, Inc., 1955. Concise discussion of offensive fundamentals.

McCreary, Jay. *Winning High School Basketball.* New York: Prentice-Hall, Inc., 1956. Offensive fundamentals are thoroughly covered in this fine book.

McGuire, Frank. *Offensive Basketball.* Englewood Cliffs, New Jersey: Prentice-Hall, Inc., 1958. Clear description of offensive skills.

McLane, Hardin. *Championship Basketball by 12 Great Coaches.* Englewood Cliffs, N. J.: Prentice-Hall, Inc., 1965. Coach E. A. Diddle on offensive fundamentals.

Newell, Pete, and Benington, John. *Basketball Methods*. New York: The Ronald Press Co., 1962. Comprehensive coverage of offensive fundamentals combined with a group of excellent pictures of players in action.

Newsom, Heber. *Basketball for the High School Coach and the Physical Education Teacher*. Dubuque, Iowa: Wm. C. Brown Co., 1952. Good coverage of offensive drills and fundamentals.

Pettit, Bob, with Bob Wolff. *Bob Pettit: The Drive Within Me*. Englewood Cliffs, N. J.: Prentice-Hall, Inc., 1966. Basic skills cleverly inserted into narrative of book.

Pinholster, Garland F. *Encyclopedia of Basketball Drills*. New York: Prentice-Hall, Inc., 1958. Excellent source of drills for the teaching of offensive skills.

Ramsay, Jack. *Pressure Basketball*. Englewood Cliffs, N. J.: Prentice-Hall, Inc., 1964. Basic discussion and tips on individual offense.

Rupp, Adolph F. *Rupp's Championship Basketball*. New York: Prentice-Hall, Inc., 1948. Offensive fundamentals plus specific hints on the proper techniques are covered.

Scholastic Coach. Scholastic Magazines, Inc., New York, New York 10036. Contains many articles dealing with offensive fundamentals and drills.

Sharman, Bill. *Sharman on Basketball Shooting*. Englewood Cliffs, N. J.: Prentice-Hall, Inc., 1965. Outstanding book devoted entirely to the individual offensive skill of shooting the basketball.

U.S. Navy. *Basketball*. Annapolis, Md.: United States Naval Institute, 1943. Clear, well-illustrated section on offensive fundamentals.

Watts, Stan. *Developing an Offensive Attack in Basketball*. New York: Prentice-Hall, Inc., 1959. Excellent material on offensive fundamentals.

Wooden, John R. *Practical Modern Basketball*. New York: The Ronald Press Co., 1966. Complete coverage of individual defense.

CHAPTER 7: Team Offense

Team offense is the co-ordinated effort of a team to move the ball down the court, to maintain control of the ball, and to score. This major objective of basketball is accomplished through a variety of systems, each in its own way designed to provide a scoring opportunity. Systems of offensive play vary from a fast break, free-lance offense to slow-down, deliberate, set offensive patterns. Also included in team offense are the special offensive situations of the out-of-bounds play, jump ball plays, free throw offense, and last-minute scoring plays.

Whether in an attempt to move the ball into scoring position or in an effort to score, the offense should be so constituted that it is prepared to meet any defensive situation: press, jump ball, out-of-bounds, foul shot, and any defense, whether it be man-to-man, zone, or a combination of the two.

▶ Basic Principles of Team Offense

Criteria for Selecting the Team Offense

The specific choice of an offense ultimately rests with the coach. The selection should be one of which the coach has a thorough understanding. Once the offense has been selected, the coach should stay with it. If the original selection was sound, it will soon be reflected in improved co-ordinated team play.

Because the opponent's defensive play is never the same from game to game, or even in the same game, a balanced attack is necessary; consequently, each coach should strive for an offense which fits his purpose.

The following criteria for selecting the team offense can be used as a standard for judging whether or not the offense is a good one.

1. *The criterion of co-ordination.* Each player is co-ordinated in his actions with every other player on the team. Each knows what the other is doing and acts accordingly. The team's actions are so co-ordinated that it moves smoothly from one phase of play to another and from one option to another.

2. *The criterion of simplicity.* The offensive maneuvers are simple, so that each player understands and is able to accomplish the required techniques. The material given should be understood and mastered before more is offered.

3. *The criterion of fundamentals.* Fundamentals taught as drills are the same as those utilized in the offense. The fundamentals and techniques necessary to the offense should be such that they can be and are mastered.

4. *The criterion of balance.* The offense is so balanced on the court that it is ready to change from offense to defense, even to the extent of anticipating loss of the ball. When a shot is taken, assigned players endeavor to control the offensive boards.

5. *The criterion of flexibility.* The offense is flexible to meet all defensive situations. It is not so rigid in its constitution that small variations cannot be made. It is ready for each offensive opportunity: jump balls, out-of-bounds, foul shot, fast break, set attack and semi-control, or absolute stall.

6. *The criterion of timing.* The offense is a smoothly functioning, co-operating unit of five players, each in the proper place at the proper time. Split-second timing and synchronized actions make this possible.

7. *The criterion of action.* The offense has a movement of the players, a movement of the ball, or a combination of the two.

8. *The criterion of surprise.* The actions of the offense are such that the defense is placed in a quandary or is forced to make adjustments. The element of surprise by an unexpected maneuver is often upsetting to the players on the defense and makes the offense more effective.

9. *The criterion of confidence.* The fact that the players have confidence in themselves and in the ability of the team offense comes from mastery of the

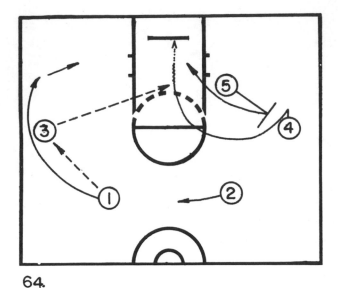

64.

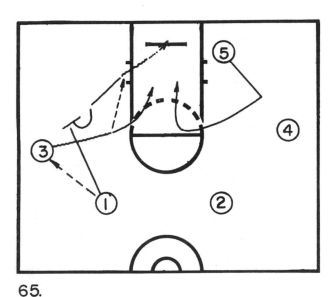

65.

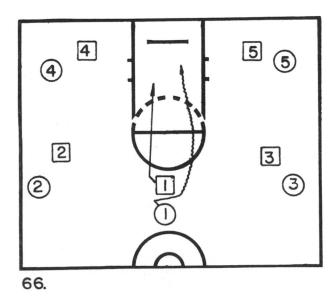

66.

fundamentals, techniques, and maneuvers necessary in the offense.

10. *The criterion of adaptability.* The offense should fit the players. It should be adapted to their abilities and capabilities. This important criteria is one which should be most seriously considered. When coaching at a large school where material is plentiful, the coach can effectively use the system he favors. But when the material is limited, and when it varies from year to year, the coach should fit the system to the players.

How to Build an Offense

Building and presenting an offense to a group is a teaching process. The following is a recommended procedure.

Explain and portray the entire offensive maneuver or pattern to the players on a blackboard and then in slow motion on the court. This material can also be distributed on sheets of paper or in a notebook.

The offense is now broken down into drills. Each drill should be an integral part of the offensive maneuver. The offense in its individual drills should be practiced first in one-on-one situations. The basic element of any offensive system of play is to obtain a situation where one man breaks free with the ball for a good shot at the basket, or at least a situation in which one offensive player is placed against one defensive player. It is at this level of play that the foundation of the offense is built. The offensive player, when he is well grounded in individual one-on-one offensive techniques, is ready to take his place in the offense.

From one-on-one drills, the teaching process moves to a two-on-two drill. Again, the drills are integral parts of the total offensive pattern. From a two-on-two, the process goes to three-on-three and four-on-four, and finally the entire five-man offense is reached. Each player, from this building and teaching process, should by now thoroughly understand his place in the team offense and be able to function efficiently as an integral part of the offense.

Often the coach has the problem of having one or two players with special abilities and the remaining members of the team just ordinary basketball players. When special situations like this exist, it is the coach's responsibility to build the offense to take advantage

FIG. 64. PLANNING THE OFFENSE: CENTER CLEARS. The center, ⑤, clears and screens for ④. ⑤ then returns to rebound.

FIG. 65. PLANNING THE OFFENSE: CENTER CLEARS. As the play develops on one side of the court, the center clears to the outside, but returns to rebound.

FIG. 66. PLANNING THE OFFENSE: CENTER OPEN. The 3-2 offense leaves the center open for drives. In this case, ① drives against his opponent in a one-on-one situation.

of the strong points and minimize the weak ones. Typical examples of this follow.

The first deals with the situation of a tall, awkward boy who is a good defensive rebounder, but not a strong offensive player. In this case it is necessary to place the boy on the team, but he should be delegated a secondary roll in the offense. Plays toward the forwards, with the center clearing to the side and then coming back for a rebound, are necessary. The center is cleared for drives, but the offensive strength is still available on the boards. Figures 64 and 65 depict such a play pattern. Another situation would be a team with no large pivot man, but a small hard-driving guard. A 3-2 offense would suit this problem. The center is kept open, and the hard driver is placed in the number ① position so that he has numerous opportunities to exploit his special abilities. Figure 66 portrays a play pattern in which player ① has a major role.

Many such personnel problems will exist, and an imaginative coach can often exploit the strengths and minimize the weaknesses by careful planning and coaching.

Principles of a Successful Play Pattern

Each offensive maneuver or play pattern should adhere to the following principles.

1. Provide good opportunity to score on the primary effort.

2. Alternate or secondary opportunities or options to score are available.

3. There is assigned strength on the offensive board, whether it be three, three and a half, or four men.

4. There is defensive balance in which men are assigned to defensive should it be necessary.

5. Each player has a part in the play and, whether it be a primary or secondary part, he is given a definite assignment.

6. Offense should make the defense do what they want them to do. They maneuver the defense and do not let the defense maneuver them.

7. The play should involve an inside attack with drives for lay-ins or short shots within the perimeter of the defense as well as an outside attack in which shots are taken from outside the defensive line of resistance.

8. The players realize that they should maintain possession of the ball if the maneuver is not successful. They should have the poise to realize that another maneuver is necessary and consequently set another planned attack, and not force the issue in a haphazard manner.

9. There should be a smooth continuity or turnover from one maneuver or play to another. Should a play fail to produce the desired attack, there should be a movement of ball and personnel in such a manner that a second attack can be smoothly co-ordinated from the first.

Signals to Designate Plays

In general, there are four methods of signaling which designate the offensive play pattern to be used. These are of the verbal, visual, ball movement, and player movement types and are usually initiated by the guard or team quarterback.

Verbal signals given by the player can be of the number, color, player's name, play name, etc. The player calls out the verbal signal and then starts the play. One difficulty with this type of signal is that the noise of the crowd can, and often does, drown out the signal so that there is a possibility that each player might not receive his cue.

Visual signals include waving an arm, holding hand over head indicating play by number of fingers extended, bouncing the ball, etc. This is a good way to indicate the play so long as the defense allows the signaler the time to give the signal. A pressure defense can make this type of signal difficult to complete.

Ball movement signals actually are the start of a particular play. If the guard passes to the guard, one maneuver or type of play is designated. Another play results when the ball is passed to the forward, and still another when the center receives a pass. This type of signal is common to teams using a more or less free-lance style of play.

Player movement signals indicate the play because of a certain path the designated quarterback takes. If he passes to the other guard and cuts to the basket, one maneuver is started; should he pass to the forward and cut around that forward on the outside, another maneuver is indicated, etc. This type of signal is used by teams using continuities as well as by those utilizing set patterns.

Maneuvers to Determine Opponent's Defense

At the beginning of each period, and when in doubt as to the type of defense being utilized by the opponent, a simple maneuver can be accomplished to determine whether the defense is of the man-to-man or zone type. All that is necessary is to have a guard cut through the defense, and if he is followed, a man-to-man defense is being used; on the other hand, should he go through unguarded, a zone is the method used to stop the attack. Some teams have such a maneuver in their repertoire of plays, but if not, one of the following type is recommended. Figure 67 (A to C) indicates such maneuvers from a double post, single post, and three-two offensive attacks with the guard passing and cutting through the defense. When the forward receives the pass, he observes the defensive players' actions, calls out the defense, and gives the

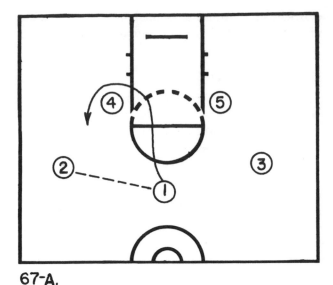

67-A.

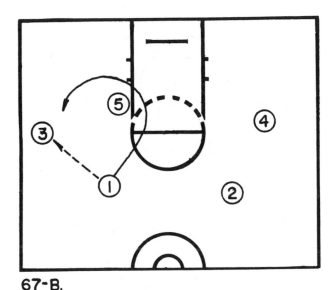

67-B.

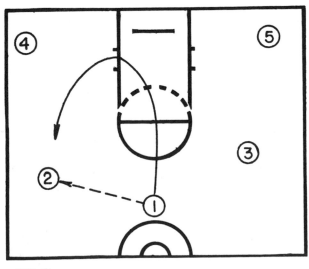

67-C.

ball to the other guard, and the offense is ready to attack a zone or man-to-man defense. Because teams are frequently changing defenses, a maneuver of this type is often necessary.

In addition to the use of this type of maneuver, the team quarterback should be observant and always be checking the defense for a change of strategy by the defensive team. This can be done by watching the actions of the defensive players. Are they following their opponents, which would indicate a man-to-man defense, or are they guarding an area of the court in a zone defense?

Special Maneuvers

There are certain maneuvers involving more than one player which are necessary for team play. These maneuvers are those which enable two offensive men to release the pressure of a tight man-to-man defense so that the regular offense can be set up and placed smoothly into operation. A tight man-to-man defense can often upset the tempo of a team's regular play, with the result that the offensive team fails to run its regular patterns and becomes ineffective. These special maneuvers are also used as offensive maneuvers which are a part of the team offense, and result in an opportunity for a score.

These basic maneuvers are between the two guards, a guard and a forward, and the problem situation of feeding the center.

Guard-to-Guard Maneuvers Used When the Defense Is Playing Tight

In-and-out. The in-and-out maneuver enables one guard to get free for a pass. Figure 68 shows this situation. The threat of a break to the basket makes the maneuver effective. The man who desires to get free breaks for the basket two or three steps, stops, and breaks back to receive a pass in the hand away from the defensive man.

Screen and change sides. This maneuver enables the two guards to change sides of the court and still make a threat of an offensive thrust. One guard passes to the other, screens, fakes to the basket, comes back out, and takes the other guard's position. The second guard dribbles around the screen, goes in for a shot, and continues for a play or stops in the other guard's original spot. Figure 69 pictures this situation.

Fig. 67. Maneuvers to Determine the Opponent's Defense. In each case, the ball is passed to the forward, who observes the defensive players' actions when ① cuts. If ① is followed, the defense is a man-to-man; but if he goes through free, the defense is some variation of a zone. The forward calls out the defense, and the offense prepares to attack that defense.

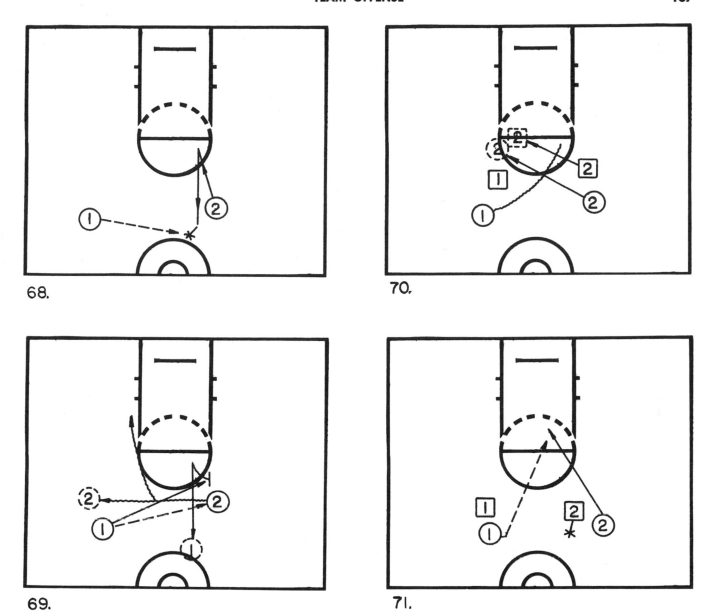

68.

69.

70.

71.

FIG. 68. SPECIAL GUARD MANEUVERS: IN AND OUT. To get free for a pass, ② cuts in several steps then back for a pass from ①.

FIG. 69. SPECIAL GUARD MANEUVERS: SCREEN AND CHANGE SIDES. ① passes to ② and screens. Two dribbles behind the screen and drives for a shot, takes ①'s spot, or starts a play. ① fakes to the basket after the screen, then comes back to be in a position to receive a pass from ②.

FIG. 70. SPECIAL GUARD MANEUVERS: THE CROSS. The man who does not have the ball, ② in this instance, cuts behind ①'s defensive man. As soon as ② is opposite ①'s defensive man, ① can dribble, using ② as a moving screen.

FIG. 71. SPECIAL GUARD MANEUVERS: THE CUT. This maneuver is designed to make an eager, aggressive man play a more cautious game. When ② plays high to prevent a pass or to intercept the ball, ② cuts for the basket, receives a pass from ①, and shoots.

The cross. This movement is initiated by the man who does not have the ball. Figure 70 shows this action as the man without the ball cuts behind the defensive man guarding the other guard. As soon as this cutter is opposite the offensive man's opponent, the man with the ball dribbles across the court using his teammate as a moving screen.

The cut. The cut, or backdoor move, is used when the defensive man plays high on defense to prevent the ball's being passed from one guard to the other.

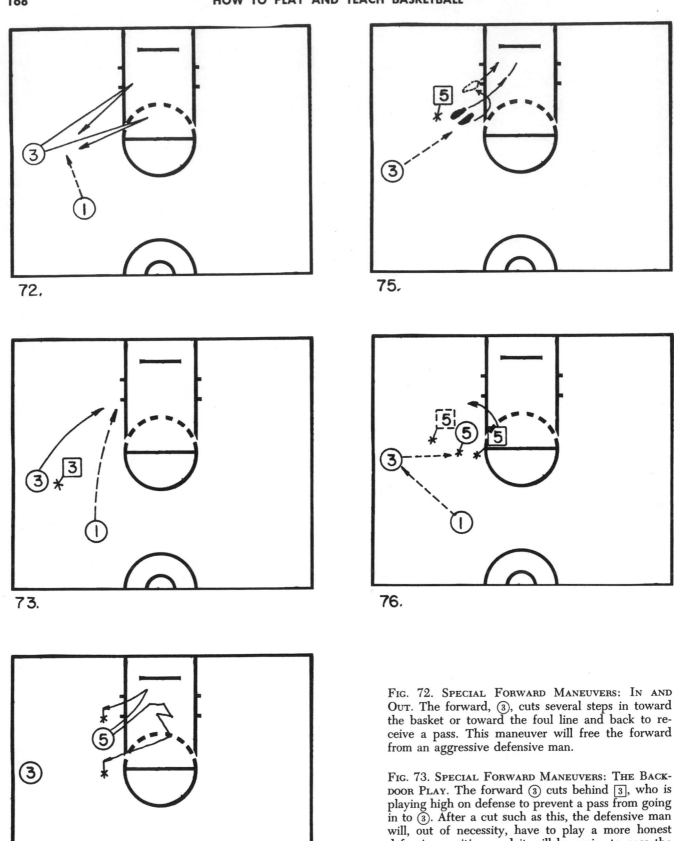

72.

73.

74.

75.

76.

FIG. 72. SPECIAL FORWARD MANEUVERS: IN AND OUT. The forward, ③, cuts several steps in toward the basket or toward the foul line and back to receive a pass. This maneuver will free the forward from an aggressive defensive man.

FIG. 73. SPECIAL FORWARD MANEUVERS: THE BACK-DOOR PLAY. The forward ③ cuts behind ③, who is playing high on defense to prevent a pass from going in to ③. After a cut such as this, the defensive man will, out of necessity, have to play a more honest defensive position, and it will be easier to pass the ball into ③.

FIG. 74. SPECIAL CENTER MANEUVERS: ZIGZAG, IN-AND-OUT CUT. The center, when he desires to receive a pass, cuts toward the basket and then reverses and moves directly toward the man with the ball. If this is not successful, he should cut in a zigzag pattern.

FIG. 75. SPECIAL CENTER MANEUVERS: THE PIVOT AND DRIVE. When the center receives the ball and the opposing defensive man is high and to one side, the offensive man can pivot and drive for the basket. A pivot will place the defensive man behind the center and at a distinct disadvantage.

FIG. 76. SPECIAL CENTER MANEUVERS: FEEDING THE PIVOT. Whenever the defensive center has to reposition himself on another side of the pivot man, it is possible to pass the ball in to the pivot man. ① passes to ③. ⑤, in an effort to obtain a good defensive position, moves to the other side of ⑤. It is at this time that ③ can pass the ball to ⑤.

Figure 71 gives an example of how the cut is effective. The defensive guard overplays the offensive guard. This offensive man cuts behind the eager defensive man to the basket and receives a pass from the man with the ball.

Guard-to-Forward Maneuvers Used When the Defense Is Tight

Often an aggressive defensive man who is tightly guarding a forward can present problems and stall offensive thrusts. The in-and-out and the backdoor play are moves designed to release the pressure of the tough defensive man and force him to play a more honest position.

The in-and-out. This action is a cut by the forward either toward the basket or toward the foul line. After two or three quick steps the forward reverses direction and breaks to receive the ball at his proper place at the forward position. Should the opposing player be a good defensive man, the ball can still be received by the forward on his outside hand; and by placing his body between the ball and the defensive man he can screen his opponent from the ball. The footwork for this move is shown in Figure 72.

The backdoor play. The threat of breaking free for a score will make the defensive man play an honest position. The backdoor play, even though it is not successful, will make the defensive man play a more cautious game. The forward moves forward as if to receive the ball from the guard, but because the de-

fensive man is playing high, the guard cannot pass the ball in. Figure 73 indicates that at this time the forward turns and cuts for the basket. A high or bounce pass from the guard often produces a score.

Feeding-the-Center Maneuvers Used When the Center Is Closely Guarded

In an attempt to keep the center from obtaining the ball, defensive centers take a high position between the ball and the offensive center. To obtain a pass in this closely guarded situation, the center should know how to maneuver in and out to get the ball, and to pivot and drive.

The in-and-out maneuver. In an effort to obtain a pass, the offensive center takes several steps toward the basket and, when the defensive man follows, reverses his direction and moves quickly toward the ball. The center will find it to his advantage to give a target to the passer by placing the palm of the hand on the side away from the defensive man toward the man with the ball. Should the defensive center be very mobile a zigzag cut is in order, with the offensive center moving in and out and from side to side in an irregular pattern, so that the defensive man will not be able to determine a pattern of action and anticipate the move. Figure 74 indicates this type of move.

The pivot-and-drive. The pivot man should be prepared to pivot and drive when he obtains a pass and is guarded to the side or high. Figure 75 shows the footwork which enables the center to maneuver inside the defensive man and toward the basket. Being guarded high and to the right, the center pivots on the right foot and points the toe of the left foot directly toward the basket. He follows with the right foot as he dribbles off his right side. This quick first step with the left foot places the defensive man in an unfavorable outside position. A large man can score from the foul line without a dribble, with a one-bounce dribble being a minimum.

Guard-to-forward-to-center. In an effort to feed the center, the movement of the ball from the guard to the forward will force the defensive center to reposition himself. As the defensive center is moving from one side of the offensive center to the other, it is possible to pass the ball in on the side opposite to where he is stationed. This method of feeding the pivot man is shown in Figure 76.

▶ Types of Offenses

There are many types of offense, each with numerous variations. Described below are basic basketball offenses classified as: the fast break attack; free-lance offense; post attacks; screen attacks; weaves or figure eights; continuities or plays with turnover; offenses

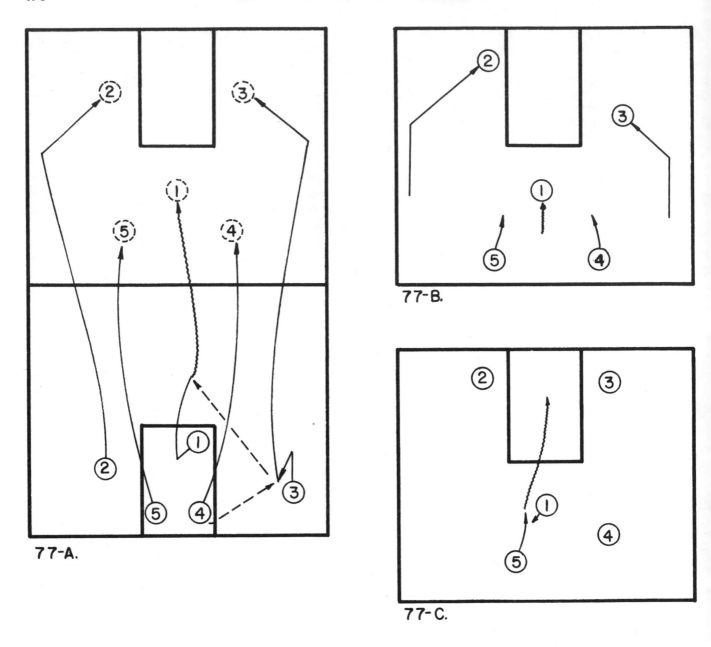

FIG. 77. FAST BREAK: THE THREE-LANE ATTACK, IDEAL FINISH, AND LATE-AND-FAST.
(A) An example of the three-lane fast break. ④ rebounds and immediately clears to ③.
③ passes to ①, who takes the ball up the middle of the court with a dribble. ② goes
down the left lane while ③ takes the right side. ④ and ⑤ come after as trailers. (B)
The ideal finish, with ② and ③ breaking for the basket. ① can give to either for a
lay-in shot. ④ and ⑤ trail the play. The late-and-fast play involves the trailers and
presents a good opportunity to score when the defense thinks the fast break has been
stopped. (C) ⑤ breaks past ① for a pass and a drive to the basket for a jump or lay-in
shot.

against presses; offenses for the shifting man-to-man defenses and special play situations such as the jump ball, foul shot and out-of-bounds plays.

Each offense will be briefly outlined, the basic plays will be explained, and personnel requirements will be discussed. For a more thorough coverage of the specific offenses, the reader should refer to the annotated references at the end of the chapter.

The Fast Break

The fast break is an offensive attack designed to obtain an easy score before the defense arrives or has an opportunity to form. The offense endeavors to force the defense into a vulnerable situation in which a man with the ball gets behind the defense and scores on an unopposed lay-in, or into a situation where only one defensive man is pitted against two offensive players or only two defensive men against three offensive players. This outnumbering of the defense is accomplished by moving the ball into a scoring position as fast as possible. The most successful fast break starts with a quick outlet pass or a fast dribble, regardless of how possession is obtained. Actually a fast break can be initiated any time the team gains possession of the ball. Thus, the break can start with a rebound, an intercepted pass, recovery of a free ball, after a field goal score, and from a made or missed free throw.

Although some coaches do not permit their players to fast break, no one can doubt the value of an easy score. Also, the fast break moves the ball quickly into the front court making the pressure defenses ineffective. Another advantage in using the fast break is that it is one of the primary weapons to be used against a zone defense. To move the ball into scoring territory before the five men forming a zone arrive to set their defense is the key to this fast break weapon.

Whether a team executes a fast break every time it gains possession of the ball or exploits a favorable situation and uses the fast break in that particular situation will depend upon the abilities of the individual players and upon the coach's philosophy.

Fast Break Philosophy

It can be stated that there are three separate and distinct philosophies regarding the fast break. The first involves no break, regardless of the opportunity. The coach exposing this idea usually is of the slow, deliberate, set offense style of play school, which believes that the ball is a precious item and that it must not be lost by mistakes or poor shots. The ball is shot only when a good percentage shot is obtained. A team using this style of play must be prepared to attack the various pressure defenses and expect to meet already formed zone defenses.

The second basic philosophy is that which utilizes the fast break as a primary team offense. Teams coached under this idea run and run and run. The mistakes made by the fast break team offense are rationalized away by the number of easy baskets obtained and the fact that many teams playing against this race-horse type of offense in turn commit mistakes and often lose their poise and become demoralized.

The third philosophy is one in which the fast break is made a part of the offense, but it is a secondary team offense. The idea is to take advantage of every fast break opportunity; but when the risk of losing the ball or committing a mistake overbalances the chance of obtaining a score, the players stop, set up their primary offense, and attempt to score by virtue of a predetermined pattern. This type of fast break is thought of as a supplementary offense to the basic pattern of offense.

Although most coaches practice specific types of fast breaks, it is recommended to take whatever comes along. Players who are alert and who anticipate their team's obtaining possession of the ball will often take the course of least resistance, regardless of the pattern practiced. On the other hand, practice inculcates into each player a pattern of action which the coach desires to use to beat the opponents down the floor. When thoroughly indoctrinated into a fast break pattern, players will unconsciously fall into the pattern, and the fast break will be a pattern which has been practiced, although it may appear to be a haphazard action.

Types of Fast Breaks

A fast break can be a free-lance type, but generally speaking they involve the short pass, the long pass, and the dribble, with the players going down the court in three straight lanes or crossing from one side of the court to the other.

Three-lane attack. The main objective of the three-lane attack is to move the ball down the middle of the court and to have men flanking the ball on each side of the court. General rules are: (1) move the ball to the middle of the court by either a dribble or a pass; (2) if the middle lane has a man in it, go to an outside, unoccupied lane; (3) dribble the ball down the middle of the court to the top of the key; and (4) when not in one of these lanes, trail behind.

Figure 77-A shows the three-lane attack, with Figure 77-B indicating the ideal finish. If there is no fast break opening in the front court, often a trailer coming late and fast can receive a pass and drive all the way. This is shown in Figure 77-C.

Whenever an opponent shoots, the front men, anticipating a recovery by their team, break down the sidelines and back for an outlet pass. The rebounders gain possession and immediately look for an opportunity to clear out the ball. The clear-out can be by way of a long pass, a short pass, or a dribble. This phase of the fast break is the most important. The quicker the ball is cleared, the greater the opportunity for the success of the fast break.

It is possible to clear the ball to one specific player,

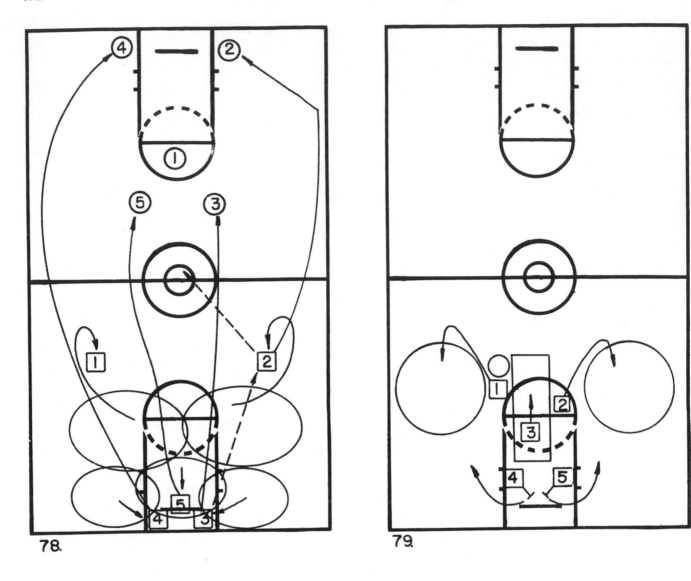

FIG. 78. FAST BREAK: OUTLET AREAS FROM A MAN-TO-MAN FAST BREAK. Players break to specific spots whenever they are in a particular area and their team recovers the ball. A player in any of the three areas under the basket rebounds and then follows the prescribed pattern. If a player is in one of the outside areas, he breaks down the court and comes back for a pass. In this instance, ③ rebounds and clears to ②. ① breaks diagonally across the court, receives a pass from ②, and takes the ball to the edge of the circle. ④ leaves as soon as ③ clears and fills the left lane. ③ and ⑤ trail.

FIG. 79. FAST BREAK: OUTLET AREAS FROM A 2-1-2 ZONE DEFENSE. Because the players are in relatively the same positions on the court all the time, each man moves to a prescribed spot after a shot. ① and ② clear out to the sides, while ③ goes down the middle. ④ and ⑤ rebound, then trail.

who takes the ball with a dribble to the middle of the court and, if contested by a defensive man, to a stop at the top of the key. If no specific man is designated, the ball is cleared to prearranged areas of the court; and when the team uses a zone defense, the players, because they are stationed at specific places on the court, can easily go to outlet areas. On the other hand, players going into a fast break from a man-to-man

defense must react depending upon their positions on the floor when their team obtains possession of the ball. Figure 78 indicates with shaded portions of the court the outlet areas. Regardless of the normal defensive position, a player goes from where he was when possession of the ball occurred to a specific area.

When a team goes from a zone defense into a fast break, the transition is relatively easy. Figure 79

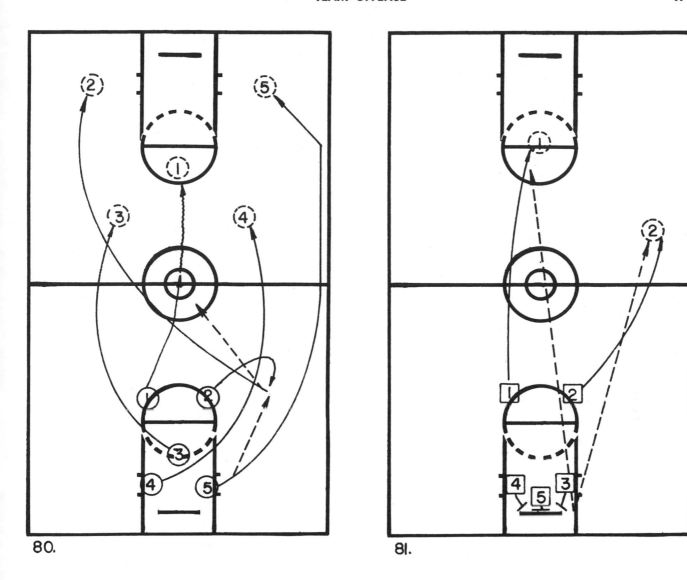

80.

81.

FIG. 80. FAST BREAK: CROSS-OVER ATTACK. ⑤ clears to ② and breaks down the side-line. ② passes to ① in the middle of the court and crosses over to the left side. ③ and ④ cross sides and trail the play.

FIG. 81. FAST BREAK: LONG-PASS ATTACK. ③, ④, and ⑤ rebound, while ① and ② release when a shot is taken. Two alternatives are shown. ③ can pass long down the sideline to ② or long down the middle to ①. If the ball is cleared to ②'s side, ② goes down the sideline and ① down the middle, and vice versa if the ball is cleared out on ①'s side.

shows how the men react when operating out of a 2-1-2 zone.

Cross-over attack. Players in this fast break offense clear the ball to a teammate ahead and cross behind the pass to the other side of the floor. This fast break pattern is shown in Figure 80. It is a good attack when the defense quickly picks up the front men. But it is slow, because the players do not move to the basket in a straight line.

Long-pass attack. This fast break is designed to throw a long pass beyond the defense for an easy score or to clear the ball out to the sideline as far down the court as possible. It is necessary, for this attack to be successful, to have rebounders who can control the defensive boards so that fast men can be released as soon as a shot is taken. Figure 81 indicates these two alternatives.

The long-pass attack is excellent to use when the

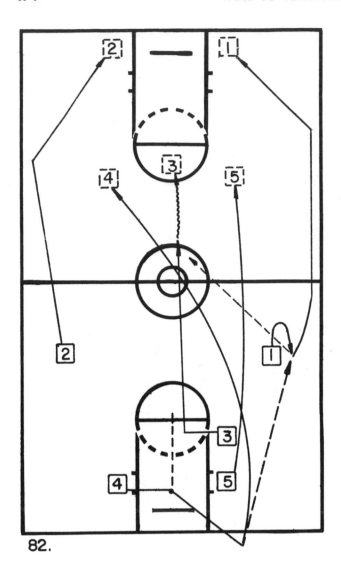

82.

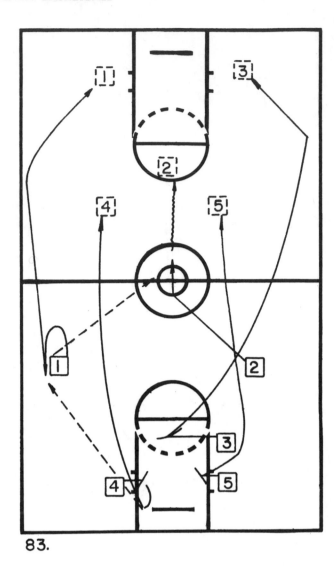

83.

Fig. 82. Fast Break: From a Foul Shot Which Has Been Made. [4] grabs the ball as it comes out of the net and jumps out of bounds ready to throw to [1]. [1] starts down the court and fishhooks back. [3] cuts off the shooter, then goes down the middle to receive the ball from [1]. [1] and [2] fill the outside lanes, [4] and [5] trail as [3] brings the ball to the head of the circle.

Fig. 83. Fast Break: From a Foul Shot Which Has Been Missed. A successful fast break can stem from a missed foul shot when each player anticipates recovery of the ball. [4] rebounds and clears to [1]. [2] breaks to the middle of the court, receives the ball from [1] and takes it to the circle. [1] and [3] fill the outside lanes, and [5] and [4] follow as trailers.

defense is in a zone press, as it is often possible to get behind the men in the press and receive a pass for a quick score.

Fast break from a foul shot. A fast break can be developed from a foul shot whether it is made or not. A pattern for a fast break from a foul shot which has been made is described in Figure 82. When a foul

shot is missed, a quick clear-out can produce a fast break. Figure 83 indicates the action involved in such an attack.

Personnel Requirements

To effectively handle a fast break, the team—or at least those carrying the main burden of the attack—should possess certain physical and mental attributes,

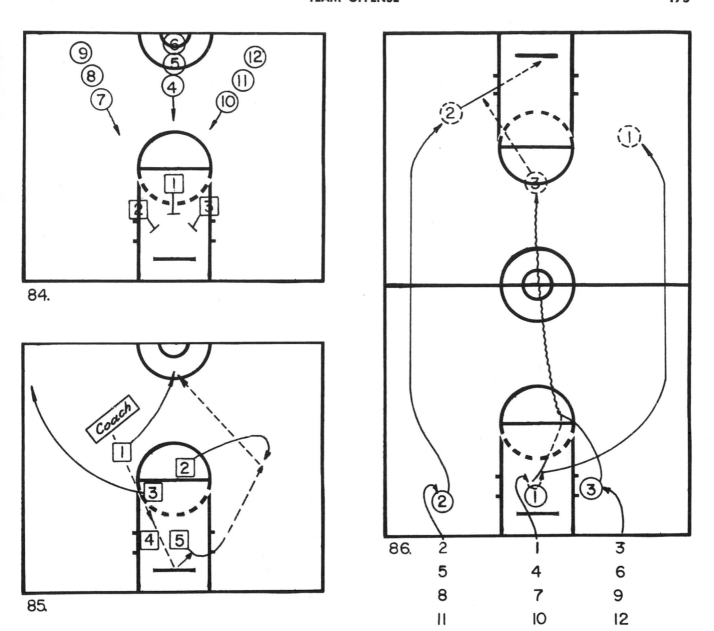

FIG. 84. FAST BREAK DRILL: REBOUND AND CLEAR PASS OUT. [1], [2], and [3] stay on defense until they have rebounded and passed the ball out five times. The first man in each line goes on offense, ⑦, ④, and ⑩ in this case. They shoot and rebound, if possible, and shoot again. [1], [2], and [3] rebound and pass out to the next man in the outside lines, ⑧, ⑤, or ⑪ and the drill continues as soon as ⑦, ④, and ⑩ have gone to the ends of their line.

FIG. 85. FAST BREAK DRILL: FROM A ZONE DEFENSE. The team is divided into teams of five on a team. The first team assumes a zone defense in front of the coach. The coach shoots; the team rebounds and executes a fast break the length of the floor. The second team, with its own ball, comes out on the court and runs through the drill. When all teams are at the other end of the floor, the coach moves to that end and the drill continues.

FIG. 86. FAST BREAK DRILL: FULL-COURT. Players ①, ②, and ③ move onto the court. ① tosses the ball up on the board, rebounds, and clears to ③. ③ takes the ball down the court while ② and ① break down the sidelines. They take a lay-in shot, rebound the ball, and clear off the court. As soon as the first group has crossed the mid-court line, the second group goes. Each group of three has a ball, and when they have all reached one end of the floor they reverse direction and come back.

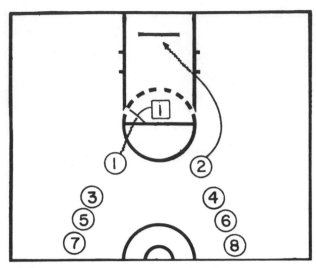

87-A.

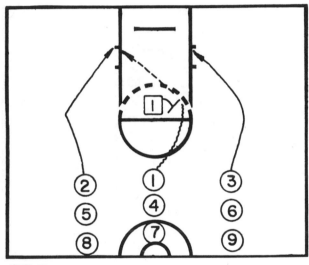

87-B.

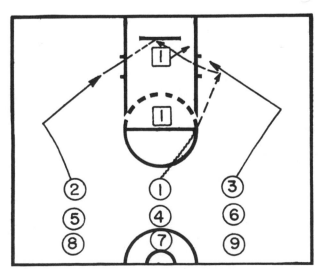

87-C.

or the attempt to fast break will result in repeated mistakes and subsequent loss of possession of the ball. These essential personnel requirements are:

1. Good rebounding and aggressive play to obtain possession of the ball.

2. Speed afoot to move down the floor.

3. Good ball handling to cut mistakes to a minimum. This includes passing, dribbling, and shooting while traveling at top speed.

4. Alertness to recognize fast break opportunities.

5. Poise to control self and the ball so that if no opportunity exists the fast break is slowed, controlled and blended into the regular offense.

Drills

Following are a few drills which aid in developing a fast break. It should be remembered that each drill should be a part of the offense that is regularly practiced. These drills are designed from and for a three-lane fast break attack.

The first deals with rebounding and immediately clearing the first pass out. Figure 84 illustrates this drill.

The second drill indicates how the fast break starts from a zone defense. This is shown in Figure 85.

The third drill deals with a full-court, three-man fast break. This is a fast-moving drill and is good for conditioning and practicing ball handling while traveling at fast speeds. Occasionally, one defensive man can be stationed at one end of the floor to make the offensive men "work for" a score. Figure 86 shows this excellent drill.

The fourth drill is concerned with the end of the fast break. Figure 87 (A to C) shows two-against-one, three-against-one and three-against-two drills.

Single Post Offense

The single post attack has many variations, each with several options. Described in Figure 88 (A to D) are basic single post offenses or maneuvers. It should be pointed out that in the series presented there are

FIG. 87. FAST BREAK DRILLS: TWO VS. ONE, THREE VS. ONE, AND THREE VS. TWO. (A) Two offensive men are placed against one defensive man, indicating a situation which often results at the end of a fast break. ① and ② endeavor to score against ⬜1. ⬜1 stays on defense for five defensive moves. (B) Three men are set against only one. (C) Three are matched against two.

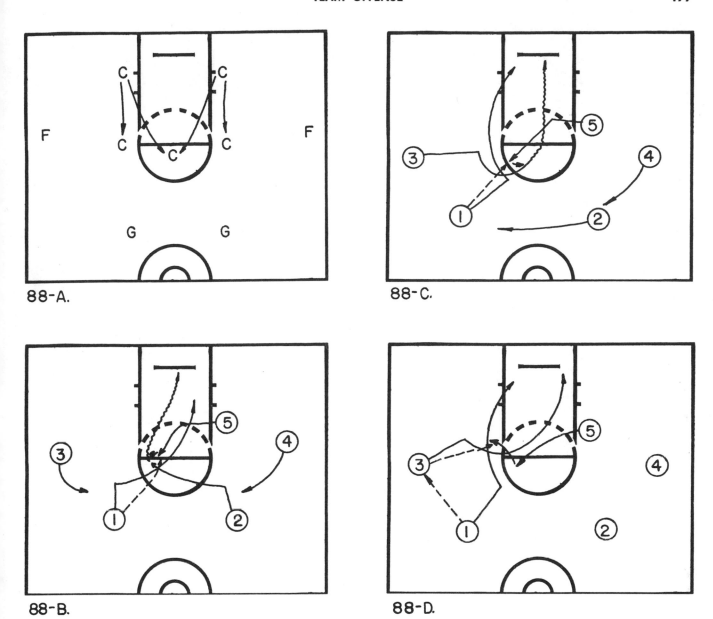

88-A.

88-B.

88-C.

88-D.

Fig. 88. Single Post Offense. A common type of single post offense is portrayed, with 88-A indicating the basic setup. (B) ① passes to ⑤, and ① and ② scissor off of the center. (C) The guard and forward scissoring off of the center. ① passes to ⑤ and cuts, followed by ③. (D) The forward passing to the center ③ to ⑤. ③ cuts off of the center, followed by ①.

always several options possible. This post type of offense is probably the most popular one in existence today.

Low Post Offense

The low post attack positions the center just out-side the foul lane in the vicinity of the basket. Figure 89 (A to D) describes this series. The main problem encountered in placing the center close to the basket is that the opposing defensive man will make every attempt to prevent a pass from being thrown in.

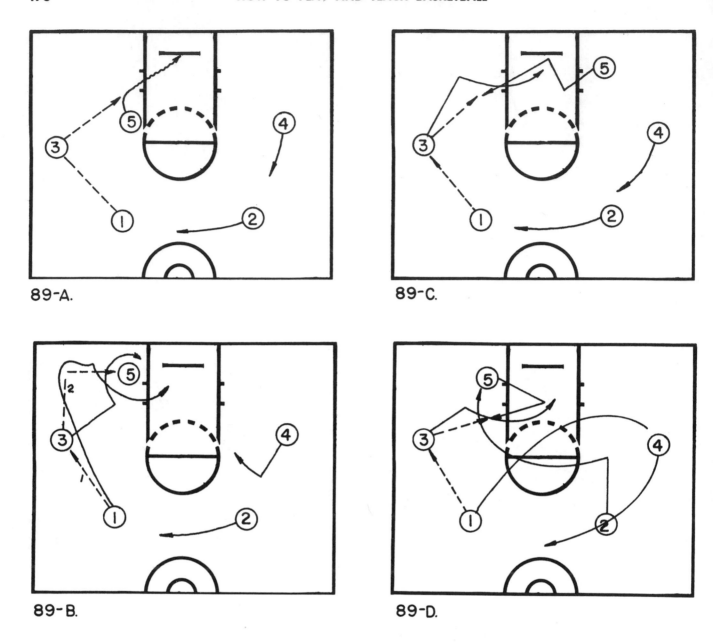

89-A.

89-C.

89-B.

89-D.

FIG. 89. LOW POST OFFENSE. Typical plays for a low post offense are shown. (A) The center moves down the foul lane and receives a pass from the forward ① to ③ to ⑤. (B) Passing into the center at a low post position is sometimes very difficult, but here the pass and play are relatively simple. ① gives to ③ and cuts to the corner. ③ returns the ball to ①. ① now passes to ⑤ on his open, unguarded side. ① and ③ scissor off of ⑤, with ① cutting first. (C) The center comes from the weak side to receive a pass. ① passes to ③. ③ hits the center and cuts. (D) A play requiring good timing. ① passes to ③ and cuts diagonally across the court. ③ passes to ⑤ and cuts off of ⑤. ② times his cut behind ① and around ⑤ to complete the play.

Good ball handling, clever footwork, and good passing can overcome this obstacle.

High Post Offense

Figure 90 (A to D) indicates a series of maneuvers with the center at a high post position in the area of the foul line. In this series, the guard initiates the pass to the center. A guard-around sequence is described in Figure 91 (A to D), while Figure 92 (A to D) portrays a center screen series.

Personnel

A strong center is necessary to make this single post attack function. He should be a good rebounder, a

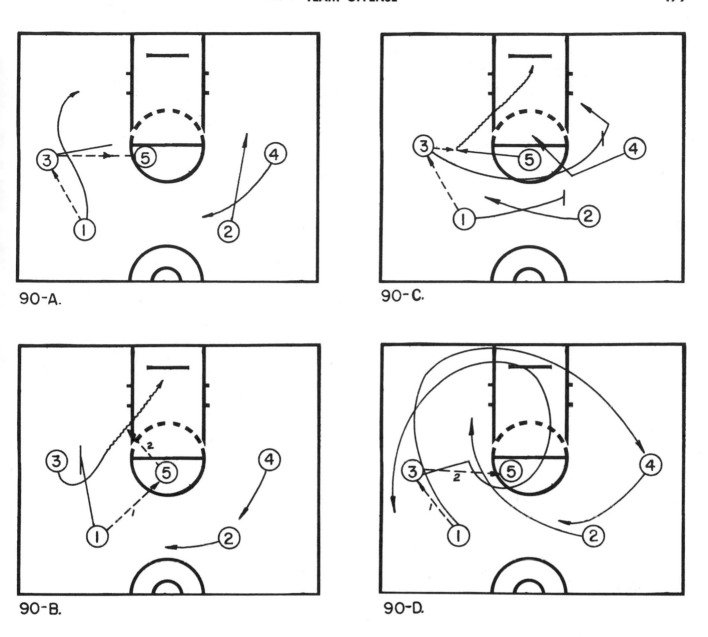

90-A.

90-B.

90-C.

90-D.

FIG. 90. HIGH POST OFFENSE. Presented are a series of plays off of a high post offense. (A) A good method of passing to the center behind a cutter. ① passes to ③ and cuts toward ③'s defensive man. ③ passes to ⑤ and cuts. (B) A screen to feed the forward. ① passes to ⑤ and screens for ③. ③ cuts behind the screen toward the basket and receives a pass from ⑤. (C) ⑤ being given half of the court in which he can go one-on-one against his defensive man. ① gives to ③ and cuts to the right, screening for ② ③ passes to ⑤ and clears to the right, screening for ④. ⑤ shoots, or drives and shoots. (D) ① passing to ③ to start the play. ① continues under the basket and around to his original position, while ③ passes to ⑤. ③ and ② cut off of ⑤ and circle under the basket and back to their original position.

good feeder, and a scorer. When one or more of these qualifications are missing, the coach must adjust the patterns accordingly. For instance, if the center is not a scorer, he can be utilized to screen for the forward to free that man in the area of the basket. The rebound strength of the center is still available. Should the center be big and slow, it is a good idea to place him in a low post, as his talents will be lost when he

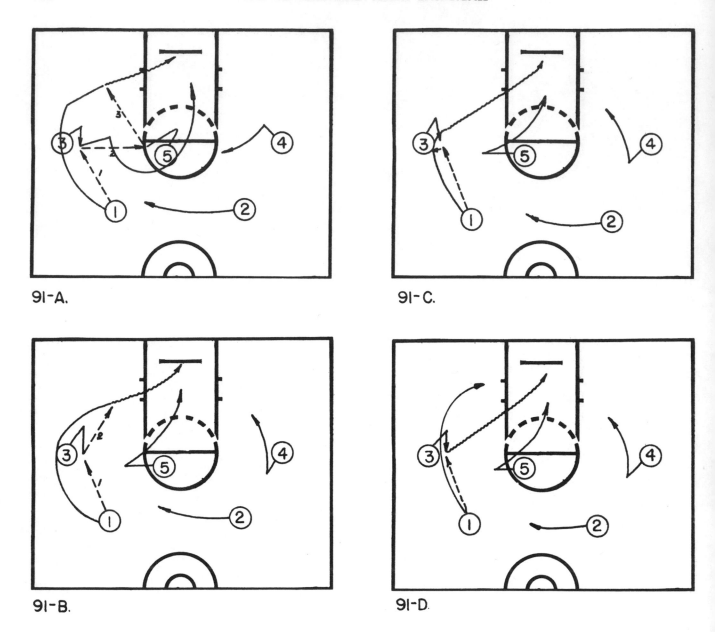

91-A.

91-C.

91-B.

91-D.

FIG. 91. POST OFFENSE: GUARD-AROUND SERIES. (A) The guard-around play. ① passes to ③ and cuts around ③ and in toward the basket. ③ gives to ⑤ and cuts off the center. ⑤ passes to ① for a lay-in shot. (B) ① passing to ③ and cutting behind ③ toward the basket. ③ fakes a pass to ⑤ and passes back to ① for a lay-in. (C) A variation of the above. ① passes to ③ and cuts behind. ③ returns the ball to ① as he cuts by for a drive to the basket. (D) ① passing to ③. ③ fakes to return the ball to ① and drives for the basket.

plays out from the basket.

The forwards should be good shooters and passers, have good rebounding ability, and should be able to drive for the basket.

One of the guards should be a quarterback to initiate the plays. Poise and good passing are essential. The ability to cut and drive with a good outside shot is desired.

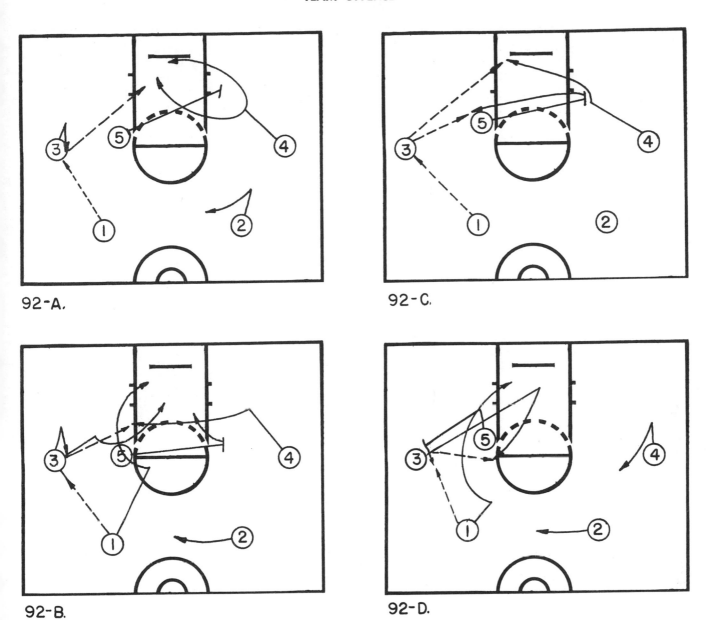

92-A.

92-C.

92-B.

92-D.

FIG. 92. POST OFFENSE: CENTER SCREEN SERIES. (A) The center-to-forward screen. ① passes to ③ at which time ⑤ screens for ④. ④ cuts to either side and to a point under the basket for a pass from ③. (B) The forward comes to the post. ① passes to ③, while ⑤ screens for ④. ③ passes to ④, and ③ and ① cut off ④. (C) When the defensive center shifts men, the center returns to the pivot position after placing a screen for ④. ① passes to ③. ⑤ screens for ④, but returns to his original position for a pass from ③. ③ has the option of giving to ④ or ⑤. (D) The center screening on the near side. The center, ⑤, screens for ③, who breaks for the basket. If ③ goes free, ① gives him the ball. If not, ① passes to ⑤ and ⑤ to ③, who has returned to the pivot spot. ① and ⑤ cut off of ③.

Double Post Offense

In the double post offense, two centers are positioned in the area near the foul lane. They can be stationed in a tandem formation, with one at a low post position and the other at the high spot, or both can be stationed opposite each other either high or low.

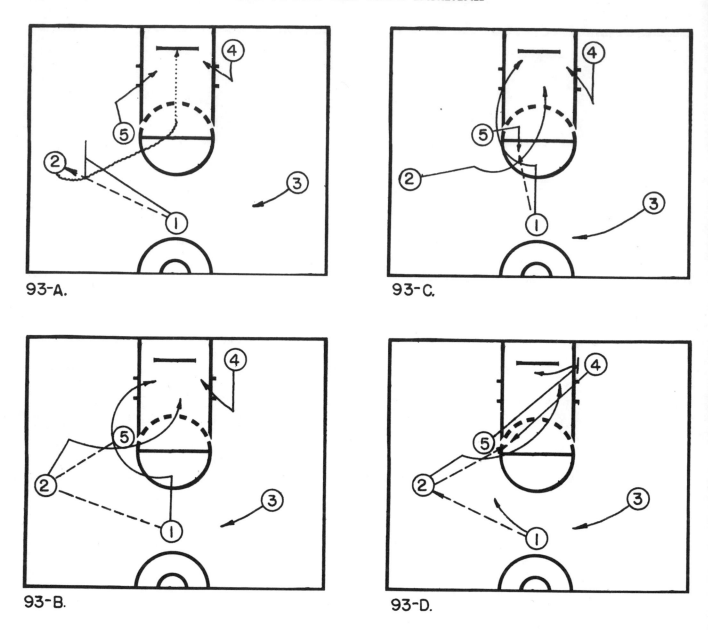

93-A.

93-C.

93-B.

93-D.

FIG. 93. TANDEM DOUBLE POST. In this sequence, one center plays high on the strong side, while the other is in a low position on the weak side. (A) ① passes to ② and screens for ②. ② dribbles around ① and around ⑤ for a close jump shot. (B) ① passing to ②. ② passes to ⑤, and ① and ② scissor off of ⑤. (C) A pass from ① to ⑤, with ① and ② scissoring off of ⑤. (D) ⑤ screens for ④. ① passes to ② and ② to ④. ② cuts off of ④. Should the defensive centers switch men, ⑤ is often left open under the basket.

The Tandem Double Post

The tandem double post offense presents many variations and good opportunities to pass the ball into the post area as is shown in Figure 93 (A to D). Good outside shooting is necessary to combat sagging on the center men.

The Low Double Post

A low double post offense is described in Figure 94 (A to D). In this offense the centers shuttle and screen for one another, which makes it relatively easy to move the ball into the area in front of the basket.

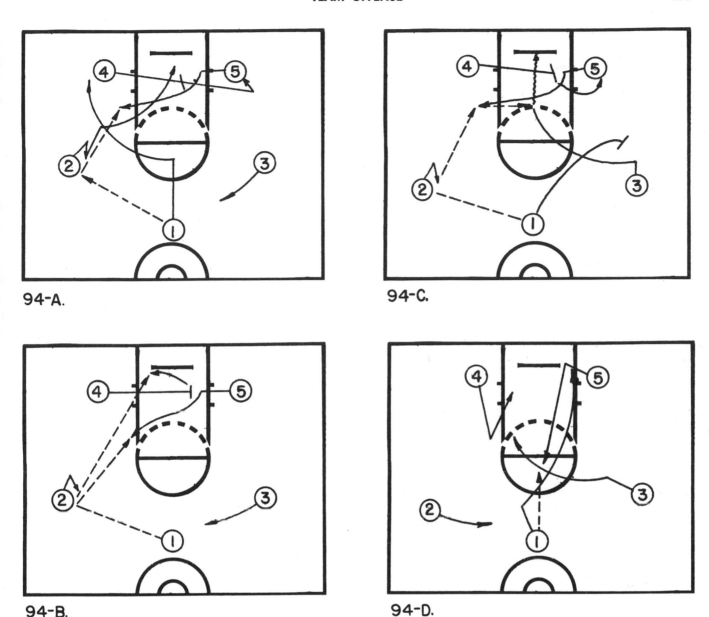

94-A.

94-C.

94-B.

94-D.

FIG. 94. LOW DOUBLE POST. (A) ④ screens for ⑤ as ① passes to ②. ② passes in to ⑤, and ① and ② scissor by ⑤. (B) A variation of 94-A. ④ screens for ⑤, while ① passes to ②. ④ rolls off of the screen and back for a pass from ②. ② can give to ④ or ⑤, depending upon the play of the defensive men. (C) ④ screening for ⑤ and ① screening for ③ to produce a lay-in shot. ① passes to ② and screens for ③. At the same time, ④ screens for ⑤. ② passes to ⑤ and ⑤ to ③. (D) ⑤ breaks up toward ①. ① passes to ⑤, and ① and ③ scissor by.

The High Double Post

Figure 95 (A to D) shows a high double post sequence which is similar to those utilized in the low double post attack.

In this double post type of attack, the two centers must be aware of the fact that they have to maneuver the men guarding them so that the defense does not clog up the middle any more than has already been done. In addition, when any player is driving for the basket, he should be ready to pass off when he finds a defensive center picking him up. When this does occur, the center is open for a close shot at the basket.

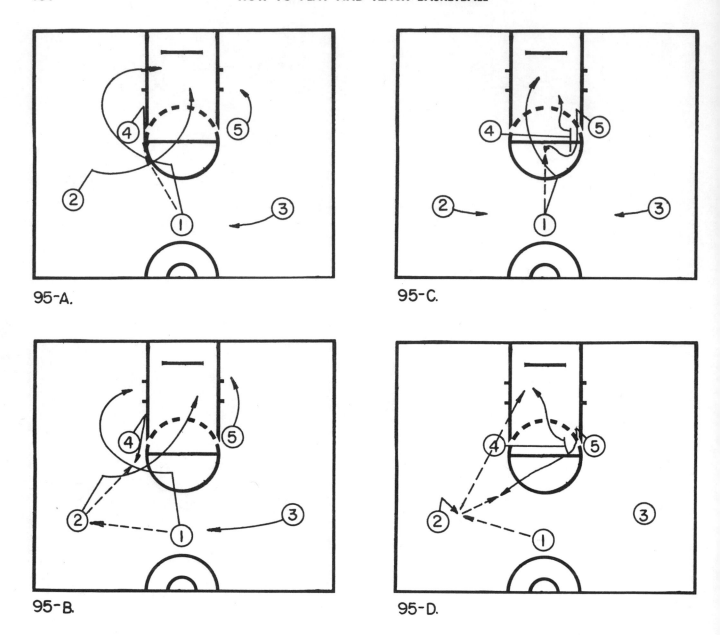

95-A.

95-C.

95-B.

95-D.

FIG. 95. HIGH DOUBLE POST. (A) ① passes to ④. ① and ② scissor by. (B) The same type of play, but the ball is passed into ④ by ②. (C) A screen by ④ to free ⑤ for a pass from ①. (D) ④ screens for ⑤ as ① passes to ②. ② can pass to ⑤ or to ④, who has rolled off of the screen to the basket.

FIG. 96. 3-2 OFFENSE. (A) The original setup. (B) ① passes to ②, screens, and rolls to the basket. ② dribbles around the screen. (C) ① passing to ③ and screening for ②. ② cuts by the screen as ③ passes to ⑤. ⑤ gives to ② for a lay-in shot. (D) The screen opposite of 96-C. ① passes to ② and screens for ③. ③ cuts by the screen and receives a pass from ②. (E) A sideline play. ② passes to ④ and screens and rolls to the basket. ④ dribbles around the screen. (F) A second man-around play. ② passes to ④ and clears to the other side of the court. ④ dribbles to the corner of the foul line and passes off to either ①, the first cutter, or ③, the second cutter, whichever is clear.

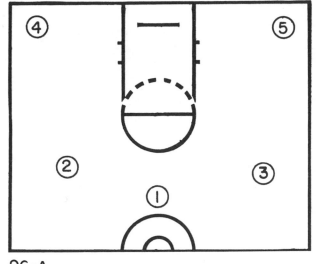

96-A.

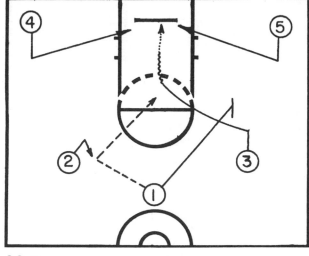

96-D.

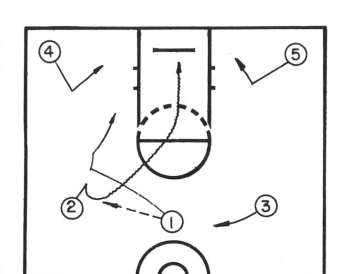

96-B.

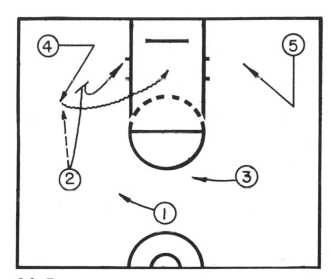

96-E.

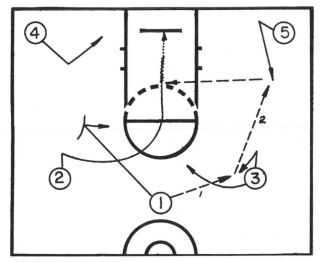

96-C.

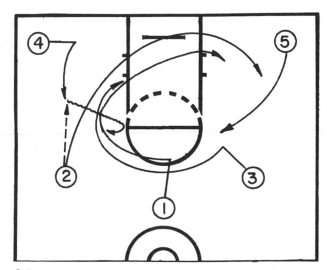

96-F.

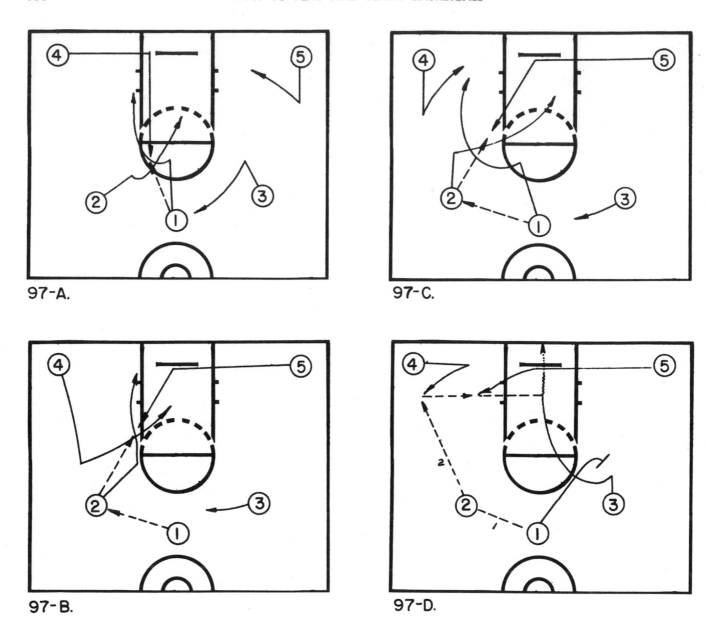

FIG. 97. 3-2 OFFENSE—FLASH TO THE PIVOT. (A) ④ flashes to the pivot. ① passes to ④, and ① and ② scissor by. (B) ⑤ flashes to the pivot spot, ① passes to ②, ② to ⑤, and ② and ④ scissor. (C) Another scissor play. ① gives to ②, and ⑤ flashes to the foul line. ② passes to ⑤, and ② and ① cut by. (D) ① passing to ② and screening for ③. ② gives to ④, who passes quickly to ⑤ in the pivot spot. ⑤ can shoot or give to ③.

Personnel

Two big centers are necessary in this type of offense. Strong rebounding is a must. The more mobile the centers, the farther they can effectively range from the basket.

The quarterback or number one guard must be the play-maker. He should have poise and be a good passer and dribbler.

The wing men should be good outside shots with the ability to pass and cut for the basket.

The Three-Two Offense

The three-two offense is essentially a wide double post attack in which the center is left open for drives up the middle or for occasional flashes to the post by either of the corner men.

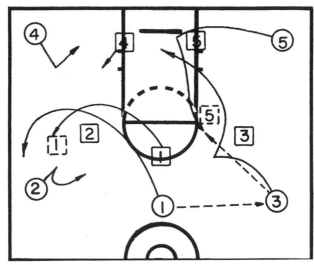

98-A.

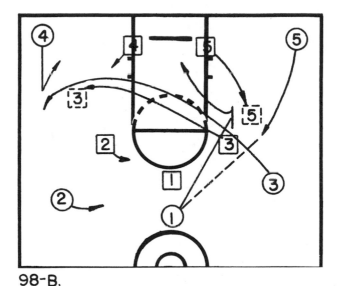

98-B.

FIG. 98. 3-2 OFFENSE VS. A CLOGGED CENTER. Often the defense will clog up the middle by sagging toward the basket. This can be countered by playing on one half of the court and clearing that half for the play. (A) ① passes to ③ and clears to the left side of the court. ⑤ breaks up the foul lane for a pass from ③. ③ and ⑤ now have one half of the court in which to maneuver. ③ cuts by ⑤. ⑤ can pass off to ③, turn and shoot, or drive and shoot. (B) ① passing behind ③'s back to ⑤. ① screens for ⑤. ⑤ can pass to ①, who rolls off of the screen, or go one-on-one.

Figure 96-A indicates the original setup, with the corner men positioned a step from the baseline and a step from the sideline. The wing men are a step in front of the middle guard and three to four steps in from the sideline.

Figure 96 (B to F) shows a sequence in which the middle is left open for driving.

When the centers flash into the post as is indicated in A, B, C, and D of Figure 97, the attack becomes similar to that of the double post offense.

It is imperative that a maneuver be installed to counter a defense which sags and clogs up the middle. Of course, the first answer is good outside shooting, but when that is not available, patterns such as are pictured in Figure 98 (A and B) should be used.

There are five main items which all players must consider in this type of offense. These are: (1) outside player movement; (2) movement of the ball; (3) feeding of the corner men by the outside wing men; (4) proper floor balance both offensively and defensively; and (5) assigned men rebounding on the offensive board.

Personnel

The number one player, the quarterback, should have poise, be a good dribbler and passer, and be able to start the plays.

The wing men should be fast, good ball handlers, hard drivers, and good outside shooters.

Corner men should be mobile and able to move into the post area and shoot or feed off.

This type of offense is often utilized when the personnel are small and no one player is strong enough to handle the post.

Free-Lance Offense

There are two distinct philosophies or theories which are of vital concern to every coach: they are the use of free-lance play vs. deliberate set patterns. A free-lance offense is one in which individual players are allowed great latitude of action. Their movements and actions are not governed by any set rule or rules of action. On the other end of the scale is the set pattern school of thought, in which each player's actions are prescribed until an opportunity to score presents itself.

Free-lance play usually stems from a regular formation such as a post or three-two setup. From then on, the players pass and cut, pass and screen, go one-on-one, shoot, and rebound strongly on the offensive board. Players work one-, two-, and three-man plays which stem from the defensive play of the opponents and from what has proven successful in the past.

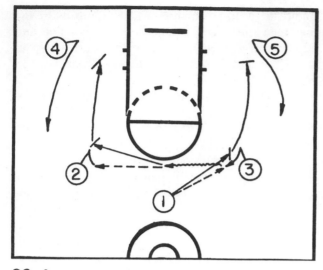

99-A.

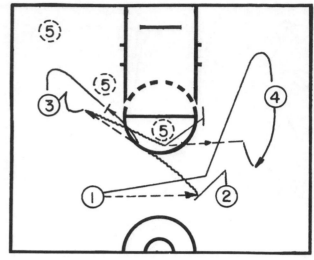

101-A.

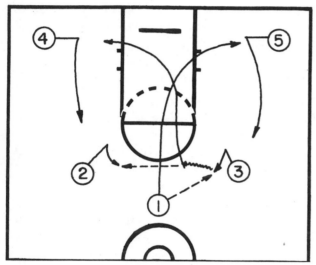

99-B.

101-B.

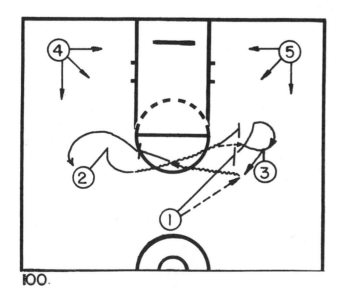

100.

FIG. 99. WEAVE: FLAT AND DEEP-CUT TYPES. (A) ① passes to ③ and screens ③'s defensive man. Each player in turn screens each time he passes an opponent in a flat type of weave. (B) The deep cut toward the basket each time the ball is passed off. ① passes to ③ and cuts directly toward the basket, ③ gives to ② and does the same type of cut.

FIG. 100. THE THREE-MAN WEAVE. ① passes to ③, screens for ③, and comes back toward ③'s original position. ③ dribbles toward ②, passes to ②, screens for ②, and comes back toward ②'s original position. This maneuver can be repeated indefinitely. Should each player cut sharply around the screen toward the basket, the figure-eight weave will move toward the basket.

FIG. 101. THE FOUR-MAN WEAVE. (A) The four outside men participate in the weave, while the center, ⑤, can be positioned in any one of a number of positions. (B) The center being used as a post man. He is stationed at the foul line, and men in the weave can use him as a screen. ③ does so in this case by dribbling as close as possible, then in toward the basket.

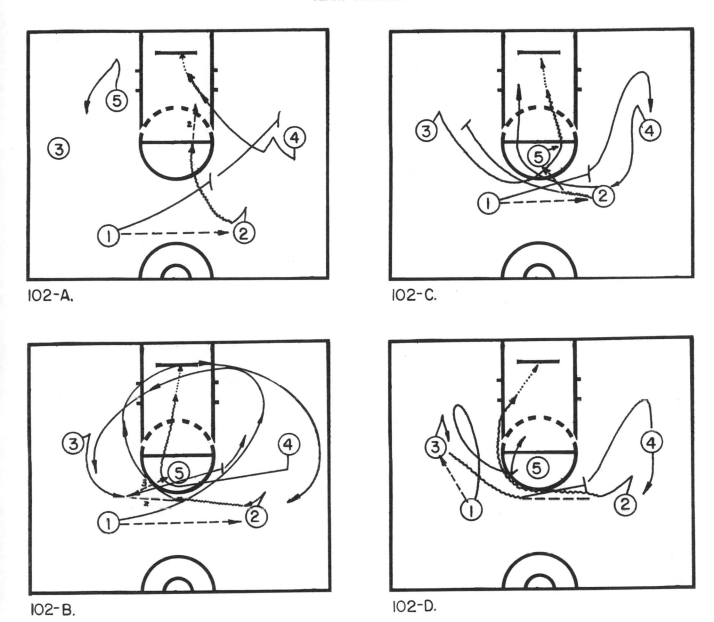

102-A.

102-C.

102-B.

102-D.

FIG. 102. PLAYS OFF OF THE FOUR-MAN WEAVE. (A) ① passes to ② and screens first for ②, then for ④. ② dribbles around the screen and passes to ④, who has cut off of ①'s screen. (B) ① passing to ② and clearing all the way. ② gives to ③ and clears all the way. ③ passes to ⑤ and screens for ④. ④ comes up the sideline and cuts by the screen by ③ and around ⑤ for a pass and a drive. (C) ① passes to ②, screens for ②, then continues on. ② dribbles, passes to ⑤, and screens for ③. ③ cuts around the screen and by ⑤ for a pass and a drive. ④ cuts off of ⑤ after ③ goes by. (D) ① starts the weave to ③. ③ gives to ② and screens for ②. ② dribbles around the screen by ③ and around a screen set by ①. Should men switch, ① will roll off to the basket.

Drills of all sorts are practiced, as is the one-on-one situation, with the players often using the drills as play patterns.

Personnel

Personnel requirements are such that good individ-ual offensive skills are necessary on the part of all the players. It is also necessary to have very strong re-bounding on the offensive board. It is imperative to have a good quarterback, so that the play does not stall. His responsibility is to "get things going."

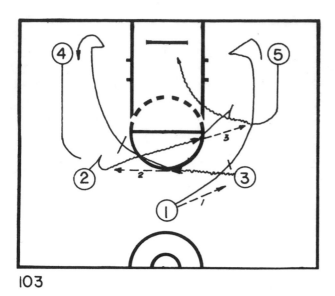

103

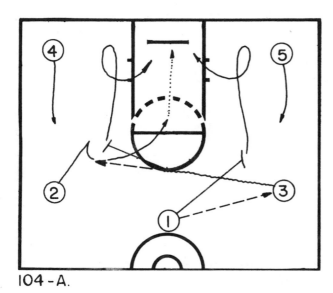

104-A.

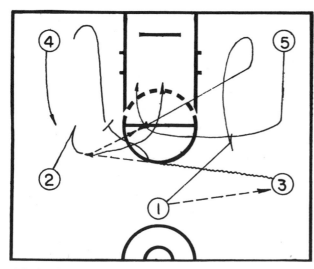

104-B.

Weaves or Figure-Eight Attacks

The weave or figure-eight attack is a continuity offense which utilizes a set or moving screen principle in which a defense is placed at a disadvantage by the movement of the offense. In general, the defensive man can be picked off, overplays, or is delayed in his movement. This type of defensive mistake enables the offensive player to get free for a shot or a drive at the basket.

The continuity of action places a burden on each defensive man, in that he has to guard men in all positions on the court, regardless of his size or normal defensive position. Each defensive man is kept busy following his man; consequently, little opportunity exists to aid other men should they need help defensively.

The continuity offense can be of the three-, four-, or five-man weave type. There can be a pivot man utilized as a post, or men can be designated who flash to the post. In addition to the above variations, the weave can be of the flat, moving screen type or of a deep-cut design.

In the flat weave, the players pass off and cut toward the defensive man to effect a moving screen every time the ball changes hands or when two offensive men pass one another. The deep cut results in a pass and a movement straight toward the basket and then back into the weave. These two distinct types of weaves are shown in Figure 99 (A and B).

The weave lends itself to situations where none, one, or two players can be left out of the weave with the continuity of movement still retaining its essential attributes.

Three-Man Weave

Figure 100 shows the three-man weave. The corner men, not being agile ball handlers, are kept out of the

FIG. 103. THE FIVE-MAN WEAVE. All five players participate in the weave. As each player passes off, he moves between the defensive man and the basket as either a stationary or moving screen. In this case, ① passes to ③, screens and goes to the corner. ③ dribbles toward ②, passes to ②, screens, and moves to the corner. ② dribbles toward ⑤, passes to ⑤, and screens. ⑤ drives around the screen for a score.

FIG. 104. PLAYS OFF OF THE FIVE-MAN WEAVE. (A) A typical jump shot from a five-man weave. ① passes to ③ and screens for ③. ③ dribbles toward ② and toward the basket, passes to ②, and screens for ②. ② comes over the screen with a dribble and gets a jump shot in the vicinity of the foul line. (B) ① flashes to the pivot position. The weave starts as in 104-A, but ① breaks from the corner toward ②. ② passes to ①, and ② and ⑤ scissor off of ①.

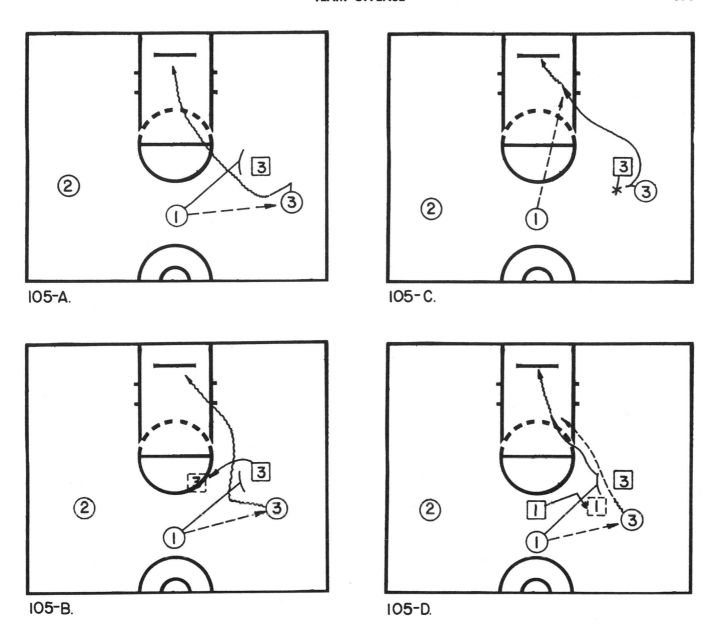

105-A.

105-C.

105-B.

105-D.

FIG. 105. MANEUVERS FROM THE WEAVE WHICH STEM FROM THE ACTIONS OF THE DEFENSE. (A) The defensive man, 3, being picked off by the screen. 3 goes free for a shot. (B) The situation of 3 anticipating a screen and getting ahead of 3. 3 dribbles, reverses, and goes in free for a shot. (C) The situation of an over-eager man who plays to intercept. 3 cuts behind and goes free for a pass for a shot. (D) The defensive men switch. In this case, 1 sets the screen and rolls off to the basket. 1 picks up 3, but the roll from the screen places 3 behind 1, and 1 goes free.

weave. They participate by cutting up the sidelines or going to the post position. This continuity with three men out can be set up with the inside men placed wide in the corners. This is the usual starting formation. In addition, the inside men can be stationed in a tandem post, a close double post, or any other position which would best suit their abilities. Of course, the main objective in weaving three men is to obtain a good percentage shot at the basket, and the best way to obtain this end is to drive up the middle; hence, the usual placement of the inside men wide in the corner.

Four-Man Weave

The four-man weave is pictured in Figure 101 (A and B). The center is positioned at the foul line to

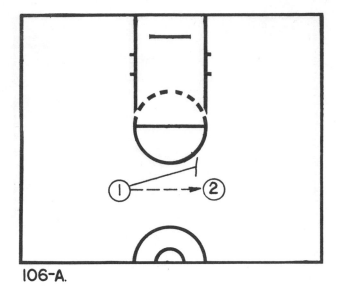

106-A.

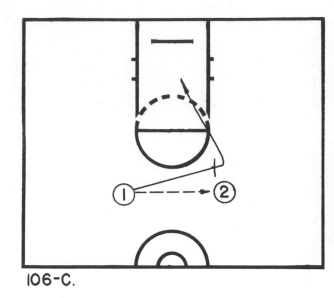

106-C.

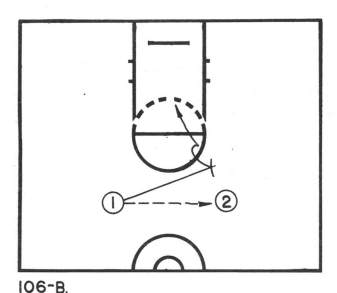

106-B.

FIG. 106. SCREEN MANEUVERS. (A) The guard-to-guard screen. (B) The guard-to-guard screen and roll. (C) The guard-to-guard fake screen and cut.

receive passes or to be a post and screen for men cutting by. He can also be placed along the foul lane or at one corner of the court. His mobility, shooting, and passing ability have to be considered when positioning him in this offense.

Basic plays off this four-man weave are indicated in Figure 102 (A to D).

Five-Man Weave

A five-man weave is pictured in Figure 103. Each man participates in the weave; consequently, each has to be a threat and a ball handler. Typical plays from a weave are shown in Figure 104 (A and B).

Often one, two, or more players are designated centers and are given the option of flashing to the post instead of coming up the sideline in the regular weave. This takes defensive men, who are unaccustomed to defensing a man in this area, into a difficult defensive situation. Flashing into the pivot also takes advantage of the special abilities of a player and allows him to have some freedom of action within the framework of the offense.

Maneuvers Off the Weave

There are various maneuvers that are utilized in conjunction with the weave. These maneuvers are counters to actions by the defense. Figure 105 (A to D) indicates four of these basic movements. When the defensive man gets picked off, the opponent drives or cuts for the basket. Should the defensive man get ahead of the dribbler, the dribbler reverses back and drives. If the defensive man overplays his opponent who does not have the ball, the offensive man cuts behind the eager defensive man toward the basket. Should the defensive players switch men, the screener immediately calls and cuts for the basket. Each player in the weave reacts to the actions of the defense in an action-counteraction type of reaction. These movements must be natural reactions; consequently, each player must know the options and react to them naturally.

Passes in the weave attack are of three general types. The first is a chest or bounce pass to the man

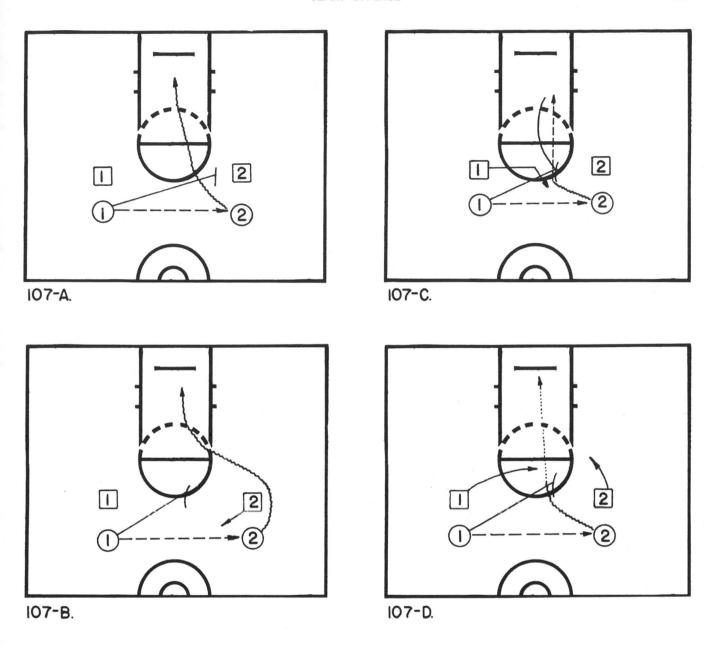

FIG. 107. MANEUVERS TO BE USED BY THE MAN WITH THE BALL WHEN A SCREEN HAS BEEN SET. (A) Dribble around screen. (B) Go away from the screen when the defensive man anticipates a screen and starts to fight through. (C) Dribble, stop, and pass off to screener who has rolled off. (D) Shoot over the screen, because defense has dropped back.

coming to meet the ball. When the defensive man is close to his opponent, the ball should be directed to the offensive man's outside hand, the one away from the defensive man. The second type of pass is the hand-off. The ball is handed to a teammate as he cuts closely by. The ball is actually handed off about waist high. The third pass is a dribble pass, in which the man coming to meet the dribbler takes the ball as it comes off the floor as a result of a dribble.

Personnel

The players in this type of offense have to be good ball handlers. They should be good at driving and experienced in the movements and reactions necessary

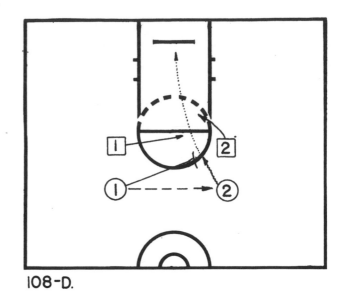

108-A.

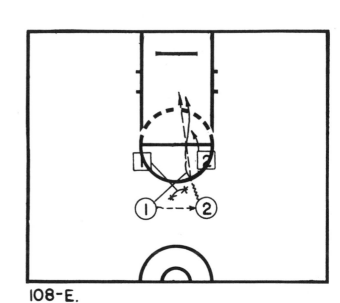

108-D.

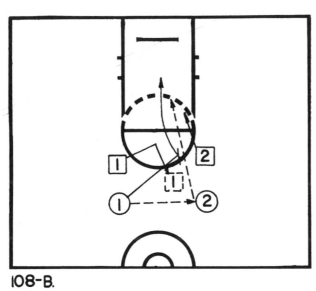

108-B.

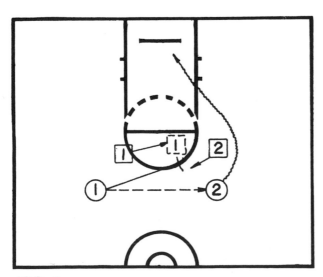

108-E.

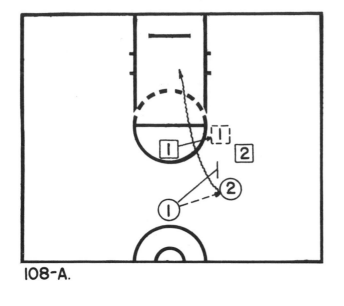

108-C.

Fig. 108. Maneuvers Which Stem from Defensive Actions against a Screen. (A) *Defense stays man-to-man.* Man with ball dribbles behind screen for drive to the basket. ① passes to ②. ② drives around the screen. (B) *Defense switches.* Screen rolls to basket. ① passes to ②, screens, and rolls. ② passes back to ①. (C) *Defense anticipates a screen and starts to fight through.* Man with ball goes opposite screen. ① passes to ② and screens. ② fights through, enabling ② to go opposite the screen for a drive to the basket. (D) *Defense goes behind the screen.* Man with ball is momentarily free for a shot over the screen. ① passes to ② and screens. ① and ② drop back, enabling ② to get off a good shot. (E) *Defense quick-shifts.* The screener rolls and the man with the ball quickly passes it off before he is tied up. ① passes to ② and screens. ① and ② quick-switch. ② passes to ①.

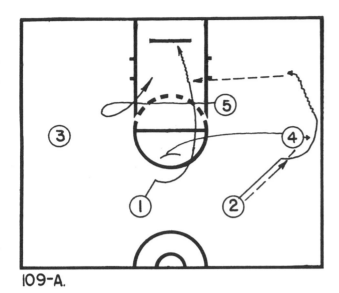

109-A.

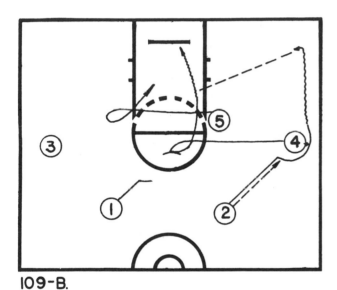

109-B.

Fig. 109. Screen Plays. (A) ② passes to ④, cuts by ④, receives the ball, and dribbles to the corner of the court. ④ moves toward the foul line and sets a screen for ①. ① cuts around ④ for a pass from ① and a lay-in shot. (B) A variation of 109-A. The play is identical except that ④ sets a screen and, anticipating the defense switching men, rolls off of the screen to the basket. ② to ④ for a shot.

for this offense. When tall men are available, they can be placed in a post, double post, or similar position to fully realize their talents. But if one is not available, a four- or five-man weave can be used. If a player does not fit into the weave because he does not have the necessary talent, he can be placed in a corner and a four-man weave developed. This variation makes it possible either to utilize the strong points of a par-

ticular player or to minimize his weak points. His rebounding and defensive abilities are still available.

Screen Attack

The screen attack is based upon the fact that a screen, an obstacle, is placed in the path of the defensive man. When the guard is forced to detour or when defensive men switch opponents, an offensive man has an opportunity to go free.

An attack of this type has many variations. Play can be with rules or set plays. Set and moving screens are used, and in addition, the offense can start from a variety of original setups.

Screen Plays

An example of play with rules would be to pass and screen. This one rule will provide a variety of situations, mostly between the guard and guard, the guard and forward, and the forward and guard. In each case, the screener can screen, screen and roll, and fake screen and cut.

Guard-to-Guard screens. Both guard-to-guard screens are described in Figure 106 (A to C). The man who sets the screen can screen, screen and roll, or fake to screen and cut.

Figure 107 (A to D) depicts the maneuvers to be made by the man with the ball, for when the screen is set the man with the ball can dribble around the screen, dribble away from the screen, pass off to the screener who has rolled off, or shoot over the screen. The same situations are presented in guard-to-forward and forward-to-guard screens, except that the screen comes from another direction.

The action of the defense presents the offense with opportunities to go free. Figure 108 (A to E) offers these maneuvers. Generally speaking, when the defense plays strict man to man, the screen should free the man with the ball for a dribble drive by the screen. On the other hand, when the defense switches, the screen-and-roll is designed to free the screener. Should the defensive man anticipate a screen and start to fight through it, the man with the ball can dribble-drive opposite the screen. When the defense attempts to evade the screen by going behind it, the man with the ball has the opportunity for a shot over the screen. A good defensive tactic is the quick or early switch. This is combated by a screen-and-roll and by the man with the ball getting it up in the air for a quick pass to the screener.

Set screen plays can be practiced and used as individual plays. Figure 109-A shows guard cutting around a *screen set behind* or on the blind side of his defensive man. Figure 109-B indicates a variation of the above play.

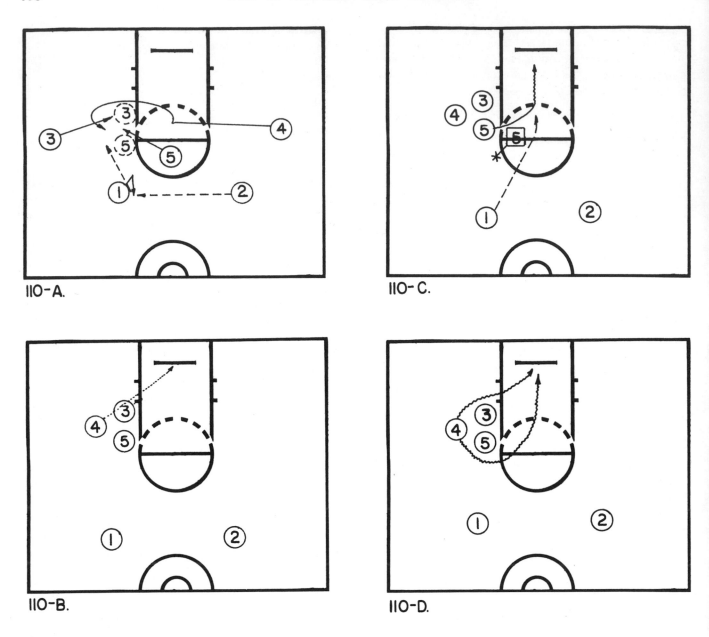

FIG. 110. DOUBLE SCREEN PLAY. The four frames show a double screen play with options. (A) How the play starts. On a signal, ② passes to ①, while ④ moves across the court. ⑤ and ③ line up outside of, but along, the foul lane. ④ breaks up behind the double screen for a pass from ①. (B) This is the setup with ④ in possession of the ball. ④ shoots. (C) When ① observes an eager defensive man trying to cut off a pass in to ④, he can give to ⑤ for a shot or a drive to the basket. (D) The last option, ④ dribbling opposite the way that his defensive man goes. He can dribble all the way or stop for a shot.

A double screen play which offers a variety of options is portrayed in Figure 110 (A to D).

An excellent play is shown in Figure 111-A, while Figure 111-B gives another screen play with its various options.

A center-to-forward screen play is shown in Figure 112.

Personnel

The personnel for a screen attack should be good ball handlers, versatile, so that they are quick to take advantage of a wrong move by the defense, and well drilled in the screen options. The forwards should be rangy, good drivers and have good outside shots. The center can be utilized to his best advantage. If he is strong and a good scorer, he can play in the pivot. If short and agile, he could play in the corner. The guards initiate the plays and must be good play-makers and drivers.

Offensive Patterns with Turnovers or Continuities

An offense of this type has player continuity in which men move to one position and then another in a regular order when one play option does not materialize. This going from one setup to another with another option available after the first has failed does not require a complete rebalance, with players going back to their original positions. Each player plays in two or more positions within the complete turnover and, in doing so, takes his guard into a defensive position to which that guard is not accustomed.

Offenses of the turnover type combine the many different methods used to score: the one-on-one, the pivot play, the screen, and the pass and cut. Also, each player is given the opportunity to participate in each within the framework of the entire pattern.

Offered in this section are five basic offenses which are used to illustrate different types of turnover patterns.

Drake Shuffle

"This offense eliminates a nemesis of set-plays—that of having to set up after the play has failed to score. Beginning with an overload on one side of the floor, the shuffle has three options in the basic pattern. Once these three options have been run through by a team, the players should be in an overload position on the opposite side of the floor ready to repeat the series with no necessity for setting up again."[1]

---

[1] Glenn Wilkes, *Winning Basketball Strategy* (New York: Prentice-Hall, Inc., 1959), p. 16.

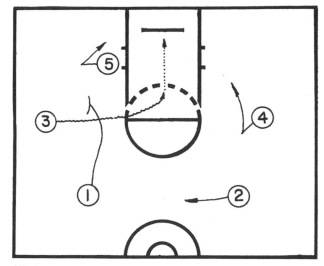

III-A.

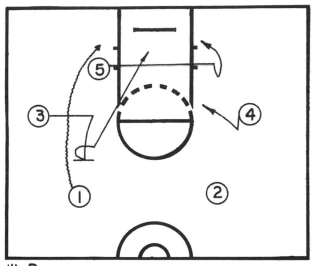

III-B.

FIG. 111. SCREEN PLAYS. (A) ① passes to ③, breaks toward the basket, and comes to a fast stop just inside an extension of the foul line. ③ dribbles around the screen for a drive or a jump shot. (B) ③ sets a screen behind ①'s defensive man. ① dribbles to the outside around the screen. ③ rolls off, ⑤ clears, and ① has the option of driving or giving the ball to ③, depending upon the actions of the defensive men.

FIG. 112. SCREEN PLAY: CENTER-TO-FORWARD SCREEN. This very popular play breaks the weak side forward clear in the vicinity of the foul lane and provides opportunities for good shots. ② passes to ④ and cuts by toward the corner of the court. ⑤ screens for ③. ③ can go to either side and goes opposite the way his defensive man goes. ④ gives to ③ for a shot or a drive to the basket.

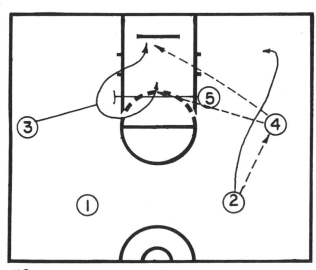

112.

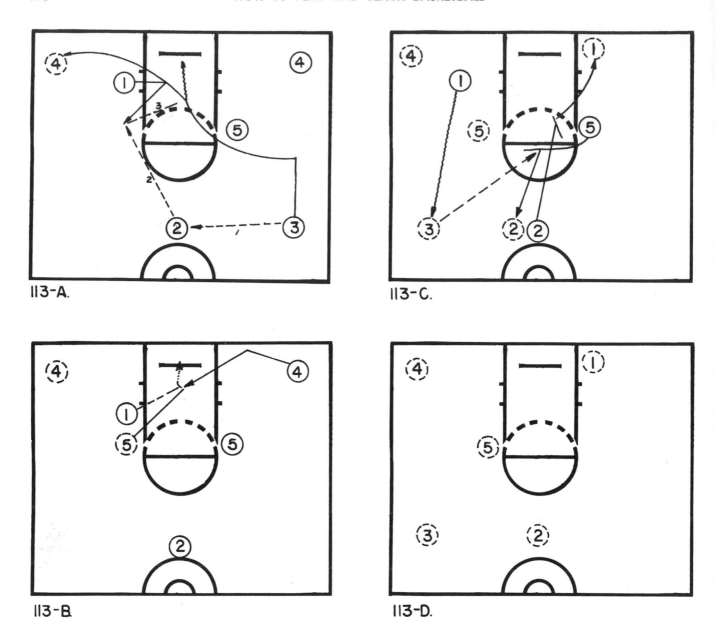

113-A.   113-C.

113-B.   113-D.

FIG. 113. THE DRAKE SHUFFLE: A CONTINUITY OFFENSE. (A) The basic pattern for the Drake Shuffle is shown from the right side of the floor. ③ to ② to ①. ③ cuts up and by ⑤ to the basket. ① gives to ③. If ③ is not clear, he becomes the new ④ on the left side of the court. (B) ① has the ball. ④ breaks toward the basket toward ①, ① to ④ for a shot. If ④ is covered, he continues to become the new ⑤. (C) ① dribbles out and becomes the new ③. ⑤ cuts around the screen for a pass from ③. If ⑤ is covered, he continues out and becomes the new ②. (D) The players are now back to the original setup, but on the left side of the floor ready to continue the offense without unnecessary movement of men.

This offensive pattern is named after Bruce Drake and was originated by him when he was at the University of Oklahoma. The Drake Shuffle offense is becoming popular throughout the United States, and many teams have used it with exceptional success.

Although there are many options, the basic pattern with its three options plus two variations will be described.

Figure 113 (A to D) describes the complete shuffle from the overload on the right to the overload on the left. Three options are available within the one turnover, and they include a pass and cut-off, a stationary screen, pivot post play, a one-on-one situation, plus a give-and-go.

Figures 114 (A and B) and 115 (A and B) offer variations to the basic Drake Shuffle pattern. In Fig-

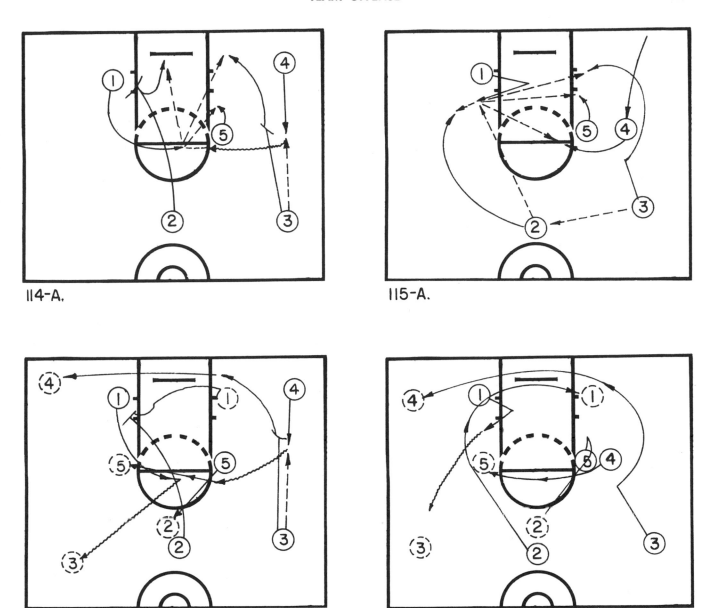

114-A.

115-A.

114-B.

115-B.

FIG. 114. VARIATIONS OFF OF THE DRAKE SHUFFLE. (A) ③ passes to ④ breaking up the sideline. ③ screens for ④, allowing ④ to dribble around the screen into the foul lane. ② screens for ① and rolls to the basket. ④ can pass to ②, ①, or ⑤. (B) If the play does not work, each player continues to his next assigned position: ① to ③, ② to ①, ③ to ④, ④ to ⑤, and ⑤ to ②.

FIG. 115. VARIATIONS OFF OF THE DRAKE SHUFFLE. (A) ④ sets up alongside ⑤. ③ passes to ② and cuts outside of ④ to the basket. ② passes to ① and cuts outside ①. ④ breaks over ⑤ to the foul line. ⑤ rolls to the basket. ① can pass to: ③ cutting around the double screen; to ④ cutting around ⑤; to ⑤ if the guards cross; or to ① for a set shot. (B) If the play does not provide a good shot, each man continues on to his next position and play continues: ① to ③, ② to ①, ③ to ④, ④ to ⑤, and ⑤ to ②.

ure 114-A, a screen is used to free a forward in the vicinity of the foul lane. Multiple options stem off this guard-to-forward screen. In Figure 115-A, the forward sets up alongside the center, with the guard cutting around a double screen. In each case, should the scoring opportunity fail to materialize, the players move to their assigned positions and play continues with the next option. Figures 114-B and 115-B show this movement.

This type of offense requires players who are good

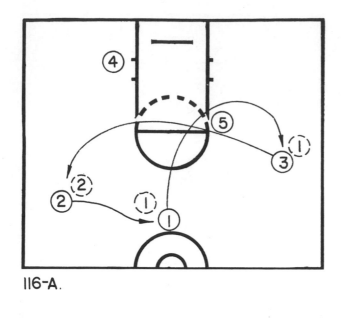

116-A.

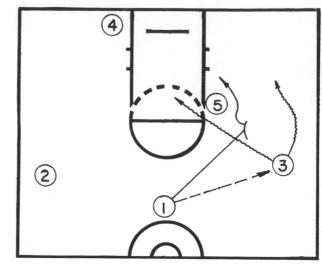

117-B.

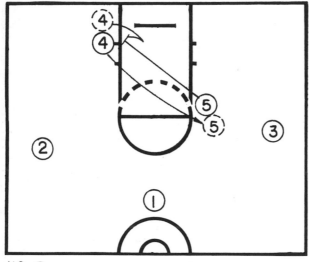

116-B.

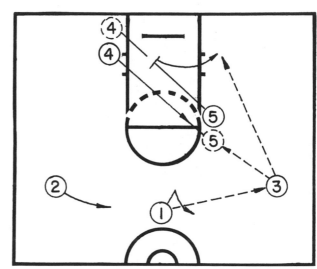

117-C.

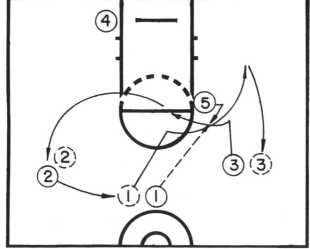

117-A.

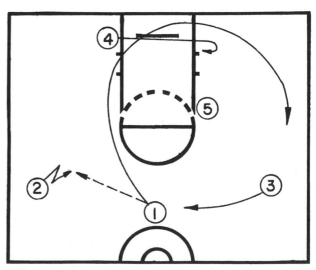

117-D.

FIG. 116. THE TANDEM POST: A CONTINUITY OFFENSE. (A) *The outside men's turn-over.* ① replaces ③, ② takes ①'s place, while ③ moves to ②'s spot. (B) *The center's movement or shuffle.* ⑤ shuttles, screens for ④, and takes ④'s place. ④ comes by the screen toward the ball. If ④ does not get the ball, he becomes ⑤.

FIG. 117. THE TANDEM POST SHUFFLE: A CONTINUITY OFFENSE. (A) *Split the post and outside rotation.* ① passes to ⑤. ① and ③ split the post. If nothing develops, ① takes ③'s position, ③ to ②'s, and ① to ③'s. They are now balanced and can start again. (B) *A screen.* ① passes to ③ and sets an inside screen. ③ has the following options: dribble around the screen and by ⑤ for a drive or a shot; go opposite the screen; or pass to ①, rolling off of the screen as the defense switches. (C) *The centers' movements when they change position.* If the defense switches as the centers shuffle, the man going toward the baseline quickly comes back for a pass, ① to ③. ③ can pass to ④, who becomes ⑤, or to ⑤ rolling back for a pass. (D) *An opportunity for a one-on-one.* ① passes to ② and clears. As ① clears, so does ④. ② now has half of the court in which to maneuver against his opponent.

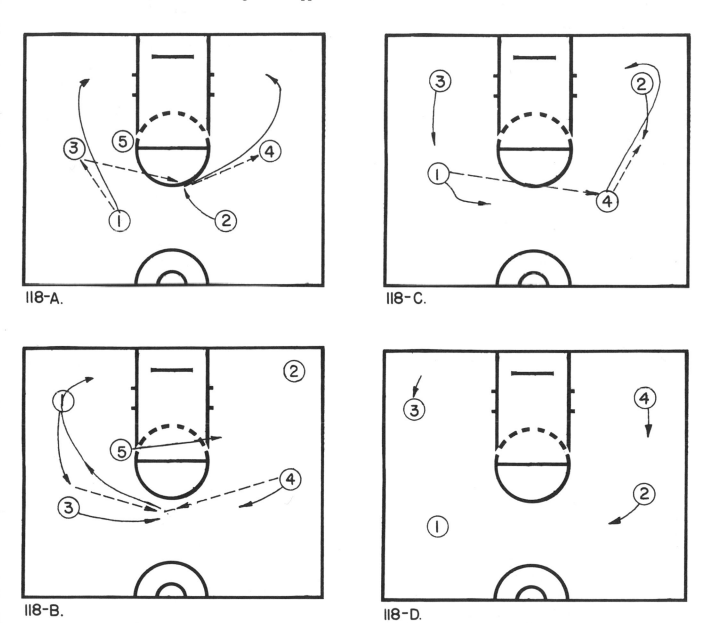

118-A.

118-C.

118-B.

118-D.

FIG. 118. SIDE SHUFFLE OFFENSE: A CONTINUITY OFFENSE. A complete turnover is shown. (A) ① passes to ③ and cuts to the corner. ③ passes to ②. ② gives to ④ and cuts to the corner. (B) ④ passes to ③. ③ passes to ① and cuts to the corner. (C) ① passes to ④, ④ to ②, and ④ cuts to the corner. (D) Players are now back to their original positions. If the defense plays aggressive ball, the side men can shuttle before they receive the ball. This shuttle will produce a screen and free the men coming to meet the ball.

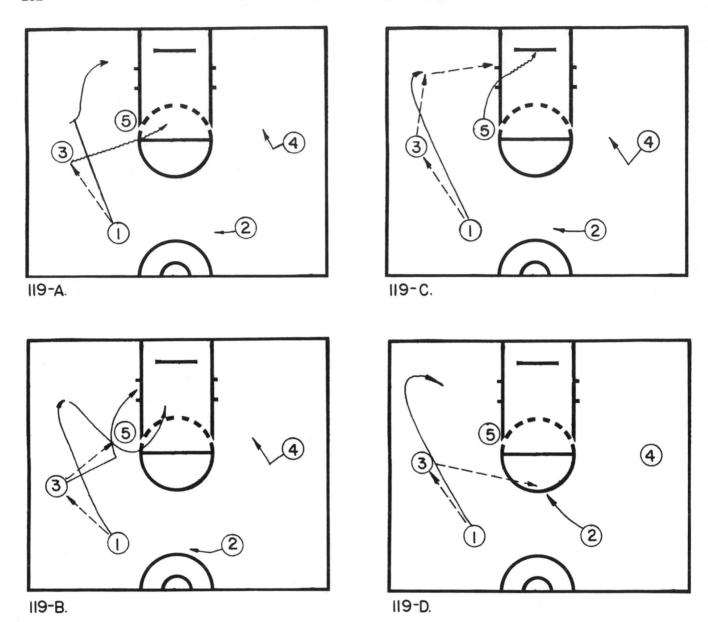

119-A.

119-C.

119-B.

119-D.

Fig. 119. Play Patterns Off of the Side Shuttle Offense. (A) ① passes to ③ and screens as he goes by. ③ dribbles around ① and ⑤. (B) ① passes to ③ and goes to the corner. ③ passes to ⑤. ③ and ① cut by ⑤. (C) ① passes to ③ and goes to the corner. ③ passes back to ①, while ⑤ goes down the foul line for a pass from ①. (D) ① passes to ③ and cuts to the corner. The defense sags. ③ passes to ② for a set shot. (E) ① passes to ③ and cuts to the corner. ⑤ clears as ④ moves into the pivot position. ③ passes to ④ and ④ to ②. ② can drive or, if the defense has sagged, shoot. (F) ① to ③ to ④ as in 119-E. If ②'s defensive man, [2], plays high to prevent a pass, ② can go for the basket and receive a pass from ④. (G) ① passes to ⑤ and cuts to the corner. ③ cuts off of ①'s heels and around ⑤ for a pass and a drive. (H) ① to ③. ③ passes to ②. ② to ④ just as if to change sides, but ⑤ moves over and down the lane for a pass from ④ for a lay-in.

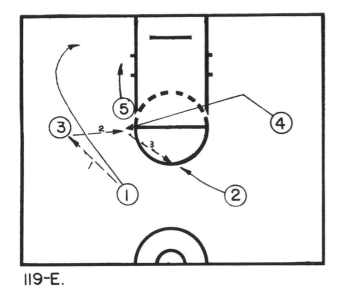

119-E.

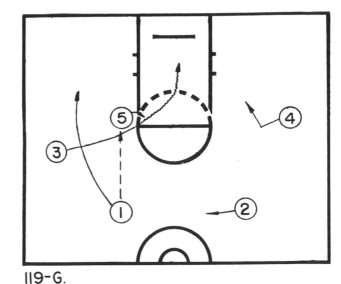

119-G.

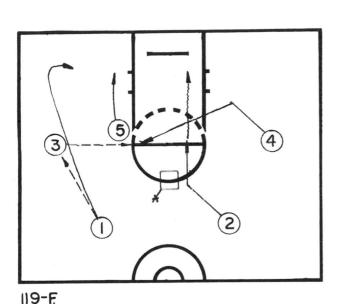

119-F.

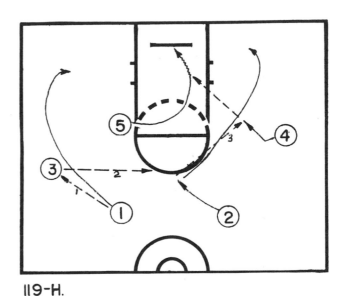

119-H.

ball handlers and who are versatile and have practiced so that they are ready to play each position with ease. Height is not necessary, and often a small guard can play in the pivot position. Balanced height would be ideal.

Tandem Post Shuffle

In this shuffle pattern, the post men shuffle and the three outside men change positions.

The outside men's turnover is shown in Figure 116-A, and the center shuffle in Figure 116-B. Play patterns from this offense are described in Figure 117 (A to D.)

Good pivot men are necessary in this offense. They

must be scorers, rebounders, and passers. The three outside men should be good outside shooters and have the ability to give and go, pass and screen, and roll.

Side Shuffle Offense

In this pattern the outside men, the guards and forwards, shuffle, while the center remains in the pivot position. Figure 118 (A to D) indicates the complete turnover back to the original position.

Figure 119 (A to H) shows the various patterns possible under this shuttle offense. The patterns are of the single pivot offense type.

A good rebounding center who can score is valu-

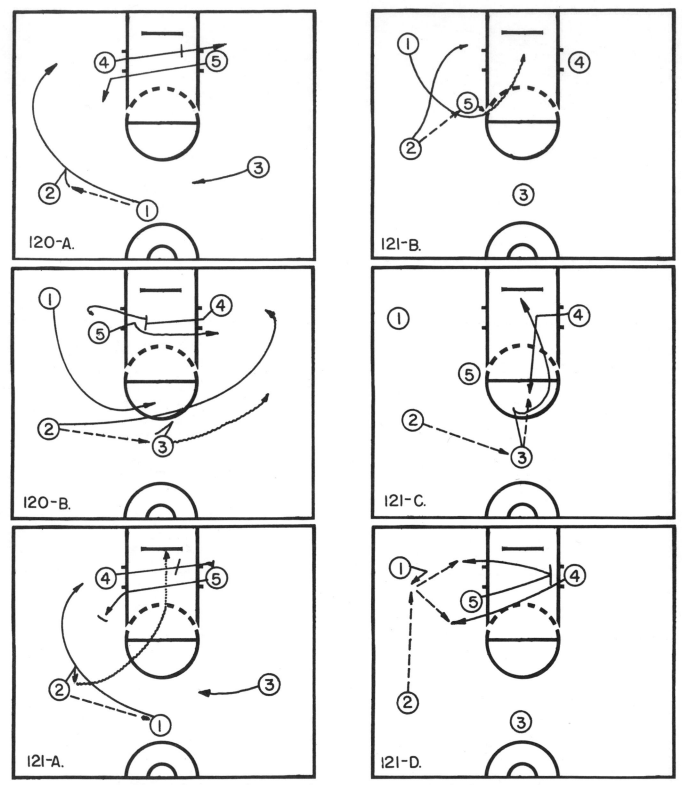

FIG. 120. CENTER SHUFFLE: A CONTINUITY OFFENSE. (A) The basic movement. ①
passes to ② and cuts to the corner. ③ replaces ①. (B) The movement to the right
side of the floor from the left side. ② passes to ③ and cuts to the right corner. ③ dribbles to his right and back to his original position. ① comes back to his original position.

FIG. 121. CENTER SHUFFLE PLAY PATTERNS. (A) ① passes to ②, while ④ and ⑤ shuffle. ② dribbles off of ①'s heels and around ⑤ for a shot. (B) ② passes to ⑤ and cuts between ① and ⑤. ① cuts off of ②'s heels and around ⑤. ⑤ gives to ①. (C) A weak-
side play. ② gives to ③. ③ feeds ④ and cuts by. ④ can either give to ③ early or
late, turn and shoot, or drive. (D) ② passes to ① as ⑤ and ④ shuttle. ⑤ comes back
toward the ball along the baseline, while ④ comes high. ① can pass to either.

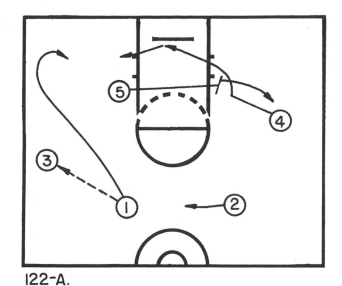

122-A.

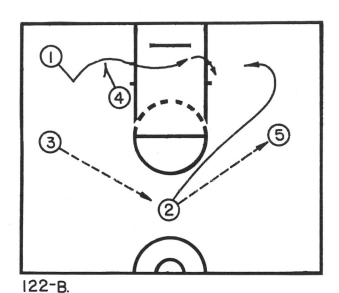

122-B.

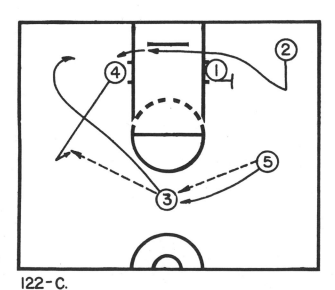

122-C.

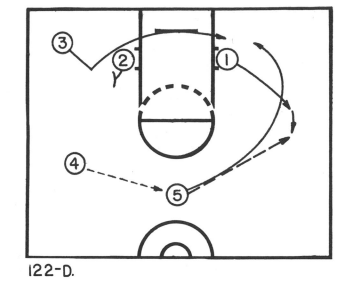

122-D.

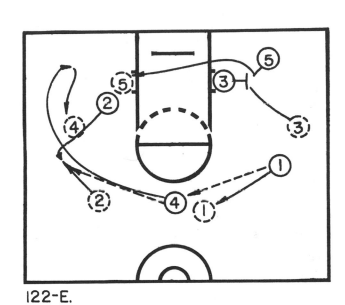

122-E.

FIG. 122. CENTER SCREEN: A CONTINUITY OFFENSE. A complete turnover from the left to the right side of the court. (A) ① to ③, ① to corner, ⑤ screens for ④. ④ is now the center, ⑤ and ① the forwards, and ③ and ② the guards. (B) ③ to ② to ⑤, ② to corner, ④ screens for ①. ① is now the center, ② and ④ the forwards, and ⑤ and ③ the guards. (C) ⑤ passes to ③, ③ to ④, ③ to corner, ① screens for ②. ② is now the center, ③ and ① the forwards, and ⑤ and ④ the guards. (D) ④ passes to ⑤ and ⑤ to ①. ⑤ goes to the corner, while ② screens for ③. ③ is now the center, ② and ⑤ the forwards, and ④ and ① the guards. (E) ① passes to ④, ④ to ②, ④ goes to the corner. ③ screens for ⑤. The players are now back in their respective positions but on the opposite side of the court.

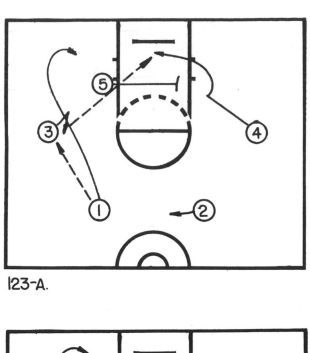

123-A.

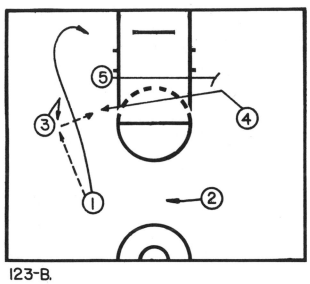

123-B.

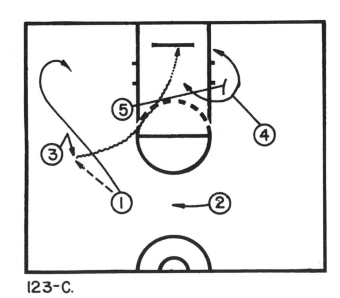

123-C.

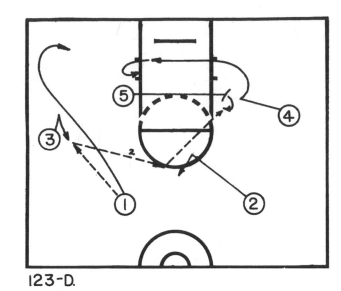

123-D.

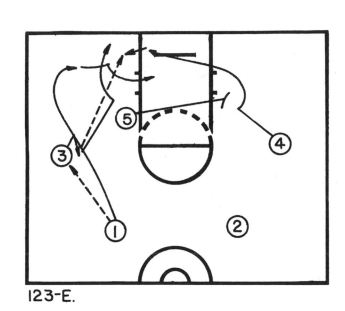

123-E.

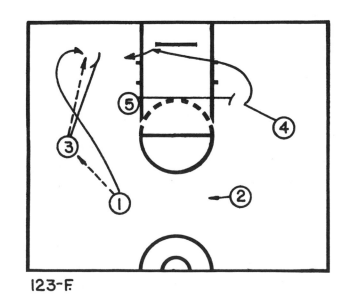

123-F.

able in this offense. The guards and forwards, because the positions are interchangeable should all be good passers, drivers, and good shots.

Center Shuffle Attack

As in the tandem post shuffle, this attack combines a shuttle of the double post men laterally and an interchange of positions between the three outside men. Figure 120 (A and B) indicates the player movement in the center shuffle attack.

This attack is essentially a double post attack, but with player movement designed to keep the defense busy following their opponents. Figure 121 (A to D) pictures basic plays from this attack. Personnel necessary are similar to that of the tandem post shuffle attack described above.

Center Screen Offense

This offense is one in which a pivot man is used in the pivot position and the player movement brings each player into this position. The center screen and side shuttle of the outside men provide player movement which is designed to keep the defense busy and concerned with the particular man he is guarding, whether it be in the guard, forward, or center positions.

Figure 122 (A to E) points out the complete turn-over and movement of each player back to the original positions. Play patterns are indicated in Figure 123 (A to F). They provide an excellent variety of offensive situations, including: the one-on-one, the screen, the give-and-go, and pivot play.

Personnel

Players in this offense must be versatile, in that they play each position. Balanced height is excellent for this attack, but if a good pivot man is available, he can be positioned in the pivot position to start the action. Good ball handling is essential.

FIG. 123. CENTER SCREEN PLAY PATTERNS. (A) *The center screen with the forward low.* ① passes to ③ and goes to the corner. ⑤ screens for ④. ③ passes to ④ for a shot. (B) *The center screen with the forward high.* ① passes to ③ and goes to the corner. ⑤ screens for ④. ③ passes to ④, and ④ can shoot or pass to either ① or ③ cutting by. (C) *The forward drive behind the screen.* ① passes to ③. ③ drives off of ①'s heels for a lay-in. ⑤ screens, which clears the middle. (D) *Center shot or drive.* ① gives to ③ and goes to the corner. ⑤ screens for ④ and steps back to receive the ball. ③ to ② to ⑤. ⑤ can shoot or drive. (E) *The center play.* ① passes to ③ and goes to the corner. ⑤ screens for ④. ③ gives to ④, and ③ and ① cut off of ④. (F) *The corner play.* ① gives to ③ and goes to the corner. ⑤ screens while ③ passes to ① and screens for ①. ① can shoot or drive by the screen.

Zone Offenses

In order to plan a zone attack, one must thoroughly understand the basic reasons a zone defense is employed. When these reasons are understood, the attack can be prepared to counter these measures.

1. Mass the defense between the ball and the basket.
2. Strong rebounding.
3. Men play the ball instead of the man and secure interceptions and loose balls.
4. Men shift in relation to the movement of the ball and attempt to cut off passing lanes into the zone.
5. When guarding the man with the ball, the defensive man can take liberties because he has teammates to back him up should he be evaded by the offensive man.
6. Change from the zone defense to offense is rapid and organized, as men are always in the same relative defensive position on the court.
7. The zone type of defense wants the opponents to: dribble, make slow passes, hold the ball, make cross-court passes, or bunch the offensive players.

Counter measures to the above defensive techniques are the answer:

1. The most effective way to attack a zone defense is to score or obtain a good shot before the zone defense can be organized. This is the fast break offense.
2. Organize a set attack which is effective against a massed defense. This can be by an overload, by the use of cuts, by a player rotation, or with screens.
3. Good ball handling, short fast passes, either high or low, and good shooting are effective measures against the zone.
4. Move the ball and wait for a good percentage shot. This will cause the zone to shift and present openings in the defense.
5. Definite rebounding assignments are made, which enables the team to have strong offensive rebounding.
6. Spread and balance the attack. Spread the defense and balance for offensive rebounding and defensive balance.

Methods of Attacking Zone Defenses

In general, there are four methods or techniques of attacking zone defenses: the overload, the cut, the rotation, and the screen. Offenses can be designed which incorporate one, two, three, or all four of these methods.

The overload principle. This method of attacking zone defenses places men in and around the zone in such a manner that the offensive men outnumber the defensive men in certain areas of the floor. Rapid movement of the ball to men in this area will sooner or later produce a good shot at the basket.

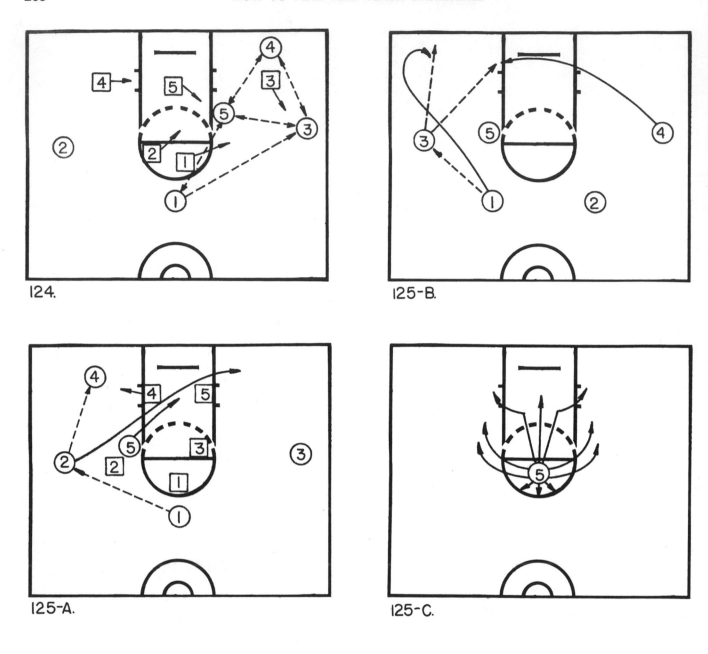

FIG. 124. OVERLOAD PRINCIPLE. ①, ③, and ⑤ outnumber ☐1 and ☐5. ①, ③, ⑤, and ④ outnumber ☐1, ☐5, and ☐3. ①, ③, ④, and ⑤ outnumber ☐1, ☐3, and ☐5.

FIG. 125. MANEUVERS USED AGAINST A ZONE DEFENSE. (A) The cut used against the zone. ① to ② to ④. ② cuts toward the basket, after which ⑤ cuts into the same path. The following options are available, depending upon the actions of the defense: shot by ④ if ☐4 does not guard him; ④ to ② cutting for the basket; if ☐2 picks up ②, ⑤ will be clear. (B) ① passes to ③ and cuts inside ③ to the corner. ④ cuts along the baseline and under the basket. ③ passes to ④ if defense covers ①; otherwise, ① will be free for a pass and a shot. (C) The position and moves possible by a center at the foul line.

Figure 124 pictures an overload with the offense in a 1-3-1 offensive setup against a 2-3 zone. Movement of the ball between men in the offense results in a percentage shot at the basket.

The cut. The cut is a means of having men cut into open areas in the zone or move between layers of the zone and force the defensive men to make a choice of whether to guard the cutter or the man already stationed in that area. These are shown in Figure 125 (A and B). The center man is in a position to be very

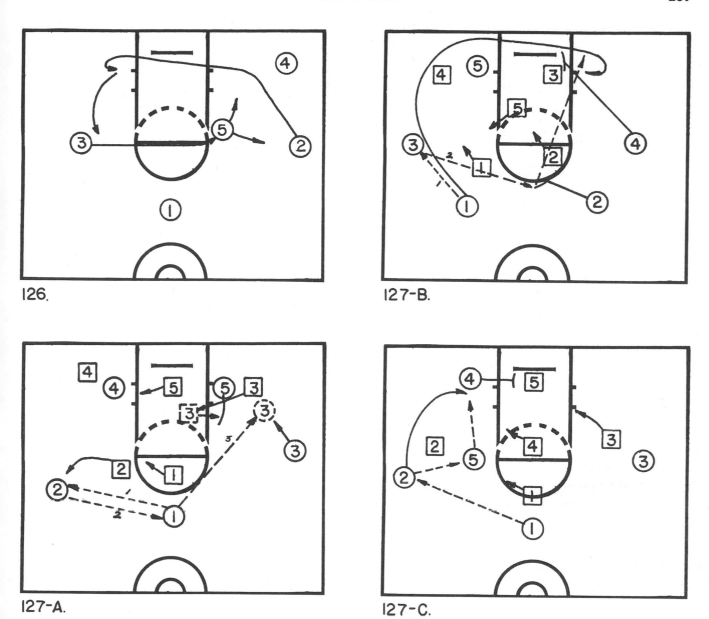

126.

127-B.

127-A.

127-C.

FIG. 126. ROTATION: AN OFFENSE VS. A ZONE DEFENSE. ②, ⑤, and ③ rotate from one position to another as indicated. The players move after the ball has been passed or as they see an opening.

FIG. 127. SCREEN PLAYS AGAINST A ZONE. (A) ③ gets a shot over and behind ⑤ against a 2-3 zone. ① to ② to ①. ⑤ screens ③. ① to ③ for a shot. (B) ① gets a shot over and behind ④ vs. a 2-1-2 zone. ① to ③. ① cuts by ③ and under the basket. ④ screens ③. ③ passes to ② and ② to ① behind the screen for a shot. (C) ② shoots from behind ④ vs. a 1-3-1 zone. ① to ② and ② to ⑤. ④ screens ⑤ while ② moves into ④'s former position for a pass from ⑤ and a shot.

effective in this method of attacking a zone. Figure 125-C shows how he can move to meet the ball from within a zone.

The rotation. This method of attacking the zone is by rotation or a continuity of movement. Figure 126

indicates such an offense, with the center and two forwards rotating from one position to another. This offense combines the cuts and the overload to produce an effective zone offense.

The screen. The zone can be screened, and there

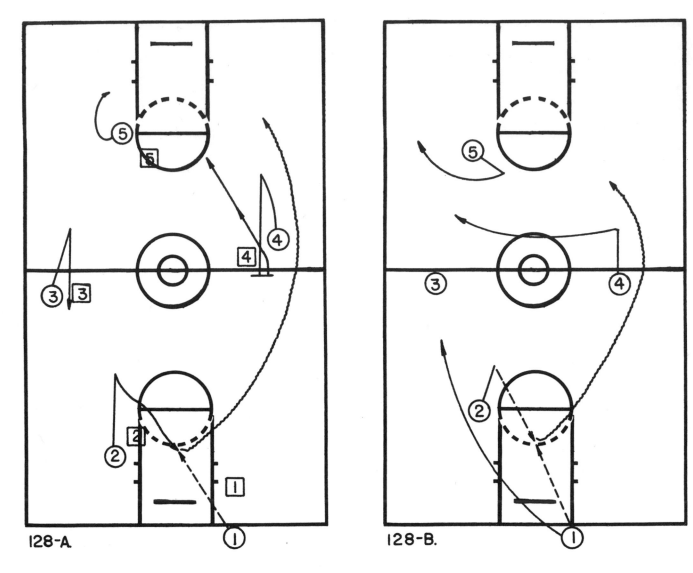

128-A.   128-B.

FIG. 128. PATTERNS AGAINST MAN-TO-MAN AND ZONE PRESSING DEFENSES. (A) *Dribble pattern vs. a man-to-man pressing defense.* ② cuts down the court and back to receive a pass from ①. ④ cuts to basket and back to set a screen and roll for ②. ② dribbles around ④ and looks for a pass to ④ if the defense switches. (B) *Dribble pattern vs. a man-to-man press.* ② cuts down the court and back for a pass from ①. ① passes to ②, and ① and ④ clear the right side of the court for a solo dribble across by ②. (C) *Pattern vs. a 2-2-1 zone press.* ① passes to ②. ② passes to ③, and ③ turns to the weak side and passes to ④ to beat the press. (D) ① passes to ②. ③ starts down the court, stops, and comes up the sideline for a pass from ②.

are many excellent patterns which produce good shots at the basket. Figure 127 (A to C) portrays three such patterns. These are play patterns especially designed to screen a particular man in a particular position in the zone.

**Offenses to Be Used Against
Both Man-to-Man and Zone Defenses**

Every coach would like to have an offense which will be effective against a man-to-man defense as well as against a zone. This perplexing problem is most

frequently solved by having one offense to meet one situation and a different offense for the other. Half the time one offense is practiced, and the remainder of the time devoted to offense goes to the other. In addition, teams will frequently play a man-to-man offense only to discover, much to their surprise, that the defense is playing a zone. Of course, the real solution is a universal offense, one which will be effective against any defense, regardless of the type. At the present time, the author does not know of a universal offense, but can recommend several offenses which have been fairly successful under these conditions.

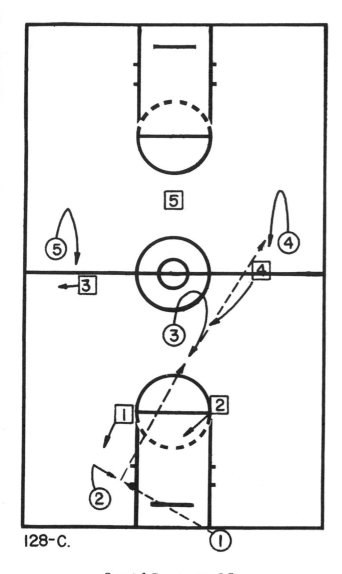

128-C.

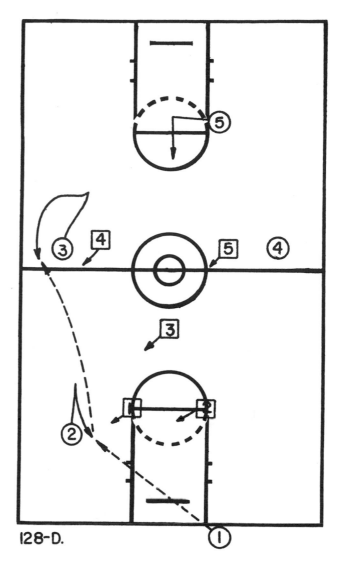

128-D.

Special Continuity Offense

This offense is described above as the side shuffle offense. It utilizes principles which are effective against both man-to-man and zone defenses. Good shots are obtained against either defense.

The Drake Shuffle

Described as the complete offense, the Drake Shuffle has proven very successful against any type of defense.

Revolving or Continuity Offenses

In general, revolving or continuity defenses are better adapted as complete offenses than other special offenses.

It should be recognized that regardless of the type of defense, the team with the ball has the advantage over its opponent. Good ball handling, poise, patience, player movements, and ball movement will sooner or later provide good opportunities to score. When this fact is recognized by the coach and each individual

player, the panic of meeting one defense or another will vanish into optimistic offensive play.

Meeting Combination Defenses

The fact that special defenses are designed and used means that the offense will occasionally encounter such a defense. Combination defenses are those which are partially man-to-man and partially zone or shifting man-to-man. Their main purpose is, of course, to muster their strong assets and minimize the weak points, in addition to presenting a perplexing problem for the offense.

Certain basic principles are pointed out which, when the offense embodies them, indicate that it will be effective against combination defenses.

1. Exhibit poise and patience.
2. Control the ball with good ball handling.
3. Make strong offensive moves.
4. Pass and make deep cuts.
5. Pass and cut away from the man with the ball.
6. Form triangles and pass the ball.

7. Screen and roll.
8. Move ball.
9. Move men.

It is recognized that it is difficult to incorporate all of the above into a play pattern; consequently, the reader will find that the continuity type of offenses come as close to fitting these principles as any offense.

Meeting the Press

At any time during the game, often the entire game and for certain when ahead late in the game, the pressing defense will be met. This often disconcerting defense can stampede a team, cause frequent mistakes, and result in a loss of team morale. This is one of the main objectives of the pressing defense; consequently, planned maneuvers are necessary so that the team knows that the press, although a bother, will not be an effective defensive maneuver.

There are many patterns, but the following basic principles are important.

1. Team poise.
2. Calm, cool, collected attitude.
3. Primary effort is to get the ball into the front court in ten seconds.
4. Scoring is secondary.
5. Plan an attack by practicing basic patterns.

Beat the Man-to-Man Press

1. Best dribbler takes the ball across. *Against the man-to-man press, dribble.*
2. Short pass and cut.
3. Long pass to free man.

Figure 128 (A and B) indicates the dribble patterns which are effective against the man-to-man press. In the first instance, the guard takes the ball across via a dribble, while the forward sets up a screen-and-roll situation near mid-court. In the second, the court is cleared for the dribbler to go on his own.

Beat the Zone Press

The following are offered as general principles which are used against the zone press.

1. Pass and cut away from ball. *Against a zone press, pass.*
2. Do not cross.
3. Dribble only in an emergency.
4. Come to meet the pass.
5. Pass when double-teamed.

Two patterns are offered which release the pressure of a zone press. The first places an outlet man in the center of the court, while the second outlets up the sidelines. Figure 128 (C and D) shows these patterns.

Following are some *do nots.*

1. Do not cross, which will allow a double-team.
2. Do not maneuver near the sidelines.
3. Do not make high cross-court passes.

Probably the best recommendation to make regarding attacking a press is: *Against a man-for-man press, dribble; and against a zone press, pass.*

Stall

The stall is designed to enable a team to control the tempo of the game and to prevent the opponents from obtaining possession of the ball. The type of stall varies from the absolute freeze, in which the team plays ball control to run out the clock, to the control stall where the tempo of the game is controlled to a slow pace and a shot is taken only when an unopposed lay-in is available.

Generally speaking, the stall is utilized in the closing minutes of a close game. The stalling maneuver forces the opponents to come after the ball, and this in turn causes them to commit mistakes or to foul. This forcing of mistakes or of fouls is to the detriment of the defensive team and to the definite advantage of the stalling team if that team can capitalize on these advantages.

General Principles of Stalls

1. Retain possession of the ball.
2. Prevent double-teaming by opponents by not going near man with ball.
3. Keep opponents busy, so that they cannot double-team.
4. Passes should be short and snappy.
5. Man receiving the pass must come to meet the ball.
6. Man must be open before pass is thrown; never force the ball.
7. Man with ball must stay away from corners, sidelines, and baselines, as they act as an additional defensive barrier.
8. Spread the defense.
9. The stall pattern must be an offensive threat.
10. Regardless of the type of stalling pattern, the players must be poised and confident in their actions.

Types of Stalls

There are many types of stalls, as there are many offenses, but stalls can be classified and placed in categories. When this is done, there are four general types: Figure-eight continuity; play-with-rules; dribbler; and set patterns.

Continuity type of stall. Figure 129-A portrays one figure-eight continuity stall. As each player passes, he cuts directly to the basket and away from the man receiving the ball. This cutting away from the man

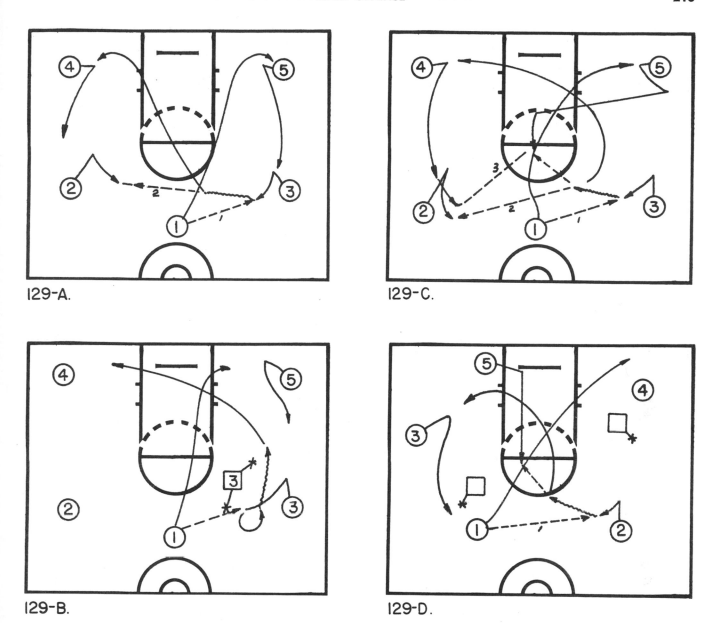

129-A.

129-C.

129-B.

129-D.

Fig. 129. Continuity Type of Stall. The figure-eight weave is used as a stall. (A) The movement of the players. A deep cut toward the basket is made to prevent double-teaming. (B) An alternative to 129-A. ① passes to ③ and cuts toward the basket. Because his defensive man is playing high, ③ reverses and dribbles toward ⑤ to continue the weave. (C) Another choice brings ⑤ to the foul line for a pass. ① to ③, ① clears. ③ gives to ⑤ or ② and cuts wide behind ⑤. ⑤ gives to ④, and the weave continues. (D) A four-man weave is used as a stall. In this case, ⑤ is used only as an emergency outlet. ② cannot pass to ③ or ④ and has no dribble. He calls ⑤ up, gives him the ball, cuts wide, and the stall pattern continues.

with the ball prevents double-teaming. Alternate maneuvers are shown in Figure 129 (A and B).

This type of stall can be executed with five men as portrayed or, if one player is not a good ball handler, with four men in the weave, with the weak man placed in the corner to be utilized only as an emergency outlet. Figure 129-D indicates this type of pattern. The same options are available as are used in the five-man figure-eight weave explained above.

Play-with-rules type of stall. In this type of stall, freedom of action is allowed within certain rules. The team is placed in positions on the floor, and their actions are governed by specific rules. An example would be to *pass and cut away from the pass.* Figure 130 (A to C) indicates the players' actions when operating under this freedom of action but within the rule *pass and cut away from the pass.*

A freedom stall of this type requires a well-rounded

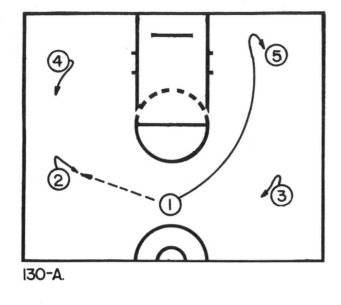

130-A.

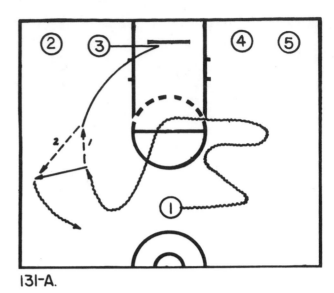

131-A.

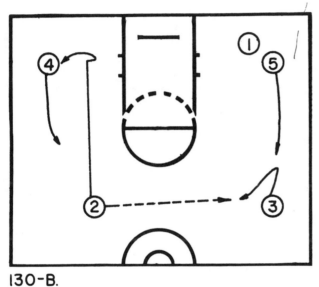

130-B.

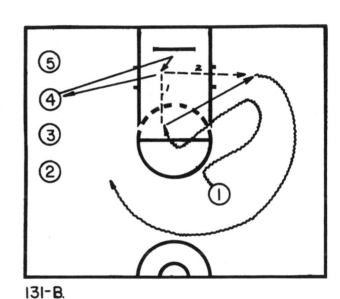

131-B.

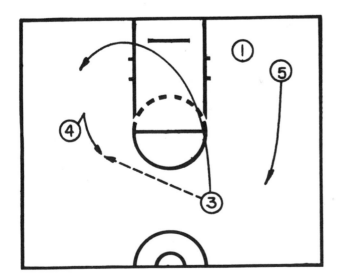

130-C.

FIG. 130. STALL WITH RULES. Pass and cut away from the pass is the rule for this stall. (A) ① passes to ② and cuts away from the pass. ④ and ③ move toward the ball. (B) ② passes to ③ and cuts away from the ball. ④ and ⑤ move toward the ball. (C) ③ passes to ④ and cuts away from the pass. ⑤ and ③ move toward the ball. (Regardless of the formation used in this type of stall, each player, after cutting away from the ball, fills the spot vacated by another player. This keeps the stall pattern well-spread and balanced.)

FIG. 131. STALL BY DRIBBLING. (A) ① dribbles until forced to stop. ③ breaks forward, receives a pass, returns the ball to ①, and the dribble continues. (B) ① dribbles until forced to stop. ④ breaks toward the basket and back for a pass. ① passes to ④, ④ to ①, and the dribble continues.

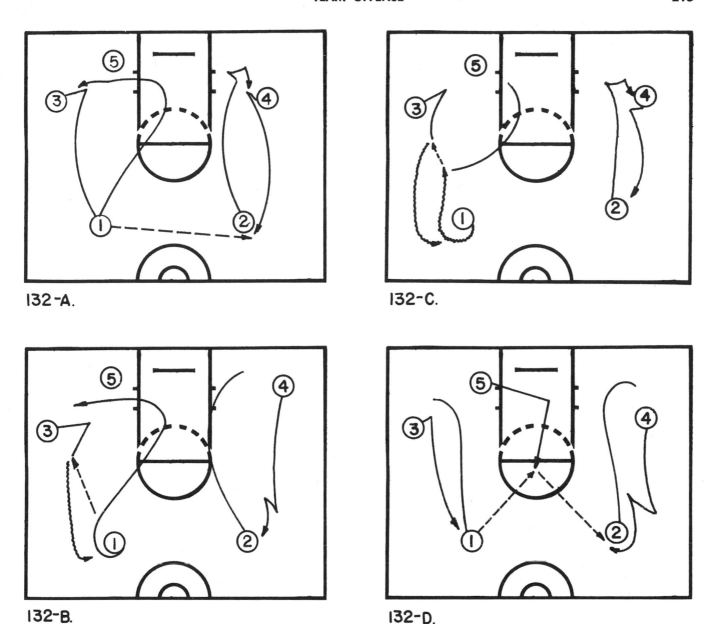

132-A.

132-C.

132-B.

132-D.

FIG. 132. SIDE SHUTTLE STALL. (A) ① is in possession of the ball, ② and ④ shuttle, ① passes to ④ and shuttles with ③. The drill continues. Players shuttle any time they are not clear to receive a pass. (B) ① pivots, passes to ③ and shuttles. ② and ④ shuttle while ③ dribbles out into the clear. (C) The third option shows ① circling back toward ③ by means of a dribble. ① passes to ③ as ② and ④ shuttle. (D) ② and ④ shuttle, ① signals ⑤, who breaks up for a pass. ① and ③ shuttle, ⑤ passes to ④, returns to his original position, and the stall continues.

group of players who are good ball handlers and who can play according to the rule while under the pressure of the defense. This stall can be set up in any formation and is frequently used in the same formation utilized as the regular offense.

Stall by dribbling. The stall by dribbling takes advantage of the attributes of a good dribbler and a good foul shooter. In this stall, one player keeps possession of the ball by his exceptional skill of dribbling while the remaining four players keep the floor clear

and their defensive men busy. Figure 131 (A and B) shows how the stall operates. In either case, should the dribbler be forced to stop, one of the remaining players, in a prearranged order, breaks to receive a pass, gives the ball back to the dribbler, and returns to the original position while the dribbler resumes the dribble. Should the other defensive player attempt a double-team, that offensive man (as shown in Figure 131-B) breaks to a prearranged spot on the floor for a pass.

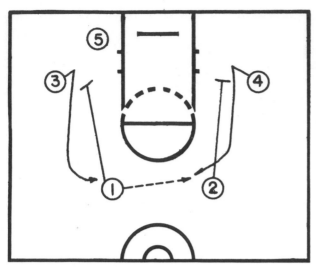

133.

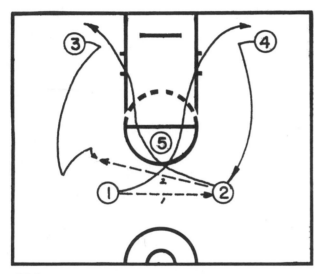

134.

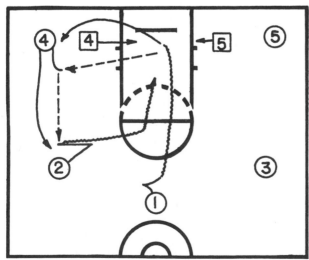

135.

This type of stall is effective if the team has a good dribbler who is also a good foul shooter. This qualification is necessary, as the dribbler will probably be fouled when the defense attempts to get the ball and he must make a good percentage of his foul shots or the defense will gain the ball by virtue of a rebound after the missed foul shot. It should be noted that the dribbler must progress toward the basket to a point at least inside an imaginary line drawn three feet above the edge of the key. If this is not accomplished and he is closely guarded, the officials will call a held ball.

Set pattern type of stall. In the set pattern type of stall, any formation and a variety of patterns can be used. Some coaches use their regular formation and their normal set patterns in stalling, but they control the ball and allow a shot only when an unopposed lay-in is available. On the other hand, many coaches prefer one which, although it has an offensive threat, has definite moves designed to keep the ball from the opponents.

The most common formations are the three men out and two in; the two men out, two in, and a high post; and the two men out, two in, and a low post. Types of patterns described are the regular offensive attack, the side shuffle, the figure-eight and the dribble drive. These three have been selected as stall patterns which are fairly common and have been very successful when executed properly.

The *side shuttle stall* is pictured in Figure 132 (A to D). The forward and guard shuttle on their side of the court in a circular motion while the other forward and guard shuttle on the other side. Any player with the ball has four options. He may pass to the man opposite (Fig. 132-A). He may pivot back and pass to the man on his side as is shown in Figure 132-B. He may dribble back toward the man on his side as is portrayed in Figure 132-C. When none of

Fig. 133. Shuttle Stall with Screens. ② and ④ shuttle. ② screens ④'s defensive man, freeing ④ for a pass from ①. ① shuttles and screens ③'s defensive man. Each player screens as he shuttles.

Fig. 134. Stall: Figure-Eight Pattern Type. ① passes to ②, cuts diagonally across the court by ⑤ to pick off his defensive man. ② passes to ③ and cuts by ⑤ to the far corner of the court. Each player continues in this pattern.

Fig. 135. Dribble Drive Stall. ① drives for the basket, and as ④ picks him up, he passes to ④. ② goes in and out and ④ passes to ②. ① takes ④'s spot, while ④ replaces ②. ② drives and the pattern continues. The driver goes to the side to which he passed off.

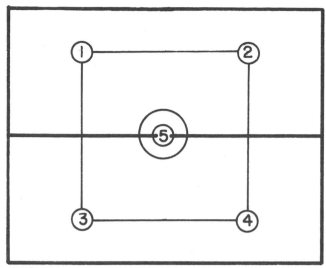

136-A.

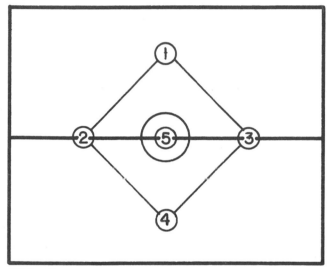

136-B.

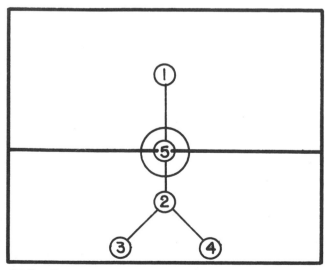

136- C.

the above options is available, the man with the ball can pass to the center at a high post position and shuttle. Figure 132-D indicates the fourth option.

The *side shuttle type of stall* can also involve *screens* in the shuttle. A caution is necessary at this point, and it concerns the possibility of fouling during a screen. Players are coached so that they *do not* foul as they screen. As they approach an opponent and attempt to screen, they should slide off on the side toward the basket. The same options are available as those explained under the side shuttle type of stall.

Figure 133 indicates the pattern of movement utilized in the shuttle type of stall with screens. As each offensive man shuttles, he moves directly toward the defensive man, presents his body as a screen, and slides in toward the basket to prevent contact. A player shuttles and screens every time he comes out and is not open to receive a pass.

Another set pattern type of stall resembles a figure-eight pattern of player movement. As each player passes, he cuts diagonally across the court and then up the sideline to receive a pass. Figure 134 indicates the player movement. Options for each player are similar to those noted above.

The *dribble drive type of stall* involves a hard dribble drive toward the basket as a scoring threat, then a release of the ball to the side from where a defensive man has been drawn. Figure 135 indicates a drive by the dribbler down the middle toward the basket. Should the dribbler drive in unopposed, he is free to score. If he is picked up by a defensive man, he passes off to the side from which that man came.

The success of this type of stall is based upon the fact that the offensive players can drive against their opponents who are anxious to get the ball. Because the defense must overplay their opponents, the dribble drive is made easier.

When utilized effectively, the control stall or the absolute freeze will disconcert the opponents, force them to make mistakes or to foul. If the stalling team makes a good percentage of its foul shots and capitalizes on the opponents' mistakes by scoring one or two easy baskets, that team should win going away.

► Special Situations

There are several special situations which occur frequently during the course of a game which, when properly executed, can mean possession of the ball

FIG. 136. JUMP BALL TO GAIN POSSESSION. Common formations to be used when control of the tip is fairly certain. (A) The box. (B) The diamond. (C) The Y (upside down).

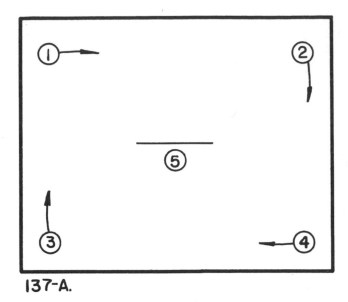

137-A.

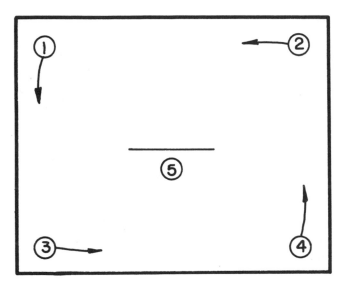

137-B.

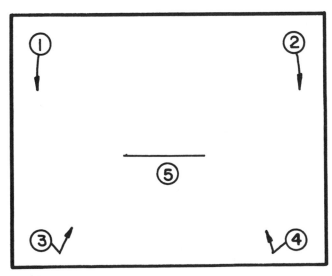

137-C.

and often an opportunity to score. These special situations involve the jump ball, foul shot offense, the out-of-bounds play, and the last shot opportunity.

Jump Ball

The jump ball situation is one in which the team controlling the tip should always gain possession of the ball. In addition to gaining possession of the ball, it is also possible to plan a scoring play. These situations involve a jump ball in which the jumper can control the tip.

A jump ball situation can occur in any one of three positions on the floor: at the center circle, in the front court foul circle, or at the back court foul circle. Although it is possible to line up in the same positions at each of these three positions, it is often advantageous to change the alignment of the players according to the position and regardless of whether the main objective of controlling the tip is possession of the ball or possession leading directly to a scoring opportunity. Controlling the tip leading to possession should be the primary objective, and a play can be attempted as the secondary objective.

Jump Ball Possession

There are many ways to align players when control of the tip is more or less certain, but in general there are three that are most common: the box, the diamond, and the Y formation. Figure 136 (A to C) indicates these positions.

The man controlling the tip should be certain to tip the ball to his own man high and away from the defensive man. This can be predetermined by a general movement of the players or by a tip to a definite position on the floor to which a particular player cuts.

When possession of the tip is desired by a general movement of the players, the man jumping can survey the defense and, knowing exactly where his men will move on the toss, tip the ball to that spot. The movement can be clockwise (Fig. 137-A), counterclockwise (Fig. 137-B), or a special move by the forward men or back men (Fig. 137-C). The direction of the move can be arranged by a signal from one of the players. Common signals are verbal calls or body movements. One effective way to indicate positions on the floor to the players is to note positions as if they are the face of a clock. Figure 138 shows these "spots" on the floor.

When the tip is directed to a particular player at a position on the floor, the move is usually directed by a signal. This move is then made in relation to where

FIG. 137. JUMP BALL: PLAYER MOVEMENT. (A) Clockwise movement. (B) Counterclockwise movement (C) Special moves.

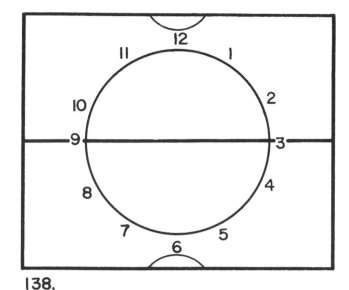

138.

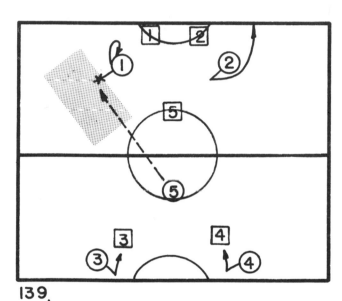

139.

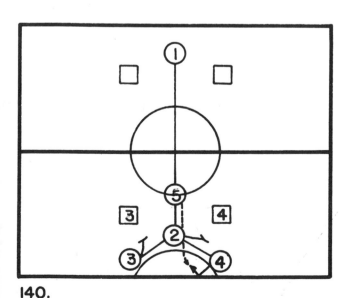

140.

FIG. 138. JUMP BALL: TIP TO SPOTS. Spots on the floor are indicated by the face of a clock. 12 is straight ahead, 6 is straight back, 3 to the right, etc.

FIG. 139. JUMP BALL PLAY: TIP TO A SPOT. ① breaks a step toward the basket and then comes back to receive the tip in the shaded area. ② starts toward the ball, pivots, and breaks for the basket. ① hooks to ②.

FIG. 140. JUMP BALL: "Y" FORMATION. Tip to the deep man, ④. ② screens ④, ③ screens ③, and ⑤ tips deep to ④, who is clear to receive the ball.

the defense is stationed. Figure 139 gives an indication of this type of play. The jumper gives a signal by placing his left hand against his left hip. This signal indicates that he will tip the ball to the left forward in the open or shaded area. The forward moves into this area as the ball is tossed and the jumper tips the ball high to the forward at that spot.

One of the best alignments to assure possession is the Y formation, with the tip going into the back center of the Y. Figure 140 indicates how this maneuver is carried out. The jumper tips the ball back to the deep men while the side men screen the opponents away from the ball. A long tip to the deep men is almost a certain way to obtain possession of the ball.

Jump Ball Plays

Following are basic plays designed to score from a jump ball situation.

Figure 141-A shows a jump ball play from the center circle of the court. This play is also a good one when the jump is in the back court foul circle area.

Figure 141-B portrays a scoring play from a diamond formation and a screen.

If the defense aligns only two players back on a tip at the front-court foul circle, one of the front men will always have an open side. Figure 141-C indicates this position, and one player is open at his left side. When the ball is tipped to this position, he can hook or take a jump shot.

Figure 141-D shows how another type of play can be developed. It results in a jump shot over a screen.

Foul Shot Offense

When a player has missed a foul shot, it is entirely possible to obtain possession of the ball even though the defense has the favorable rebounding positions. It is possible to obtain long rebounds, or if not certain of possession, the player can tip the ball either back to the shooter or long to the guards.

Now that there is a twelve-inch buffer zone between the defensive and offensive rebounders on each side of the foul line, it is very important that the proper movement be made for the offensive re-

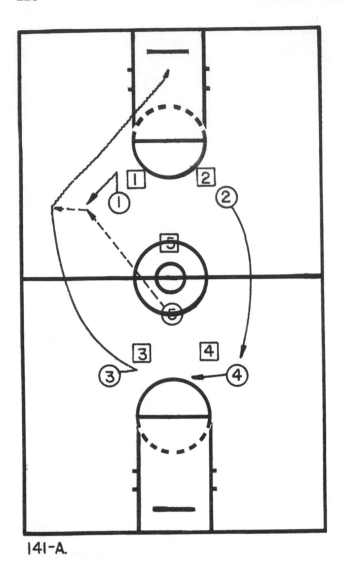

141-A.

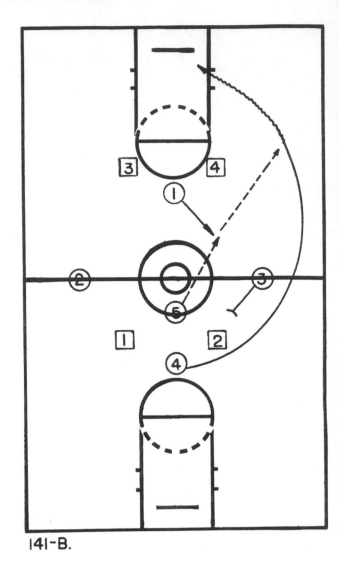

141-B.

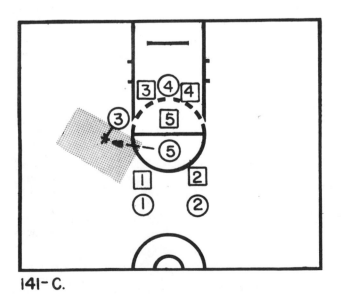

141-C.

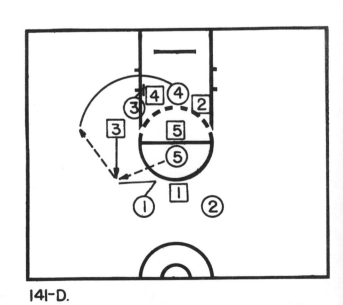

141-D.

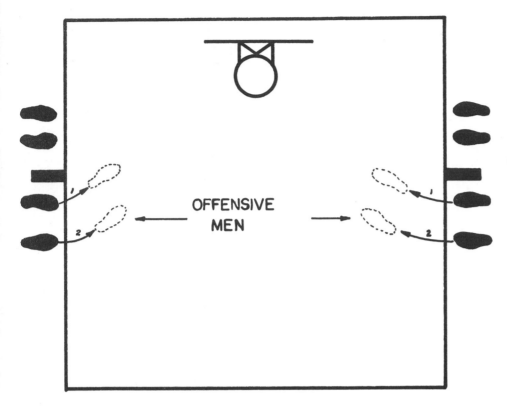

Fig. 142. Offensive Rebound-ing: Footwork. The offensive player on the right side steps first with his right foot and then with his left. The player on the left steps first with his left foot. The objective is to gain a position alongside of the inside defensive men and not behind them.

bounder to obtain the most favorable rebounding position possible. As soon as the ball hits the rim, the offensive player on the right side should step with his right foot and the player on the left with his left foot. This first step should counter the first step by the defense, and several quick shuttling steps should place the offensive rebounders in the positions indicated in Figure 142. The proper position is alongside the defensive man and not behind him. In this position, a rebound off the side can be contested and one off the front can be controlled.

Out-of-Bounds Plays

Out-of-bounds plays are designed to get the ball into the court within five seconds and then, if possible,

Fig. 141. Jump Ball Plays. (A) ① starts toward the basket but returns for the tip from ⑤. ③ starts to his right, reverses, and cuts around ① for the ball. (B) ⑤ tips to ①, ③ screens ② while ④ breaks around the outside. ① passes to ④ for a lay-in shot. (C) ④ takes the middle spot, ③ the side, while ③ and ④ take up defensive positions. With only two men back, ③ and ④, ③ is open on one side. The ball is tipped to this free side, and ③ can hook or take a jump shot. (D) ⑤ tips to ①. ③ screens ④, ④ comes around the screen for a pass from ① and a shot.

to score. The defense is placed in a special situation, and unless their play is clever, good maneuvers should present a scoring opportunity.

Plays from out-of-bounds situations originate from three places on the court: baseline in front court, sideline in front court, and baseline or sideline in back court. Out-of-bounds plays are successful when the timing, cuts, and passes are executed with precision and good form. It is usual for the man who takes the ball out of bounds to signal the play. A strategic move is for teams to use one play with alternate options the first half and a different play the second. Whatever the method, proper execution is what is important.

Front-Court Baseline Plays

Excellent scoring plays have been designed which produce a good primary scoring effort, a secondary option, and a safe outlet pass. Figure 143 (A to D) offers four different types of plays from the baseline. These patterns involve screens, cuts, drives, and split-second timing.

Front-Court Sideline Plays

When the ball is obtained out of bounds at the sideline in the front court, possession inside the court is

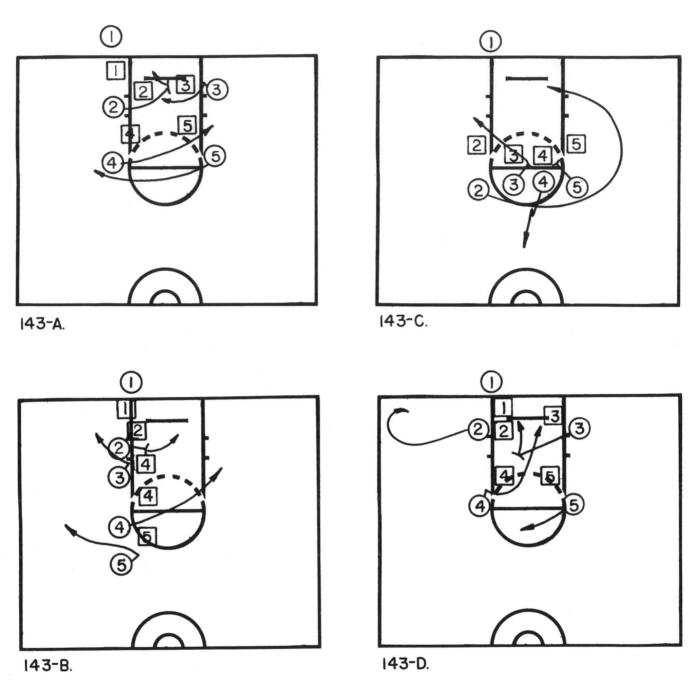

143-A.

143-C.

143-B.

143-D.

FIG. 143. OUT-OF-BOUNDS PLAYS FROM THE FRONT COURT, BASELINE. (A) Screen and roll. ② screens for ③ and rolls back toward the ball. ③ cuts around the screen. ① can pass to ②, ③, or ⑤, the outlet man. (B) ② screens for ③ and rolls to the basket. ③ cuts toward the ball. ① can pass to ②, ③, or ⑤, the outlet man. (C) ② cuts behind ③, ④, and ⑤ to the basket. ③ and ⑤ screen ④. ③ slides off of his screen toward the ball while ④ steps back. ① can pass to ②, ③, or ④. (D) ③ screens for ④ and rolls off to the ball. ④ cuts to the right as ② clears. ① can pass to ③, ④, or outlet pass to ② or ⑤.

usually considered the primary objective; but a scoring play from this position on the court is valuable, particularly when the defense is forced to apply pressure to obtain possession of the ball. Figure 144 (A to C) offers three plays which have proven successful.

Back-Court Baseline or Sideline Plays

Out-of-bounds plays are used in this situation when the time in a period is short or when it is necessary to score against a pressing defense.

Because the ball is awarded out of bounds after a foul by a player while his team is in possession of the

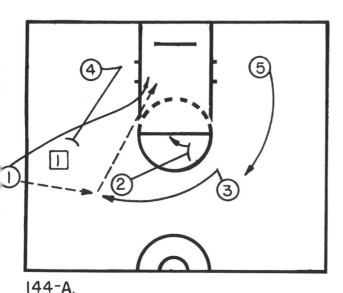

144-A.

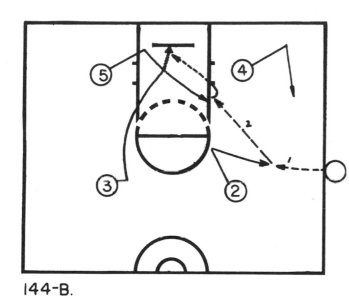

144-B.

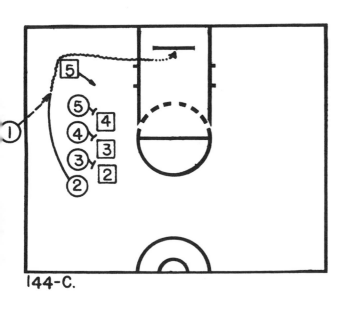

144-C.

ball, many such out-of-bounds situations will occur. A play in this instance could mean the difference between a win or a loss. Figures 145 A and B offer two simple plays. They can be very effective, but only against a tight, man-to-man defense.

Last Shot Opportunity

In a game played in quarters there are four times in which a team will have the last shot opportunity, while in a game played in halves this opportunity comes only twice. In addition to having the last scoring opportunity, the strategic situation often exists in which it is advantageous to hold the ball and then make every effort to score on the last shot. This would involve a game which is tied going into the last seconds of play.

The main question to be resolved in this last shot opportunity is whether to use a regular offensive pattern or to have a special play for this purpose. Whether the regular pattern is used or a special play, several items must be considered which will contribute to the success of the play.

1. Each of the five players must know the exact play to be used and his part and position in the pattern.

2. The individual or quarterback starting the play must have the poise and experience necessary to get the play off to a good start. He has to know the time left in the game and the amount of time the play takes.

3. The play should produce the primary scoring effort which is a good percentage shot, the best being a lay-in shot.

4. The play should have a secondary option which will produce a good scoring opportunity.

5. The player involved in the primary scoring effort should be a calm, cool, collected individual who never misses when under pressure.

6. The play should be practiced under situations which simulate game conditions: score tied and twenty seconds to go, one point behind and ten seconds to go, etc.

Figure 146 (A to F) portrays special scoring plays for this last shot opportunity. They are offered from a variety of original setups and are given names which stimulate the imagination of the players.

Fig. 144. Out-of-Bounds Plays from the Front Court, Sideline. (A) ② screens for ③, ③ cuts to receive the ball from ①. ④ screens ①, ① cuts outside and toward the basket to receive the ball from ③ for a lay-in. (B) ① passes in to ②. ⑤ comes up high toward the foul line. ② passes to ⑤. ③ cuts and ⑤ gives to ③ for a shot. (C) ③, ④, and ⑤ screen ②, ③, and ④ respectively. ② cuts around ③, ④, and ⑤ to receive a pass from ① for a scoring shot.

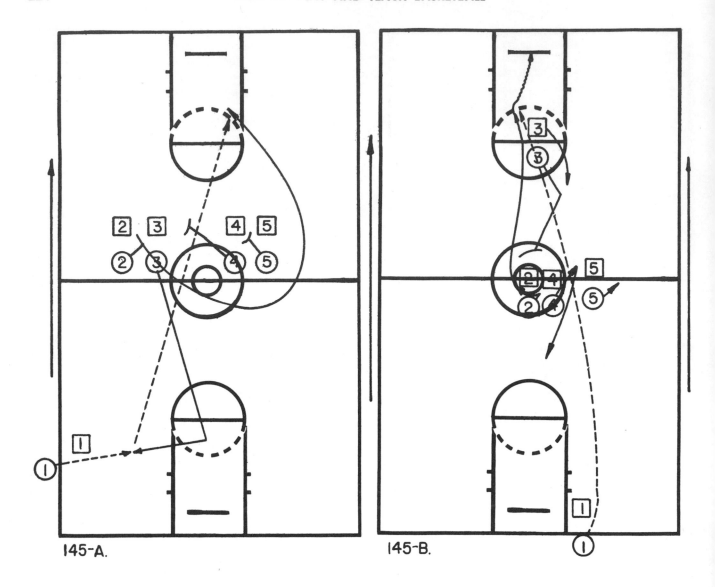

145-A.   145-B.

FIG. 145. OUT-OF-BOUNDS PLAYS FROM THE BACK COURT. (A) ② screens for ③, ④ screens ③ and ⑤ screens ④. ③ breaks back for a pass, while ② slides off of the screen and circles ④ and ⑤ to the basket. ③ tosses a high pass to ② for a shot. (B) ③ comes back up the court and screens ②. ② rolls around the screen and breaks toward the basket. ① throws a long pass to ② for a shot.

FIG. 146. LAST-SHOT PLAYS. (A) *Blind Pig.* ⑤ clears and ① passes to ④ at the foul line. ② cuts when his defensive man, the blind pig, tries to locate the ball. ④ gives to ②. A good option involves ③ cutting around ⑤'s screen for a shot at the basket. (B) *Wheel.* ① passes to ③ and cuts by ③ all the way under the basket and out again. ③ dribbles off of ①'s heels to the foul line, stops, and pivots as ② cuts by. ③ can give to ②, turn and shoot, or give to ④ for a jump or set shot. (C) *Double screen.* ① passes to ③ and screens. ③ dribbles around ① and ⑤ for a drive to the basket. ① rolls off of his screen and provides an option for ③ should he be stopped. (D) *Cross for two.* ① passes to ③ and screens for ②. ② cuts for the basket. ③ can pass to ② or to ①, who rolls off of his screen. (E) *Cut.* ④ breaks to the foul line to receive a pass from ①. ① cuts by while ② cuts, but stops behind ④. ④ can pass to ① or give to ② for a jump shot. (F) *Weave.* ① passes to ②, screens, and breaks up to the foul line. ② passes to ③, hesitates while ③ passes to ①. ② then cuts by a screen by ③ for a pass from ① for a lay-in shot. ① can also pass to ③, who slides off of his screen and around ① toward the basket. An alternate play would be for ② to give to ③ and screen for ③. ③ to ① and back to ③ as ③ cuts by ②'s screen and around ①.

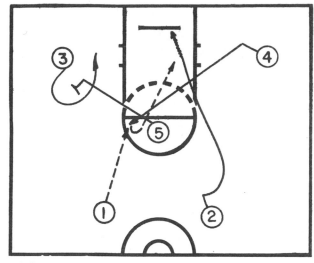

146-A.

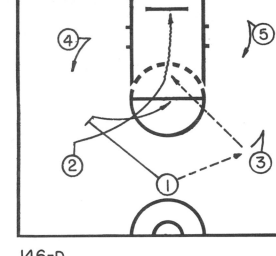

146-D.

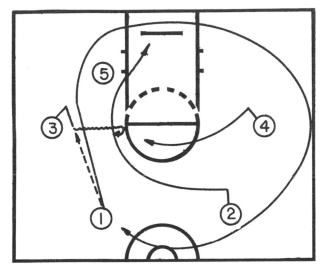

146-B.

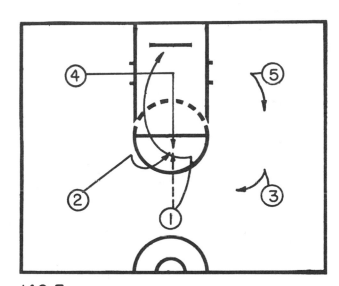

146-E.

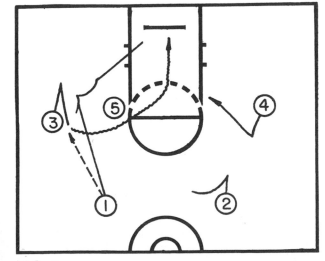

146-C.

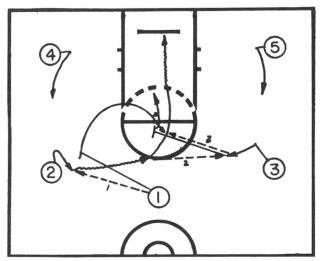

146-F.

► Summary

Team offense is the effort of a team to move the ball into scoring territory, to make a co-ordinated attempt to control the possession of the ball and to score. This offensive action is concerned with system of offensive play and special situations: the jump ball situation, foul shot offense, the out-of-bounds play, and the last-minute scoring play.

Team offense is based upon certain basic principles which act as guides for effective action. Within the framework of these principles there are many systems of play, each with numerous options. These vary from the fast break offense to the set, control tempo type of offense, with the great majority of offensive systems of play between these two extremes.

► Study
Questions

1. Select the one most important criterion for selecting a team offense and explain why it is the most important.
2. Diagram a play which is designed to determine the opponent's defense.
3. List the ways used to signal the designation of a play.
4. Diagram the basic options which stem from a figure-eight weave.
5. A guard to forward inside screen will cause the defense to maneuver in a variety of ways. What are the offensive countermeasures?
6. Diagram two out-of-bounds plays for use in the front court: one to be used from the baseline and one from the sideline at the extension of the foul line.
7. Your team is facing a jump ball situation at center court in which the tip will be controlled by your team. How will you line up the team and what techniques will be utilized to gain possession of the ball?
8. What advantages are there in flashing one or two men to the post from a figure-eight weave, from a 3-2 offense?
9. Describe the overload principle. What other means are there to combat the zone?
10. What are the advantages of a 3-2 offense: Why is it used?
11. State a general rule regarding the method of beating a press.
12. Your team has possession of the ball with ten seconds left in the game, and is behind one point. What is the strategy regarding the play to be used?
13. Describe a stall pattern. Does it have the threat of a score?

► Projects for
Additional
Study

1. Following a logical progression, develop a team offense. Break this offense down into specific practice drills.
2. Diagram the complete turnover of a continuity offense.
3. Using the above diagrammed continuity offense, take one setup and describe possible options.
4. Discuss the philosophies of the free-lance offense vs. control ball offense.
5. Diagram and describe a stall pattern. Does it have any unique features?
6. What are the options which result from the first option of the Drake Shuffle?
7. Describe or diagram a complete or universal offense.
8. What basic ways can the centers be deployed in a double post offense?

9. Using the offense described in Question 2 above, explain how it meets the criteria for selecting the team offense.

10. With a single post offense, explain how to use the strong attributes of a big center. On the other hand, how would you minimize the center's play when he is a very weak offensive man but a strong rebounder?

11. Observe a basketball game and determine the offensive patterns of one team. What type of set play was used? Did the team fast break? Give a critical analysis of the offense with regard to the ability of the players and the defense encountered.

12. You have the following personnel which make the first team: two short, aggressive, fast guards; a big, aggressive, awkward center who is a good rebounder but a poor shooter; and two rangy, hard-driving forwards, both good outside shooters. Design an offense to fit this personnel.

13. Outline a ten-minute practice session during which time a stall is practiced.

► Selected References

Athletic Journal. Athletic Journal Publishing Co., Evanston, Ill. Contains many fine articles dealing with all types of team offenses, philosophy, and principles.

Auerbach, Arnold. *Basketball for the Player, the Fan and the Coach.* New York: Pocketbooks, Inc., 1952. Excellent material on team offense.

Basketball Coach's Digest. Huntington Laboratories, Huntington, Ind. Yearly Journal which contains many fine articles dealing with all types of team offenses, philosophy, and principles.

Bee, Clair. *Man to Man Defense and Attack.* New York: A. S. Barnes & Co., 1942. Comprehensive coverage of all types of man-to-man offense.

————. *Zone Defense and Attack.* New York: A. S. Barnes & Co., 1942. Comprehensive coverage of all types of zone attacks.

————. *Winning Basketball Plays.* New York: A. S. Barnes & Co., 1950. A compilation of every conceivable type of offense offered by America's foremost coaches.

Bunn, John W. *Basketball Methods.* New York: The Macmillan Co., 1939. Contains valuable information on the general principles of team offense, specific team offense, and the fast break.

————. *Basketball Techniques and Team Play.* Englewood Cliffs, N. J.: Prentice-Hall, Inc., 1964. Excellent, concise explanation of various types of team offenses.

Dean, Everett S. *Progressive Basketball.* New York: Prentice-Hall, Inc., 1950. Excellent material on a specific offense, three-man figure-eight offense, fast break, zone offense, and offense for pressing defenses.

Eaves, Joel. *Basketball Shuffle Offense.* New York: Prentice-Hall, Inc., 1960. Comprehensive description of the Drake Shuffle. Excellent portion on general offensive theory.

Gardner, Jack. *Championship Basketball with Jack Gardner.* Englewood Cliffs, New Jersey: Prentice-Hall, Inc., 1961. Detailed treatment of Utah's fast break, man-to-man attack, attacking the zones, the stall and the freeze, and situation offenses.

Hobson, Howard A. *Basketball Illustrated.* New York: A. S. Barnes & Co., 1948. Basic information on what a team offense should consist of, the fast break, and set plays.

Jucker, Ed. *Cincinnati Power Basketball.* Englewood Cliffs, N. J.: Prentice-Hall, Inc., 1962. Excellent on Cincinnati's swing-and-go offense, the backdoor trap, the high post pattern combating the press and attacking the zone.

Julian, Alvin F. *Bread and Butter Basketball.* New York: Prentice-Hall, Inc., 1960. Excellent coverage of different types of offensive systems of play.

Loeffler, Ken. *Ken Loeffler on Basketball.* New York: Prentice-Hall, Inc., 1955. Loeffler's specific ideas on offense. Good description of the 3-2 offense with the flash to the pivot.

McCracken, Frank. *Offensive Basketball.* New York: Prentice-Hall, Inc., 1955. Fine description of Indiana's offensive system.

McGuire, Frank. *Offensive Basketball.* New York: Prentice-Hall, Inc., 1958. Entire book is devoted to offense. Clear concise picture of how McGuire does it.

McLane, Hardin. *Championship Basketball by 12 Great Coaches*. Englewood Cliffs, N. J.: Prentice-Hall, Inc., 1965. Coach Ed Jucker on Cincinnati's swing-and-go offense. Coach John B. McLendon, Jr., on championship fast break. Coach Hank Iba on attacking the press. Coach Ken Norton on special situation plays.

Newell, Pete, and Benington, John. *Basketball Methods*. New York: The Ronald Press Co., 1962. Good material on how to assemble an offense, set offenses, and the fast break.

Newsom, Heber. *Basketball for the High School Coach and the Physical Education Teacher*. Dubuque, Iowa: Wm. C. Brown, 1952. Good material on various offensive systems of play.

Ramsay, Jack. *Pressure Basketball*. Englewood Cliffs, N. J.: Prentice-Hall, Inc., 1964. Team offense dealing with fast break, multiple man-to-man offense, a low post attack and the freeze offense and zone freeze.

Rupp, Adolph F. *Rupp's Championship Basketball*. New York: Prentice-Hall, Inc., 1948. One of America's most successful coaches offers his version of all phases of offensive basketball.

Scholastic Coach. Scholastic Magazines, Inc., New York, N. Y. 10036. Contains many fine articles dealing with all types of team offenses, philosophy, and principles.

Watts, Stan. *Developing An Offensive Attack in Basketball*. New York: Prentice-Hall, Inc., 1959. Thorough and concise coverage of the basic offensive systems of play.

Wilkes, Glenn. *Winning Basketball Strategy*. New York: Prentice-Hall, Inc., 1959. Contains some excellent material on specific offensive preparations such as selecting the offense and types of offenses and personnel required.

Wooden, John R. *Practical Modern Basketball*. New York: The Ronald Press Co., 1966. John Wooden's man and zone offenses plus his concept of other types of successful offenses.

CHAPTER 8: Strategy of the Game

Although the players pass the ball, dribble, and shoot the baskets, the coach is actually the behind-the-scenes strategist. He is responsible for the operation, adjustments, moves and countermoves which govern the playing strategy. The strategies set the defense, unleash the offense, make the substitutions, fully utilize the time-outs and, in general, mastermind the play. What defense should be used against an opponent with a high-scoring center? When to apply the press? When to control the ball? When to go into a freeze? To fast break? These and many more questions demand answers during the course of the game and in many instances immediate decisions are necessary. Every strategic situation is impossible to cover, but many are offered with possible solutions.

▶ Playing Strategy

Playing strategy involves certain general principles of team play, the specific preparations necessary to play a game against an opponent, and decisions which are made during the course of a game.

General Principles

Listed below are some tried and true general principles, or tactics. It must be realized that they are general statements and should be adapted to fit the particular situation.

1. Make the opponents play in a way in which they are not accustomed. This is to control the tempo of a game. Play slow against faster opponents and fast against slower teams.

2. Force the opponents and individual players out of their normal operational areas. If a player drives the baseline, force him to the middle. If a team attacks down the middle, force them to the sideline.

3. Run against teams that appear tired.

4. Slow down a fast breaking team.

5. Press an inexperienced team.

6. Mass the defense in the area near the basket on poor outside shooting teams. This is done by using a zone or a sagging man-to-man defense.

7. If your team is small and fast, press.

8. Play a different pattern or different offensive option each half.

9. Alternate defenses to confuse the opponent.

Preparation for the Game

All preparation for the game to be played is not in the form of practice on the floor. The coach and players should know the opponent and themselves. Knowledge of the opponent stems from scouting and is concerned with an appraisal of the opponent's offense, defense, and personnel. Although this is discussed in more detail in Chapter 9, some mention must be made of matching players. When the opponents have been appraised, the coach can match speed with speed, height with height, best defensive man against opponent's star, etc. A pride in wanting to be matched with an opponent is what is desired.

Knowledge of self is the appraisal of the team by the coach to determine their abilities and capabilities. It is foolish to break and run if the team cannot handle the ball at top speed. It is useless to full-court press when the team is tall and awkward. The knowledge of knowing what a team can do and cannot do is important, as these facts limit the actions of the team.

Playing the Game

First Half

During the first half it is possible to ascertain the opponent's offensive patterns, defensive setup, out-of-bounds plays, tip off plays, and strength on the offensive and defensive boards. Also observed is the effectiveness of our team's offense and defense.

Half Time

During this short period of time, the players rest and are refreshed; but in addition, certain pertinent information is offered which will make the team play more effectively during the second half. Although specific information which is given the team during this valuable respite was listed in Chapter 3, it is worth relisting here:

1. Tell players of fouls and fouls on opponents.

2. Inform players of leading scorer on each team.

3. Indicate opponent's offense and make necessary defensive adjustments.

4. Indicate opponent's defense and make recommendations concerning offensive adjustments.

5. Inform team of second-half starting line-up.

It should be added that it is useless to try to improvise. Stay with what the team has practiced and can handle and their second-half play will be up to their capabilities.

Second Half

It is during this period of time that the coach has important decisions to make. These can involve a press, control offense, a freeze, whether or not to foul, and the last shot opportunity.

When ahead late in the game, with the opponents closing the gap, it is often wise to play a *control offense* in which only a good percentage shot is taken. Play is slowed down and the ball is controlled. This type of offense frustrates the opponents and consumes time. The opponent cannot score unless he has the ball and the objective is not to give it up unless two points have been scored.

The next stage of strategy, when ahead only by five to ten points in the game, is the *freeze*. Again the situation dictates the choice, but the freeze should be applied whenever the lead is still sufficient to win the game. It is recommended that the freeze include the option of shooting an unopposed lay-in should the opportunity arise.

When behind late in the game, the question of whether or not *to foul* has to be decided. Of course, the object is to force a man to the foul line hoping that he will not score or will score only one point, after which possession of the ball can be gained. The question of ethics arises, and this must be decided before game time. Should a player foul, though, and the official observe that it is a deliberate action, the penalty is two foul shots. Smart playing would advise a player, if he is going to foul, to foul a player who is a poor foul shooter. The player who commits the foul should be one who is not in danger of fouling out of the game.

The *last shot* can be a very important one when the score is within three points and the playing time is short. When the opponent is in possession of the ball and is behind by three points with only a few seconds to play, allow the man with the ball freedom of action and do not get near him when he shoots be-

cause of the danger of drawing a foul. If the shot is made, the opponent relinquishes his possession of the ball still one point behind. Again, when the opponent is behind one or two points and in possession of the ball, and the playing time is less than ten or fifteen seconds, the best defense is to play the man with the ball tight while everyone else sags toward the basket to prevent a second shot attempt and to gain possession of the ball. The opponent should not get off an uncontested shot, but the word is *caution against fouling*.

When in possession of the ball and behind by three points with the time left for only one good shot at the basket, every attempt should be made to score and have the opponent foul. The best opportunity for this situation is to drive for the basket and hope to be fouled when the shot is taken.

Two points or one point behind with only time for one shot requires a well-run pattern which results in a good shot. Whether it be a regular offensive pattern or a special play as discussed in Chapter 7 is significant, but what is really important is that the attempt be made as a co-ordinated, confident team effort.

When in possession of the ball with the score tied, work on the basis of obtaining the last shot, and then the result will be a win—or at least the game will go into overtime. This situation could exist where the ball would have to be worked for a minute or two and then the last shot would be taken with the special play starting at ten seconds left in the game.

When ahead by four, five, or six points late in the game, stall and be satisfied to win by that margin. Instructions should be to take only good shots and to rebound. No mistakes.

Substitutions

An ideal situation would exist if five players could play together at full strength and maximum effort the entire game. This is seldom seen for one reason or another, and sooner or later substitutions are necessary. No one will ever be certain that the substitution made has solved the problem; consequently, experience is necessary in evaluating the result of the action.

Rules for Substitution

In order to make substituting effective, it is possible to follow certain basic rules. These rules do not fit all situations, but can be used as general guides for substituting players.

1. Replace a tired player.

2. Take out a player who is not playing up to his ability.

3. Substitute for a man who has three fouls in the first half.

4. Put a "fireball" into the game to get things roll-

ing or to put some pep and aggressiveness into the team.

5. Substitute when a commanding lead has been built up. This will develop reserves and make the substitutes happy.

6. When ahead in the first half, substitute judiciously so that a commanding lead is not lost and so that the opponents do not gain confidence in their ability.

7. Replace players for strategic reasons. Small, fast, aggressive men for a press; a tall man for rebound strength, certain men for their defensive ability, etc.

In some offenses it is feasible to first substitute the sixth man on the team, regardless of the man's position he replaces. On the other hand, it is often necessary to substitute the third guard or forward and the second center. In this case, each player in a particular position has a substitute playing behind him who takes his place.

Each coach has to know his material and has to develop his plan for substituting accordingly. The team personnel, and consequently the substituting plan, will change from year to year, but it should still be within the above general framework of rules.

Time-Outs

Time-outs can be very valuable late in the game; therefore, every effort should be made to save them except when absolutely necessary. It is sometimes possible to use the opponent-called time-out, but when necessary one has to be taken. It should not be necessary to call a time-out to rest the team unless the game has been a strenuous one or has gone into overtime. There has to be a good reason to take a charged time-out. It is possible for the coach to legally signal for the players to take a time-out; thus there are very few times when players, on their own volition, request a time-out of an official. In fact, many coaches will not allow their players that option and call all time-outs from the bench.

Rules for Calling Time-Outs

1. When it is necessary to put in a substitute.
2. To change the playing strategy, whether it be offensive or defensive.
3. To run a special play pattern.
4. When the opponents score three or four consecutive baskets and it appears that your team is demoralized and on the run.

When a time-out is called, each coach should have a standard operating procedure. The following is recommended. The team on the floor comes to the bench. They receive wet towels and are quiet. The players on the bench join the huddle so that they are in on all playing strategies, and because it brings them right into the spirit of the game. This makes those sitting on the bench feel as close to being in the game as possible, and should one be sent into the game, he will know exactly what his playing actions should be.

One of the most important time-outs is the first one, whether it is taken by the opponents or by your team. If affords the coach the opportunity to briefly clarify the opponent's defense and offense and to take countermeasures if necessary. Patterns, maneuvers, and player actions can be briefly described or diagrammed, and in addition to a brief rest, the team has profited from the knowledge imparted to them by the coach.

Special Situations

Following are several special strategic situations which are worthy of consideration.

The first has to do with the critical situation of the star or valuable player having four fouls. One more foul and his services are lost for that game. In this case, it is often a good move, if possible, to change into a zone defense where this one player can play a more passive and "safe" defense. He has to be cautioned not to foul, though, and often a player can play a remarkably long period of time with four fouls hanging over his head.

The second strategic move should be made when the team goes behind by ten points. At this place in the game, some change should be made. The defense should be changed, the offense modified, a player substituted, a time-out taken, or something done that might turn the tide of the battle. Each situation of this kind will call for a different reaction, but the important thing is to make some effort to rally the team and reverse the course of the game.

The third strategic plan of action offered is that of a change in defense as a second-half surprise for the opponent. They will not have ample opportunity to adjust as they would during half time and will of necessity have to make their countermoves during a charged time-out. A surprise defense can often upset the opponents, particularly if they have not expected it.

The fourth situation involves the use of one offensive pattern the first half and a second one the second half. When the offense is kept fairly basic and simple, this is not too difficult for the team to accomplish, and the opponents will have to be ready for two offensive patterns. In addition, any defensive adjustments made by the opponents at half time will be of no avail, since what they adjusted for has now been changed. This same principle is suggested for out-of-bounds plays. Run one the first half and a different one the second half. The opponent will not have the opportunity to adjust, and several baskets might result from this strategic move.

▶ Summary

The individual coach is responsible for the strategy of team play. The operation, adjustments, moves, and countermoves are his concern. Each situation will necessitate a thorough knowledge of the entire problem, and each will probably require a different course of action.

There are general principles that can be followed which cover situations that occur frequently in the course of a season. The most important of these is to endeavor to make the opponent play your type of game.

Playing strategy deals with problems encountered in conjunction with preparation for the game and playing the game. Under this category come such problems as when to press, when to control the play, and when to stall.

Substituting players and time-outs can be accomplished within the framework of general rules. These rules of action help the coach and relieve him of the costly gamble of guesswork.

When special situations arise during the course of a game, recommended courses of action often help solve the problem with a suggested change of strategy.

Basketball is like a chess game, with its move and countermove, and the experienced coach with a thorough knowledge of the problem will be the one to solve it realistically and successfully.

▶ Study Questions

1. Define strategy as the term refers to basketball.
2. Explain tempo and why it is important in team play.
3. List two general principles, or tactics, which require a decision on the part of the coach.
4. Why is an appraisal of the opponent's players important? Give a hypothetical example.
5. What valuable information can be gathered concerning the opponent during the first half?
6. Outline the half-time procedure.
7. Is there any set rule which gives the time when a team should stall or press? Why or why not?
8. You have a time-out. What instructions do you give to the team that is behind three points and has eight seconds to go?
9. Would you take a player from the game when he has fouled three times in the first half? If so, why?
10. Is it a good idea to substitute freely in the first half when a lead of fifteen points has been built up?
11. You, as coach, will call all the time-outs. What rules of action will you follow?

▶ Projects for Additional Study

1. Look in the sports page of a newspaper for articles reporting basketball games and find in them references to strategy. Find one which was successful and one which failed.
2. In the above newspaper reports, on a game which ended within four points, did either team stall or press?

3. You are to play a fast breaking team. In preparation for the game, what tactics would you give to the team to slow the opponent down?

4. Situation: behind two points, opponent's ball in back court, and only five seconds to play. Give instructions to the team.

5. Set up two hypothetical situations in which you are behind, and plan the strategy which could enable the players to win or tie the game.

6. Interview two basketball coaches and determine their rules for substitutions and time-outs.

7. Ask these two coaches their theories regarding action when behind by only a few points late in the game. Is there a hard and fast rule of action?

8. The opponents are ahead at half time by ten points and have been driving the baseline with set plays. What adjustments could be made at half time? Were these maneuvers practiced by the team?

► Selected References

Athletic Journal. Athletic Journal Publishing Co., Evanston, Ill. Contains many individual articles dealing with all aspects of strategy.

Auerbach, Arnold. *Basketball for the Player, the Fan and the Coach.* New York: Pocket Books, Inc., 1952. Contains a list of 57 psychological and strategic moves.

Basketball Coach's Digest. Huntington Laboratories, Huntington, Ind. Yearly journal which contains many of the best articles dealing with strategy.

Bee, Clair. *Winning Basketball Plays.* New York: A. S. Barnes & Co., 1950. Has excellent material on the strategy of team play.

Bunn, John W. *Basketball Methods.* New York: The Macmillan Co., 1939. Excellent sections on team strategy and tactics to be used.

Dean, Everett S. *Progressive Basketball.* New York: Prentice-Hall, Inc., 1950. Has an entire chapter of excellent ideas devoted to strategy and psychology of playing basketball.

Gardner, Jack. *Championship Basketball with Jack Gardner.* New York: Prentice-Hall, Inc., 1961. Basic information on team strategy is covered.

Julian, Alvin F. *Bread and Butter Basketball.* New York: Prentice Hall, Inc., 1960. Contains a good discussion on game procedures and strategy.

Loeffler, Ken. *Ken Loeffler on Basketball.* New York: Prentice-Hall, Inc., 1955. Excellent suggestions regarding substitutions and time-outs.

McGuire, Frank. *Defensive Basketball.* New York: Prentice-Hall, Inc., 1959. Deals with defensive strategy and the rating and the matching of players.

_____. *Offensive Basketball.* New York: Prentice-Hall, Inc., 1958. Deals with offensive game strategy, substitutions and time-outs.

McLane, Hardin. *Championship Basketball by 12 Great Coaches.* Englewood Cliffs, N. J.: Prentice-Hall, Inc., 1965. Coach John W. Bunn on winning basketball strategy.

Newell, Pete, and Benington, John. *Basketball Methods.* New York: The Ronald Press Co., 1962. Contains a fine discussion of strategy and game tempo.

Rupp, Adolph F. *Rupp's Championship Basketball.* New York: Prentice-Hall, Inc., 1948. Rupp's own ideas on substitutes and time-outs.

Scholastic Coach. Scholastic Magazines, Inc., New York, N. Y. 10036. Contains many individual articles dealing with all aspects of strategy.

Wilkes, Glenn. *Winning Basketball Strategy.* New York: Prentice-Hall, Inc., 1959. Excellent book dealing entirely with basketball strategy.

Wooden, John R. *Practical Modern Basketball.* New York: The Ronald Press Co., 1966. Basic strategy on playing the game.

CHAPTER 9: Scouting and Game Statistics

The collection, analysis, and use of information concerning both the opponent and one's own team are extremely valuable and, when intelligently utilized, can aid the coach in many different ways.

Information and statistics can be collected on an opponent and effectively used in preparing to play that opponent. This information is usually gathered on a scouting report form.

Statistics on all aspects of playing the game, on each player on the home team and regarding the opponents' play, can be compiled from scrimmages, intersquad games, and actual competition. These objective figures will give the coach and the players facts concerning individual and team play.

▶ Scouting the Opponent

Collection of Data

Scouting is a method of securing pertinent information on the opposition, and it can be accomplished by several methods.

Personal observation by coach or team scout.

Movies of opponent.

Independent scout, friend, fellow coach, etc.

Observation of opponent during game with that opponent.

The first three will give specific information on the opponent, while the latter justifiably surmises that because a certain defense, offense, or strategy was used by that coach and team the first half of that game, it will be used again the second half, during a second game that season, or the next season.

The Scouting Report

Generally speaking, scouting reports can be divided into two types: the brief, short form and the comprehensive, long form.

Short Form

This form is designed to collect the basic information on an opponent. Two such forms are shown in Figures 147 and 148, and they indicate the basic information gathered.

Opponents' offense. Offensive patterns, fast breaks, out-of-bounds plays, jump ball organization, foul shot offense, and stall.

Opponents' defense. Basic team defenses, free throw defense, and press.

Personnel. Name, number, height, weight, and individual characteristics of important players.

Comments. Opponents' weak and strong points, plus how they might be exploited.

Long Form

This type of form is designed to collect comprehensive information on the opponent. Reports run from two to eighteen pages in length and call for specific information on all aspects of the opponent's team and individual play. Figures 149 and 150 indicate typical comprehensive long-form scouting reports used at Indiana State University and Brigham Young University.

Comprehensive scouting reports, regardless of their individual make-up and form, specifically ask for information on the following.

Personnel appraisal. The individual personal characteristics of each player and his replacement.

1. Name, number, height, and weight.
2. Offensive characteristics. Specific information on individual maneuvers, speed, strength, favorite shots, and whether right- or left-handed. Strong points and weak points.
3. Defensive characteristics. Specific information on regular position, rebound strength, strong and weak points.

SCOUTING REPORT

.... vs. ....

Date ....

PERSONNEL

PLAYER Name, number, height, weight, position.	SHOOTING STYLES	REBOUNDING STRENGTH	BALL HANDLING	COMMENTS

OFFENSE:

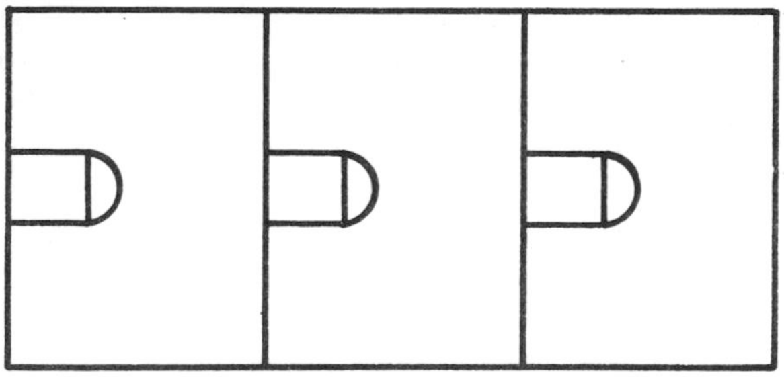

DEFENSE:

COMMENTS:

OUT OF BOUNDS

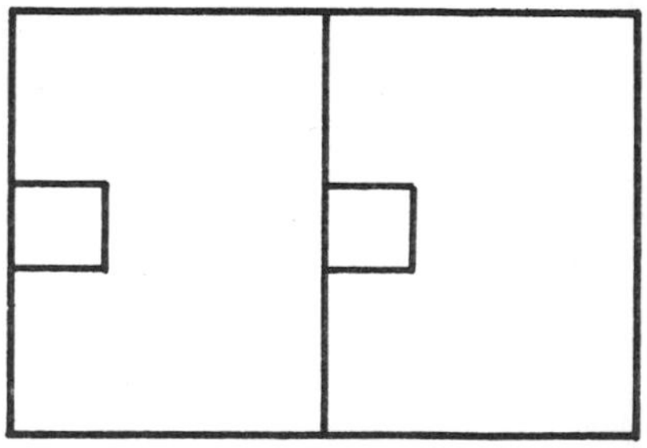

JUMP BALL

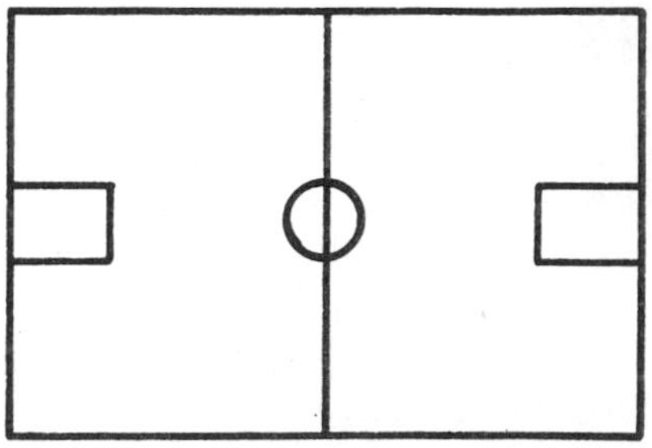

Fig. 147. Scouting Report: Short Form.

SCOUTING REPORT

_____ vs. _____ Date_____

OFFENSE PATTERNS   **SPECIAL**

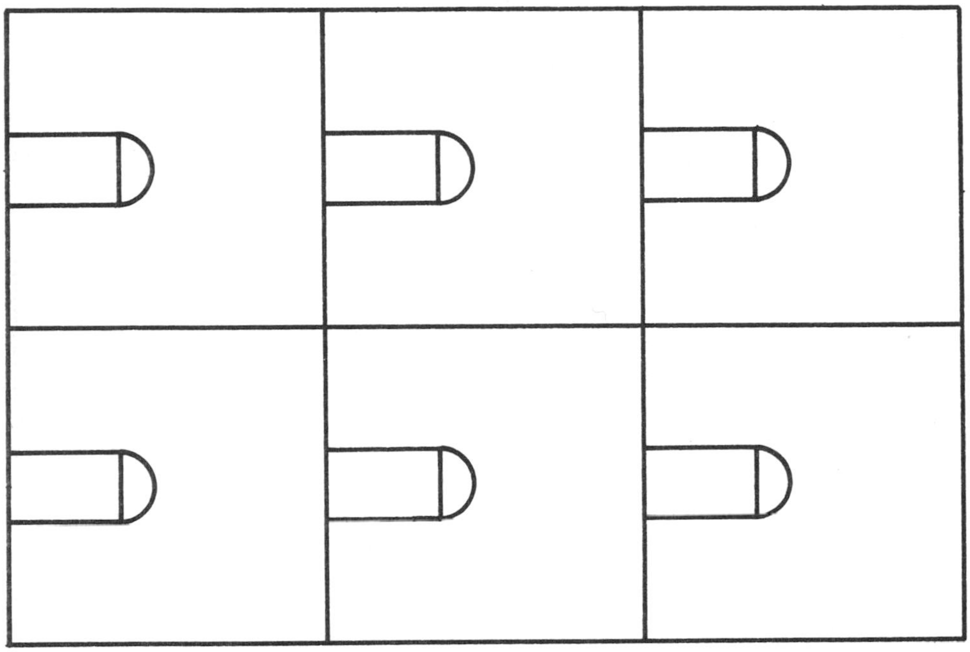

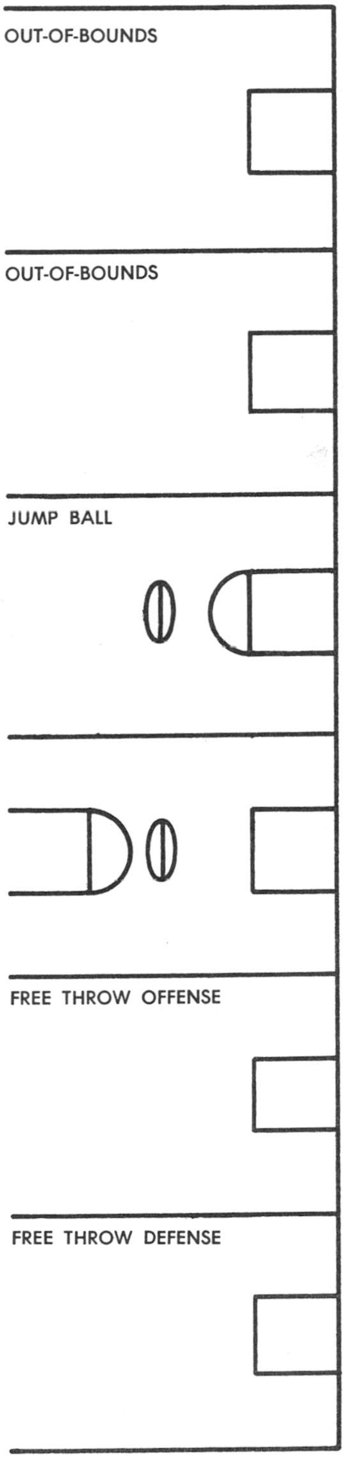

DEFENSE

PERSONNEL   Name   No.   Ht.   Wt.   Characteristics

C
F
F
G
G

COMMENTS

Fig. 148. Scouting Report: Short Form.

INDIANA STATE SCOUTING REPORT

-- vs. ---

At ---

Date ---

Officials ---

ROSTER

Starters

-- ----------

-- ----------

-- ----------

-- ----------

-- ----------

Scorers	Post Men
Fast Men	Outside Shooters
Good Dribblers	Rebounder
Cutters	Weak Defense

Replacements

Individual Notes

-- ----------

-- ----------

-- ----------

-- ----------

-- ----------

FIG. 149. SCOUTING REPORT: COMPREHENSIVE FORM. (*Courtesy, Branch McCracken, Basketball Coach, Indiana State University.*)

INDIVIDUAL CHARACTERISTICS

No.	No.	No.	No.	No.	No.	No.	No.	No.	No.

GENERAL

Height									
Weight									
Is he in good condition?									
Is he a good team man?									
Is he fast?									
Is he a good rebounder?									
Does he have good competitive spirit?									

OFFENSIVE

Is he aggressive on offense?									
Is he a good offensive man?									
Is he a good dribbler?									
Does he dribble through fast and hard?									
Is he a good ball handler?									
Is he a good passer?									
Does he look to pass to cutting teammates?									
Does he attempt "up and unders"?									
Does he attempt "give and goes"?									
Does he cut through hard and fast?									
Is he a sleeper who does not get back?									
Is he deceptive?									
Does he change direction on cuts?									
Does he try to bump his opponent into mates?									
Does he screen for teammates?									
Is he a good scorer?									
Is he a good set shooter?									
Does he take left-handed shots?									
Does he take right-handed shots?									
Does he shoot a lot?									
Is he a good foul shooter?									
Does he try to tap in rebounds?									

DEFENSIVE

Is he aggressive on defense?									
Is he a good defensive player?									
Does he get back fast on defense?									
Is he easily feinted out of position?									
Does he turn his head on defense?									
Does he watch the ball on a shot?									
Does he switch well?									
Does he fight hard for defensive rebounds?									
Is he a ball hawk?									

FIG. 149 (continued)

TEAM CHARACTERISTICS

	YES	NO

GENERAL

Is the team big? ....

Is the team fast? ....

Is the team aggressive? ....

Is the team in good condition? ....

Does the team have good competitive spirit? ....

Do the men fight hard for rebounds? ....

Are the reserves good? ....

OFFENSIVE

Does the team have an offensive pattern? ....

What type of offense is used? ....

Is the "post" used? ....

Where does the "post" man play? ....

How are passes made to the "post" man? ....

Does the "post" man shoot a lot? ....

Is it a good ball-handling team? ....

Is the team deliberate? ....

Does the team use a fast break? ....

Do the men "cut" a lot? ....

Do the men use "give and goes"? ....

Do the men use "up and unders"? ....

Do men set up plays for teammates? ....

Do they use a sleeper? ....

Do the men shoot a lot? ....

Do the men take a lot of set shots? ....

Do the men take many one-handed shots? ....

Do they attempt to tap in rebounds? ....

Do the men dribble through a lot? ....

DEFENSIVE

What type of defense is used? ....

Does the defense withdraw? ....

Do the men get back to defensive positions fast? ....

Is a zone defense used? ....

Is an all-court press used? ....

Are set shooters given much room? ....

How is the post man played? ....

Do the men switch? ....

Are dribblers boxed out? ....

Do the men ball-hawk? ....

Do the men slide well? ....

Do screens work on them? ....

Do the men turn their heads? ....

Do the men follow the flight of the ball on a shot? ....

Are they aggressive on defense? ....

Do they rebound well defensively? ....

FIG. 149 (continued)

FIG. 149 (continued)

BRIGHAM YOUNG UNIVERSITY
SCOUTING REPORT FORM

_____ vs. _____
Visitors   Home Team

_____   _____
Played At   Date

_____
Name of Scout

Starters and Their Substitutes	Jersey Number	Height	Weight
FORWARD			
Sub 1			
Sub 2			
FORWARD			
Sub 1			
Sub 2			
CENTER			
Sub 1			
Sub 2			
GUARD			
Sub 1			
Sub 2			
GUARD			
Sub 1			
Sub 2			

OFFENSIVE ALIGNMENT

DEFENSIVE ALIGNMENT

INDIVIDUAL CHARACTERISTICS

List the important characteristics of each player. We would like to know the strength and weakness both offensively and defensively and what he likes to do most. Is he fast or slow? Clever? Quick? Can he hit from outside? Does he drive much? What type of shot does he use the most? Is he right- or left-handed? How much game experience? Is he fundamentally sound? In what area does he do most of his shooting? Can he maneuver to get his shots or does he need help from teammates, such as an inside screen?

Fig. 150. Scouting Report: Comprehensive Form. (*Courtesy, Stan Watts, Basketball Coach, Brigham Young University, and Jack Gardner, Basketball Coach, University of Utah.*)

INDIVIDUAL CHARACTERISTICS (Please list each member of the personnel and the important information about each.)

-- -------- -------- --------
                    Player   **No.** **Hgt.** **Wgt.**

-- -------- -------- --------
                    Player   **No.** **Hgt.** **Wgt.**

-- -------- -------- --------
                    Player   **No.** **Hgt.** **Wgt.**

-- -------- -------- --------
                    Player   **No.** **Hgt.** **Wgt.**

Fɪɢ. 150 (*continued*)

INDIVIDUAL CHARACTERISTICS (Please list each member of the personnel and the important information about each.)

Player	No.	Hgt.	Wgt.

Player	No.	Hgt.	Wgt.

Player	No.	Hgt.	Wgt.

Player	No.	Hgt.	Wgt.

FIG. 150 *(continued)*

INDIVIDUAL SHOOTING CHART

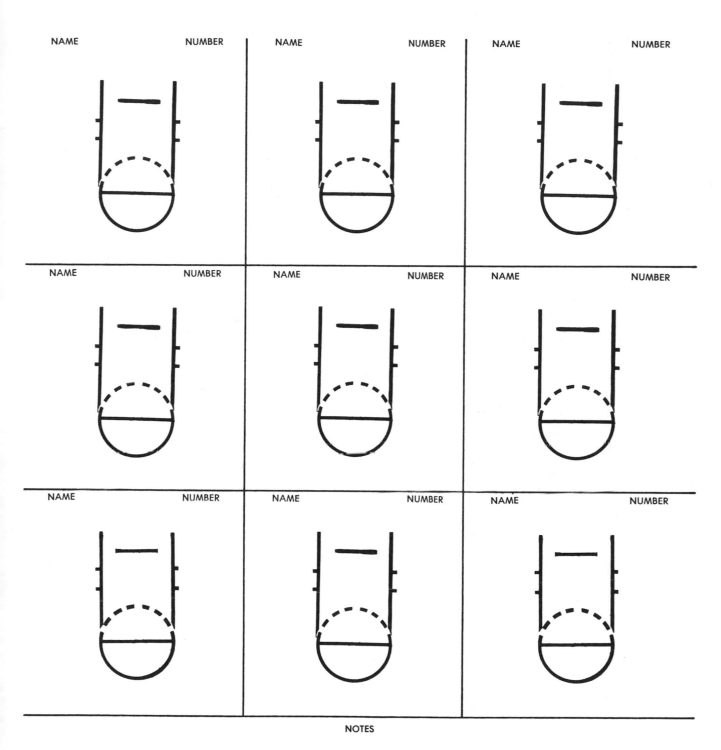

NOTES

FIG. 150 (continued)

OFFENSIVE PATTERN OF PLAY

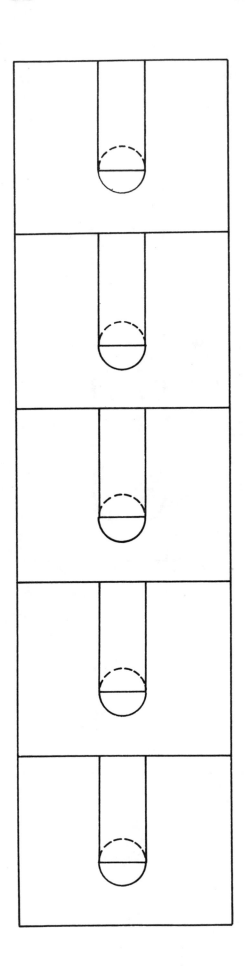

Fig. 150 (continued)

OFFENSIVE PATTERN OF PLAY

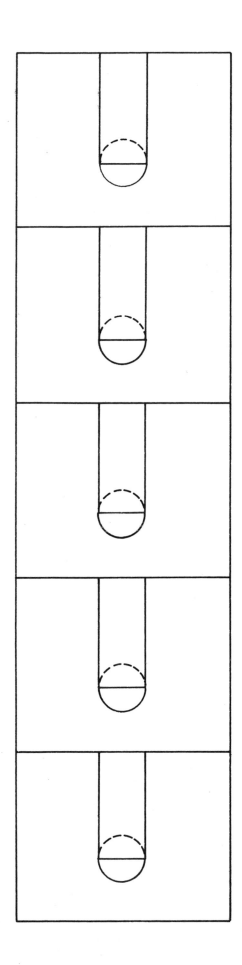

FIG. 150 (continued)

OFFENSIVE PATTERN OF PLAY

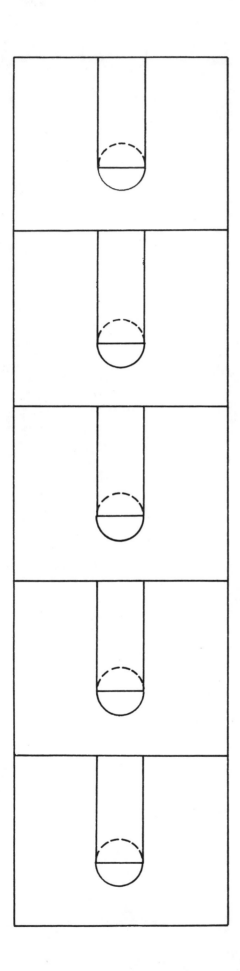

Fig. 150 (continued)

OUT-OF-BOUNDS PLAYS AND CENTER JUMP

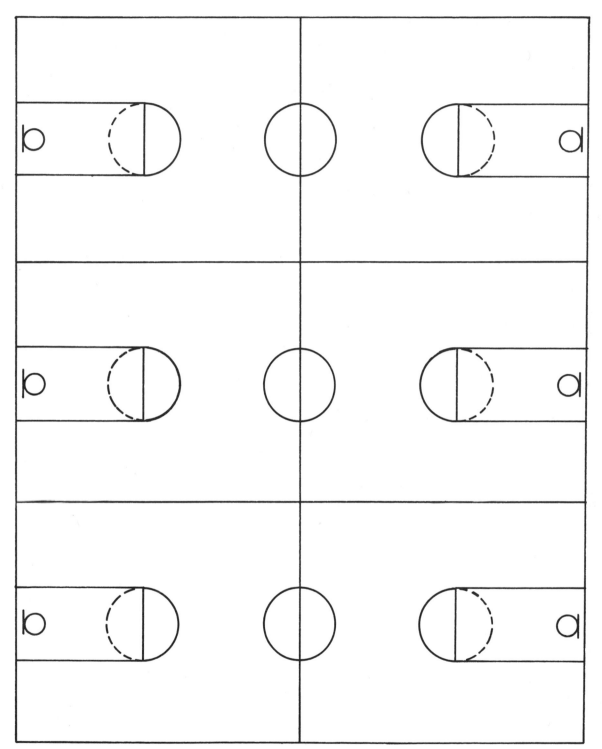

1. What formation do they use when they have the height advantage on the held ball?
2. Where do they like to tip?
3. Do they like to tip to any particular man?
4. How do they line up for a defensive tip?

FIG. 150 (continued)

OPPONENTS ON THE OFFENSE

Write a concise report on their strengths. Are they a breaking ball club? How strong is their backboard play? Would they rather hold up the ball in the back court and then come down and run set offense? Do they use ball control?

1. What is their main offensive threat?

2. Do they like to break fast or would they rather bring the ball down slowly?

3. Are they clever and free shooters or do they stress picks or screens to get off their shots?

4. How many and what players rebound on the offensive board?

SET OFFENSE

1. What formation do they set up in? 3 in and 2 out? 2 in and 3 out? 1-3-1?

2. Where do they line up? (See the front-page diagrams.)

3. Are they a blocking or screening team?

4. Who are their best shooters? From what part of the court do they like to shoot, and what type of shots do they take?

5. Who are their fastest men?

6. Do they fake and dribble? How well?

7. Who are their best and most dangerous men? (Suggest defensive assignments.)

FIG. 150 (continued)

DO THEY USE A STALL GAME?

1. What is the continuity of the stall game? (4-man weave; 5-man weave, etc.)

2. Is it a team movement or does one man use a possession dribble game?

3. Could they be pressed?

4. When during the game can you expect them to go into their stall game?

PLEASE DIAGRAM STALL PATTERN

OUT-OF-BOUNDS PLAYS

1. Do they have an organized out-of-bounds setup?

2. Under their basket (the basket they are shooting at), who takes the ball out? Do they have a signal to start the maneuver?

3. What do they use from the sideline? Is it a play carrying a scoring threat from out of bounds or is it to get the ball in and start their regular offense?

4. Do they have a formation and method of bringing the ball in from the far end line when the opponents are putting on a full-court press? If so, please diagram?

FIG. 150 (*continued*)

DEFENSE

1. What type of defense do they use? Man-to-man? Zone? Combination?

2. Do they usually shift on screens or block plays?

3. Where does the front line usually pick up? Do they press or sag?

4. Do they use a pressing defense when behind? Is it man-to-man or zone? If man-to-man, do they switch or cross over?

5. Who plays in the front line?

6. Who tries to cover the post? How do they play the post man? In front, to the side, or behind? Is he easily fooled by fakes? Does he get help from his teammates away from the ball?

7. In general, do you consider them a good defensive team? What are their weaknesses?

8. Who are their strong men? Who are their weak?

9. How tough are they on the defensive backboard? Can we fast break on them? Do they loaf changing from offense to defense? Are they slow getting back?

10. Please write a brief summary of their set defense.

FIG. 150 (*continued*)

General team appraisal. A summary of the better players in each category:

Scorers	Outside shooters
Post men	Fast men
Rebounders	Slow men
Drivers	Good defense
Cutters	Weak defense

Offensive team appraisal. General and specific information on the opponent's offense. Diagrams are included where possible.

Offensive alignment.

Plays or patterns. Include against what type of defense.

Fast break.

Jump ball plays. Tip-off first and second half. Tip to one man or a play?

Out-of-bounds plays: from baseline and sideline.

Stall game.

Patterns vs. press. Include type of press.

Foul shot alignment: offensive.

Strength on offensive board. Number of men and who they are.

Free-wheeling or percentage shot team.

Strengths.

Weaknesses.

Defensive team appraisal. General and specific information on the opponent's defense. Diagrams are included where possible.

Basic defense.

Secondary defense.

Where does front line pick up man with the ball?

Jump ball defense.

Foul shot alignment: defensive.

Type of press.

Strength on defensive board. Who?

Strengths.

Weaknesses.

Suggestions and strategy.

1. What of ours will work offensively: set offense, fast break, out-of-bounds plays, press offense, stall, and jump ball plays?
2. What of ours will work defensively: man-to-man, tight, regular or sag defense, zone, front line pick-up point, press, and combat stall?
3. How do we combat their strengths?
4. How do we exploit their weaknesses?

Analysis and Use of Scouting Report

When all the information has been compiled on an opponent, there should be a rating of the players offensively and defensively, an appraisal of the team's offense and defense, and suggestions to combat the strengths and to exploit the weaknesses. It is at this point, when the coach has an intimate knowledge of the situation, that he plans the strategy for that game. Now a coach can effectively match his strong defensive players against the opponent's and arm his players with information concerning the individual opponent and the team. Strong defensive men are pitted against high scorers, tall men versus tall men, and the like. Also desired is specific information on the playing habits of the opponents. If a player constantly drives to his right, the defensive man can stop this drive by playing a half a man strong to that side. If a player does not have a strong outside shot, he can be played weakly on the outside and strongly when he gets inside, etc.

Probably the best plan of action is to give the players an honest appraisal of the situation and to present to them material with which they can cope.

There is a certain minimum knowledge which each squad should possess regarding its opponent. This would include what to expect offensively and defensively, and a personnel report. Players are matched, and the coach informs the players of their tactics and strategy for the game. It is at this point that the coach endeavors to combat the strengths and profit by the weaknesses of the opponent.

In addition to the minimum knowledge which each squad should possess, more information can be given if time allows and the individual team members can understand and cope with it. This information pertains to the specific individual questions which deal with particular aspects of the opponent's offense, defense, and strategy. It amounts to presenting the comprehensive scouting report to each team member for study and specific information.

Game Statistics

The compilation of statistics regarding the play of the individual members of the team, the team itself, or of the opponents, provides vital objective data which indicates specifically the value of each man and how the game was played.

Statistics should be accumulated on field goal shooting, foul shooting, personal fouls, rebounds, assists, mistakes, and recoveries.

_____ vs. _____   Date: _____

F.G.A.

F.G.M.

%

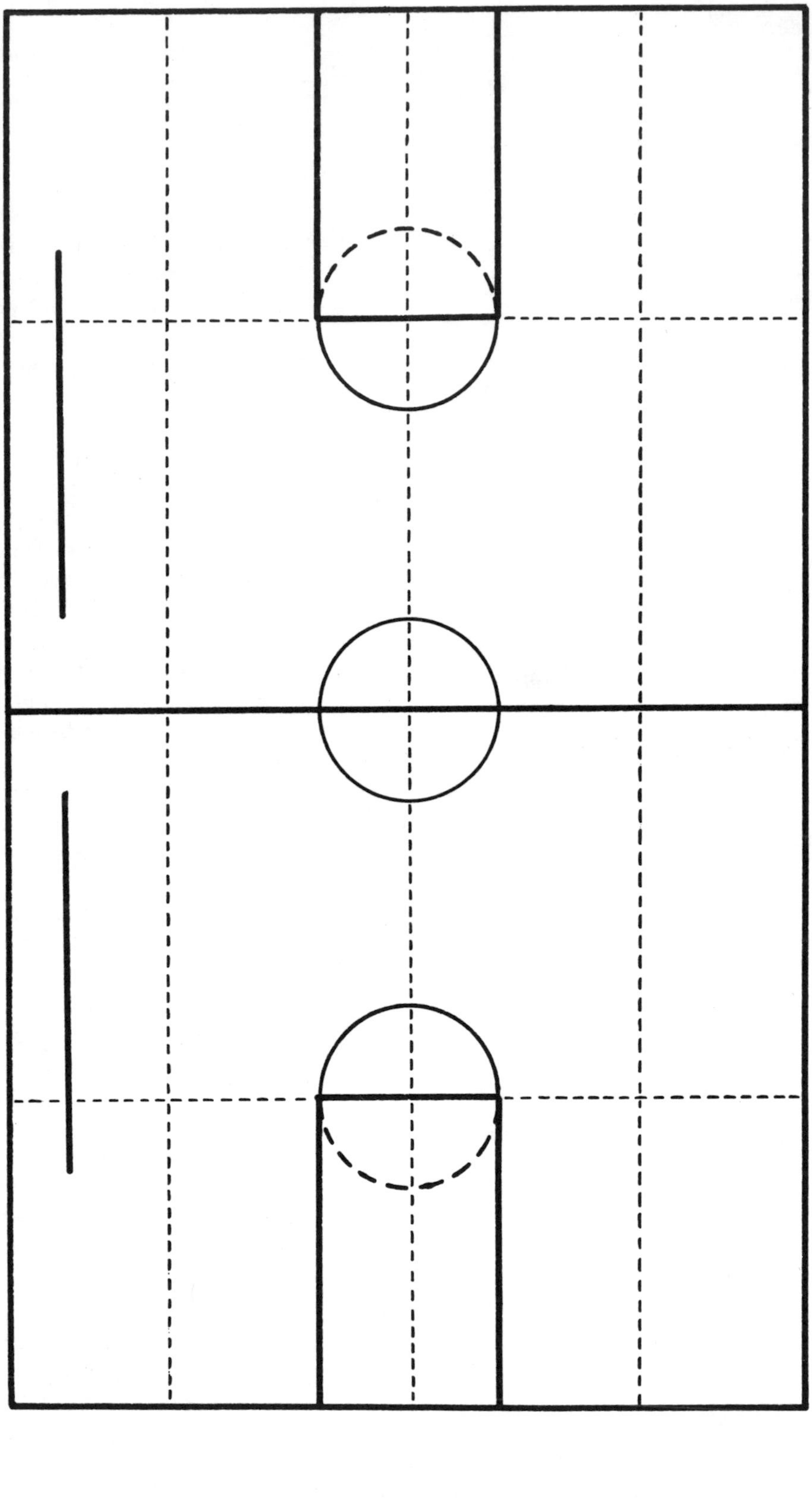

F.G.A.

F.G.M.

%

CHART X. SHOT CHART

Field Goal Attempts

The results of field goal shooting are obtained from some type of a shot chart (Chart X). Pertinent information is gathered on the number of attempts by each player, shots made, and the shooting percentage. Also noted is where the shots are taken by individuals and by the entire team. Is there a pattern which indicates that a player has a favorite spot, or are a team's attempts so grouped as to reveal that they run everything, for instance, to the right? Such information can aid in planning the defense.

Foul Shooting

The importance of foul shooting cannot be minimized. The free throws can account for many points during one game, and often close games are decided at the foul line. The number of foul shots attempted and made, and the shooting percentage for an individual or team, clearly indicate how good the foul shooting is.

Personal Fouls

Players who foul consistently are not only jeopardizing their opportunity to stay in the game but are allowing the opponents to add to their point total one by one by foul shots. A team that fouls a great deal will give the opponent many points, and frequently the difference is costly.

Rebounds

Basketball games are won on the boards; consequently, this important statistic can indicate which players are doing yeoman work. Rebounding can be broken down to offensive rebounding and defensive rebounding. In order to account for every shot that is missed, team rebounds also have to be counted. These include instances in which a shot rebounds out of bounds, is deflected out of bounds before there is possession, and a free throw attempt misses the rim and is awarded to opponent out of bounds.

Assists

An assist is credit given to the player who passes to a player who in turn scores. The score resulting is directly from the pass. Players who accumulate a great number of assists are valuable men on the team, and conversely, an opponent who has a great number of assists should be guarded with this in mind. Keep the ball from him; either prevent or hinder his passing by aggressive guarding.

Mistakes

It is in this category that bad passes, violations, and fumbles are recorded and assessed against that player.

If a player has a large total in this category, his play should be closely scrutinized with the idea in mind of his improving his play or of replacing him.

Recoveries

Recoveries are recorded for a player, and they include tie-ups which result in a held ball and recoveries by intercepting passes or recovering fumbles. Recoveries are an indication of heads-up, aggressive play. It is possible to classify rebounds as recoveries, although most coaches prefer to consider this aspect of recoveries separately.

Charts

There are many types of charts, each designed for a specific purpose. The "Basketball Profile" Statistics Chart and the "Basketball Profile" Statistics Chart Summary respectively are probably two of the best charts designed to easily collect and record basketball statistics. Information is gathered on the former (Chart XI) during the first half by a team manager or an assistant. A duplicate copy is made for the opposition during home games as a courtesy. This information is available then for half-time use. After the game, the information is placed on the summary chart (Chart XII). There is no doubt as to the relative value of one player's playing up to capacity in any one game as compared with the season's average.

Chart I (shown in Chapter 2) is a different type of chart, an individual statistics chart. It is maintained during the game and as a player shoots, rebounds, etc.; a tally is placed in the appropriate column. These are totalled at half time and at the end of the game.

An individual shot chart is shown in Chart X. Whenever a player shoots, his number is placed on the chart at the place corresponding to his position on the court. If the shot is made, the number is circled. Totals, which include one's own and opponent's attempts, shots made, and percentages are registered for the first half, and a second chart is used during the second half.

Analysis of Game Data

Game data can be used immediately or recorded and filed for future use. Immediate use would include half-time analysis and preparation for that particular game. Chart XIII offers a form which can be used for recording information for half-time use. Shooting percentages indicate players who are doing well, rebounding figures reveal who is getting the ball, etc. Future use involves the next game on the schedule, the next game against that particular opponent, or even for use the next season. Each category utilized will reveal specific information for the coach's analysis and use.

"Basketball Profile" Statistics Chart

Date _____ School _____ vs. _____ at _____ Score _____ Half-Final _____

AGAINST

SHOTS

School _____

ATT. _____
Made _____
Pct. _____ Half _____

BAD PASSES	VIOLATION	FUMBLE	HELD BALL	RECOVERY	ASSISTS

OFFENSIVE TEAM

FOR

SHOTS

School _____

ATT. _____
Made _____
Pct. _____ Half _____

DEFENSIVE TEAM

REBOUNDS

Offensive	Defensive

Personal Fouls

REBOUNDS

Offensive	Defensive

Personal Fouls

FREE THROWS

Score _____ (quarter) _____ Half _____ Score _____ (quarter) _____ Half _____

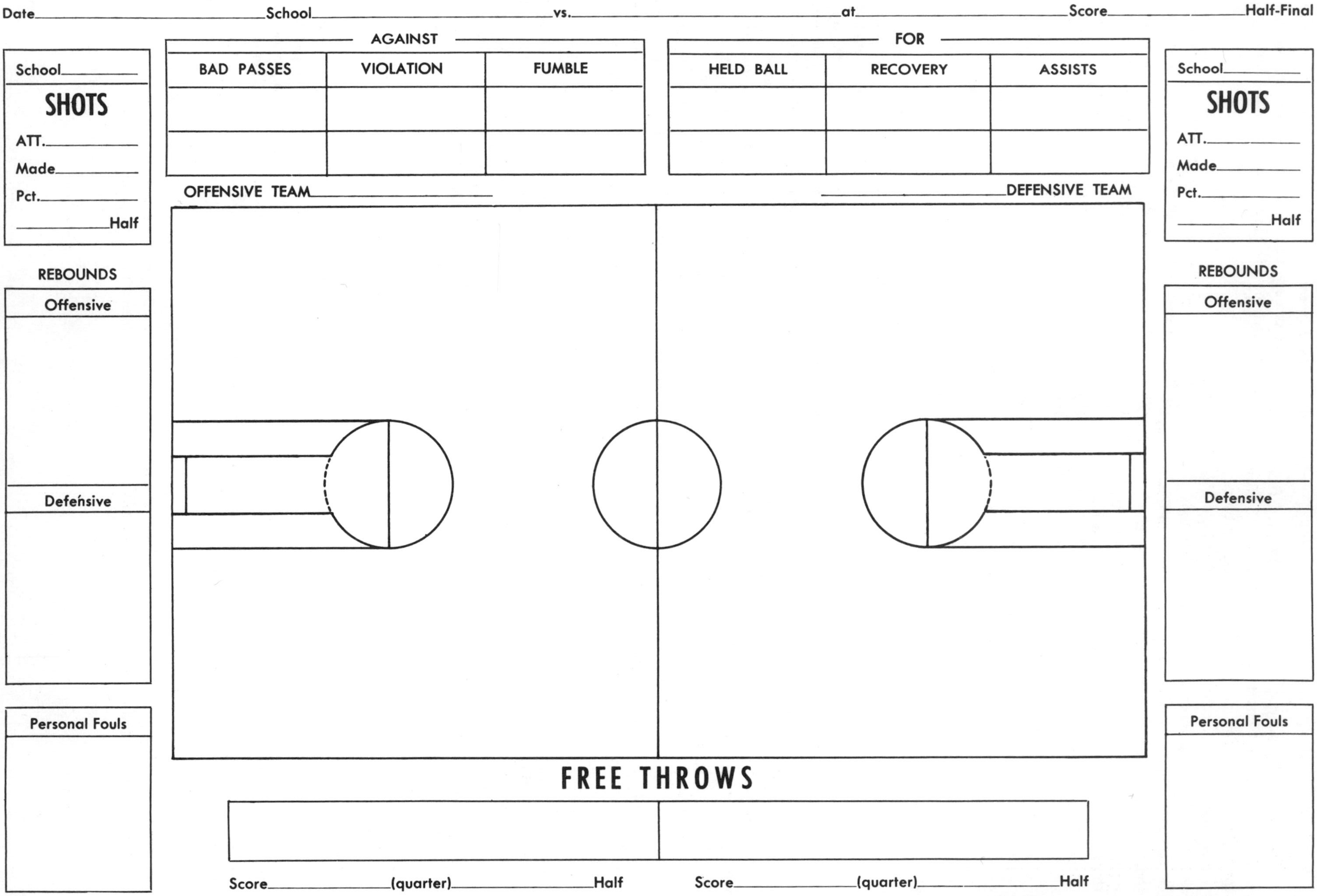

CHART XI "BASKETBALL PROFILE" STATISTICS CHART (Courtesy Statistics Chart Com-

"BASKETBALL PROFILE" STATISTICS CHART SUMMARY

DATE _____ TEAM _____ VS. _____ AT _____ SCORE _____ OBSERVOR _____

| PLAYERS | | SHOTS | | | FREE THROWS | | | REBOUNDS | | P.F. | AGAINST | | | FOR | | | Plus or Minus Points |
NUMBER	NAME	SA	SM	PCT.	SA	SM	PCT.	OFF.	DEF.		Bad Pass	Viol.	Fumb.	Held Ball	Recov.	Assists	
SCHOOL	TOTAL																
SCHOOL																	

CHART XII. "BASKETBALL PROFILE" STATISTICS CHART SUMMARY (*Courtesy, Statistics Chart Company, 105-107 Fourth Ave., Peoria, Ill.*)

HALF-TIME INFORMATION CHART

Compile from box score and statistics chart on both teams.
When home team, make duplicate copy for the opponents.

	HOME	OPPONENT
HALF-TIME SCORE		
FIELD GOAL ATTEMPTS		
FIELD GOALS MADE		
FIELD GOAL PERCENTAGE		
FOUL SHOTS ATTEMPTED		
FOUL SHOTS MADE		
FOUL SHOT PERCENTAGE		
REBOUNDING: Individual		
Team		
Total		
INDIVIDUAL SCORING LEADERS		
INDIVIDUAL REBOUNDING LEADERS		
PLAYERS WITH 3 OR MORE FOULS		

COMMENTS:

Defense _____

Offense _____

Strategy _____

Chart XIII. Half-Time Information Chart

► Summary

Scouting involves the collection, analysis, and use of information concerning the opponent. Strategic use of the data and the information given to the team should involve an honest opinion and that with which the squad can cope.

Statistics concerning the playing of the game include: field goal shooting, foul shooting, rebounding, mistakes, recoveries, assists, and personal fouls. This information reveals objective data on how each player, as well as the team, is playing the game.

► Study Questions

1. Outline the pertinent information compiled by the short-form type of scouting report.
2. As a coach, what minimum essential information would you desire to know regarding your next opponent?
3. It is revealed in the scouting report that one of the opponents always drives to his right. How will you use this information?
4. You know the basic patterns the opponent uses for his offense. How will you utilize this information?
5. Why is the recording of "recoveries" important? What is included in this category?
6. What does the shot chart reveal for half-time use?
7. Mistakes can be recorded as game statistics. What is included, and why are mistakes important?
8. A shot chart indicates that the opposition shoots primarily from the right side of the court and one player takes half the shots. Defense this team.

► Projects for Additional Study

1. Attend a basketball game and scout one of the teams. Use one of the long type of comprehensive forms.
2. From the data obtained in Question 1, fill in a short type scouting form.
3. Using a theoretical team, you as coach analyze the information gathered in Question 1 and indicate what information you will give to your team.
4. Chart shots for both teams for an entire basketball game. Analyze the statistics after you have summarized them. Are there any obvious conclusions you can make?
5. Visit two different coaches and question them regarding the following: (a) How do they scout? (b) What forms do they use? (c) What information do they give their squads? (d) What game statistics do they maintain? (e) What use do they make of this data?

► Selected References

Athletic Journal. Athletic Journal Publishing Co., Evanston, Ill. Has occasional articles which deal with scouting and the use of statistics.

Dean, Everett S. *Progressive Basketball.* New York: Prentice-Hall, Inc., 1950. Good information on scouting the opponent and the use of the report.

Gardner, Jack. *Championship Basketball with Jack Gardner.* New York: Prentice-Hall, Inc., 1961. Thorough coverage of scouting, scouting techniques, and scouting forms.

Hobson, Howard A. *Scientific Basketball*. New York: Prentice-Hall, Inc., 1949. Comprehensive treatment of scouting, statistics, and their use. Entire book deals with this subject.

Julian, Alvin F. *Bread and Butter Basketball*. New York: Prentice-Hall, Inc., 1960. Contains scouting information and useful charts.

McCreary, Jay. *Winning High School Basketball*. New York: Prentice-Hall, Inc., 1956. Good source of information on scouting.

McGuire, Frank. *Offensive Basketball*. New York: Prentice-Hall, Inc., 1958. Scouting and rating the players and the offense are clearly presented.

McLane, Hardin. *Championship Basketball by 12 Great Coaches*. Englewood Cliffs, N. J.: Prentice-Hall, Inc., 1965. Coach Brian McCall on charting and scouting.

Rupp, Adolph F. *Rupp's Championship Basketball*. New York: Prentice-Hall, Inc., 1948. Good material on scouting.

Scholastic Coach. Scholastic Magazines, Inc., New York, N. Y. 10036. Has occasional articles which deal with scouting and the use of statistics.

Wilkes, Glenn. *Winning Basketball Strategy*. New York: Prentice-Hall, Inc., 1959. Excellent coverage of strategy by scouting and strategic use of charts.

Wooden, John R. *Practical Modern Basketball*. New York: The Ronald Press Co., 1966. Scouting, practice and game statistics, forms and charts and, in general, excellent material.

CHAPTER 10: Conditioning and Training

"The game of basketball demands the finest type of mental alertness in a physically fit, well co-ordinated body."[1]

"Stamina, muscle co-ordination, good mind, and agility are prerequisites of a good ball player. As basketball is played today, it is one of the most strenuous of team games. Every player must be in top physical condition."[2]

"Efficient performance is attained through a carefully planned program of progressive practice which will perfect co-ordination, eliminate unnecessary moves, accomplish results at the expense of a minimum of energy, and condition the muscle structure and the circulation to withstand without harm the intensive demands made upon them."[3]

These three statements perfectly illustrate the point that basketball is a strenuous game and that each player must, to play efficiently, be in good physical condition.

Physical condition can be defined as the state of efficiency of the body with regard to participation in basketball. Training is the means whereby the body is physically conditioned. Training in this regard involves exercise, diet, sleep, and mental attitude.

▶ Pre-Season Training

Each basketball player should, by the first game, have the physical condition necessary to play an entire game at full speed. This involves the stamina, endurance, and mental attitude to stop, start, run, and stop and start again for a complete game. A player in good physical condition will accomplish this task and will rapidly recover from fatigue after the game.

There seem to be two general theories regarding pre-season training. The first theory is that each player should report to the first day of practice in top physical condition, while the second considers that physical conditioning is attained through basic drills, fundamentals, and scrimmages, with the players gradually being brought to top physical condition in time for the first game.

It is generally agreed that once top physical condition is reached, regular well-conducted practices will maintain this condition as long as the players do not have a prolonged lay-off.

Pre-season training is usually unsupervised participation and up to the individual player, although often a coach can suggest a course of action which he feels will help that player. Following are listed the common

activities engaged in to maintain physical condition or to train for a higher degree of condition.

Shooting

This is one activity in which the players will participate without any encouragement. Basketball players seem to gravitate to the gymnasium for a pick-up game of basketball or just to shoot baskets. In some instances it is necessary to lock the gymnasium to keep them from practicing.

Because shooting is so important to playing the game of basketball, this type of pre-season practice should be encouraged. In addition to maintaining a shooting eye, the feet are kept in condition and a certain amount of physical training is obtained.

Weight Training Program

Weight training is now recognized as a program that is very effective in increasing strength, jumping ability, endurance, and speed of movement. Programs

---

[1] Clair Bee, *The Science of Coaching* (New York: A. S. Barnes & Co., 1942), p. 44.
[2] Branch McCracken, *Indiana Basketball* (New York: Prentice-Hall, Inc., 1956), p. 16.
[3] John W. Bunn, *Basketball Methods* (New York: The Macmillan Co., 1939), p. 60.

designed specifically for basketball players develop the muscles of the shoulder girdle, arms, hands, fingers, and legs. Sills and O'Connor[4] developed a program for basketball players that is very effective. Murray and Karpovich have done similar work and recommended a similar program. After five weeks of a weight training program, basketball players gain in jumping ability, are stronger, have more endurance, and in general play a better brand of basketball.

A typical program would include weight training Monday, Wednesday, and Friday and exercises Tuesday and Thursday for five weeks prior to the start of the season. Normal basketball workouts will maintain the strength and endurance levels developed by the weight training program.

Equipment

Weights and dumbbells are required, with bar bells ranging in weight from 20 to 250 pounds. An ideal setup would have individual bar bells with the weights welded on, ranging in size from 20 to 250 pounds. Dumbbells should range from 10 to 30 pounds. Chart

XIV indicates a record sheet in which the basketball player records his best weight and number of repetitions for each exercise each day.

A touching board is necessary to record the heights jumped in Exercise 8. The illustration indicates such a board. This touching board is a blackboard with the height measured off on it. It is dusted with chalk and the highest jump is noticeable where the chalk dust is rubbed off by the fingers.

Recommended Weight Training Program

Following is offered a weight training program for basketball players which has proven very successful. It is directed to the basketball player.

The purpose of this program is to develop the muscles of the shoulder girdle, arms, hands, fingers, and legs. Increased endurance, strength, jumping ability, and speed of movement will result from the program.

[4] O'Connor and Sills, "Heavy Resistance Exercises for Basketball Players," *Athletic Journal*, June, 1956, p. 7.

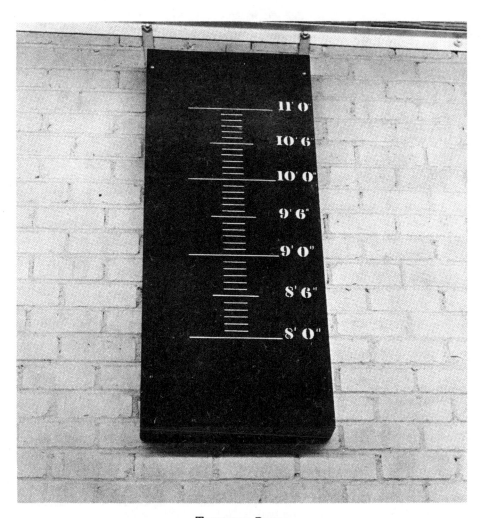

TOUCHING BOARD

WEIGHT TRAINING PROGRAM—RECORD SHEET

NAME _____

Record your best record each day.

	1st Week						2nd Week						3rd Week						4th Week						5th Week			
	M T		W T		F F		M T		W T		F F		M T		W T		F F		M T		W T		F F		M T		W T		F F
1. CLEAN AND PRESS																													
2. CURL																													
3. LATERAL RAISE																													
4. FORWARD RAISE																													
5. SQUAT																													
6. PULLOVER																													
7. QUICK PARTIAL BENDS																													
8. JUMPING TO TOUCH	R L	R L	R L	R L	R L	R L	R L	R L	R L	R L	R L	R L	R L	R L	R L	R L	R L	R L	R L	R L	R L	R L	R L	R L	R L	R L	R L	L

Exercises on alternate days:
1. Jump to touch backboard or rim—10 times without stopping.
2. Sit-ups—25 1st week and add 5 each week.
3. Squat jumps—25 1st week and add 5 each week.

CHART XIV. WEIGHT TRAINING PROGRAM—RECORD SHEET

Instructions

Each of the eight exercises will be executed with a weight which will hold you down to a maximum of from seven to ten repetitions. When you can do ten repetitions, add weight and start again. This procedure is called the overload principle. If you can do more than ten repetitions, you are not receiving full benefit from the program.

Each exercise is listed with the number of repetitions and the weight to add.

Do these exercises three times a week—Monday, Wednesday, and Friday. Continue for a period of five weeks, then stop.

Record the weight and the number of repetitions on the record sheet after each exercise, so that you will know where to start the next time (Chart XIV).

Warm-up

Stand close to a bar bell that is well within your ability to use in any exercise (30 to 50 lbs.).

Lower the hips and grasp the bar bell with palms toward your legs at shoulder width.

WARM-UP 1. Maintain a straight back and straighten fully. Lean back slightly with the weight hanging across the thighs. Repeat three to five times.

WARM-UP 2. Do not set the weight down. Increase the action by pulling the bar bell to the chest. Repeat three to five times.

Exercises

Exercise 1   Ten repetitions
CLEAN AND PRESS   Two sets

Grasp the bar bell with the palms toward the legs and pull it to the upper chest. Push it to fully locked arms overhead, lower to chest, and repeat the overhead lift. Start with 25 to 50 pounds. Add 10 pounds.

Exercise 2   Ten repetitions
CURL   Two sets

Bar bell is grasped with palms away from the legs and is raised to a position across the thighs as the exerciser stands erect. It is then raised to the chest by flexing the arms, elbows remain at the sides. Start with 25 to 50 pounds. Add 10 pounds.

Exercise 3   Dumbbells
LATERAL RAISE   Ten repetitions

Stand at attention with the dumbbells held at the sides, arms straight. Keeping the knuckles up, raise the dumbbells directly from the sides in a full semicircular arc until they are fully overhead. Start with 5 to 10 pounds. Add 5 pounds.

Exercise 4   Dumbbells
FORWARD RAISE   Ten repetitions

Same as Exercise 3 except raise the dumbbells in an arc forward to an overhead position. Start with 5 to 10 pounds. Add 5 pounds.

Exercise 5   Ten repetitions
SQUAT   Two sets

NOTE: Do Exercise 5 once, then 6 once, then 5, then 6.

The bar bell is placed on the shoulders at the back of the neck by a partner or oneself by pressing. Keeping the back straight and the chest high, the exerciser lowers into a full squat and rises, repeating for the desired number of counts. Start with 40 to 75 pounds. Add 10 pounds.

Exercise 6   Ten repetitions with a light weight
PULLOVER   after each set of squats

Lie on back, the bar bell grasped at shoulder width, with arms stretched fully over (behind) the head. After inhaling fully, pull bar bell to a position directly above the chest, exhaling as the weight rises in an arc. Then lower bar bell to the starting position with accompanying full inhalations as it is lowered. Arms should remain rigid. Start with bar alone. Never use much weight on this exercise.

Exercise 7   Ten repetitions
QUICK PARTIAL BENDS   Two sets

With bar bell on shoulders, dip to approximately one-quarter squat or as though to jump at center or try for a rebound. Straighten up and repeat. Start with 40 to 75 pounds. Add 10 pounds.

Exercise 8
JUMPING TO TOUCH

Jump to touch on the blackboard as high as possible. Ten jumps to touch with the right and ten with the left. Highest jump progress with each hand should be recorded. Do not crow hop. Come down and go right up again. Rest several seconds before proceeding with the other hand. Chalk the board so you can see where your fingers touch.

Exercises on alternate days

Three exercises are performed on Tuesdays and Thursdays:

EXERCISE 1. Jump to touch backboard or rim ten times without stopping.

EXERCISE 2. Sit-ups. Do twenty-five the first week and add five each week.

EXERCISE 3. Squat jumps. Do twenty-five the first week and add five each week.

Calisthenics

Calisthenics are physical exercises which, when done properly, can aid in developing the physical condition of a player. These involve push-ups, push-ups on the finger tips, sit-ups, squat jumps, and the like. When performed regularly and when progressively increased in number, they can aid in strengthening various parts of the body. Exercises which strengthen the fingers and hands, the arms and shoulders, the ab-dominal muscles, and the legs are of particular value to a basketball player.

Running

Many coaches recommend that basketball players do cross-country running to strengthen their legs. This is an individual preference, and many other coaches believe the time can be better utilized in other activities. Wind sprints, stops and starts, and changes of direction are other forms of running which are often used as pre-season activities.

Games

Volleyball and handball are games which require footwork and hand-eye co-ordination and which, because they are fun to play, are often recommended for basketball players. They are a different activity, but help keep the feet and legs in shape.

► Early-Season Training

It is during this period of time that the players work out under the direction and supervision of the coach. The definite objective of the training part of each practice is to bring each player up to a state of physical condition so that he will be able to play an entire game.

Practices with a gradual increase in the intensity of the physical activity until a peak is reached are what is desired. This is accomplished under somewhat the same ideas as those which prevail in the pre-season training. The first idea is to supplement the practices with special activities designed to develop a high degree of physical condition. These activities include medicine ball drills, calisthenics, running up steps in the gymnasium, weight training, and the like. On the other hand, coaches who have the opposite point of view work the players hard and fast in the regular drills and fundamentals to accomplish their purposes. It is difficult to recommend one over the other, but the following is a known fact. Some players who are awkward, heavy, unco-ordinated, etc. benefit from the weight training and special activities type of training. But well-co-ordinated individuals seem to have no trouble getting into condition with a minimum amount of effort. Probably a position between the two extremes can be taken, with special activities recommended where they appear to be necessary. It should be noted that weight training programs which are carried on for a period of five weeks during the pre-season and then carry on into the early-season training period have proven to be very successful. It is hard to overlook the fact that jumping height has been improved two inches and that the program also increases the lung capacity and subsequent endurance of the players, plus increasing strength in the fingers, hands, and arms. In addition, once the program has been concluded, the regular practice sessions maintain the level of physical condition of each player.

► In-Season Training

Once the schedule of games is in progress, practices with regular fundamentals and drills should prove sufficient training to maintain a high level of physical condition through to the end of the season.

Whenever a team has a prolonged lay-off, such as over a Christmas vacation or finals period, it is necessary to again increase gradually the tempo and strenuousness of the drills. In addition to increasing the intensity of the drills, it is an advantage to use a variety of drills plus some new ones to stimulate interest.

► Mental Attitude

The attitude of the coach toward physical condition and the reactions of the players are of extreme importance in developing a high state of physical condition in the squad. It takes will power and self-discipline on the part of each player to work hard on a particular drill and then to work harder. This produces stamina and endurance, and an attitude of *it can be done* always shows up in successful basketball teams.

This attitude is reflected in the training rules which were discussed in Chapter 2. Here the coach sets the standards, and the mental attitude on the part of the players is reflected in their standards of conduct.

► Diet

Whatever influences the condition of the body has an influence upon the physical condition of the player. What a person eats is of concern from two points of view: regular diet and the pre-game meal.

Regular Diet

Probably the best advice to give to a basketball player is to eat what he normally has provided in his home or wherever he eats. All food, no matter when eaten, should be consumed in moderation. What is important is that a good balanced diet is obtained and that sufficient calories are obtained for an active player.

Alcohol, smoking, and drugs are considered to be a negative part of the diet, and participants in athletics should refrain entirely from such non-nutritious habits which are detrimental to the body.

Pre-Game Meal

The pre-game meal should be eaten from three to four hours prior to the game. This is customary and is probably a good practice. The meal itself should contain what is regularly eaten by the athlete and should not contain highly spiced or greasy foods. The individual should eat and drink in moderation. Following is an example of a typical pre-game meal.

> Fruit cocktail or juice
> Jello Salad
> Toast or melba toast and butter
> Baked potato
> Green Vegetable
> Small steak
> Milk, water, or tea
> Ice cream for dessert

► Sleep

Regularity is the clue to good sleeping habits. Although eight hours is the recommended length of time for most individuals, some need more and others can get along on less. A growing young man will require more. What is required by the individual should be obtained each night at regular hours.

In addition to regular sleeping hours, it would be excellent if each player could rest for an hour before dressing for the game. This is not always possible, but should be practiced whenever feasible.

► Staleness

Staleness is a condition of not being up to par mentally or physically. The individual is moody, tired, irritable, and restless, and consequently is not in the proper condition to give his best in a basketball game.

There are probably a hundred and one causes for staleness, but one's mental and physical state can be improved by any one or all of the following: complete rest, shorter practices, practices motivated with fun games, change of drills, change of recreation, change of diet, or any activity which will relieve monotony or cause the individual to have fun. It is hoped that these practices will relieve the mental and physical strain and return the player to his former condition.

Actually, a good coach will not wait for a state of staleness to set in, but in his practices will regularly do just those things which are used to combat staleness.

► Summary

The physical condition of the individual basketball player is important, and each should be at such a peak of physical condition that he can participate in a full game without noticeable loss of efficiency.

Training is the means whereby the body is physically conditioned. Training can be accomplished during the pre-season, but is actually increased in strenuousness during the early-season, regular practice schedule. Sleep and diet are a part of training, as they affect the physical condition of the individual. Moderation and regularity are the best recommendations for diet and sleep. No player should indulge in alcohol, tobacco, or drugs.

► Study Questions

1. Define physical condition.
2. What is meant by training?
3. What does training involve?
4. Describe staleness? What techniques can be used to alleviate this condition.
5. Order a pre-game meal. What important items should you consider?
6. Is a pre-season training period necessary?
7. List several games which are recommended for basketball players.
8. What is the overload principle?
9. List the important items which should be considered in relation to diet.

► Projects for Additional Study

1. Ask a basketball coach his theory regarding training for physical condition.
2. Look in the literature for a book on weight training. How does the program for a basketball player differ from that designed for baseball or football?
3. Plan a training program for the entire basketball season including the pre-season period.

4. Discover a book which deals with diet. What is important in regard to diet and strenuous work?

5. Check a high school and a college basketball schedule with reference to away and home games. Can a player plan to rest an hour before each game?

► Selected References

Athletic Journal. Athletic Journal Publishing Co.: Evanston, Ill. Occasionally has pertinent articles dealing with all phases of conditioning and training.

Auerback, Arnold. *Basketball for the Player, the Fan and the Coach.* New York: Pocketbooks, Inc., 1952. Offers an excellent list of reasons why a player should be in condition.

Bee, Clair. *The Science of Coaching.* New York: A. S. Barnes & Co., 1942. General information on training and conditioning is presented.

Belik, S. E. *The Trainers Bible.* New York: T. J. Reed & Co. Information for the trainer and coach.

Bevan, Rollie. *The Athletic Trainer's Handbook.* New York: Prentice-Hall, Inc., 1955. Information for the trainer and coach.

Bunn, John W. *Basketball Methods.* New York: The Macmillan Co., 1939. Contains excellent material on training and conditioning.

Dean, Everett S. *Progressive Basketball.* New York: Prentice-Hall, Inc., 1950. Valuable hints on conditioning and training are clearly presented.

Hobson, Howard A. *Basketball Illustrated.* New York: A. S. Barnes & Co., 1948. Brief comments on training are offered.

Loeffler, Ken. *Ken Loeffler on Basketball.* New York: Prentice-Hall, Inc., 1955. Loeffler's own opinions regarding conditioning are presented.

McCracken, Branch. *Indiana Basketball.* New York: Prentice-Hall, Inc., 1955. Pertinent common sense views on conditioning and training with general advice on training.

McCreary, Jay. *Winning High School Basketball.* New York: Prentice-Hall, Inc., 1956. Valuable discussion of training and the prevention of injuries.

McGuire, Frank. *Defensive Basketball.* New York: Prentice-Hall, Inc., 1959. Excellent comments regarding conditioning and training.

————. *Offensive Basketball.* New York: Prentice-Hall, Inc., 1958. Excellent comments regarding conditioning and training.

McLane, Hardin. *Championship Basketball by 12 Great Coaches.* Englewood Cliffs, N. J.: Prentice-Hall, Inc., 1965. Coach Bill Gardiner on Loyola's (New Orleans) isometric basketball program.

Newell, Pete, and Benington, John. *Basketball Methods.* New York: The Ronald Press Co., 1962. Outstanding information on conditioning and training.

Ramsay, Jack. *Pressure Basketball.* Englewood Cliffs, N. J.: Prentice-Hall, Inc., 1964. Team training by isometric exercises is explained.

Rupp, Adolph F. *Rupp's Championship Basketball.* New York: Prentice-Hall, Inc., 1948. Contains valuable facts and information on conditioning and training.

Scholastic Coach. Scholastic Magazines, Inc., New York, N. Y. 10036. Occasionally has pertinent articles dealing with all phases of conditioning and training.

Ward, Charles R. *Basketball's Match-up Defense.* Englewood Cliffs, N. J.: Prentice-Hall, Inc., 1964. Scouting and charting are presented, particularly for use of the match-up defense, but also good for general ideas and philosophy.

Wooden, John R. *Practical Modern Basketball.* New York: The Ronald Press Co., 1966. Good material on training and conditioning and the philosophy of coaching, with pointers for the player and coach.